MODERN DRAMA

by

MARTIN LAMM

Translated by

KARIN ELLIOTT

FOLCROFT LIBRARY EDITIONS / 1971

Limited to 150 Copies

MODERN DRAMA

by

MARTIN LAMM

Translated by

KARIN ELLIOTT

PHILOSOPHICAL LIBRARY
NEW YORK

Published, 1953, by the Philosophical Library, Inc.,
15 East 40th Street, New York 16, N.Y.

Printed in Great Britain for Basil Blackwell, Publisher

CONTENTS

v

PREFACE

IN calling this book "Modern Drama" I do not wish to suggest that it is a comprehensive survey of all European and American dramatic writing to date. Such a work might easily become nothing more than an annotated bibliography in which the reader loses his way among a multitude of names and titles. I should then be compelled, too, to comment on authors whose career has not yet ended.

My aim has been to describe the development of modern drama during the hundred years between the début of Scribe and the present day, in a series of portraits of dramatists. The selection is based entirely on my own estimate of their significance for world drama. Sardou, though he is primarily a technician, has therefore been included, while his numerous followers in various countries have been omitted. Those dramatic works which were mainly intended to be read, and have not played any significant part in the development of drama, I have ignored or only mentioned in passing, as also those plays which have not often penetrated beyond the borders of their own country, and have failed to create any great impression. The only Scandinavian playwrights who exercised a wide influence during this period were Björnson, Ibsen and Strindberg, and they are therefore the sole representatives of Scandinavian drama in this book.

The amount of space which I have given to various writers has not been determined by the importance which I attach to them. As this book is written primarily for the Swedish reader, I have contented myself in the Strindberg chapter with indicating his international significance and the main features of his dramatic work. Ibsen, whom I regard as being, with Strindberg, the greatest dramatist of the last hundred years, has been treated in greater detail: as, however, his plays and his personality are

familiar to the reader I have devoted relatively more space to
other authors of less significance, in order to describe the content
of their work and the setting in which they wrote.

My book is not a history of the theatre, though I have occasionally had to refer to aspects of that subject when they have
affected the writing and international reputation of a play.

Stockholm, *September,* 1948.   Martin Lamm.

INTRODUCTION

DURING the first half of the 19th century there was in most European countries a wide gulf between the drama which formed the regular stock-in-trade of the theatres and the dramatic works of great authors, which were only occasionally performed and rarely retained their hold on the stage.

The separation of stage drama from literary drama had already begun in the latter part of the 18th century. The new art-form, which occupied a place half-way between tragedy and comedy, and which was known as *drame*, suited the actors better because it lent itself to outward effect, to exciting plots and impressive spectacles. Its setting was often domestic, and even when the action was supposed to take place in historical times it saw these through contemporary eyes. Many of the great actors were themselves authors of such plays; Schröder and Iffland, for example, in Germany, and in France, Monvel, whom Gustav III invited to Sweden. The other actors, too, wholeheartedly favoured the *drame*, which gave them rewarding parts.

During the last quarter of the 18th century the *drame* had found itself a new public. The large masses of lower middle-class patrons who thronged the theatre yards in Renaissance times disappeared in the 17th century, when theatre-going became a fashion in high society. By the end of the 18th century, however, the pendulum was beginning to swing back again, even in the theatres of the great capitals. Contemporary witnesses tell us that the bulk of the audience at the Théâtre Français consisted of soldiers, artisans and clerks. This new public wanted to hear everyday problems treated in the theatre, and to see heroes drawn from its own ranks. It wanted more action on the stage and less discussion. It was the popular play in its many forms which held the day. Beside the sentimental or comic domestic *drames* we find plays about knights and robbers, and strange combinations of all these types.

The plot of a domestic *drame* should be taken from everyday life, but the stock themes were soon exhausted, and the taste for extravagant and fantastic situations soon gained the upper hand: the domestic *drame* was gradually becoming completely eccentric. Nothing could be more remote from ordinary domestic life than the *drames* of Kotzebue, which were greatly admired by his contemporaries, were translated into every language, met with resounding success in every theatre in Europe, and even found their way to America. *Menschenhass und Reue (Misanthropy and Repentance)*, his most famous play, aroused the same kind of extravagant response as greeted Goethe's Werther. Just as the "Werther coat" became the fashion for men, so the ladies adopted the "Eulalia hood", so called after the heroine of the play, the once faithless but later penitent wife.

The historical *drame* also treated thrilling subjects, in a very thin historical guise. New features appeared in them, horror and adventure. The knight and robber plays made generous use of trap-doors, dungeons and poison. Secret societies and tribunals were prominent in these plays, which gave a grimly realistic picture of the cruelty of the Middle Ages and the early Renaissance.

By the end of the 18th century an even less artistic form of popular play had developed out of the French domestic and historical *drame*. It was called melodrama, and dominated the theatre well into the 19th century. As it developed further it received impulses from various sources, including the novels of Walter Scott, but remained basically unchanged. During their 'Sturm und Drang' period Goethe and Schiller had produced *drames* both of the domestic and the knight and robber type. Goethe's *Götz von Berlichingen* and Schiller's *Die Räuber (The Robbers)*, and *Kabale und Liebe (Intrigue and Love)*, can serve as examples. The French neo-romantic writers were also strongly influenced by the stage drama. Victor Hugo's prose plays are most properly regarded as melodramas, and so are almost all the works of the elder Dumas.

The modern drama of contemporary life, which first appeared in France in the middle of the 19th century, with the younger

Dumas and Augier as its foremost exponents, inherited the traditions of the bourgeois *drame*, as was clearly recognized at the time. The younger Dumas himself emphasized this connexion when he named one of his plays *Le fils naturel* (*The Natural Son*), a title which Diderot had used before him. Ibsen, too, used as a sub-title for his play, *Gengangere* (*Ghosts*), the phrase 'domestic drama', which was commonly given to the German bourgeois *drames*. One part of this heritage from the bourgeois *drame* was a concern for social problems and reforms. In the hands of serious authors such plays became significant contributions to the development of thought, and sometimes helped to bring about changes in the law and in public opinion generally. Throughout the latter half of the 19th century the theatre exercises an influence on public opinion unequalled at any period in its history. The realistic drama of contemporary life can be said to have achieved the aim which Diderot had set himself, and which his successors had failed to achieve.

The playwrights of the Second French Empire continued to use much of the technique of the bourgeois *drame*, but in so doing improved its quality. Most of the plays of the younger Dumas and Augier have happy, or at any rate harmonious, endings. Some of the sentimentality of the bourgeois *drame* is still evident in their emotional outbursts, and they still allow their characters, heroes and villains alike, to suffer a change of heart. In these respects even Ibsen, in his first social drama, is bound by tradition. *Samfundets Stötter* (*Pillars of Society*) still retains much of the bourgeois *drame*: Bernick openly confesses his sins and receives absolution for them from the noble characters, Lona Hessel and Johan Tönnesen. Even in *Et dukkehjem* (*A Doll's House*) the spiteful Krogstad is converted in an instant and becomes engaged to Nora's friend, Mrs. Linde, one of those busy moralists of whom the early writers of bourgeois *drame* were so fond.

Already, however, a new influence became noticeable in the French dramatists, and still more in the first plays which Björnson and Ibsen wrote about contemporary problems—an influence derived equally from neo-classical and neo-romantic drama, hitherto a rare visitor to the large theatres. The younger Dumas and Augier mostly followed their own French models, the classical writers, the Romantics, and those writers of the classical reaction, such as Ponsard, who followed the Romantics. Outside France, on the other hand, the determining influence was that of the German neo-classical and romantic schools.

During their neo-classical period, Goethe and Schiller despised the public theatres, which, with excellent actors and a constant flow of patrons, offered nothing but cheap and trashy plays. When Goethe became director of the Court Theatre at Weimar, their plays could be produced in the old-fashioned, stylized manner which they preferred. Bad taste, however, could not be excluded, even from this stage, dedicated though it was to neo-classicism, and both great authors wrote their later plays without giving much thought to stage production. Literary drama in its purest form was the medium through which the first generation of the Romantics developed: they despised the theatre on principle. The legendary plays of Tieck were no more intended to be acted than *Lycksalighetens ö* (*The Isle of Happiness*) or the plays of Ling and Stagnelius. Writers of real dramatic genius, such as Kleist and Hebbel, naturally wanted their works to be staged, but only rarely were their plays performed, and then often without the success for which they had hoped.

The very fact that the major playwrights were largely excluded from the popular stage, and were forced to address themselves to the reading public, meant that they could escape from the rigidity of current theatrical convention. As a result of this freedom they exercised an extremely powerful influence on modern drama as it developed in the second half of the 19th century.

This new form of drama was composed for production on the stage but its authors made it a point of honour to address themselves to the reader at the same time. Even the plays of the younger Dumas have the long witty prefaces for which Shaw later became famous. Ibsen was not fond of acting as his own interpreter, but the text of his plays, both in his own day and in later times, has meant at least as much to his readers as to his audiences. Our parents and their contemporaries can tell us how they used to fight each other for a copy of Ibsen's latest play in the bookshops of Stockholm and the university towns, and how eagerly they discussed it and argued about it.

The public had learned that plays could be read, and at long last theatre directors had also come to realize that what they had regarded as literary dramas could be staged. Kleist and Hebbel were already dead when their greatest stage triumphs were achieved, and Musset had fallen on evil days by the time that the comedies and the *Proverbes Dramatiques* which he had written for the *Revue des Deux Mondes* became part of the regular repertoire at the Théâtre Français.

The development of drama during the last hundred years— what is here called modern drama—has at the same time brought about a stage revival of neo-classical and neo-romantic drama, because it derives as much from this school as from the bourgeois drama. Already in neo-classical drama we discover trends which have become significant in modern drama. Goethe created what became the established pattern for the 19th century 'drama of ideas'. His *Faust* was clearly the chief model for *Brand* and *Peer Gynt*, two plays which were also intended primarily for reading. Other modern dramas of ideas derive from Byron's *Manfred*.

But Goethe's dramas of ideas had another important effect on the stage plays of the late 19th century. In *Iphigenie* and *Tasso* there is one characteristic which can be described as new; they are self-revelations in dramatic form. An author must of course always reveal himself to some extent in his work, but this characteristic is less evident in older plays than we are inclined to think. In 19th century drama we have become accustomed to look for the author's own portrait and experience disguised in the character of his hero. Ibsen's later plays and Strindberg's *Till Damaskus* (*To Damascus*) are typical examples.

Goethe was the first to discard everything external as unimportant: with him drama enters the realm of psychological experience, with the hero suffering a spiritual development, or rather crisis, for Goethe's insistence on the temporal unity, particularly marked in his classical plays, forbade any more profound delineation of character. This tendency to lay the main stress on psychological analysis, whether the characters analyse themselves or are exposed to the shrewd observations of other characters in the dialogue, later becomes so significant for modern drama that we forget that it did not occur, for instance, in Elizabethan drama. The French classical tragedy, on the other hand, from which Goethe was not far removed, has in the works of its foremost exponent, Racine, a psychological basis which is often very subtle. But deliberate psychological analysis is not found in Racine, nor indeed in Molière.

In Goethe's treatment of the Iphigenia in Tauris legend the basic story—if we discard all the dramatic trimmings—is that Orestes is freed from the pangs of conscience by the calmer influence of his sister, Iphigenia. This story would be better expressed in narrative form; Orestes' change of heart could more easily be analysed in continuous prose than in monologues and dialogues.

Modern drama has followed in Goethe's footsteps in so far as from the beginning it took as its foundation the novel and the prose story. *La dame aux camélias* (*The Lady of the Camellias*) is a dramatized novel, and Augier's *Le gendre de M. Poirier* (*The Son-in-law of M. Poirier*), another play which points the way to modern drama, is based on a novel by a contemporary of Balzac. Zola constructed his plays from his own novels, beginning with *Thérèse Raquin*, when he wanted to create models for the naturalistic drama. Symbolic dramas are clearly even more closely allied to the novel as an art-form: one has only to remember Maeterlinck, or the later plays of Strindberg. In Goethe the historical element is often no more than a sort of disguise. The court scenes in *Tasso*, for instance, resemble those of Weimar rather than Ferrara. The clash of ideas presented in the play, the conflict between poetry and reality, was a problem for Goethe and his contemporaries, not for his character, Tasso. This topical interpretation of historical material is even more obvious in Schiller—a more significant figure than Goethe for modern drama.

Unlike Goethe, Schiller was profoundly interested in the theory of drama, and his plays, together with the illuminating correspondence about them, serve also as a guide to playwriting. The modern theatre has inherited from Schiller this concern with questions of form.

Earlier authors had contented themselves with selecting persons and events from history or legend and presenting them in psychological conflict. Schiller, on the other hand, wanted to explain the historical event itself. *Wallenstein* is an attempt to recreate history in dramatic form, to allow the various factors in history, personified in his characters, to contend directly with one another. This is already plain in the prologue, which describes the conditions in Wallenstein's army, and is even clearer in the two succeeding plays of the trilogy which describe the rivalry between the army leaders, and the intrigues of diplomacy. The climax of the drama comes with the fall of Wallenstein, the result of his equivocal position between the contending powers. Many attempts have been made to imitate this magnificent trilogy. Björnson tried to do so in *Sigurd Slembe* (*Sigurd the Bastard*), Ibsen in *Kejser og Galilaeer* (*Emperor and Galilean*), and Strindberg in his three first plays from the Vasa story, to name only Scandinavian examples. Schiller's successors, however, all lacked his peculiar qualities, the combination of real historical insight with great dramatic talent.

But Schiller was not merely a historian; he was a philosopher of history, and from the first we can detect in his work qualities which were later to make this new type of historical drama no longer purely historical. The conflict of ideas in Schiller's plays becomes at the same time a conflict of ideals. World history for Schiller had a moral content: "Die Weltgeschichte ist das Weltgericht".

Wallenstein is a series of moral debates, often almost forensic in tone. This tendency to transform a historical drama into a trial before a court of morals was carried a stage further by Kleist, whose first play, *Der Prinz von Homburg* (*The Prince of Homburg*), culminates with an actual representation of a court scene. In Hebbel the historical conflict of ideas is treated according to Hegelian principles and therefore remains valid for all time, as Hegel held that history always develops on the same lines. There is therefore no inconsistency when Hebbel, in *Maria Magdalena*, presents the same conflict of ideas in a modern bourgeois setting.

Partly, but not entirely, as a result of Hegel's influence, the lively moral debates of the historical plays had found their way into contemporary drama. The younger Dumas, Ibsen, Strindberg, Shaw and Galsworthy are names chosen at random to show the development of drama into a setting for moral debate, a court where prosecution and defence can argue out their case. Never has the theatre staged so much earnest discussion on morals as it did in the later part of the 19th century, beginning with the drama of the Second French Empire. It was to this tendency that

Brandes was referring in his dictum in *Main Streams of Literature in the 19th Century,* that a literature lives by raising problems for debate. He proved a true prophet a few years later when Ibsen's *A Doll's House* caused fierce discussion throughout the whole civilized world.

This antagonism between conventional and instinctive morality, on which Ibsen constructed *A Doll's House* and his other social plays, can already be seen in Schiller's *Wallenstein.* In the second part, the sober, prudent Octavio Piccolomini is contrasted with his idealist son, Max. They represent different modes of behaviour and different outlooks on life. Schiller himself in a letter to Goethe wrote that all poetic characters are symbolic beings and represent universal types.

This is true not merely of dramatic characters but also of dramatic events. What happens is that which must happen. It is the compulsion of external events which drives Wallenstein to become a traitor, but the stars symbolize the dark fate in which he believes, and which at the same time torments him and gives him a fatalistic calm: "Nacht muss es sein, wo Friedlands Sterne strahlen".

Occasionally, even in Schiller's works, events seem to have been so arranged as to bear an allegorical interpretation. Max Piccolomini the idealist, nauseated by the intrigues of both sides, rides at the head of his men seeking death. He falls from his horse and is trampled to death by the riders behind him. Wallenstein's daughter, who loves Max, laments the fate which causes him to die by the hooves of his own horses: "Das ist das Los des Schönen auf der Erde". Ibsen, too, throughout his life as a writer shows a liking for situations which could also bear a symbolic significance. When the "breaking of the bridges" is mentioned in *Kongsemnerne (The Pretenders),* the phrase has both a literal and an allegorical significance. In *John Gabriel Borkman,* the timid old man Foldal is run over by the sledge which is carrying the younger generation away from their gloomy home; Borkman concludes, "Oh, we are all of us run over some time or other in life".

When Schiller had finished *Wallenstein* he declared that the *Oedipus Rex* of Sophocles had been his model. He described the Sophoclean play as simply a tragic analysis, in the sense that what

happens on the stage is the development of events which have
occurred before the play opens. In Schiller's tragedy this method
of analysis is only employed in so far as Wallenstein's decision to
go over to the Swedes is made before the trilogy opens, and has
been revealed by spies to the court at Vienna. The drama begins
in the middle of the disaster, and Wallenstein dies before he has
had time to accomplish his plan. The revelations which occur
in the course of the play compel him to abide by his decision, as
all ways of retreat are barred. From the Sophoclean original the
trilogy derives its atmosphere of brooding and foreboding. In
Die Braut von Messina (*The Bride of Messina*) Schiller follows the
pattern of the Oedipus drama very closely, with the single
difference that in his tragedy Destiny is revealed in a dream, and
not by an oracle. All the other elements of a Sophoclean drama
are present, family guilt, incest, tragic irony, and above all the
doctrine proclaimed by the chorus, that any effort to forestall
fate's decrees only serves to make its blows more merciless.

The Bride of Messina still has some of the qualities of a literary
experiment, and it was reserved for a later generation of playwrights to succeed in depicting that crushing yet cleansing power
which Schiller himself has described in a much quoted passage
about fate, "welches den Menschen erhebt, wenn es den Menschen
zermalmt".

Both directly, and through the medium of Romanticism, the
neo-classical drama of Goethe and Schiller exercised a powerful
influence on all dramatic work in the century that followed. In
individual cases it is of course often impossible to determine
where modern dramatists have found their inspiration. Many of
them produced their first efforts in the guise of classical drama or
historical tragedy, and subsequently turned to contemporary
forms. This is true of authors as widely different as Hebbel,
Augier, Björnson, Ibsen and Strindberg. Others, the younger
Dumas and Shaw for instance, adopted the contemporary idiom
from the very start, though they shared Goethe's liking for the
classical unities and the limitations they imposed on the actions
and the numbers of characters.

Schiller's use of "the tragic analysis" as found in the *Oedipus
Rex* has been imitated even in dramas which are not concerned
with classical themes. In general it is safe to say that modern

drama is more concerned to reveal what lies behind the facade of
the characters or the events of the past than to present an exciting
action on the stage.

Modern drama, is, however, often concerned with those
ingredients of classical tragedy to which Schiller gave new life.
Family guilt, incest, nemesis, hubris and peripeteia are themes and
concepts which recur continually both in drama and in discussions about drama, though of course they have suffered some
modification in the light of recent increases in scientific, philosophical and psychological knowledge. Heredity, for instance, is
the explanation given for family guilt in Ibsen's *Ghosts* and
Rosmersholm, and, in a slightly different sense, in Strindberg's
Fröken Julie (*Miss Julie*). Taine's theories about environment and
Darwin's teaching about the struggle for survival were woven
into the pattern of classical tragedy during the heyday of naturalism. Symbolism, which also claims associations with classical
drama, reintroduced, in the writings of Maeterlinck, the classical
conception of destiny, with all its mystery and foreboding. The
20th century saw the introduction of new factors; Strindberg's
plays, starting with the three parts of *To Damascus*, combined the
notions of hubris, guilt and retribution with Christian and
Sweden-borgian conceptions.

In modern drama's latest masterpiece, *Mourning becomes Electra*,
written in 1931, Eugene O'Neill starts with the same assumptions
as Schiller did when he wrote *The Bride of Messina*. He is trying to
create a modern psychological equivalent of the Greek belief in
fate, which shall be acceptable to a public which no longer
believes in supernatural retribution.

O'Neill chose Aeschylus's *Orestes* instead of *Oedipus Rex*,
which had served as a model for Schiller and Ibsen, but he
modernized his theme in the same way. He made use of the current theories of heredity, but also allowed his characters to be
influenced by the old puritanical faith which held that man is
doomed to sin and punishment. In the same way Ibsen wove
into his plays the two strands of heredity and rigid morality. In
the last part of O'Neill's trilogy the Oedipus concept is interpreted
in the light of Freudian psychology.

As a century and a half had passed since Goethe and Schiller
wrote their classical plays, it is obvious that O'Neill went straight

to the Greek tragedies for his inspiration. It is, however, equally clear that he made a thorough study of Goethe and Schiller: his next play, *Days without End,* is a modern version of the Faust legend. O'Neill explains that in his own trilogy the Furies are within Orestes himself, are in fact his conscience. This is the same reinterpretation of the old myth which Goethe adopted in *Iphigenie auf Tauris (Iphigenia in Tauris),* and which drew from Schiller the criticism, "ohne Furien kein Orest". T. S. Eliot, in *The Family Reunion,* also introduces the Eumenides in a modern setting.

The influence of the neo-classical drama of ideas and of the historical drama is present in the work of all modern playwrights, though like a hidden spring which flows beneath the ground it very rarely comes to the surface. Without this continuous source of strength, modern drama might well have remained mere entertainment, without pathos or real tragic force, and without any appeal for an educated public. It would also lack some of the common elements which, despite the diversity of the various schools, do in fact characterize modern drama.

This is most plainly observed in the bias which modern playwrights display against action on the stage, and their desire to translate everything into psychological analysis, and to allow their heroes, Hamlet-wise, to prefer speculation about life to action. Maeterlinck, whose idiosyncrasies are in fact typical of the fundamental trends of modern drama, speaks of most classical tragedies as static and unmoving; there is no action in them. Their beauty and grandeur are to be found in their language and not in their plot. This also points to a significant characteristic of modern drama. Those who in 1881 were shocked at Ibsen's *Ghosts,* and twenty years later at Strindberg's *Dödsdansen (Dance of Death),* hardly seem to have noticed that these plays contain practically no action. The terrifying impression they create is the result of what is said, and even more of the implication behind what is said, the "inner dialogue", as Maeterlinck calls it.

It may be objected that film technique must inevitably increase the demand for action. Perhaps it has even done so in some cases, including some of the very best works. But it is certainly significant that the most powerful modern play which owes its inspiration to the film, and indeed can hardly be produced without its aid—*The Emperor Jones*, by O'Neill—is almost entirely static. Apart from the introduction and the finale, the play consists almost entirely of monologues by the unhappy negro emperor, struggling with shadows of the past, his own and that of his race, which are as unreal as the apparitions in *Macbeth*. Pursued by these hallucinations, he runs in circles through the maze of the tropical jungle, and finally into the arms of his pursuers. *The Emperor Jones* is a perfect example of modern drama: its action takes place in a man's mind, and it ends as it began.

SCRIBE AND HEBBEL

THE juxtaposition of these two names in the title of this chapter may seem strange. There is a vast gulf between the elegantly constructed comedies of Eugène Scribe and the weighty bourgeois tragedy, *Maria Magdalena*, by Hebbel. But these two, each in his own fashion, helped to prepare the way for present-day drama, and for Ibsen, its first great exponent.

Hebbel writes in his diary; "A real drama can be compared with a big building, which has as many rooms and passages under the ground as above it. Ordinary people only see the latter, but the builder knows both".

Scribe never wrote a "real drama" in this sense. There are no underground passages and rooms in his works; everything is above the ground. He took to heart La Bruyère's maxim, that writing a book is as much a craft as making a clock. In his chosen craft, moreover, Scribe achieved a mastery which was to stand his successors during the next fifty years in good stead. In particular, his skill in the construction of plots provided a firm framework which the shapeless bourgeois dramas had previously lacked. He succeeded in writing plays which gave a real impression of contemporary life; he dealt with live issues in a way which made the stage seem their natural setting. It remained for the next generation of playwrights to give the stage drama greater depth. Scribe was not the man to compose literary drama; he wrote for a wider public. To some extent he resembles those playwrights who created the folk drama of the late renaissance in Spain and England. Like them he was an educated man and had originally intended to become a lawyer. Economic reasons had compelled him to turn to playwriting. He wrote his plays to be acted, not to be read, but he knew how to use his education to the best advantage. He was the first of the 19th century playwrights to succeed in living by his pen alone. Hitherto authors had received only a single and very meagre payment for their plays. Scribe however introduced a system of royalties which made him a millionaire and the owner of a great chateau in France. He also formed an association of playwrights to defend their interests against the theatre directors, thanks to which dramatic authors were enabled for the rest of the century to devote themselves wholly to their craft.

It was this system of royalties which Scribe introduced that enabled the younger Dumas, Augier and Ibsen to live a life free from financial worries.

The changes which Scribe introduced into the drama were the most valuable of all reforms during this period. There had been no lack of good poets, shrewd psychologists and profound thinkers ready to try their hand at drama in the early 19th century. The majority, however, had little stage sense, or if they had, stifled it with their theories. Scribe had no great gift for characterization, no high moral or philosophical ideas; he had no style, and was indifferent to all aesthetic theories; but he understood stagecraft better than anyone. His skill at weaving plots was such that he gave to the 19th century drama just what it had hitherto lacked—a firm internal structure. It is surprising to note how rapidly modern drama developed after Scribe, though his disciples soon revolted against the excessive artificiality of their master's plots.

Scribe's dramatic works, including those which he wrote in collaboration with other authors, are estimated at three or four hundred. Not all of these are plays. Scribe also completely transformed the libretti of opera and opéra comique. Opera had not yet shaken itself free from the classical subjects, and the same situations and themes were repeated again and again. Scribe was the creator (as far as the text is concerned) of Grand Opera, his first work being *La Muette de Portici* (*The Mute From Portici*). Later he wrote some of the best-known operas of his day, *Les Huguenots* (*The Huguenots*), *Le Prophète* (*The Prophet*), *L'Africaine* (*The African Woman*), and many more. As an opera librettist, his taste was for romantic and colourful subjects, though otherwise he was no romantic. Many of his libretti were not original, but adaptations of others' work; he even had the courage to rewrite

Shakespeare's *The Tempest* as an opera. Of all Scribe's works, his elegant comic operas have perhaps held their place on the stage longest—*La dame blanche* (*The White Lady*), *Le domino noir* (*The Black Domino*), *Fra Diavolo,* and many others.

It was for the half-musical Vaudeville theatre that Scribe wrote his first and most of his later plays, and it was here that he first won his reputation. Vaudeville was a light form of drama, dating back to the 17th century. The name really referred to the couplets which occurred in it. For instance in Beaumarchais' *Le mariage de Figaro* (*The Marriage of Figaro*), which is a comedy, there is a vaudeville, that is a series of couplets, at the end of the play. During the 18th century the name came to signify a short musical play with a delicate and sometimes improvised plot, with interspersed couplets, which often have a topical or political significance. During the 18th century this peculiarly French form spread all over Europe.

The reason why Scribe came to write so many vaudevilles or vaudeville-comedies was that the Théâtre Français had special privileges for the production of both comedies and tragedies. But Scribe was too prolific a writer for the Théâtre Français to take all his works. He had therefore come to an agreement with the Director of the Gymnase Theatre, whereby the latter undertook to stage all Scribe's vaudeville plays—an arrangement, incidentally, which made this director a multi-millionaire.

Scribe was least happy as a writer of lyrics, and he gradually whittled away the couplets until he had removed from vaudeville the last traces of the pastoral drama and the rural idyll. Instead he invested it with a lively Parisian atmosphere. He devoted his attention to devising more elegant and ingenious plots, based on stories both old and new, real and imaginary. Even at this stage he was giving expression to a sober bourgeois attitude that was later to be reflected in modern French drama.

It was above all as a writer of vaudeville that Scribe made his name. In this capacity he became a master from whom Heiberg, Hertz and Hostrup learned much, as did also the distinguished Swedish vaudeville playwrights of whom Blanche was the best. Even when, in his more serious plays, he deals with social problems, there always lingers a faint echo of the gaiety of vaudeville.

Scribe's straight plays are either historical comedies or domestic dramas. In both types his technique is the same, but as his historical plays have retained their popularity longer it is proposed to deal first with them, and in particular with his play *Le Verre d'Eau* (*The Glass of Water*). This drama was first produced in 1840 and is still being played to-day. This play gives in essence Scribe's whole philosophy of dramatic art, in so far as he can be said to have had one.

The Glass of Water has the high-sounding sub-title, *Les effets et les causes*. A glass of water spilt on Queen Anne's dress by the Duchess of Marlborough is the cause of her own disgrace, the collapse of the Whigs, the rise of Bolingbroke and ultimately a revolution in English foreign policy. Scribe wishes to show that from the most trivial incident can result the most catastrophic reversals of fortune. This point of view is put by Bolingbroke himself in his famous tirade in the first act; he concludes it by telling how he became a statesman and a Minister of the Crown because he could dance a saraband, and was dismissed because he caught a cold.

This discovery made by Scribe and Bolingbroke is as old as the hills, and many authors at many times have expressed it in more or less the same terms. Scribe found it first in Voltaire who had previously quoted this very same historical incident, the spilling of a glass of water.

In direct contrast to Schiller, Scribe conceived a historical event as the result of cunning intrigue, and as set in motion by trivial causes such as personal ambition or vanity. This conception naturally deprived his plays of all semblance of historical reality, but enhanced their dramatic quality. About the actual clash of ideas behind the conflict between Bolingbroke and his enemy we learn nothing.

Significantly enough, it is only against the Duchess of Marlborough that Bolingbroke is fighting; as plotters and counter-plotters they are well matched in cunning. The remaining characters—the Queen who is always vacillating, and the young lovers, Masham and Abigail Churchill, are mere puppets in their hands. The whole play hinges on the rather improbable supposition that Masham is the unconscious object of admiration of two rivals, the Queen and the Duchess. Bolingbroke contrives to make good use of their jealousy, and by the fourth act causes a quarrel to break out between them, at the very moment when the Queen bids Masham hand her the fateful glass of water. The jealous Duchess seizes it and spills the water over the Queen's dress.

Scribe often builds his plays round two young people who fall in love, and are happily united at the end of the fifth act. But their fates are playfully interwoven with serious political struggles and they are used as catspaws by both sides for their own ends. The general idea is to allow the characters to fall victims to all kinds of misunderstandings, which the audience knows all about already and therefore finds all the more entertaining to watch as they see the characters becoming innocently and unconsciously embroiled. If Masham is anxious to confide in one or other of the noble ladies, or they are about to confess their affection for him, the author is sure to interrupt their conversation by some device which leaves them with false impressions of each other's feelings. Letters are intercepted, secret whisperings overheard and misunderstood, assignations are made, but the person who turns up is always the one whose presence is least desired; this is all according to the convention.

Plots of this kind go far back into dramatic history, and are to be found fully developed in the French playwrights of the 18th century, Marivaux and Beaumarchais. One can even find 18th century examples of comedy based on some historical incident —a type of which Scribe was so fond. What was new in Scribe was the importance which he gave to the plot. In *The Glass of Water* the love of the Queen and the Duchess of Marlborough for Masham is regarded solely as a factor in the development of the plot, and the author makes no effort whatever to explain their motives in psychological terms.

The Exposition, which was such an important element in most 19th century drama, is almost entirely missing in Scribe's works. He plunges straight into the action, and from the first moment dramatic tension is high. Scribe then gives himself plenty of time; the real climax is not reached until the fourth act, the fifth being reserved for setting all to rights. Meanwhile the audience is held in suspense. Every new character who appears on the stage adds a new twist to the plot, and leads the audience to look for a solution in a different quarter. To ensure that they fully appreciate the dangers of the situation, the author allows the principal characters to exchange asides which show how the game is going. At the end of the third act Bolingbroke whispers to Abigail, "The match goes well". "It is lost", says Abigail. "It is won", answers Bolingbroke.

At the end of the fourth act comes the big scene which everyone has been waiting for, the same which later on, in the plays of Dumas the younger and Augier was to be known as the *scène à faire*. In *The Glass of Water* we have in this scene the fateful glass of water which brings disgrace to the Duchess of Marlborough. The purpose of this technique is of course to ensure that right up to the moment when the curtain rises for the last act the spectator's heart shall be in his mouth. Plays were constructed on this principle not only by the younger Dumas and Augier, but also by Ibsen in his earliest plays.

The last act, however, always brings a happy solution to every problem. The plot is by now so complicated that the audience is quite incapable of guessing the solution, though at the same time entirely confident that all will be well in the end. The dramatic critic Sarcey, who, unlike his contemporaries, cherished an abiding affection for Scribe, was very irritated when the great tragic actress, Madame Bartet, overacted her part in one of Scribe's plays and gave her despair too realistic an expression. The incident occurred in a scene in *La bataille de dames* (*The Ladies' Battle*), when her lover was being dragged away to execution by the police. So movingly did the actress depict the agony of young Léonie that Sarcey felt himself compelled in the name of the public to reprove her. "Dear Lady", he said, "Pray do not be so anxious. You are in M. Scribe's hands; he is a fine fellow and he won't let you down. In the last act he will restore your handsome lover and see that you are married. Your young man pretends to put his head on the block, and we pretend to believe that he may lose it. You must pretend to be anxious, because courtesy demands it, but if you are more than reasonably anxious you embarrass both the author and all of us. The emotion that you show must bear some relation to the truth of the situation—and the truth is that none of this is really true: it has never happened".

This passage shows the atmosphere of unreality which pervades Scribe's plays. They are good theatre, and good theatre they are meant to be: they have no pretensions to reality.

The last line of a Scribe play often contains some allusion to the title. In *The Glass of Water*, Bolingbroke hands Masham his seals of office, and receives the answer, "And all this thanks to a glass of water". *The Ladies' Battle* ends in the same way; "It's not enough to play well in order to win", says the triumphant Countess. "True", replies her opponent, "you need to hold the aces and kings". At which the Countess, with a glance at the happy lover, exclaims, "Especially the King, when ladies wage war". Allusions to card games or chess are characteristic of Scribe, and may be noted in as late a play as Strindberg's *Gustav III*.

Plots such as those of Scribe would seem quite incredible if he had not also created characters expressly for them. These characters fall into two categories, the intriguers and their victims.

At the centre of his plays there is always a brilliant conspirator, who carries on his intrigues for the sheer joy of intriguing. To enable him to display his art in all its glory, it is necessary that the other characters shall be, if not fools, at least easily led and unsuspecting. The audience are in the chief conspirator's confidence from the very first moment, and by means of his asides they are kept informed of the progress of his plots. Thus they can derive great amusement from the spectacle of those poor credulous wretches who think they are behaving as heroes, when in fact they are being used as pawns by others, or else are chivvied along in ignorance of the fearful dangers around them, until at last they are safe in their lovers' arms, as happens to Masham in *The Glass of Water*. If ever Scribe tries to create a real character he fails miserably, and his dramas are almost always at their best when they are so full of incident that no one has any time to gain a real impression of the characters.

The dialogue is also determined by the plot. In no way does it resemble ordinary conversation—indeed, it hardly pretends to do so. A typical dramatic dialogue of Scribe's is one where the brilliant characters sparkle like fireworks, while the stupid, the pompous and the gullible betray themselves in every sentence they utter. Scribe's style is considered to be dull, but it is at any rate economical: it carries the reader straight into the action and anchors his attention there.

It is above all in these historical plays that Scribe's virtuosity as a constructor of plots is made plain. For the development of modern drama, however, his contemporary plays have been of at least equal significance. On the whole they are written after the same pattern; but however slight their connexion with real life, these plays, because of the subject with which they deal and the technique employed, have had a considerable effect on modern drama as developed by Augier and Dumas the younger.

The construction of *La Camaraderie* (*Comradeship*) is similar to that of the historical plays. Conspiracy and intrigue are represented in a contemporary setting of cliques and coteries. The play introduces us first to a group of people who have made a compact to secure each other's advancement to posts of honour and profit by every available means. To this end they influence opinion in journals and salons, and whisper confidences in the ears of ministers—with such success that all members of the group achieve fame and distinction, while outsiders are discredited and disgraced. As the leader of the conspiracy we find Madame de Mirémont, a former schoolmistress, who has succeeded in marrying a peer of France. There is also a hero, an honest young lawyer who is pushed forward to advancement without his being aware of it. Exactly like Masham in *The Glass of Water*, he falls in love with a girl, and to win her hand must secure election to Parliament. To achieve this his friends succeed in persuading the influential Mme. de Mirémont that he is in love with her. The ruse is not discovered until too late, when she can no longer take counter-measures, and in the final scene the hero makes this naive recantation: "How wrong I was to lament my fate and the wickedness of mankind. Why, even this morning, I was cursing the age for its plots and intrigues. Now I perceive that friendships can indeed be disinterested, and that one may succeed without recourse to cliques and shameful manœuvres". The play was immensely popular because it openly satirized the cliques which have always flourished in French politics. It is superficial, but it is also witty and entertaining, and it is certainly a forerunner of the "Comedy of Manners," in which Augier was later to display the sores on the body of French society.

Une Châine (*A Chain*) is probably the play of Scribe's which most foreshadows the dramas of the younger Dumas, a playwright on whom Scribe's technique was to have great influence. It tells of a young man who falls in love with a girl, but feels himself still bound to a former mistress, as if by a heavy chain, and it introduces several characters who are later to become stock figures in modern French drama; the *grande dame* who falls in love with a young genius, the deceived husband whose duelling pistols are always cocked, the innocent girl led to the altar without knowing anything about her husband or the extent of his affections, and finally the honest and prosperous father-in-law from the country. The issue is really a profoundly serious one, but Scribe cannot resist the temptation to contrive intrigues and really succeeds (without unduly straining our credulity) in presenting a series of highly dramatic situations.

The play shows both Scribe's strength and his weakness. It was written in 1841, and portrayed both characters and situations with a realism that modern drama was not to develop to the full until ten years later. As soon as the complexities of the plot begin to appear, the atmosphere changes, the characters become mere puppets in the author's hands, and the whole thing becomes just an ingenious piece of stagecraft. The novel at this period had already achieved a much higher degree of realism. Ten years before *A Chain* appeared, Stendhal had written in France *Le Rouge et le Noir*, a study of a similar situation, but executed with supreme realism and with very shrewd psychological insight.

The attention which Scribe gave to his plots was a very necessary element in the reform and growth of drama, which needed to recover some of the logic it had lost since the great days of the French classical period. The trouble is, however, that the mechanism of Scribe's plots is too obvious, and dramatic tension becomes the dominating factor in his plays. The play becomes a sort of chess problem where the spectator is presented with a situation for which there seems no solution until the author's skill suddenly reveals the move which resolves it. Scribe was once watching a performance of one of his own early plays whose plot he had forgotten; turning to his neighbour he said, "I am curious to see how I got myself out of this one". Perhaps it is the weakness of Scribe's plays that the spectator is more interested in the author's solution to the problem than in the psychological consistency of his characters' behaviour.

Scribe was very fond of placing one character at the mercy of two powerful personalities, each pulling him in a different direction. The typical example of this is *The Glass of Water*, where young Masham is tossed like a shuttle between the Duchess of Marlborough and Bolingbroke. Again in *Comradeship* the hero is placed between two intriguing ladies, and with various modifications the same situation is found in most of his main plays. The solution is usually so contrived that the main con-spirator achieves his object, and removes the last obstacle to the union of the young lovers in the final scene.

By his skill in the construction of plots Scribe became the obvious teacher, to whom young dramatists of succeeding generations looked. It is said of Sardou, his most faithful disciple and the heir of his crown, that he began his career by reading the first act of a Scribe drama with which he was not familiar, then composing the rest of the play, and finally comparing the result with Scribe's original.

The more ambitious playwrights of the realistic modern drama school which followed Scribe also made use of his technique. This holds true even of the younger Dumas, who rather ungrate-fully described Scribe as the Shakespeare of the shadow theatre, the master who could construct plays with characters who never came alive. Naturally Björnson and Ibsen were not such close intimates of Scribe, but in their young days, when they were theatre directors, they came much under his influence, because the Norwegian repertory gave pride of place to his plays. Björnson, indeed, in his early theatre reviews expressly warned his contemporaries not to omit that stage in development which could be described by the name of "the man with the new theatre machine". The influence of Scribe on Björnson's plays is apparent, not only in the early Norse dramas, but also in later contemporary plays. In his great feminist play, *Leonarda*, a forerunner of Ibsen's *A Doll's House*, the resemblance to *The Ladies' Battle* was so plain that he found it advisable to make one of his heroines say that she had just read the play.

The influence of Scribe also dominated Ibsen when he wrote his early historical plays, especially *Fru Inger til Östråt* (*Lady Inger of*

Östrât), while his first contemporary play, *De unges forbund* (*The League of Youth*), has as its hero, Stensgård, a mere puppet of the Scribe type who is tossed to and fro between two experienced plotters, Daniel Hejre and Lundestad. Gradually Ibsen cut the threads that bound him to Scribe's involved plots, but he never quite succeeded in freeing himself entirely from the tendency to over-elaborate his plots. Without those years of apprenticeship to Scribe, however, he might never have become the greatest master of technique in modern drama.

While Scribe was king of the French theatre, a poor German poet, Friedrich Hebbel, was completing his play, *Maria Magdalena*, in Paris in 1843. It was the greatest of the plays that fore-shadowed Ibsen's social dramas, and though it was described in the title as a domestic drama, it differed greatly from earlier German dramas. As Hebbel wrote in his diary while he was finishing the play, he hoped that there would be a new birth of domestic drama which would free it from excessive sentimentality and the rigid limitations which had come to hamper its growth.

Maria Magdalena shows some of the grey, northern, winter atmosphere that we find later in Ibsen. To some extent it resembles *Vildanden* (*The Wild Duck*), but it lacks altogether the sardonic humour which makes that play slightly less shattering to the audience. It also shares with Ibsen's modern plays the absence of any reconciliation, indeed the complete absence of any factors that might lead to a reconciliation. This play is also a forerunner of Ibsen, in that within the framework of ordinary domestic life it deals with problems that are fundamental to our whole conception of society; just as in Ibsen a single story is treated in a larger context and made typical of the outlook of a whole generation.

According to Hebbel himself, the story in *Maria Magdalena*, which centres round a joiner's family, is taken from real life. Klara's father, Anton, is a carpenter, honest but abnormally morose and surly. He is supposed to represent Hebbel's own father, and the joyless family life of the play is taken as representing that of his home.

The plot in essence is quite simple. Hebbel was beginning to work out a technique that Ibsen was to develop further in later domestic plays. The significant events have already occurred before the play starts, and it is their consequences as they are gradually revealed to the characters that shape the play.

Klara, the daughter of Anton the joiner, has fallen in love with a young man, referred to in the play as the secretary. But he has gone off to a university and nothing more has been heard of him, so she has become engaged to the writer, Leonard. Then the secretary returns and Leonard becomes jealous. To reassure Leonard, Klara agrees to become his lover; there is no risk as they will soon be married.

In the actual play we learn that Klara, who is expecting a child, is deserted by Leonard, a miserable fortune-hunter. He becomes engaged to the hunchback daughter of the Mayor, a very profitable undertaking for him. The secretary, an attractive young man, then asks for Klara's hand in marriage, but withdraws his offer when she confesses the truth. "No man could get over that".

Now there is no way out for Klara but death, and a death which will arouse no suspicion of suicide in her father. When she is told to go and fetch some water, she feels that fate has given her a signal; she can throw herself into the well and her father will not suspect that she has killed herself. When she has left the stage, her father enters with the secretary, who has been wounded. He has killed Leonard in a duel, but has himself received a fatal thrust. From him the father learns the secret that has so carefully been kept. Shortly after comes a message that Klara has been seen to fall into the well.

"It is you who showed her the way to death", says the secretary to Anton, "and I, I am the cause that she did not turn back. You, when you perceived her wretchedness, thought of the tongues that would hiss behind you, not of the vileness of the serpents to whom they belong. And I, I should have held her in my arms when she opened her heart to me in her bitter sorrow, but all I could think of was that villain's mocking laughter". But Anton remains standing, stiff and uncomprehending. Not until his daughter's body is carried in does he utter a word, and then, with great deliberation, he speaks the last line of the play. "No longer do I understand the world".

Maria Magdalena is no masterpiece in execution. The play is in prose, the costumes are modern, and Hebbel's inability to write good dramatic dialogue is more apparent than in his verse plays. His simple citizens often find themselves delivering long orations. The characterization is often rough and crude. Some of the characters, Klara, Anton and his son Karl, are well drawn, but there are no subtle shades. In the final act events pile up with such power and speed that the audience is given no breathing-space.

The greatness of the play lies in its fundamental idea, and the way in which Hebbel has succeeded in expressing it in a domestic setting. In the preface to the play he pointed out that the domestic tragedy had fallen into disfavour in Germany, on the grounds, he believed, that it had been dealing only with external elements, the contrast between poverty and plenty, and above all the social distinctions between the Second and the Third Estate. Such subjects could arouse sorrow, but were not the stuff of tragedy, for tragedy depended on inevitability. The conflicts in the earlier domestic dramas could have been resolved if the hero had had another thirty thaler in his pocket at the crucial moment, or if the girl he wished to marry had been of noble birth. Such is not the material of great dramatic art. A real domestic tragedy must be created round conflicts which arise within the domestic world, and which are peculiar to it. Only thus can the life and fate of an individual become universal symbols, and only thus can the strokes of blind fate seem as real in a picture of our everyday world as they do in classical tragedies.

It was Hebbel's great achievement that he was the first to succeed in this. The modern dramatists who followed Scribe never managed to reach the real heights of tragedy, though they often display quite a shrewd insight into social problems. This preoccupation, however, is the kind which Hebbel describes so bitingly when he says that poor-law guardians and unmarried daughters would be more grateful for it than lovers of the theatre.

There is another way in which *Maria Magdalena* grips us, despite its uneven quality and its improbabilities. The problem which it treats is timeless and universal, as are those in the plays of the great tragic poets and Ibsen. It attacks a fundamental human weakness, that in everything we do we are more concerned with our neighbour's opinions than with the intrinsic rightness and value of our actions.

A false code of morals and a false sense of honour—these are the motive forces behind action. It is these which drive Klara, when she is deserted by one lover, to become engaged to Leonard. Old Anton has only one emotion left, fear of disgrace, or what his fellow-men should say, whether justified or unjustified. "I can bear anything—I've shown that—anything except disgrace. Lay on me what burdens you will, but do not cut the nerve which holds me up". When the secretary hears of Klara's plight, his first thought is not to save her but to silence her faithless lover. Meanwhile the unhappy Klara, lest her father should seek refuge from disgrace in suicide, has tried to persuade Leonard to marry her, though far from loving him she loathes him. When this attempt fails she drowns herself, in the vain hope that her death will seem to be an accident. By morning the whole town is full of gossip.

If the characters had shouted the scandalous story through loud-speakers, it would have not been more widely known than it became through their anxiety to conceal it. They are smitten by all the blows of fate, because they try so hard to avoid them, just as Oedipus did, whom Hebbel mentions in the preface to his play.

The principle at stake in *Maria Magdalena* is precisely the same as that in Ibsen's social plays, namely the immorality of con-ventional morals. We allow our nearest and dearest to die, to be sacrificed to our false moral code. Our homes may collapse over our heads, but we still cling doggedly to our false convention and the best we can hope to attain is the negative attitude expres-ed in Anton's last words.

Hebbel also said in his preface that he was hoping to bring out in *Maria Magdalena* the same point which he had made in his historical plays, namely the contrasting attitudes of an older and a younger generation, and the merciless suppression of the younger pioneers. In the event we find ourselves not far removed from the historical drama of Schiller and Kleist, where the char-acters are the mouthpieces of various schools of thought, and the play is a conflict of ideas. Oehlenschläger, who was Hebbel's patron during his visit to Copenhagen in 1842-3, stood nearer Hebbel in this respect, for in his plays we often find characters representing successive generations.

This, however, was not enough for Hebbel. Inspired by Hegel, he wished to show the conflict between the community, representing one stage of historical and social development, and the individual, fighting, it may be unconsciously, for the next stage in social growth, and going down in the struggle. He made it plain in his preface to *Maria Magdalena* that this was also his intention in his domestic tragedies. Anton's final words show that we are at the end of one period of social culture and at the beginning of the next. Klara's sacrifice opens the way to a new conception of morality.

FRENCH DRAMA OF THE SECOND EMPIRE

(i) *Alexandre Dumas the Younger*

THE school of drama which flourished under the Second Empire, and which, from Paris, influenced drama throughout Europe, was known as Realist. It was contemporary with the Realist novel, and was much influenced by it. The playwrights shared the novelists' interest in social problems, and by their success and popularity in the European theatre they came to exercise an even more powerful influence. The younger Dumas was particularly conscious of this power, as we can see in his long prefaces.

When naturalism became the fashion, doubts arose whether this school had in fact achieved true realism, and it was felt that the plays were in this respect much inferior to the novels. The playwrights of the next generation did their best to free themselves from the limitations of the Augier-Dumas pattern and the technique of plot-construction which they had inherited from Scribe. But as long as people believed with Dumas that there was a special *don dramatique*, a natural instinct for dramatic presentation, which had very little to do with poetic talent, it was almost impossible to disentangle oneself from the toils of French salon comedy.

With all its defects, however, this type of comedy did allow the theatre to become a forum for the discussion of social problems. In Dumas and Augier we see people of the period struggling with such problems, but it is not really surprising that to a later generation they should look rather like professional debaters and the world in which they moved like a conventional stage setting.

The neo-romantics who preceded Dumas and Augier tried by every means to represent the period of their plays faithfully. Dumas and Augier were tired of such attempts and thought that if they chose contemporary settings for their plays, there would be no real need to reproduce them in any great detail. The stage was usually set as a salon, with a double door at the back and side-entrances, corresponding rather to the *antichambre* of French classical tragedy. This taste for the simple and conventional was to recur despite all the efforts of the Naturalists, in Strindberg's dramas of the Eighties.

The rather extravagant air of the characters who exchange witty conversation in the salons of Augier and Dumas is derived directly from French neo-romanticism, as is also the taste of these two authors for sentimental scenes and declamatory tirades. Actually they are more characteristic of Dumas the younger than of Augier.

Dumas the younger was the son of the author of *The Three Musketeers*, and was born, out of wedlock, when the latter was an unknown, twenty-year-old clerk in a lawyer's office. His mother was a sempstress, eight years older than his father. After his first literary success, in 1831, the elder Dumas acknowledged his son but did not marry the mother. Consequently, Alexandre Dumas the younger had to suffer many jeers from his school-mates. His concern for unmarried mothers and illegitimate children was founded on his own experiences; indeed he says as much in several prefaces to plays, and in his novel, *L'Affaire Clemenceau*.

After a time he took his place in his father's household. By the standards of the day, Alexandre Dumas was extremely wealthy, but he was also recklessly extravagant, and in 1852 he had to flee to escape his creditors. In his old age his son had to support him, and Dumas the younger has described the remarkable friendship between father and son in his play, *Un Père prodigue* (*A Prodigal Father*).

Dumas the younger became very rich himself after some early years of struggle and stress, partly thanks to his own theatre royalties, but also to the royalties from successive editions of his father's novels. His preoccupation with courtesans and the bohemian world which he had frequented during his father's lifetime soon vanished, but throughout his life he retained a sympathy for unmarried mothers and illegitimate children, and the propaganda in his plays is considered to have helped greatly to improve their legal status.

Dumas never came into real contact with the bourgeois world whose spokesman he wished to be. In his youth he lived with the bohemian society which he christened, with his own word, the *demi-monde*, and he ended his life as a guest in the salons of the real aristocracy, notably in the literary circle which grew up around Princess Mathilde. The world that he depicts therefore seems unreal to us, and indeed, except for one or two plays, his work never had as much influence outside France as that of Augier, whose scenes from bourgeois domestic life appeared much more convincing.

Among the many plays of Dumas the elder, there was one, *Antony,* dealing with a contemporary story, which achieved great success. It was first staged and met with an excellent reception in 1831, the year after *Hernani* appeared, and though it has no literary value whatever, it foreshadows in some respects the work of the author's son. The hero, with the title part, is born out of wedlock and is consequently despised in the salons of Paris. He takes as his mistress the wife of a Colonel in Strasbourg. Towards the end of the play the two lovers realize that the Colonel is bound to discover them. The wife knows that her husband will kill her, but is chiefly grieved because her daughter will then become an outcast from society, as Antony has been. To save his mistress's reputation Antony shoots her just as the Colonel enters the room. "She resisted me", he declares, "and so I killed her".

It was for this final statement, psychologically incredible but dramatically effective, that Dumas the younger expressed his admiration in a preface. There was a sort of logic in it which appealed to him. Antony is a replica of Didier in Hugo's *Marion Delorme*, but without the period costume. Dumas the younger was affected by the play because it dealt with illegitimate children and their difficulties in society, and he was particularly moved by the notion that the Colonel's wife sacrificed her life to preserve appearances and enable her daughter to enter society unblemished.

Dumas the younger only turned to play-writing by chance. His first publication was a collection of verses, his second a novel, rather in his father's style. The novel he published in 1848 with the title *La Dame aux camélias* was directly inspired by his own experiences though greatly romanticized. At the age of twenty he had met one of the most famous courtesans in Paris, Marie du Plessis. She was the daughter of a seaman ; she entranced everyone by her beauty and won sympathy because she was consumptive. She was extremely extravagant, and in less than a year Dumas had to break off the connexion. A few years later, in 1847, she died at the age of 23.

It was, then, a recent and true story that Dumas told in his novel. At the suggestion of a friend he dramatized the novel, but the censors forbade the performance of the play. This of course caused the book to be talked about even more, and several more editions were printed. Finally, though, its popularity was completely overshadowed by that of the play, which had its première early in 1852.

The play, which is still being performed in theatres all over the world, is much more loosely constructed than Dumas' later plays. The first act merely introduces the characters and the setting, and the final act might also be said to be dramatically unnecessary. It shows the heroine on her bed of sickness, visited by her lover Armand Duval, and dying after she has been reunited with him.

There is a shimmer of belated romanticism over this play. Marguerite Gautier might have been one of those virtuous courtesans of the old romantic days. Dumas' work in its setting and characterization is also intimately linked with that of another late-flowering off-shoot of romanticism, Murger, and his *Scènes de La Vie de Bohême*, where the heroine, Mimi, also dies of consumption.

Dumas lacked Murger's poetical gifts, and his attempts to portray two visitors from the gay world of Murger's Bohemia, eking out a poverty-stricken existence in a garret, were not successful. No less artificial was the gaiety in Marguerite Gautier's salon, where the guests are counts and barons who sign cheques for twenty thousand francs without turning a hair.

In the faded romanticism of Dumas' heroic world we find ideals and sentiments that strike us as strange. An aged and noble duke discovers that Marguerite Gautier is the image of his daughter who died of consumption, and he invites her to consider herself as his child. It is also rather difficult to understand how or why the diffident, melancholy Marguerite came to adopt this way of life, and why she has to lead such a hectic and extravagant existence. The only answer we receive is that it is because consumption will soon carry her off.

Through the Duvals we get a glimpse of the life of a prosperous bourgeois family in the provinces. Armand comes into Marguerite's salon, talking about his dead mother; this is his custom whenever he finds himself in bad company. Indeed it is a habit which becomes universal among all Dumas' heroes from the country. They express their innocence by speaking, at the most unsuitable moment, of their mothers. This notion is to be found in other playwrights of the period, and even in Augier who usually has a more realistic understanding of what goes on in the average family.

After the first performance one critic maintained that the motivation was weak in the great scene where Armand's father secures a promise from Marguerite that she will reject Armand's advances because otherwise his sister's engagement may be broken off. The sister's fiancé belongs to a family so respectable that they will not allow their son to marry the sister of a notorious courtesan's lover. Yet it was sentimental scenes such as this that maintained the play's great popularity.

Above all, the audiences of the day appreciated *The Lady of the Camellias* as a realistic play. They had not been spoilt by many such vivid presentations of real life on the stage, and already visits were being paid to the grave of Marie du Plessis, and poems written in her honour.

What survives, with poetic vitality, in *The Lady of the Camellias* is the portrait of the young girl herself, refined and weary of life, her character so out of tune with the setting in which she has been placed. In contrast to those noble stage courtesans of earlier days, the lady of the camellias does not indulge in the rhetoric of pathos. She does not accuse society or her fellow beings. Only at one moment, when her suffering is at its height and she is talking to Armand's father, does she allow herself a gentle reproach against the cruelty of the world. Usually, however, it is not her exclusion from respectable society that distresses her. She is tortured by the emptiness and the lack of human feeling which she finds in her world: "We seem happy, and people envy us. The truth is that we have lovers who ruin themselves, not for us, as they claim, but for their own vanity. In their conceit we come first; in their respect last. We have friends whose friendship means only servility, never disinterested devotion. Around us there is nothing but ruin, shame and deceit". It is Armand's heart, not his name that she wants. She longs to meet a lover who will not ask about her past, but who will love her thoughts, her inmost being, a man in whose presence she can feel a breath of country air, of clean air, of childhood. "We were all children once, whatever we have become since".

What grieves her is the feeling that she is shut out from the world of real action and true feeling, and has to live in a society where every tone, every word, every gesture is false. Dumas' loathing of the sham and deceit of the world he lives in is already apparent here, and it will be even plainer in his next great drama, *Le Demi-Monde*.

The Lady of the Camellias started a new fashion in contemporary society and the great courtesans became all the rage. So much so that in 1855 Augier wrote a play, *Le Mariage d'Olympe* (*Olympia's Marriage*), in which an old marquis asks why a well-known *cocotte* in Paris should suddenly become world-famous and receive so many tributes at her grave. He is told that everyone these days is passionately interested in the salvation of fallen women, and that every author is making speeches about the virginity of the soul "and other such-like metaphysical paradoxes".

When Dumas wrote *Le Demi-Monde* in 1854 he created a drama which has been held to be his masterpiece. He wrote others later, with better constructed plots, and scenes with more dramatic tension, but he never wrote another where setting, action and purpose were so well fused into a harmonious whole.

In this play we meet for the first time several situations and characters which are to recur frequently in Dumas' plays and those of his school. It has met with more popular acclaim than any other of his plays except *The Lady of the Camellias*.

This play also is based on personal experience. In a later preface Dumas described the originals of his characters and the setting in which he placed them. By the time he wrote this preface the word which he had coined and given as a title to his play had taken on another meaning than the one he had intended. This may have been the reason why in the Swedish version of the play in 1880 it was called *Falska Juveler* (*False Jewels*); for it was a world of false jewels that Dumas wished to portray, a society of people who had sunk below their proper class, of counts and marquises with remarkable luck at cards, of marchionesses and countesses who either imagined they had had husbands, or if they ever did, had lost them. This small world had to all appearances retained the fashions of the great world, and a newcomer would have no means of telling that he was not in the most exclusive society.

In the days of naturalism, this picture of earlier times seemed old-fashioned. But we are so far removed from the Second Empire that we can appreciate it as a historical document, and admire the skill with which Dumas has presented in dramatic form a period piece which ought really to be a novel. Naturally some sacrifices have to be made to theatrical convention. Dumas must have someone who can explain to us the strange life of make-believe that is going on before our eyes. So he has created the greatest of his 'raisonneurs', Olivier de Jalin.

The raisonneur has a long history in the theatre. He is to be found in Molière's comedies, as well as in those of the Roman comic playwrights. He is the personification of common sense, and serves as the author's own mouthpiece. As a son-in-law or an uncle in a family he lets fall his asides, often directed straight at the audience. He was of course a familiar figure in 19th century comedies, before Dumas, though Scribe usually makes one of the chief conspirators play this part. In *The Demi-Monde* Olivier has both these functions to fulfil. He is the master of ceremonies in the play, who introduces young Raymond, but he also has to show the audience what goes on behind the scenes. He also plays the part of Providence, and rescues those who have come into the demi-monde by mistake from becoming entangled in its toils. He allows Raymond to discover what Suzanne d'Ange, the girl he loves, is really like, and saves the young and innocent Marcelle from the demi-monde by marrying her himself. He also expresses the author's point of view, not merely about the demi-monde, but about moral problems in general. He has too many functions to perform, and cannot really appear as a consistent character; and people who know everything are always irritating. Never-

theless, Olivier is one of the wittiest and least irritating of Dumas'
raisonneurs.

These characters are of course to be found in all his plays, and
they vary with his interest of the moment. At one stage, when
Dumas was particularly concerned with feminine psychology,
the raisonneur was usually a professional 'ladies man' such as de
Ryons in *L'ami des femmes* (*The Friend of Women*), produced in
1864, who refused to marry because it would hamper his study of
women.

In Dumas' earlier plays the raisonneurs have incomes of sixty
thousand francs, and need therefore have no occupation. As time
passed, however, Dumas began to feel that they ought to have a
respectable occupation, and in the play of 1876, *L'Étrangère* (*The
Fair Stranger*), the raisonneur appears as the family doctor. This
change made his constant presence in the house a good deal more
probable than hitherto. He was also able to comment on events
with the cool impartiality of a physician, and with the cynical
scepticism which the Seventies and Eighties found so attractive.
These same doctor-raisonneurs reappear in the Scandinavian
dramas of Björnson and Ibsen.

Dumas also made his raisonneurs responsible for pitching the
note, as it were, of his play, for explaining the title and its significance. In the second act of *The Demi-Monde* Olivier produces
his famous description of the demi-monde, comparing it with a
basket of peaches in a fruit shop. Only a single black spot distinguishes the bad from the good peaches. In one form or another
this introductory speech recurs in most of Dumas' plays. It appears
at the beginning of every play with the same regularity as the
cadenza in the first movement of a concerto, and for the same
purpose—to allow the soloist to show his skill. It is also of course
a commentary on the play, inserted by the author to enable him
to make his point plain, without actually appearing in person.
Scribe in his day also made use of this device: at the beginning
of *The Glass of Water* Bolingbroke makes his point about small
causes and great effects, which later proves a clue to the whole
play. An instance of the same technique in later plays can be
found in *The Wild Duck,* where Dr. Relling speaks of the need
for the 'life lie'.

Next to Olivier, whose didactic voice echoes through the

whole play, the most important character is Suzanne d'Ange. She is the soul of the demi-monde, the embodied spirit of its corruption, as Olivier is its deadly enemy.

The struggle in the play rages round Raymond de Nanjac, another familiar type from Scribe, the naive young man who is thrust into perils of which he is never aware, but who is piloted to safety by the raisonneur. He arrives in Paris, straight from ten years' service in the garrisons in Africa. A few years before *The Demi-Monde* was written, Algeria had been finally conquered by France, and with this acquisition of a colony French drama acquired a new type of hero, the conquering hero, the Chasseur d'Afrique, who preserved in the field the innocence of a Rousseau, and knew nothing of the decadence of Paris society. When he went out of fashion, he was succeeded by other types, each in his turn becoming equally conventional. There was, for example, the brilliant young man of humble birth, serving as secretary in the home of a stupid millionaire and naturally falling in love with his daughter; and the young engineer who arrived in Paris with epoch-making discoveries, and ran the risk of having them stolen by some swindler, or getting involved in dangerous love affairs, or being challenged to a duel. Among the Scandinavian dramatists we find similar types.

The plot involves an attempt to lure Raymond to marry Madame d'Ange, but, just as in Scribe, there is a parallel plot interwoven with the main one. A pure young girl, Marcelle, lives in the demi-monde because she is the niece of the gaming-house proprietress, but she loathes the life that she is compelled to lead. Olivier has told her that her reputation will be compromised if she stays, and has tried to rescue her. In return, she has fallen in love with him. At the decisive moment she avows her affection for Olivier, who is not quite certain about his own feelings. She is another stock figure in the plays of Augier and Dumas. We might imagine that the young girls of the Norwegian drama, who make proposals of marriage and take their fates into their own hands, are a new type, whereas in fact these lively young ladies had already made their appearance in French drama.

The factor which produces the highest degree of dramatic tension in most of the plays of Dumas and his successors is the fear of scandal. This was true in Scribe's day also. The terror of compromising oneself ruled the hearts of all women. Their male protectors were ready to sacrifice life and honour to save them from such a fate, and their enemies knew how to use this powerful weapon to the full.

Another device is the intercepted letter. In the French dramas of this period, the heroes and heroines are always writing letters, often in disguised hand-writing, without any address. They usually fall into the hands of those who should not see them, and the most terrible complications ensue, in which the writers have to adopt every means to explain away their real significance. The most dramatic scenes are those where a man and a woman fight for the possession of a letter, as in the fourth act of *The Demi-Monde*. One of these classic scenes of French drama has been brilliantly parodied in Strindberg's *Det nya Riket* (*The New Kingdom*).

The duel also, an inevitable element in the drama of the Second Empire, occurs in *The Demi-Monde*. In the plays of Dumas and Augier it serves as a kind of Divine Judgment, in which the guilty always perish.

Dumas' earlier dramas were first and foremost descriptions of environment. Three years after writing *The Demi-Monde*, however, he broke fresh ground with *Le Fils naturel* (*The Natural Son*), a social problem play. From then onwards, though in varying degrees, he used the stage as a pulpit from which he preached his social sermons. This period of Dumas' play-writing foreshadows the work of Ibsen. But Ibsen succeeded in achieving what Dumas in his last years had bitterly to acknowledge he had failed to do, namely to make the stage a public platform for the discussion of social problems.

Dumas' failure was due to the defects in his programme as well as to artistic weakness. He went straight into the attack against notorious social injustices, demanding amendment of certain specific sections of the law. Ibsen's greatness lay in posing a problem without giving specific answers. He realized that it was not for him to play the part of a reforming legislator, but rather to stimulate the public conscience. His plays can never become dated, for they deal with fundamental human problems. Dumas' plays, on the contrary, lose their topical significance as soon as

the reforms for which he pressed have been carried out. Divorce
was legalized in France in 1884, a reform in which his influence
may have played some part, but as the community came to take
better care of unmarried mothers and illegitimate children so his
concern for them came to seem less important.

In spite of the narrowness of his social interests, Dumas did
undoubtedly pave the way for reforms in the status of women.
He considered that existing laws, framed by men for men,
weighed most injustly against women, but he weakened the
effect of his pleas by continually citing extreme and unusual
cases. *The Natural Son* is a good instance of this. Diderot
before him had endowed his natural son with excessive nobility;
for his friend's sake he denies his affection for the girl whom he
loves, and who loves him. Dumas' hero is not only equally
noble, he is also an intellectual genius, while his father, oddly
enough, is a perfect fool. The play ends with a scene where the
son, famous now and admired by all France, refuses to acknowledge his father or to use his name. We are left with the undeniable impression that illegitimate children have greater talents
than others.

In his later propaganda plays, Dumas avoided the ingenuous-
ness and unevenness which marred *The Natural Son,* but the
basic faults were still there. This was true even of the play *Les
Idées de Madame Aubray* (*Madame Aubray's Ideas*) written in 1867,
which the historians of French literature regard as his most mature
work. The chief character expresses Dumas' own reforming
zeal; Mme. Aubray devotes her life to rescuing fallen girls and to
caring for illegitimate children. Her young son is fired by the
same zeal, and falls in love with one of his mother's protegées
Jeannine, an unmarried mother whom they met at a seaside resort.
For a moment Mme. Aubray hesitates—can she accept the practical consequences of her own faith, and respect a woman who in
youthful folly committed one error, for which she should not
have to pay with a life of misery? In the end, her better instincts
win the day and she consents to the marriage. 'This is too much',
are the final words of the play spoken by one of her friends, and
that also appears to have been the attitude of contemporary
audiences. A present-day reader is probably more disconcerted
by an earlier passage, in which the son declares his readiness to

accept in marriage, blindfold, a woman who has made a mistake, if his mother desires it. Mme. Aubray and her whole circle, quite contrary to their author's intention, create a comic impression by their determination to meddle with the most intimate affairs of others, and settle them in accordance with their own theories.

In his prefaces Dumas maintains that the most important quality in a playwright is logic. From the first word in a play to its final denouement, logic must be consistently maintained. Act must fit on to act, scene on to scene with mathematical precision, and the final solution must be as inevitable as the answer to a problem in algebra. "A solution should never be changed", says Dumas. "A solution is a mathematical answer. If the answer is wrong, it means that the problem has been wrongly worked out. Indeed, the play should begin with the solution, or rather, one cannot begin to write until the final scene, the final gesture, the final words are clear".

Dumas has with reason been compared to Corneille. Like Dumas, Corneille plans his characters in situations which are very difficult to resolve. The conflict in Dumas usually lies between conscience and social conventions. In words which foreshadow Ibsen he says, "there are two moralities, the absolute, and the legal." Dumas was not worried, any more than Corneille had been, when rigorous logic led him to absurd conclusions. With plots constructed in this spirit the characters are bound to display the inflexibility of something cast in one piece. They do not change in the course of the play and there is little light and shade in the drawing of their emotions. Corneille and Dumas present above all characters with real personalities. When a play is constructed in this way no side issues and no minor episodes can be permitted, for the spectator must be allowed to follow the logical development of the story undistracted. Indeed in several of his later plays Dumas returned to the conception of the three classical unities; in particular the time allowed for the action of the play seldom exceeds the permitted twenty-four hours. Occasionally he nearly attains the ideal of the unity of time, when the action of his play is conceived as taking no longer than the actual performance. Zola, Ibsen and Strindberg were to do the same thing in later years.

The strong points of this technique are its clarity and its dramatic concentration; the weaknesses are its rationalism, its crude characterization and its liking for paradox and stage situations which are psychologically improbable and artistically disturbing. It was this logical extravagance which brought about Corneille's fall, and Dumas developed in exactly the same way.

External circumstances also combined to develop Dumas' dramatic work in this direction. The war of 1870 and the internal struggles which followed it in France moved Dumas very deeply. He thought much about the causes of France's defeat and discovered them, as did various contemporaries, in the moral corruption of the Second Empire, in its love for luxury and in the dissolution of family life. He wrote a pamphlet on this subject, with the title *L'Homme-femme*, and developed the same theme as a play, *La femme de Claude* (*Claude's Wife*) in 1873. The hero is an inventor who discovers his wife in the act of selling his secrets to the agent of a foreign power, and shoots her on the spot. The only significant point about this highly coloured play is the symbolism whereby Dumas makes the wife represent the moral corruption which has been ruining France.

The influence of Dumas' changed attitude to women upon Strindberg is plain from the latter's admiring references to Dumas. Whether the symbolism in Ibsen's social plays owes as much to him is more doubtful. Some Scandinavian literary critics have suggested that the character of Hedda Gabler owes a good deal to the heroine of one of Dumas' most successful later plays, *The Fair Stranger*, which appeared in 1876. Dumas was led to write this play partly by his general hatred of women, but also by a desire to provide a part for Sarah Bernhardt, who loved to play the roles of extravagant and fantastically cruel women. In the play the heroine recounts her own history; she was half-negress by birth, the daughter of a plantation owner and a slave. Shortly after her birth her father sold mother and child as slaves. When she grew up the girl swore implacable vengeance against the man. The old raisonneur in the play, Rémonin, an old family doctor, is her opponent. He speaks of certain malignant germs or bacteria which attack the body from within. Like Ibsen in *En folkefiende* (*An Enemy of the People*), the doctor points out the symbolism, how in the body politic there are also hostile germs which seek to destroy it; but the body does not wish to be destroyed—it wants to live. Therefore it renders the germs susceptible to their own poison.

Dumas combines his scientific knowledge, newly acquired from Pasteur, with his old liking for happy endings. It is now almost a law of nature that virtue must triumph.

With this play Dumas has come full circle back to his beginning —to romanticism. His exotic heroine with negro blood in her veins is in some way a reflection of himself. It was the inherited negro blood, the restless mulatto spirit coming into its own at last, with its taste for the bizarre and the violent.

(ii) *Emile Augier*

Emile Augier was born in 1820, and was consequently four years older than Dumas, but his début as a writer of prose plays came much later, and his success, unlike that of Dumas, was not immediate and brilliant. Outside France his plays, which were concerned with politics and class conflicts, had more influence than those of Dumas and from 1860 to 1880 he was received with deeper appreciation in France itself. He was the sober son of middle-class parents, and was brought up to follow his father's profession of the law.

Dumas was an aristocrat even when he fought for social equality, and something of a romantic even when most realistically painting the contemporary scene. Augier, by his whole nature and inclination was a democrat who had no use for romanticism. This is not to say that he was in any way bigoted; no one dealt shrewder blows at philistinism, the abuses of modern political democracy or a prosaic attitude to life. His fundamental attitude, however, was always bourgeois and unromantic.

This is already apparent in the verse comedies, which were the first works he wrote for the stage. Dumas was a child of the romantic drama; Augier sprang from the reaction against it. The first playwright to give expression to this reaction was Ponsard, who made some not very successful attempts to revive the French classical tragedy. Augier began as his pupil with some short sentimental verse comedies, rather in the vein of Musset's *proverbes*. *Gabrielle,* which appeared in 1849—the same year as *The Lady of the Camellias*—shows Augier's attitude very clearly.

The plot is the theme of *L'École des Maris* (*School for Husbands*) in reverse. Julien wins back his wife, Gabrielle, who is on the point of running away with his secretary, by his nobility and his spiritual superiority. Without betraying the fact that he knows whose lover the secretary is, he delivers to him—and to Gabrielle who is listening behind the door—a homily on the unhappy results of free love, and an eloquent hymn of praise about the beauty of home life. Gabrielle, who is left to choose freely, bids the secretary farewell for ever, and praises her husband, whom she now sees in a new light, before an assembled gathering of all the family: "O père de famille, O poëte! je t'aime".

This glorification of the father of the family and of family life is also to be found in the domestic drama of the 18th century. Diderot's *Le père de famille* (*The Father of the Family*) concludes with a line spoken by the hero: "How sweet and yet how cruel it is to be a father". Since the Romantics had preached free love and the rights of lovers with such zeal, there was need for a new apotheosis of family life. The revolutionary effect of Augier's drama on his age may well be seen in the complaints of one Romantic critic, that he presented passion and poetry as ridiculous fantasies, and pandered to the low taste of the public. The play was, however, very successful in France and even more so in Scandinavia, where the idea of home has a much richer meaning. It contributed something to Björnson's first play, *Mellem Slagene* (*Between the Battles* (1856)), and his first contemporary play, *De nygifte* (*The Newly-married Couple*). In Ibsen's *Kjaerlighedens Komedie* (*Love's Comedy*), the spirit of Augier's play can be discerned, and in Guldstad's final speech there are arguments which had been used by Julien. One can even see traces of *Gabrielle* in *Fruen fra havet* (*The Lady from the Sea*).

For his first comedies Augier used a kind of verse, which ran the constant risk of degenerating into rhyming prose. When, following Dumas, he turned to the realist prose drama, he achieved in his very first play the masterpiece of his life, *Le gendre de M. Poirier* (*The Son-in-law of M. Poirier*).

Augier found the idea for his play in a novel by Sandeau, *Sacs et Parchemins*, and Sandeau collaborated in the writing of the play. The theme to be treated was the relation between the aristocracy of birth and the oligarchy of wealth, and in the conditions

of the day it was a topical one. During the July Monarchy and
the Second Empire, the Third Estate had steadily increased its
powers, while rich upstarts were coming forward in a steady
stream to enjoy themselves at the expense of the old nobility.
Many of the latter had emigrated, while the influence of the
remainder was much diminished owing to the so-called 'inner
withdrawal' or retirement of members of noble families who
felt constrained by their legitimist principles to refuse public
office. One result of this attitude was an irritability, resulting
from enforced idleness, which young noblemen in Dumas' plays
were always displaying. When they had spent their patrimony,
there was nothing else for them to do but marry into the families
of the new financial magnates. These plutocrats had a great
weakness for such alliances, and the most famous of them—Augier
wrote about him in one of his plays—the great financier, Mirès,
would not accept as a son-in-law anyone less than a prince of the
blood. In Augier's play Poirier, a wealthy merchant, gives his
daughter in marriage to a marquis, Gaston de Presles. The conflict between him and his father-in-law is the conflict between
the titles of nobility and the money-bags of commerce.

This main conflict is, as always in Augier, closely bound up
with a love story. The theme is the same as in *Gabrielle,* but the
roles are reversed. Gaston de Presles, newly-married, has deserted
his wife for a lady of fashion, but she wins him back by the same
means as Julien wins Gabrielle, by native dignity and nobleness of
mind. Antoinette, however, acts on impulse, and it is her natural
instincts that bring her victory.

The construction of the plot, and the representation of the
characters, recall the works of the French classical period by their
symmetry. There are two representatives of the nobility, one
wise and one foolish, and similarly two business men. Poirier,
vain and pompous, has a wise business friend, Verdelet, while his
son-in-law, a proud and wanton dandy, has for a friend the
Duke of Montmeyran, a man who has overcome prejudice
against his noble birth by serving as a common soldier with the
Chasseurs d'Afrique. This is an arrangement with which we are
familiar in Molière. Each of the chief characters has a confidant
who provides a refreshing contrast of good sense, and to some
extent plays the part of a raisonneur. The simplicity of the plot

is also reminiscent of Molière. It is Poirier's own daughter, the Marquis's deserted wife, who by her understanding of both sides succeeds in reconciling the two parties.

Because of its clear and comprehensible plot, the play became immediately popular not only in France but all over Europe. It was performed in Sweden as early as 1855, and was frequently revived, whereas it was much longer before Dumas' plays were as warmly received. The simple structure of the play had one further advantage, in that it left the playwright plenty of time in which to develop its characterization in greater detail.

The best character is that of Poirier himself. He is the self-made man, so often found in later plays and novels. The type is essentially a product of 19th century industrial progress, but is not unknown in earlier works; Molière's Georges Dandin and Jourdain in *Le Bourgeois Gentilhomme* (*The Bourgeois Gentleman*) are direct predecessors of Poirier. Augier saw this connexion quite clearly. In the very first scene of the play he makes Gaston say about his father-in-law, "to describe him in a word, he is Georges Dandin as a father-in-law". Indeed, Augier originally meant to call the play *Georges Dandin's Revenge*.

But Gaston is quite wrong in imagining that he has a mild version of Dandin to deal with, for as the play develops Poirier shows his claws more and more. He is genial or harsh in response to whatever emotion is roused in him, and can be both sympathetic and forbidding at one and the same time.

His counterpart, Gaston de Presles, displays the same subtle mixture of strength and weakness. He is superficial, an idler and a bully, with the exaggerated sense of honour typical of his class. But he shows his breeding in the assurance of his manner, his wit and charm, and his gallant and graceful bearing.

Poirier's daughter, Antoinette, is also an admirable character, a middle-class girl—every inch of her—but sensitive and imaginative enough to rise above her prejudices and read her husband's inmost thoughts.

Gaston has regarded his marriage as a commercial transaction which will enable him to pay his debts, and has devoted no attention to his wife. He continues his bachelor ways, and three months after his wedding is prepared to fight a duel with a rival for a gay countess of fairly easy virtue. He regards it as a point of honour to pay his debts and meet his social obligations, even to the extent of a duel. It has not, however, occurred to him that he has any obligations to the woman he has made his wife; the one act of raising a daughter of the people to the rank of a marquise is enough in itself. Moreover, it was Poirier who had been tempted by the title, and arranged the marriage before Antoinette fell in love with him.

Antoinette is now determined to win his heart, and she succeeds because she can understand, as her father cannot, the aristocratic notions of honour by which Gaston is moved.

The final act brings the climax of the plot. Antoinette commands Gaston, if he wishes to earn her forgiveness, to withdraw from the duel for the countess's good name, and to apologize to his opponent: there follows a bitter struggle in Gaston between his love and his sense of honour. Exhausted, he sinks down at last into a chair and bids his friend convey his apology. Immediately Antoinette goes over to him, kisses him on the forehead and says, "Now, go and fight".

It is a real *scene à faire*, which French literary historians have compared with the finest scenes in the classical tragedies. To secure a happy ending, Augier has recourse to the device of an apology from Gaston's opponent, with the result that the outcome is, if harmonious, also somewhat of an anticlimax.

Augier is happiest when he has numerous characters to manipulate. His technique, unlike that of Dumas, is not based on logic and a conflict of wills, but rather on a kind of internal balance which ensures that every character gets what he deserves. The advantage of this technique is that it affords greater opportunities for introducing a variety of types, and displaying their qualities in all their facets. This indeed is Augier's chief delight. He often writes a whole episode or whole scene merely to throw light upon some quality in his characters. A good instance in this play is the famous 'picture' scene. Gaston has bought a modern landscape painting, and a whole group of people has gathered round to examine it. The two noblemen express their opinions rather too confidently, but with fine taste and judgment. Antoinette shows the warmth of her feelings, Verdelet his sound common sense. Poirier finds the picture uninteresting, and speaks of an etching of his own, a dog barking at a sailor's hat on the shore: that is something a man can understand, it has a story to tell, it is simple and moving. He is shocked at the price Gaston has paid for this picture—fifty golden louis. "Fifty louis to a poor fool who is starving. By dinner-time you could have had it for twenty-five".

After the production of *The Son-in-law of M. Poirier* Augier's reputation rose to heights which almost overshadowed that of the younger Dumas. In his social comedies he castigated the moral corruption of his age, and upheld the claims of the family against the tyranny of the courtesan and the speculator in the France of the Second Empire. In his political dramas he branded parliamentary and political corruption.

These political dramas, which had a particularly strong influence on subsequent Scandinavian playwriting, consisted of a series of three plays, *Les éffrontés* (*The Impertinents*), *Le fils de Giboyer* (*Giboyer's Son*), and *Lions et Renards* (*Lions and Foxes*). The plays are not connected, but certain characters appear in all three, and they all tell of the struggles in France between the Clerical and Radical parties, a conflict which raged throughout the 19th century, and was not finally resolved until the Dreyfus affair. They have been variously judged by French critics. From a literary point of view they might be said to constitute a novelty, for political issues and personalities had not appeared on the French stage since the days of Beaumarchais. These political issues Augier regarded essentially with the eye of a moralist, and always combined them with a love-story. His example had a stimulating effect on the whole development of European drama, and Björnson and Ibsen were clearly inspired by him when they wrote their political plays.

In *The Impertinents* (1861) Augier presents the political decay of his age with some excellently conceived characters, moving through one of his most elaborate and complicated plots. Vernouillet, a speculator on the Bourse, is his chief character. This man has founded a bank, and at its crash has succeeded in enriching himself at the expense of his shareholders by as much as eight hundred thousand francs. At the beginning of the play Vernouillet is a wealthy man but despised and opposed by all. Suddenly he hits on the idea of buying a newspaper; "With my money I can then possess myself of the one instrument of power which money has not conquered—public opinion. The Press is a wonderful instrument whose powers no one yet realizes; so far, journalists have been mere hacks—make way for Paganini".

By allowing his assistants to spread inaccurate reports of foreign affairs, he contrives to direct operations on the Stock Exchange to his own advantage. He declines for his paper the grant which the authorities have been allowing, and transfers its allegiance to the opposition party. Now the Government regards him with a very healthy respect. By using every section of his paper to serve his own ends, he regains his position in society. Friends he secures by printing favourable notices about the dancers and actresses who are their mistresses; his enemies he holds in check by threats of publishing information about scandals in their past. With unparalleled audacity he even turns to his own advantage the awkward situations caused by his libellous articles. In the final act, to be sure, his marriage plans go awry, but he has won complete control over public opinion, and is about to extend his influence and reputation by the purchase of another paper.

For some years before the appearance of *The Impertinents* the Paris press had been in the hands of a number of financial sharks who made use of their newspapers for advertisement and exploitation. The original of Augier's Vernouillet was a financier and newspaper magnate called Mirès. He owned several Paris papers, carried on financial transactions with foreign powers, had a say in all important appointments and consorted with princes of the blood and noblemen of the highest rank. The very year before this play was produced his daughter married the Prince de Polignac. The following year he was charged with fraudulent practices and finally sentenced to a month's imprisonment. Augier needed courage to point him out so plainly.

An even better portrait than that of Vernouillet is that of his assistant in the world of journalism, Giboyer. In *The Impertinents* in particular this character is one of the liveliest and most original ever conceived by Augier. Giboyer is the first instance in the theatre of a type which later became very common, the bohemian journalist. He wears a shabby frock-coat, and carries a pipe which he cannot bear to be parted from, even when entering the elegant ball-rooms of the aristocracy. Augier seldom allows his characters to show their individuality by their manner of speaking, but he endows Giboyer with a racy style that is all his own, full of sardonic wit and lively journalese. Politically he is a Socialist at heart, and he loathes the community which has so signally failed to live up to the ideals of 1789. Still—one must live—and he is prepared to work for middle-class papers, liberal or conservative, and to write about anything from current political or financial problems to society gossip and fashion notes, using different signatures and pseudonyms, and without any concern for the good or bad effects of his writing—as long as he is paid. One reason for this attitude is that as a Socialist he hates existing society, but a more powerful reason is that this society has treated him so cruelly that he no longer recognizes any obligations towards it. There is one scene in which he describes to Vernouillet and the Marquis de Auberive, who is the raisonneur, the sad story of his life, with his usual sardonic humour. He was the son of the concierge at the Marquis' home. Against the latter's advice his father sent the talented boy to a headmaster who was prepared to teach him as an advertisement for his school. When he left school he got a job as an assistant master with a salary of six hundred francs. He soon became dissatisfied, and cast himself adrift to seek other employment: the path of education he discovered to be a blind alley. After that he lived a very varied life. The Marquis commented that he had also had his vices. Giboyer answered abruptly, "Damn it, of course I had my vices. So have you. Do you think privation spoils a man's appetite? If only I had nothing but my vices, which didn't cost much, to burden me, all would have been well. Unfortunately, there was also a virtue, the only one I never gave up. I was a good son—I wouldn't let my father go to the workhouse—pure childishness of course—but what will you?—Nobody is perfect. He was inconsiderate enough to live to a good old age, and I was simple enough to weep at his death".

Giboyer, like Figaro, comes from the lower class, a man of talent who has been prevented by prejudice and social injustice from rising in the world. Like the unhappy Figaro, he has had to serve counts and barons in their more or less praiseworthy enterprises. Like Figaro he has tried his hand at everything, and has endured many humiliations. But, also like Figaro, he has retained a sense of superiority over his masters and has remained faithful to his ideals, though he has had to betray them in practice. It has often been said that Figaro sounded the reveille for 1789; Giboyer proclaims that the revolution of 1789 has still to be completed. An aristocracy of wealth has replaced one of birth, and a brutal lust for profit rules all. What is needed to resist the power of wealth is a new aristocracy, based this time on personal merit.

A fierce newspaper war followed the production of *The Impertinents*. In their attack on Augier the journalists made Giboyer their chief target, for they considered his character a direct insult to their profession, and were in no way appeased by the amiable character of another journalist whom Augier had been careful to include in the cast as a counter-weight.

When Augier produced his next play, *Giboyer's Son*, in 1862 there was an even greater sensation. Not since Molière's time had there been so much controversy in the theatrical world about a play.

After *The Son-in-law of M. Poirier*, *Giboyer's Son* is Augier's finest play. Moreover, it is the play which exercised the greatest influence on the Scandinavian dramatists. Björnson imitated it very closely in *Redaktören* (*The Editor*) and *Det ny system* (*The New System*).

Augier was a fervent supporter of the government, and an opponent of the Clerical opposition. In this play he attacks the leading opposition publicist, Louis Veuillot, under his pseudonym 'Deodat'. In the first act of *Giboyer's Son*, Deodat is supposed to be dead, and a group of Clericals are mourning the loss of this staunch defender of orthodoxy. Fortunately, however, the Marquis of Auberive has found a successor to Deodat in Giboyer, with his cynical, diabolical pen, which spreads filth and poison with every word, a contemptible creature who would fry his own father for a few pence, and eat him with salt for a few more.

It was this unconcealed attack on Veuillot which produced so many angry articles, including one by Veuillot himself. In the preface to the play, Augier defended himself in advance by claiming that his were legitimate reprisals against a scurrilous pamphleteer, who was in any case well able to protect himself. It can scarcely be denied that here Augier has gone too far.

As in most of Augier's plays, there are in *Giboyer's Son* two plots; the political one moves round Maréchal, one of Augier's best bourgeois characters. He is wealthy, pompous, and particularly addicted to the company of marchionesses and countesses. Not much effort has therefore been necessary to lure him over into the Clerical party. On the occasion of the opposition's main attack on the government in the Chamber he is to be the main speaker. He has had a speech written for him by the versatile Giboyer, and he is so pleased that he is constantly repeating phrases from it.

Then comes a party conference in which the speech is taken away from Maréchal and given to someone else to deliver, much to Maréchal's disappointment. Giboyer, who has retained his radical sympathies, manages to rouse Maréchal's irritation to such a pitch that he decides to answer the original speech which Giboyer wrote for him. For this purpose, Giboyer lets Maximilien, Maréchal's secretary, write a new speech which Maréchal delivers with great effect in the Chamber. Maximilien, although he does not know it, is the natural son of Giboyer, but in the end he is united with Maréchal's daughter. The young couple have long cherished each other in secret.

An old-fashioned plot of this kind has its weaknesses. Maréchal has to be a complete simpleton to allow himself to be tossed about by both parties. The two chief plotters are not as diabolically cunning as those of Scribe, nor are the young couple steered through their difficulties as in *The Glass of Water.*. But it is the same old plot. The play derives its strength from the scenes between Giboyer and his son.

Maximilien has grown up in the belief that Giboyer is his uncle. By dint of accepting any work, however degrading, and by enduring the most extraordinary privations, Giboyer has succeeded in bringing up Maximilien so well that he is now three times a doctor, and no one has any idea who his father is.

The finest scene in the play comes at the end of the third act, and is played between Giboyer and Maximilien. Maximilien has been so impressed with the first "Clerical" speech, which he had been instructed by Maréchal to copy out, that he has abandoned his liberal convictions. Giboyer is very distressed, and admits that he wrote it for payment. Maximilien in his turn is very distressed that Giboyer should be practising such a trade. When Giboyer asserts that it was for his sake, he replies "For my sake? By what right do you do such dishonourable service? How do you know that I would not prefer poverty?" Giboyer collapses into a chair and Maximilien adds, penitently, "Forgive me, old friend, you didn't know what you were doing".

For the first time Giboyer gives vent to his emotions, and complains about his lot. "I knew I was sacrificing myself for you, and that I had to preserve your youth from the trials that had ruined mine. I have eaten the dust that lay in your path, and it is not for you to reproach me. My pen is not the first thing that I sold for your sake; I had already sold my freedom. I went to prison for two years and was paid a year's salary by a newspaper for so doing, and all to pay your school fees. But what does it matter? I'm just a criminal, and you want no more of me. Oh —God is too hard. I'm not a bad man—only an unfortunate one. My responsibilities have been too heavy; they have ruined me. First I had to labour for my father, and then for my . . ." Here his voice breaks, and Maximilien, who has guessed the secret, throws himself into his arms and interrupts "for your son". It is a 'scène à faire', but a moving one. Björnson followed it closely in *The New System*.

Augier's later social dramas are also very important. In *The Son-in-law of M. Poirier* he took up a position of neutrality between the aristocracy and the bourgeoisie. As time passed he became more and more the spokesman of bourgeois morality, *vis-à-vis* the decadent aristocracy of the Second Empire. He was one of the first to observe shrewdly a fact that was commonly acknowledged after the defeat of 1870, namely that the cancer in the body of France was the immorality of the nobility which came to infect the middle classes also. The remedy he preached was moral regeneration. Dumas had said the same thing earlier, but in his eyes the problem was almost entirely one of relation between the sexes. Augier struck not merely at sexual laxity, but also at political corruption, social injustices and above all at the tyranny of wealth.

Money had been the focal point of Balzac's novels, and he was also the first playwright to introduce a modern business setting on to the stage. He did this in *Mercadet,* where a speculator seeks by various shady tricks to avoid the bankruptcy that is threatening him. He is finally saved by a former friend, on condition that he promises never to speculate again.

Augier, on the other hand, appears to have been a typical French 'petit bourgeois', who would never dare to risk any money in speculation. In his plays, however, he delighted in wild and extravagant speculations, which spread all over the world and engulfed whole families and business firms in a welter of destruction. But somehow he never quite succeeded in making clear to his audiences the economic implications of the plays.

Nevertheless, his plays exercised a powerful influence, particularly in Scandinavia. The first great modern play of Björnson, *En Fallit* (*A Bankruptcy*), deals with precisely this sort of topic and presents a bankrupt business man as its hero.

Occasionally Augier allows his financial magnates to meet brilliant inventors and engineers, whose ideas they exploit or suppress with the help of their financial resources. This is a situation which recurs in several plays by Björnson, the earliest instance being *The New System*. The railways of Norway were being constructed at this period, so it was on their affairs that Björnson concentrated his critical attention.

Elsewhere in Europe great interest had been aroused by the construction of the Suez Canal and similar projects. Such a project is the subject of a play to which Augier gave the symbolic name *La Contagion* (*The Contagion*) in 1866. The hero is a young engineer called Lagarde, and his epoch-making idea consists of a plan to build a ship-canal across the Algeciras peninsular, thereby ending Gibraltar's domination over the only entrance to the Mediterranean. He comes from the country and looks like a foreman. Like a Dumas hero, he begins by weeping over his mother's death; then he is introduced to the sinful society of Paris, where an English secret agent nearly succeeds in extracting the canal concessions from him for a sum of a million-and-a-half francs. Our young hero from the country is all but succumbing to the lust for gold, when suddenly his eyes are opened. In the final act we see in him a predecessor of Doctor Stockman from *An Enemy of the People,* inexorably advancing to battle against the evils which threaten the community.

Augier has been using a very old-fashioned technique. Unlike the younger Dumas, he soon realized this. His final play was extremely successful in the theatre, but in 1879 he gave up playwriting with the feeling that a new generation, with modern resources, was ready to step into the breach: "Sometimes I feel rather as Bayard's charger might have done if he had been confronted by modern artillery".

It has already been suggested that Augier's conceptions of the moral decadence of the Second Empire had some influence on playwrights in other countries, where social conditions were hardly the same. It is significant that the first contemporary plays of both Björnson and Ibsen depict a fever for speculation and a moral corruption, to such an abhorrent degree that one is driven to ask whether conditions could really have been so bad in the small coastal towns of Norway, where life was still rather simple. Did they not simply, though unconsciously, transfer the atmosphere of the French decadence of the Second Empire straight to Norway? It took a little time before Björnson and Ibsen achieved a genuine Norwegian tone in their plays of contemporary morals and manners.

(iii) Mechanistic Drama, Farce and Operetta

In Victorien Sardou the school of drama which we have been describing reached the peak of its popularity. No other playwright of the 19th century has had his works so frequently performed on both sides of the Atlantic, or seen so many of his plays translated into so many other languages. Not even Scribe was so great a king of the theatre. Like Scribe, however, Sardou's literary reputation sank lower as his theatre successes grew, and with more reason. Scribe has an originality which Sardou lacks. Scribe invented the technique of modern drama; Sardou merely exploited the new invention.

As an artist Sardou has no claim to be included in this survey of the best that modern drama has to show. But for historical reasons he cannot be omitted. If he had never existed, it would be extremely difficult to understand the violence of the reaction that the Naturalists initiated against their predecessors. Moreover, since even first-class drama cannot help being affected by stage success, traces of Sardou's dramatic devices are occasionally found in the work of later writers.

Sardou's youth was a constant struggle for survival. His family had been ruined, and he took jobs of many kinds, including one as a writer of advertisements in a newspaper concern. He was driven to playwriting by sheer necessity, and even after he had established himself as a playwright the habit of advertising remained with him, and he built up an elaborate system of publicity for his plays.

Gradually Sardou's dramatic skill began to surpass that of Scribe. His plots were better constructed, and he had even fewer scruples about giving a final twist at the crucial moment in the direction which the audience would least expect.

To regard Sardou as purely a constructor of plots is not quite fair. He was too shrewd not to realize that the whole-hearted concentration on action which distinguished the plays of Scribe and Dumas after him contained an element of risk. Audiences were finding that a state of uninterrupted tension was beginning to pall. They were also beginning to want to see something else on the stage, apart from the elegant drawing-rooms which provided the setting for most of Dumas' and Augier's plays, and were growing tired of the brilliant cut and thrust of their dialogue. Sardou could write a play just to show life in a small provincial town. He let the public see gambling-rooms, railway stations, hotel vestibules, firework displays and balls on his stage. These reforms may seem modest, but they did contribute a new element to modern drama.

Sardou made his début more or less at the same time as the naturalistic novel. His own principles were profoundly different, but he used any trick of the Naturalists which might increase his own popularity. His press-agents, for instance, spread rumours that he undertook special factual studies for every new play, just as the brothers Goncourt and Zola were supposed to do. He built up a dossier for each character, drew plans of the sites where the action of his play was to take place, and worked out every episode in minute detail.

In his choice of subjects, Sardou was completely up-to-date. His first real success came from a play in which he beat Scribe on his own ground. Sardou had perceived the excellent results Scribe could achieve with a compromising letter. In his *Les pattes de mouche* (*A Scrap of Paper*), such a love-letter is itself the chief character. It is used to light a lamp, is screwed up by an entomologist to preserve a beetle, and has a declaration of love scribbled on its back page by a schoolboy. All the women in the play are suspected of having written it. In the end, it is burned in error by the jealous husband whose wife has in fact written it. It is believed that Ibsen had this play in mind when he wrote *The Pretenders*. Bishop Nicholas keeps Skule in a state of intolerable suspense, threatening him with the letter from the priest of Trond, which is to make plain the facts of Håkon's birth. Finally, he persuades him to burn it, still unread.

In the 1860's Sardou wrote plays about morals after the fashion of Dumas. They had magnificent women's parts, were extremely successful—and are now completely forgotten. He also imitated Augier's social satires. The play of this type that held the greatest significance for Scandinavian drama was *La famille Benoiton* (*The Benoiton Family*, 1865). Here we are introduced to a family with a father who has earned millions by manufacturing rubber mattresses, and judges the state of the world according to his ability to dispose of them. The suitor, to whom he sells his daughter, sits, pen in hand, reckoning to the last centime how much dowry she brings with her, and how it can most profitably be invested. The sons of the family are chips of the old block, even the youngest, only six years old, who in an unguarded moment, climbs into his father's money chest and exclaims, "Oh papa, how lovely they are, all these money-bags!" The ladies of the family have their heads quite turned by fashion and pursuit of pleasure. The mother is always out, so we never see her on the stage. The daughters appear in costumes which must have seemed extremely daring to an audience in the 1860's, and carry on an improper conversation, which after eighty years has lost its capacity to shock the reader.

During the last two acts, various events shatter the fortunes of the family, and its members react in different ways. The three daughters forswear all luxury, and we see them dressed in plain muslin dresses.

This feeble comedy of manners had the most fantastic success in all the theatres of Europe. One of the first results of the play, perhaps significantly, was the launching of a new set of fashions. For instance, the muslin gowns worn by the daughters in the last

act were found to be so becoming that they were soon all the
rage amongst ladies of fashion. The play was performed very
successfully in Sweden in 1865, and had similar results. A year
later, Strindberg wrote in an article, "*The Benoiton Family* was
intended to express disapproval of the excessive preoccupation
of the French bourgeoisie with their wealth (for once the aristocracy was left in peace), but when it was produced here, the only
result was that the whole Swedish public began to wear Benoiton
collars, Benoiton charms and such-like. Benoiton was a pass-
word for fashion. And this was the reply to a sermon!"

Naturally the play became a model for writers in many
countries. It is particularly interesting to note that the first great
contemporary play of the Scandinavian theatre, *A Bankruptcy*
(1875), was strongly influenced by *The Benoiton Family*, and this
play by Björnson was a direct precursor of *Pillars of Society* and
the whole of Ibsen's social drama.

Augier's success with his political plays also stimulated Sardou.
Since, however, he had no sense of political issues, his efforts in
this direction were clumsy caricatures. After the Franco-Prussian
war and the Commune, he wrote a play called *Rabagas,* where he
depicts Napoleon III, Garibaldi and Gambetta in the thinnest of
disguises. Björnson may have been to some extent influenced by
this work where he wrote his singular play, *Kongen* (*The King*).

During the last years of his life (Sardou was writing up to his
death in 1908), another factor had come to affect his production
—his relations with the great actors of his day. To an even greater
degree than Scribe, Sardou was incapable of creating characters.
His stage people are pure marionettes, carefully dressed men of
straw, who can move and talk like real people—thanks to his
theatrical skill and stagecraft—but cannot think or feel.

For Sarah Bernhardt, Sardou wrote parts demanding pathos
and gallantry, as for instance in *Fedora,* the story of a courtesan
on an imperial throne, and *La Tosca,* which Puccini made famous
in his opera. For Coquelin he wrote plays with a role for a master
plotter and intriguer. A further instance of his ability to create
parts made to measure for actors is the fact that for a long time
he supplied Sir Henry Irving with his leading roles. These plays
were translated into English before publication and had their
premières in London.

It might well be supposed that this period of drama has now been forgotten, but in fact two of Sardou's plays have kept their hold on the stage with remarkable tenacity and are frequently revived, especially where a box-office success is needed. They are *Madame Sans-Gêne* (1894) and *Divorçons* (*Let's be Divorced*) (1880).

For the most part, the great ladies of the theatre demanded poetic roles, but Réjane, on the other hand, looked for middle-class vulgarity in her parts, with a touch of the hoyden. Her fellow-actors were not outstanding and appeared at their best in costume parts, and Sardou hit on the idea of letting her play the role of the pretty young washerwoman, later to become a duchess, who consorts with the wicked Napoleon and his marshals, and the cunning Fouché. As literature *Madame Sans-Gêne* is worthless, and historically it is ridiculous, but in Stockholm it has been revived more than two hundred times. *Let's be Divorced* was written in 1880, when divorce was a burning issue in France. Sardou was a conservative, opposed to reform, but in his play he seems to support it by showing that the right to divorce can repair a marriage that threatens to break up. The husband tells his foolish wife, Cyprienne, that he is prepared to take advantage of the new laws to allow her to unite her fate with that of her young cousin, Adhémar. At that instant the flirtation loses its romantic charm for the lovers; the young man is by no means prepared to face the consequences of his actions, while Cyprienne's contempt for her husband turns into admiration. She persuades him to take her out to supper at a restaurant, where it is Adhémar's turn to play the jealous husband, and finally to be dismissed without ceremony. The plot derives partly from Augier's *Gabrielle* and partly from a charming little comedy by Meilhac and Halévy, called *La Petite Marquise* (*The Little Marchioness*). By the use of cruder effects than those of either of his predecessors, Sardou succeeded in outstripping them in popularity.

The first master of the new light comedy was Eugène Labiche; he was a contemporary of Dumas and Augier, the oldest of the three, born in 1815, and his best vaudeville-comedy, *Le Chapeau de paille d'Italie* (*The Italian Straw Hat*) dates from 1851, a period in which Dumas and Augier were producing their first really significant plays. Labiche has shared the fate of other writers in the same vein, namely to be under-estimated at first, and then to be ridiculously over-valued. Towards the end of his life he was being seriously compared with Molière—which is absurd, though it is a point of view still maintained by certain French literary historians. However, among the authors of that period, he is certainly, after Sardou, the one whose plays are most frequently performed, and also the most widely read—which Sardou's plays never are. In many countries *Le Voyage de M. Perrichon* (*M. Perrichon's Journey*) is used as a textbook for the teaching of French, and is probably the best known of all the plays of this period.

M. Perrichon's Journey (1860) is really a *proverbe*. During the 18th century, the *proverbe* was really a sort of game played on social occasions; familiar proverbs were acted, and the audience had to guess them, as in charades. The composition of such pieces soon took literary form, and the proverb which provided the theme of the play was printed at the head or the end of the play. Musset used this device solely to present psychological situations and scenes in dramatic form. *M. Perrichon's Journey* is not bound up with any particular proverb, but with a psychological maxim uttered by one of the characters at the end of the play. "People do not feel affection for us because of services we have rendered them, but because of services they have rendered us".

This truth is illustrated by Perrichon's feelings for the two suitors who are seeking his daughter's hand. Armand is a decent fellow who rescued him at the risk of his own life on a precipice on Mont Blanc, but Perrichon finds that the burden of gratitude, of which he is continually reminded by Armand's presence, becomes almost intolerable. The ingenious Daniel, however, falls into a crevasse, to give Perrichon the satisfaction of rescuing him, and thereby wins his heart completely. Henceforth Perrichon owes to him "the most beautiful emotions of his whole life" as he says himself. French has even come to use the expression "Perrichonisme" to signify both the desire to protect others, and a reluctance to be oneself protected by others.

To condemn the plot of *Perrichon* as improbable is unreasonable: the play is a farce, not intended to be probable. A more reasonable objection is its length, for Labiche tended to make his plays too long. The weakest part of the play is its finale, never a strong point with Labiche; in this instance Perrichon, from behind a door, hears the conversation of the young lovers and learns of Daniel's cunning ruse.

Zola praised this plot because it marked a departure from the standardised pattern of Dumas fils, Augier and Sardou. This praise is undeserved: the play is conceived in the good old style, strongly reminiscent of Scribe. Just as Bolingbroke and the Duchess of Marlborough engage in a tug-of-war for the possession of the fickle Queen Anne in *The Glass of Water*, so the two suitors fight for Perrichon. Perrichon is the only live character in Labiche's play: the words of the other players are only memorable when they refer to Perrichon, as for instance Daniel's famous remark about the picture he intends to paint, and exhibit in the salon in memory of his preservation: "a very small Mont Blanc and an immense Perrichon".

Poirier is a genuine representation of a self-made man from the middle classes, slightly exaggerated but on the whole fairly true to life. Perrichon is admittedly a caricature, but perhaps for that very reason possesses a universality which Poirier cannot claim. Typically French, however, is the combination of bourgeois absurdity with a love of great words, and in almost direct line of descent from Perrichon we find Daudet's Tartarin.

Labiche's other type of play, the vaudeville, contains no hidden significance. It evolves from a comic situation, not from a psychological hypothesis, and from the situation follow the inevitable consequences.

Labiche has a real gift for grotesque comedy. What is lacking in his more literary comedies is that trace of melancholy which made Molière great. For that matter, Labiche realized this himself. He once admitted to Zola that he could never really take anybody seriously.

The vaudeville farce, with its free and easy manner and readiness to burst into music, soon developed into operetta, of which at this period Meilhac and Halévy were the chief exponents, besides being excellent writers of comedy.

A renewed interest in Rococo was characteristic of Paris at this date. In some spheres ambitious attempts to capture this interest were short-lived. The heavy furniture, for instance, bulging pieces cluttered with gilt ornament, was soon banished to the attics. The crinoline and similar dress fashions, modified versions of 18th century styles, did not flourish for long, while the literary salons of that century received their death blow in the Franco-Prussian war.

The best interpreter of the Rococo spirit in the field of art was Carpeaux. He could handle marble and bronze like wax, carve every feature in detail, create figures that moved and danced, and faces sensitive and alive, almost capable of speech. Anyone who looks at his sculptures is acutely aware of their playful sensuality, their watchful eyes and smiling mouths. His work on the façade of the Opera, "*The Dance*", is a personification of this gay if somewhat artificial period, denounced as Sodom by the great moralists of the theatre.

The literary equivalent of this piece of statuary is to be found in the works of Meilhac and Halévy. They wrote one profoundly serious play in which a young girl dies on the stage amidst sentimental speeches of the *Dame aux Camélias* type, but the heroine was called Froufrou to recall the impression of rustling silk skirts. A door opens, the rustle of skirts is heard, she glides down the stairs, speaks, quarrels, laughs, sings and dances—and is gone in a moment.

From the comedies of Meilhac and Halévy, many of them single-act plays, we get a vivid impression of the Rococo period of Napoleon. There is in them the same combination of psychological realism and deliberate acceptance of convention, of real and artificial, as in the comedies of Marivaux, the masterpieces of 18th century Rococo. The characters are half way between the silhouettes of the *Commedia dell'arte* and people taken from real life. Their struggles are ours, but they are viewed through a prism which causes them to appear moving as well as laughable. The action of the plot seems quite whimsical, unhampered by any of the strict rules of dramatic composition laid down by contemporary critics.

In *The Little Marchioness*, we have a worried couple who are making every conceivable effort to free themselves from each other. They are grotesque caricatures—but they are alive. The Marquis is an absent-minded scholar, who wishes to remain undisturbed in his study of Troubadour poetry. His featherbrained little wife loathes him with all her heart, and has for

six months allowed herself to be pursued by the insipid Viscount
Boisgommeux. She does her very best to deceive her husband
with Boisgommeux. She takes three cabs, one after the other, to
reach the flat which he has hired for their meetings. But events
conspire against her; her maid looked very oddly at her when
she left, and people on the street seemed to whisper as she passed,
"There's the little Marchioness going off to a rendezvous".
When at last she reaches the flat and is about to ring the bell, her
heart fails her. She turns round and goes home again, leaving
Boisgommeux to sit and wait for her.

Now the Marquis is anxious to bring things to a head. His
lawyer advises him that for a divorce to be granted he must
either beat his wife in the presence of witnesses, or be discovered
with a mistress in his own home. The Marchioness is not prepared
to agree to the first condition, so he has to try to achieve the
second. He hires a chambermaid to play the part, but in fact
she has to pass the time looking at the manuscript of his work on
the Troubadours. Meanwhile the Marchioness, in eager expectation, drives away to Boisgommeux's castle in Poitiers to inform
him of his good fortune. The happy man, however, is quite
appalled at the news that the declared object of all his dreams is
within his grasp, and can only stammer, "I loved you as a man of
the world". She has to catch the next train home.

In the final act all is as it was at the beginning of the play.
Boisgommeux resumes his natural role of despairing lover,
while the Marquis turns back to his scholarly meditations on the
Troubadours. The Marchioness has a moment of insight when
she realizes that he is more tolerable than her deceitful lover, but
she comes to hate him more than ever.

The Little Marchioness, like Musset's *Proverbes*, points a moral:
"Stolen fruit is the sweetest. When it hangs within our reach we
no longer want it". We deceive each other with our protesta-
tions of affection and profess emotions which we do not feel.

The pointing of a moral, after the manner of Musset, is even
more significant a part of two other operettas by Meilhac and
Halévy, which were set to music by Offenbach, and which after
nearly a century are still unexcelled as models of a style which
seemed purely ephemeral. *La Grande Duchesse* (*The Grand Duchess*)
is constructed round the final words of the heroine, "Quand on

n'a pas ce que l'on aime, il faut aimer ce que l'on a". The setting is a petty German prince's court, as fantastic as Bavaria in Musset's *Fantasio*. The period is Rococo, and the characters are amusing caricatures of the same kind as the old gentlemen in *On ne badine pas avec l'amour* (*No Trifling with Love*), or the comic prince and his minister in *Fantasio*. The Grand Duchess is a lovesick ruler who has fallen in love with an ordinary soldier and promoted him to be a general. He fails to understand her purpose, however, and returns to the ranks, while she gives her hand to Prince Paul, a simple shy man, in the hope that thereby she will secure the handsome Baron Grog, his companion, for her lover. All the honours of the degraded general are heaped on Grog, before it is discovered that he is married, with three children. This time, however, the Duchess has to rest content with her unfortunate prince, and the play ends on the note of resignation, that "il faut aimer ce que l'on a".

The finest libretto for an operetta that Meilhac and Halévy wrote is undoubtedly *La Belle Hélène* (*Fair Helen*) 1864. It belongs to another category, the parody of classical antiquity, of which Holberg's *Ulysses fra Ithacia* (*Ulysses of Ithaca*) is a good Scandinavian example. Here the author even took the trouble to insert the actual lines from the Iliad where Helen's character is defined. They come in a passage where Helen enters with her maids, and Priam declares, "There is no guilt in thee; all the blame rests with the gods".

Theatre-goers who have seen only modern productions of *Fair Helen*, with clumsy revue technique, cheap humour and topical jokes, can have no conception of the spirit of the original version. Not that topical references were lacking, for the heroes of the Trojan war passed the time in charades and verse games, as was the custom of Napoleon III's Court. Achilles, forever quarrelling, wandered about on the pebbly shore of Nauplia, nursing his sore heel, rather like the Duc de Morny at Étretat. Helen, in a most proper way, puts on a long high-necked dress when Menelaus departs to Crete, but is nevertheless discovered in a tender scene with Paris when he returns home unexpectedly.

But the anachronisms of the play, which now seem to endow it with a curious period flavour, do not really rob it of its fundamentally Rococo atmosphere. Helen is a poor sinner, doomed ever since she was sixteen by the edict of Venus to frequent lapses from virtue: "I should have been an ordinary housewife, married to a Mitylene merchant, but instead what a fate is mine!" After many shipwrecks she believes she has at last found a safe harbour with King Menelaus—"Yes a good man, an excellent man ... I have tried all I could to love him ... I couldn't ... I couldn't". She falls a victim to the wiles and charms of Paris, but in her heart she does not feel guilty: "C'est la fatalité".

Paris describes them as having spent a month in the romantic atmosphere of Marivaux, and in truth the play manifests far more of the charming but artificial love-scenes associated with Marivaux than the crude brutality of modern productions.

There is one more great name of the Rococo period that one cannot fail to call to mind when reading *Fair Helen*, namely Watteau. It is in his spirit that Paris and Helen in the final scene embark on a galley with Cythera's banner floating at the stern. Venus herself through her emissary, Paris in disguise, commanded the journey. When the boat casts off, he lays aside his disguise and stirs the kings to anger, thereby causing the whole Trojan war. All this is regarded as inevitable, in a world of temptation where the Queen of Beauty holds sway. "The Goddess Venus", says Agamemnon, "has sent forth her slender airy shafts, which tempt men to forsake their wives, and wives to forsake their husbands". So it was in the days of old, and so it is in Paris of 1860: C'est la fatalité.

THE RISE OF NATURALISM IN FRANCE

BY 1875, when the first play of the Naturalist school was performed, the status of the theatre had reached new heights. Hitherto, the playwright had been just a humble member of the literary fraternity; now he was a king of the theatre, drawing a rich harvest of royalties from the stages of all Europe and America. Modern drama had suddenly become an article of international trade.

One result of this was that all writers carefully checked through their plays to remove all purely national qualities which might hinder their world-wide success. At first everybody tried to copy the French Salon comedy. The degenerate aristocracy, the aspiring middle classes, the blatant demi-monde, all reappeared in the drama of other countries, though with a more or less provincial flavour. But reaction followed swiftly.

The first attack was directed against the stereotyped structure of French plays. A completely unexpected turn of events is very rare indeed. The followers of Dumas and Augier were of course right when they charged the new Naturalist school with portraying exceptional characters and events. But the characterization of Dumas, Augier and their successors was by no means profound; the "cris de cœur" which made their plays so famous smack of the theatre. Individuals may act impulsively or nervously, but they do so according to a pattern. If a young aristocrat is confronted with the news that the lady of his choice is wealthy, ruined or compromised, his reactions are exactly predictable. The words used may differ, but that is all.

Without such sensitive characters, ruled by such an exaggerated code of morals, the playwrights would never have succeeded in constructing plots which moved swiftly from phase to phase, offering a new catastrophe of some kind every minute. The

worst fault of these plays was the over-elaboration of their plots.
The younger Dumas and the dramatists of the second Empire
regarded a play as a kind of problem which could only have one
correct solution. There was of course formal acknowledgment
of the fact that motives are psychological rather than logical, but
in practice they tended to forget that the human spirit is a highly
illogical mechanism, and that no one can prophesy how a man
will behave under a given set of conditions, without an intimate
knowledge of him and his character. That is why the characters
in this period of French drama, as in the earlier classical period,
remained abstract types.

The "art of preparing the audience" was still in high repute.
The older generation of playwrights and critics disapproved of
plays which did not provide audiences with the necessary fore-
knowledge of the actions of their heroes, condemning them as
lacking in psychological insight. This is a faulty criticism, though
it is still to be found in modern histories of literature. By revealing
the psychological elements in a situation, a playwright can show
convincingly how a character with certain qualities will act. To
give the impression that he must act in a particular way is impossible without reducing the situation to absurdity, and ignoring
psychology for the sake of effect. Even Zola, however, subscribed
to some extent to the theory of "preparation"; but the greatest
playwright of the French Naturalist school, Henri Becque,
abandoned it both in theory and practice.

Over a period of many years, theatre audiences had grown
accustomed to the stilted construction of modern French plays,
to their conventional characters and stage effects. The first
naturalistic plays, which lacked an elaborate plot and were merely
intended to show a story of real life, were very coldly received.
Their simple plots were considered to be crude, lacking the
aristocratic refinements and witty conversation of plays by
Augier or Dumas. Conservative critics concluded from their
unpopularity that the new plays were not in accord with the
eternal principles of drama.

Twenty years later, people were discovering to their surprise
that the public had changed its mind, and found the old-style
plays dull: "Une pièce bien faite", the highest compliment a
critic could bestow, came to have a derogatory significance.

The first deliberate assault on conventionalism in the theatre came from Zola. Unfortunately he possessed neither the necessary dramatic talent nor the critical insight which would have enabled him to give the public a clear idea of the new drama he wished to create. Also it was more difficult to make headway in France than elsewhere. Nevertheless, his value for modern drama as an iconoclast and a catalyst was outstanding. In reading his prefaces and programme notes of the period 1873-82 one must never forget that they were composed before Ibsen's plays had begun to make their impact on European drama.

In his critical writings, Zola took his stand on the differences between modern drama and the modern novel. Flaubert's "Madame Bovary" was published at about the time when Augier and the younger Dumas produced their first plays, and the peak of their popularity coincided with triumphs of the naturalistic novel-writers. One must agree with Zola when he claimed that drama was half a century behind the times, and would soon be no more than a field in which the skilful constructor of plots could exercise his art. Zola attacked the dramatists for their mechanical plots, their stylized characters and their weakness for presenting popular characters in a favourable light. They conceived their dialogues as a firework display, and of real life they knew nothing. Against the orthodox critics he maintained obstinately that there is no reality in the theatre distinct from the reality of real life, nor any laws of aesthetics absolving the theatre from the aesthetic laws by which other literary works are judged.

"Am I more foolish than the critics?" he wrote at the end of one essay. "I do not think so. It is only that I have no interest in clockwork, and a great deal of interest in truth. Yes, your drama is a fine mechanism, but I should like it to live proudly. I want life with all its terror, breadth and power—the whole of life".

What Zola wanted to produce on the stage, instead of 'salon' dramas, was something to correspond with the naturalistic novel. It would resemble this in having as its foundation the principles of heredity and environment and the positivism of the novel, and above all in adhering ruthlessly to realism and objectivity in every representation. The object of drama should be a complete and unflattering reflection of reality. As a model for modern drama, Zola pointed to the Elizabethan playwrights, though he was less familiar with their works in the original than in the pages of Taine's *History of English Literature*. In them he felt there was proof that powerful drama need not be tailored to fit the current theatrical convention.

What Zola failed to realize was that his reforms could not be carried through in a day. His own novels and stories he rewrote in dramatic form, and believed that thereby he had done enough to ensure that the play would satisfy the requirements of naturalism and science, and would become a piece of real life. By flouting the conventions at every point, and by adopting from Elizabethan drama a motive here, a trick of technique there, he believed he had laid the foundations of the new forms.

His own natural gifts inclined more to the broad sweep of an epic novel, and he was never fully at ease within the limits of drama. Further, once he had adopted one point of view, his obstinacy and dogmatism would never allow him to deviate from it for one step. There is never any development from one play to the next, and only the first one, *Thérèse Racquin* (1873), need receive serious consideration. This is not an easily read play, and is probably no easier on the stage, but it has a certain originality and some fundamental power which gives it greater significance than his later plays. However slight the value it may be considered to have as a model of naturalistic drama, it served as a starting-point in several countries.

Thérèse Racquin was based on a novel by Zola, and follows it closely. It is a story of criminal acts, told in the play, as in the book, in all their detail, and without sparing the melodramatic effects which Zola had condemned in theory. It is a heavy, inartistic, painful piece of work, but no one can deny that it was epoch-making.

Recent drama had concerned itself with the upper or the lower middle classes. Here we find ourselves with the lowest classes of the community, in a damp dark room behind a little shop, and here we stay for the four acts of the play. It is a world crude in its manners and way of life, crude even in its sentiments. Pleasant characters have all been swept away. In the world which Zola depicts there are only crude bestial desires, barely concealed by a veneer of civilization, and continually struggling against traditional morals. His characters are not carefully analysed individuals; they are not persons but temperaments. Zola is less concerned with the detailed psychological motives behind their actions, and more with bringing out the elemental force of their instincts, and with showing how their psychological structure is linked with environment. We recognize the same world which we discovered in Zola's novels, and which we shall meet again in the proletarian drama of the Russians and of Hauptmann.

A brutal murder and its consequences are laid before the spectator. Thérèse Racquin conspires with her lover, Laurent, to murder her husband Camille, a weak and feeble creature, by drowning him during a boating trip. The two criminals escape detection and marry one another. On the wedding night, as they are returning to the old home, the memory of the murdered man comes between them and kills their love. They give themselves away to Camille's mother by accident and, fearing that she will denounce them, haunted by remorse and with mutual recriminations, they finally commit suicide.

Plays of violence of this sort were popular in Elizabethan days, and again in the *bourgeois* drama of the 18th century, but since then they had been relegated to the repertory theatres of the suburbs. Quite frequently Zola sinks down to their level: his taste was uncertain, and he had a liking for strong effects. Camille's mother in particular, who becomes paralysed and speechless when she learns how her son was murdered, and then tries to reveal the crime by spelling out letters on the oilcloth table cover, reminds one of the vengeful characters of Kyd's and Shakespeare's early plays. The horror scenes of the final act are crudely sensational, while the characters mostly speak in a style of bombastic rhetoric which is the very reverse of naturalistic. But if the play is inartistic in its choice and treatment of subject, it is also free from the conventionalism of its predecessors. There is not a trace of Scribe's intrigues. The plot is not like a chess-problem with a neat solution, and the drama is never tendentious. With all the comprehensiveness and thoroughness of a court trial, we are shown a case history of a crime, the preparations for it and its consequences. It is the crime and its psychology which interest the author, a theme which we shall see treated with much greater artistic skill in other naturalistic plays, notably *Vlast tmi* (*The Power of Darkness*) by Tolstoy.

Zola's greatest fault was that he did not understand, did not even wish to understand, the need in drama for a concentration, an economy of effect which the novel, with its freedom from limitations of time and space, does not require. He maintained the unity of place, to give the audience an opportunity of living itself into the gloomy setting. It was also a perfectly sound instinct which led him—as he explains in the preface—to choose for his characters foolish and worthless individuals, so that the impression of the banality of life could remain with the audience. He wanted them to live, not to act. It does not, however, seem to have occurred to him that the theatre could not by a stroke of the pen return to its original primitive simplicity, that in fact it was quite unnatural to present on the stage a novel whose events are spread over several years, and whose themes are many and various without any more adaptation than recasting the most significant passages in dialogue form. Any knowledge that the audience might require of what had happened in between was clumsily worked into the conversation of the characters.

Both too much and too little happens in the play. Too much, because many of the events which precede the play, and their superficial consequences, seem irrelevant to an audience whose attention has been caught by the main issue—the psychology of a guilty conscience. Too little, because in spite of all these events the play seems to be standing still. Zola was unable to produce a dramatic crescendo. In the scenes of action he fails to make proper use of the means at his disposal, and in the quieter scenes he fails to maintain the tension and the sense of horror, often descending to a meticulous and uninteresting delineation of types. There is one scene in particular where several characters are playing dominoes at a table. Their conversation about the weather is tedious and irrelevant; cooking is going on in one corner; the bride is being attired in another; and the whole effect is merely to retard the action of the play without giving an ounce more of life. Zola's instinct was right when he resisted the current tendency of playwrights to limit dialogue to such remarks as would directly contribute to the understanding of the action or of the characters. He had a faint glimmering of the truth which

Maeterlinck twenty years later expounded more methodically, that only those remarks by characters in a play which at first seem irrelevant really count in the end. But if such apparently pointless dialogue is to have any ultimate significance, it must contribute to the creation of atmosphere, and at least give the illusion that the characters are saying one thing and thinking another. In one or two places Zola achieved this necessary condition. There is one scene after the wedding when the couple embrace each other with many expressions of affection, and then suddenly turn to speak of the weather and ladies' fashions on the boulevards. One gets the impression, however, that dark thoughts of the deed they have committed have intruded, and then Thérèse suddenly says, hoarsely, "Be quiet. Why did you let loose these memories? I hear them knocking at my head, and then the whole horror comes before me again. Behind the words you speak I can hear others. I know what you are thinking but not saying". At this point, even without Thérèse's explanation, the audience has a distinct impression of a silent transference of thought occurring during very ordinary everyday conversation. Here Zola really foreshadows the modern dramatic technique of indirect allusion. In earlier dramatic dialogues characters tend to display a frankness and eagerness to say everything that is in their hearts, which is highly improbable and theatrical. But Zola was not able—as were his successors, Strindberg and Chekhov—to maintain dialogue at this level.

On the whole, then, it may be said that the reputation of *Thérèse Racquin* depends more on its value as an experiment in a new and unfamiliar technique, and in subjects unexplored by contemporary playwrights, than in its intrinsic value as a work of art. Its brutal and elemental force held a promise for the future of drama.

The chilly reception given to *Thérèse Racquin,* both by the critics and the public at large, did not daunt Zola's unquenchable spirit, and he did not modify his principles by as much as a hair's breadth. He did, however, lose some of his interest in drama. His next two plays, clumsy comedies, one of them strongly influenced by a Ben Jonson play, were vastly inferior to *Thérèse Racquin,* and give the impression of being mere 'pot-boilers' written in spare moments. Zola did not really achieve success in

THE RISE OF NATURALISM IN FRANCE   59

the theatre until he began to dramatize his famous novels. But even he must have realized that this success depended entirely on the popularity of the novels, and not on the artistic merits of the dramatic version, and it was not long before he left to others the task of adapting his novels for the stage.

Other novelists of the naturalistic school also wrote plays— but these do not merit long consideration. They were mostly content to adapt their own novels and stories for the stage, with varying degrees of skill and success. Some appeared earlier than *Thérèse Racquin*, and have therefore been hailed as foreshadowing the naturalistic drama. In 1863, for instance, the brothers Goncourt had already produced their play *Henriette Maréchal,* which was claimed by Zola as the first instance of naturalism on the stage. The setting has indeed some of the qualities of naturalism, but the actual plot is a traditional one, and ends in the fine old style with a melodramatic pistol shot. Daudet's *L'Arlésienne* (*The Woman of Arles*), produced the year before *Thérèse Racquin* in 1872, is a charming piece, based on a provincial tale from *Lettres de mon Moulin*, but it has very little connexion with naturalism, consisting as it does of a string of long lyrical monologues. In any case, and in spite of Bizet's enchanting music, it met with very little success.

In fact it was a man who did not belong to the naturalistic school who was to determine the future course of French drama, Henri Becque. Almost every French realist playwright of any significance followed the lead which he gave, while outside France his influence was also considerable. After Augier and Dumas he was undoubtedly the greatest realistic playwright that France produced.

His story is a remarkable one. He was born in 1837, the son of a poor bank clerk, and destined by his father to become a civil servant. He was 44 when his first masterpiece, *Les corbeaux* (*The Vultures*), was produced at the Théâtre Français in 1882. Three years later he wrote his second and greater play, *La Parisienne* (*The Woman of Paris*). The rest of his life—he died in 1899—he spent in collecting material for a great play about a financial scandal, but he never completed it, though various parts were collected and pieced together by other hands after his death.

In his own day and afterwards, Becque was hailed as the greatest playwright in France. He was compared with Molière, but he only wrote two plays of any significance, and these two did not meet with immediate success in the theatre; only after a time was their reputation established. In many ways they were old-fashioned for their day, particularly in construction. In order to keep the reader acquainted with the situation, Becque makes excessive use of long monologues, descriptions and asides, at a time when other dramatists of the Second Empire had already abandoned this practice. Nor does he move out of the setting with which they were familiar. It is Augier's domestic scenes that we meet in his plays, and his characters come from the middle classes and the aristocracy of the *ancien régime*. Becque was a shrewd psychologist with none of the blurred outlines which characterized the work of his predecessors. His dialogue is heavy and clumsy, lacking their wit but also their rhetoric. Sometimes his sober objectivity seems too good to be true, but on other occasions his lines throw a cold and harsh light on a situation. It is in dealing with action that he differs most from the traditional school. The plot advances by leaps and bounds, and practically every turn of events is unexpected. In *The Vultures* we have a plot from a novel treated in a way which older dramatists regarded as indefensible. In *The Woman of Paris* we come nearer to the traditional plot, but it is a very much simplified one. In both plays it is apparent that the plot itself is only of minor importance; the main problem is the presentation of characters and the pointing of a moral.

In Becque's drama there is a strong moral sense, though it is never expressed in pious sentiments, as in the typical finale of the old school, in which virtue is triumphantly rewarded. On the contrary, it is wickedness that triumphs, but not the deliberate wickedness of Dumas' or Augier's conspirators. Becque's two chief characters, Teissier in *The Vultures* and Clotilde in *The Woman of Paris* act according to their consciences and appear to be quite satisfied with what they are doing and with the success they achieve. The author does not disturb their complacency with any moral reflections, nor does he give their victims the redeeming grandeur of tragedy. It is through the deeply moving quality of these final scenes and the way they conflict with every human sense of justice, that the author reveals the dominant note

in his character, a bitter and fierce irony. Becque's sense of
humour is not French, but dry and sober.

Becque did not belong to the Naturalist school, as Zola and the
brothers Goncourt conceived the term. He admired Balzac and
Flaubert, but held the failure of the brothers Goncourt with
Henriette Maréchal to have been well deserved, and Zola's dramatic
theories and experiments as having missed the mark. He spoke
appreciatively, though with some reservations, about plays in the
older tradition of Augier and Dumas. Sardou, who had been his
patron, he admired to an extent which passes comprehension.

His divergences from the traditional style of playwriting were
caused partly by a singularity of temperament, and partly by his
inability to write as other men did.

Becque was quite ready to observe the unity of place—in *The
Woman of Paris* there is one setting throughout, and in *The
Vultures* only a single change of scene—but he does not seem to
have done so for any particular reason, for he attacked directly
the general principle of the three unities. The setting of his plays
had evidently far less significance for him than it had for Zola,
for his stage décor was the usual one, with a door at the back and
two side entrances. His characters are different from those of his
predecessors, rather because he looked at them in a different way
than because he chose different types or described them differently. The action is different too, though not necessarily more
true to reality, or even striving to be so. It is not concerned with
theatrical effects, and still less with the desire of an audience for
excitement and change. On the other hand it does not run free
or seem like a piece of real life. Becque might be called a classical
writer as properly as a naturalistic one. Of all the 19th century
writers who have been compared with Molière, it is he who best
stands up to that comparison. There is something of Molière's
greatness in his grasp of the subject, but it is a Molière who is
petrified and has never developed his talents, a Molière without
imagination or fantasy, without lightness or grace.

Becque's earlier pieces show how difficult it was for him to
find his proper field and his natural tone. He started by writing
a vaudeville farce in the crazy style of Labiche, which is entirely
worthless. It met with some success, however, and enabled
Becque to produce, at his own risk, his first serious play, *Michel*

Pauper (1869). This proved to be an utter failure, deservedly so in some ways, as the play is immature and full of reminiscences of Byron. The title-role is played by a variant of the traditional inventor hero, a man of humble birth and rough-and-ready manner. His genius has enabled him to discover a way of crystallizing diamonds from coal. He is deceived by his wife, and is about to die after an orgy of drinking when his wife, now penitent, comes to seek him on his death-bed. He does not recognize her, and believing that she has come to steal his secret, rushes to the table where he keeps the diamonds, and pulls away the cover. Then he falls dead and the room is lit up by the blaze of diamonds: "the world has lost a great man, and science a great secret".

Apart from Pauper's discovery and other fantastic elements in the play, the story might well have been taken from real life and retold for the stage. The two chief characters, Michel Pauper and the girl he loves, become blatantly unreal the moment the author allows them to speak, but there are vestiges of originality in the two personalities which they reveal, an originality which is lacking in the general run of contemporary dramatic characters. There is a real personality within the heroine who speaks the dreadful stilted lines, a creature consumed with thirst for life, uncompromising, yet weak when mastered by passion. Michel Pauper is not a mere abstraction either. With his brutality and frequent changes of mood he presents quite a fair picture of a man who makes good, thanks to his natural gifts and the education he has fought for, but who can never wholly erase all traces of his origin. He is the first working-class type in French drama. *Thérèse Racquin* was still to come.

After another play had failed, Becque turned to the Stock Exchange, where he tried to earn a living. This experience left him with a loathing for speculators and profiteers, which was to be the mainspring of his masterpiece, *The Vultures*. It was written in 1876 but not produced till 1882, and if Balzac and Augier lashed the world of finance with whips, Becque may be said to have used scorpions.

The story of *The Vultures* is very simple. A prosperous factory owner dies, and his widow and daughters are faced with complete bankruptcy. All the vultures with whom the deceased had had dealings appear with outrageous demands. At their head is Teissier, once a good friend, who has actually bribed the family's confidential advisers, an architect and a lawyer. Meanwhile Teissier has taken a liking to one of the daughters, who has a better business head than the rest of the family, and to save them she accepts his hand in marriage.

The final scene is a masterly one. Teissier solemnly kisses his fiancée on both cheeks, and tells her that the wedding will take place in three weeks' time. Suddenly another of the 'vultures', a paperhanger, comes in to present a bill for which he demands immediate payment. The wretched girl tries vainly to convince him that the bill has already been paid. Teissier then steps forward and offers a cheque for two thousand francs, with a reminder of the risks involved in accepting payment for a bill that has already been paid. This goes straight to the mark; the tradesman declines the cheque and is hastily shown out of the room, while Teissier turns to the girl with the final words, "Ever since your father's death, my child, you have been surrounded by scoundrels". The poor girl is fully aware that Teissier is the worst of them all.

The world of *The Vultures* is a very different one from that of Björnson's play, *A Bankruptcy*, written two years earlier, though subject and structure are similar. In Becque there is no trace of romantic or poetic feeling; most of the play is taken up with business conversations. The whole family realizes that Tessier's manœuvres have brought them to the brink of ruin, but there is . nothing they can do about it. As the sole surviving partner in the factory he can sell out without regard to their interests, and indeed threatens to do so. To save the others, poor Marie has to agree to marry Teissier. Unlike her narrow-minded mother or her more romantic sisters, she has no illusions or passions. She knows what Teissier is and what her fate with him is likely to be. Without her help, however, the family would be completely lost.

Teissier's character is also worked out with the same calm psychological competence. Unlike the many characters in French drama made to this pattern, he is neither a beast in human shape nor a caricature of a miser. He is a disagreeable, sulky and suspicious old curmudgeon, but he has none of the pompous mannerisms of a self-made man, nor is he guilty of cruelty for cruelty's sake. He does not derive a sadistic pleasure from ruining his old friend's family; he is merely pursuing his normal course of acquiring wealth for himself. As long as he is uncertain how his suit will be received, he continues his preparations for the ruin of the family. When he is accepted, the family's interests automatically become identified with his own. One gets the impression that if his offer of marriage had been turned down he would have taken the news with sardonic calm, and continued undisturbed to compass their ruin. Really there is nothing to distinguish him from the other vultures; only his status as a good friend of the head of the family gives him more power.

Although Becque did not strive for the naturalistic ideal of a play without a plot, one does get the feeling that this play is a fragment of real life; it has the same gloom and even the same monotony.

Later playwrights like Strindberg and Hauptmann use darker heavier colours, and often, without any more elaborate plot, succeed in creating an atmosphere of concentrated anguish. Such an atmosphere is entirely lacking in this play, and it is therefore less powerful than one might have expected. Becque lacked sensitivity, and there is a heaviness in the conception which does not allow reader or spectator to be entirely carried away by this otherwise faultless play.

Becque's second masterpiece, written in 1885, the comedy *The Woman of Paris,* is of the same calibre. The technique here is slightly changed, and Becque has deliberately moved closer to the *salon* comedy of the Second Empire.

The first scene of *The Woman of Paris* is famous. We see the heroine conversing with an agitated gentleman who wishes her to open her desk and hand over a suspicious letter. He is exceedingly jealous, and does not allow himself to be soothed by her assurances: "Do not give way to that lust for adventure which nowadays claims so many victims. Resist, Clotilde, resist! As long as you remain faithful to me, you will be an honest and respected woman. The day you betray me . . . " At that moment Clotilde interrupts, "Beware, my husband is coming". It is not Clotilde's husband, but her lover who has been indulging in these jealous charges.

The husband is a complaisant ass, incapable of noticing anything. His ambition is to write works on political economy, and as long as there is peace in his house, and the children are not too neglected, he is content. The lover, Lafont, appears in the role of his best friend, and Clotilde's husband is sure of her fidelity, especially as she shows a certain—to his mind unjustified—dislike of Lafont. Her relationship with Lafont has therefore assumed for Clotilde almost the place of a marital relation, with its attendant disadvantages.

Clotilde leads her life in this *ménage à trois* with a perfectly clear conscience, and without having advanced views on any subject whatever. On the contrary, she tells her lover that she is a good conservative, approving good order, peace and sound principles. She reproaches him for being a democrat and a free-thinker. "I believe you would get on very well with a lover who had no religion. It's detestable".

The reason for Lafont's present jealousy is that for some time Clotilde seems to him to have been behaving oddly. This is because, in the interests of her husband's career, she is called upon to make a sacrifice. He is seeking a position in the Ministry of Finance, and to secure for him the necessary patronage, Clotilde has entered into relations with an influential young man. The husband, of course, suspects nothing, but Lafont has his doubts: "It is impossible in Paris to keep a mistress who has any sense of decency. It's just impossible. The more decent she is, the less chance there is of keeping her".

In order to dispose of the awkward Lafont, Clotilde arranges for a grand quarrel scene where she bursts into tears at the thought that for his sake she has deserted her husband and children. He leaves her for some months. In the final act we see her first of all saying farewell to the new lover, who is leaving Paris. Her husband has been appointed and her conscience is clear because she has done her duty by him. Nor does she feel any grievance against the young man, who has behaved well and been useful though rather foolish with his craze for hunting. At the right psychological moment her old lover, Lafont, appears, not indeed entirely cured of his jealousy, but anxious for a reconciliation. After a brief argument he is reinstated in his old position, and all that remains to be done is to explain to the husband the reasons for Lafont's absence from the house during the past months.

In this play there are practically no signs that the author has tried to conform to naturalistic principles. Indeed, Becque deliberately selected the salon-comedy as his vehicle, the better to attack its style and moral code.

We are shown the courtiers and lovers of recent drama in all their nakedness, effeminate and unglamorous, together with 'La grande amoureuse' as she really was—an ordinary middle-class housewife, sufficiently experienced to keep two love affairs going at the same time, orderly enough not to confuse her appointments, but with no other ideas at all about the world around her. There had been no lack of moral indignation among earlier playwrights about the rottenness of Parisian society. Both Dumas the younger and Augier include in their plays sermons against the behaviour of married women, but they seem thereby only to have invested it with a certain false glamour. In Becque there is no shadow of reproof, but the cool, dispassionate and penetrating way in which he analyses the familiar scene robs it of every trace of glamour. His characters are no pathetic relics of a dying aristocractic culture; they are prosaic and sturdy, ridiculously conventional, but firmly convinced that the moral degradation in which they live is some kind of privilege of breeding which in no way dishonours them.

The Woman of Paris exercised nearly as much influence on contemporary French playwrights as *The Vultures*, but it was not in itself so significant. Becque himself used to refer slightingly to it, "Ah, mon dieu, La Parisienne was a bagatelle; it was amusing to write it, just to show the wits that one wasn't more stupid than they". By the time he had completed this comedy he was already at work on another play which would have served better as a sequel to *The Vultures*, a great play of morals and manners, *Les Polichinelles* (*The Puppets*), dealing with the Paris Bourse and the web of political corruption which was spun round it. Theatrical circles were eagerly awaiting this play. Becque had read aloud scenes from it to various friends, and they were convinced that it was going to prove his masterpiece. During the last year of his life, however, he began to lose interest in the play and even to be unwilling to have it performed. "I have always been too good a prophet" he said, "and a man should not be that in his own country". He did not wish to complete his play because by its picture of corruption it would have furnished the opposition with a useful weapon.

Becque left behind two complete acts and one unfinished one; of the two last acts only two or three scenes had been completed. The chief character is Tavernier, a swindler. He appears as a perfectly convincing figure from real life, in no way exaggerated or caricatured. He is the sort of banker who, according to his mistress, is penniless one day, and the master of millions the next. When he first appears on the scene, the bank has only two or three francs to its credit. But one is convinced that by the end of the play he would have triumphed by hook or by crook, and be as calm and confident as ever. By his side stands his vulgar but gifted mistress, Marie; she is an actress, and Tavernier is always afraid that she will disgrace him by appearing in some shameless naturalistic play. His business friends include a decayed marquis, who serves as his cover, and a helpful member of parliament who agrees to provide him with contacts in the Government, in return for a promised share in the profits of his transactions on the Bourse. What Becque wrote is lively and vivid, but there is no sign of any action, no suggestion of dramatic plot.

The play was completed by other hands, and given a plot not unlike that in the first of these financial plays, *The Impertinents* by Augier. Whether Becque would have approved is doubtful. It seems more likely that he wanted to anticipate the later naturalistic school, with their purely descriptive and completely plotless plays, but never dared to challenge the public with such a departure from all tradition.

Becque's two great plays pointed a way for French naturalistic playwrights, a way which they could follow and produce great work. His psychological technique and his method of composition appeal to the French with their demand for sharp outlines. He himself was not the man to achieve greatness; he was too sterile, too little a poet and too little a man of the theatre.

Zola's essays and plays, together with those of Becque, created a new theatre which was to be of the utmost significance for the development of naturalistic drama in France and elsewhere. A gas-works official with a passion for the stage, called Antoine, combined with some like-minded friends to found Le Théâtre Libre in Paris in 1887. It was a small, intimate place, where the

performances were more or less private, and therefore not liable
to be censored. Expenses were met by subscriptions; audiences
did not buy tickets, but received invitations to a soirée. By this
means the theatre attracted a select public which remained faithful
in its support. The management was obliged to present a suc-
cession of new plays, but was also freed from the necessity of
building up a repertoire which had to attract the public. Stage
and scenery were completely naturalistic, without footlights,
and presenting as close an illusion of real life as possible. The
actors also used a new technique, eschewing the customary
high-sounding rhetoric, and aiming at a personal and intimate
style of diction. Above all, they tried to avoid facing the audience
squarely during their speeches, and preferred to deliver them in
any other position, often indeed with their backs to the audience;
Antoine's back became quite famous.

The repertoire included plays from many countries. It was the
Théâtre Libre which staged the first foreign productions of plays
by Ibsen, the naturalistic plays of Strindberg, *The Power of Darkness* by Tolstoy, *Die Weber* (*The Weavers*) by Hauptmann, and
many others. In French drama the opening of the Théâtre Libre
meant that Zola, and above all Becque, had many imitators. One
style of play in particular, the *comédie rosse*, flourished there as a
result of Becque's *The Woman of Paris*, and one or two of his one-
act plays. This is a drama presenting scenes of violence and great
emotion in a bitterly ironic way. The one-act plays, with a
simple but extremely violent and often satirical content, were
especially popular; often they seemed like dramatized trial
scenes from real life. One can get a good impression of the
repertoire by reading the one-act plays that Strindberg wrote for
his experimental theatre from 1880 to 1890 and after, *Paria* (*The
Pariah*), *Inför Döden* (*Death*), *Debet och kredit* (*Debit and Credit*),
etc. The French models are not up to this standard, but the same
spirit is there. They represent a deliberately callous outlook on
life and the characters who play their parts in it, an attempt to
draw aside the veils which give a false impression of beauty. It is
easy for us nowadays to see the artificiality in these plays, most
of which are forgotten. In France itself the reforming spirit which
was fostered by the Théâtre Libre did not lead to any real re-
creation of drama in general, though most of the younger play-

wrights learned their trade there, and a considerable modification of taste became noticeable. In other countries the result of Antoine's experiments were more considerable; in Germany, England, Russia, and later in the U.S.A. and elsewhere, similar theatres were founded.

These intimate experimental theatres have been the breeding-grounds of modern theories of acting and directing, and not only, be it said, in naturalistic vein. Shortly after the first rise of symbolism, Lugne Poë founded the Théâtre de L'Oeuvre, as the symbolist counterpart of the Théâtre Libre. From that time these two theatres have continued to maintain repertories representing respectively the Symbolist and the Naturalist schools of drama. The smallness of the auditorium enabled such a theatre to develop a more discreet style of acting, and to pay more detailed attention to the decorations and stage properties of each scene. Above all, the company of actors, which was more or less permanent, was able to build up a tradition of acting, a greater sense of playing together than was possible in the big theatres, for there—except in the official State theatres—a fresh company was assembled for each season, often indeed, in London and Paris, for each new play. Naturally they often presented plays that were bizarre, sensational and quite unorthodox, but it was thanks to them that the deadening routine of the theatre at last died a natural death, and that demands for reform were answered. It was in France, where theatrical taste has always been conservative, that resistance was most stubborn. The best new plays for the Théâtre Libre came from abroad. It was a long struggle, but in the end naturalism emerged victorious in France.

The playwrights of the Realistic school, who really took Becque as their model, did not contribute anything vital to the development of French drama. Their work represents a compromise between his plays and those of the Second Empire. This was partly due to the attitude of the public and the critics, but also to the fact that during this period there was a good deal of talent to be found in the ranks of contemporary French playwrights, but no artist of genius, nor indeed any great personalities. They could create more amusing characters, and plots more thrilling than those of Becque, but none could match his psy-

chological shrewdness, and no one could establish the same sense
of relentless irony.

One writer who made a place for himself was François de
Curel. He was influenced by the problem plays of Ibsen, and
wrote long dialogues with discussion of ideas, often casting
himself as one of the characters who took part. The moral and
intellectual calibre of his work is considerable, but he dealt with
exceptional people and exceptional problems. In his taste for
paradoxical situations he resembled the younger Dumas, but he
lacked gentleness. His ideas were not particularly original and his
imagination was limited.

Among the French dramatists who followed their own native
tradition, there were several who achieved success in all the
theatres of Europe. Mirbeau was the most popular playwright
in the style of Augier and Becque, and his *Les affaires sont les
affaires* (*Business is Business*) has been included in the permanent
repertory of the Théâtre Français ever since 1903. As in *The Son-
in-law of M. Poirier*, the hero is an upstart, by name Lechat, who
has two children, an extravagant ne'er-do-well son, and a
daughter who is the very reverse. She falls in love with a chemist
employed by her father in an agricultural experiment. She runs
away from home and the son is killed in a motor accident, but,
despite his grief, Lechat manages to do a good bit of business with
two financiers who hope to profit by his bereavement.

This final scene is extremely good, but in the rest of the play
Lechat is not a particularly convincing character. Mirbeau
exaggerated his plebeian qualities quite grotesquely, and also his
almost bestial passions, but his characters are nowhere near those
of Strindberg, who achieved the same result with very much less
effort. The play is a good piece of apprentice work in the school
of Augier and Becque—but no more.

There are, of course, many examples of the sort of play for
which Dumas provided the model, and which dealt with 'the
trinity of modern drama'—husband, wife and lover, as Faguet
once called it. The writers, however, are clearly trying to escape
from the constricting plots of an earlier period, to simplify and
to probe deeper into psychology. But threads of the old material
nearly always show: there is nearly always a trace of Dumas'
wordy rhetoric, and something of his paradoxical attitude to love.

The most typical play in this genre is *Amoureuse* (*A Loving Wife*) by Porto-Riche, which was produced for the first time in 1891, and then revived time and time again. The plot is simple, the psychology subtle, and Porto-Riche expounds the truth that from the beginning there has been conflict between a man's work and a woman's love.

There is a stormy discussion in which Etienne tells his wife that she is plaguing the life out of him and spoiling his scientific work by her incessant demands that he be her devoted slave, and by her jealousy in forbidding him any contact with other scientists. In his bitterness he even goes so far as to tell her to start an affair with his best friend Pascal, who has long been in love with her. With equal bitterness, Germaine avenges herself by taking him at his word. She then admits openly to Etienne that she has done so, not through any affection for Pascal, but solely to punish him. She is on the point of leaving her home, but Etienne calls her back; he feels he cannot let her go. "We have wounded each other like enemies", he says. "Words have been spoken which cannot be unsaid. I have failed to appreciate you. You have betrayed me. And yet here I am. I believe we are chained together by all the evil we have done each other, by the abuse we have hurled at each other". Germaine now beseeches him to let her go: "Just think, Etienne, you will be very unhappy". Without daring to look at her, without approaching her, Etienne answers resignedly, "What difference does that make?"

The play reminds one of later dramas about married life, such as Strindberg's *Bandet* (*The Link*, or *The Bond*), or O'Neill's *Welded*, but Porto-Riche is more bound than they by an old-fashioned theatrical technique. He is unable to exclude the sententious and the rhetorical from his dialogue, and succumbs to his liking for dramatic scenes in the style of Dumas.

It is these attempts at naturalism which were never whole-heartedly carried through that have caused French plays produced at the turn of the century to date so quickly and to seem so artificial. In spite of many efforts, writers never quite escaped from *la pièce bien faite*, with its skilfully designed plot, its tension and vitality, the uninhibited speech of the characters and its sparkling dialogue. The French temperament is clear and rational, addicted to grace and wit, and does not feel at home in the greyness of everyday life.

France is the country where the idea of naturalistic drama was first conceived and proclaimed, and where the first attempts to express it were made. It remained for other countries to create the masterpieces inspired by that idea.

NORWEGIAN DRAMA

WHILE the drama of the Second Empire was still dominating the stages of Europe, if not of the whole world, it found a brilliant rival in the drama of Norway. As late as 1890 the contemporary plays of Björnson and Ibsen were still being received with scornful superiority by leading French critics. They were regarded as mere imitations of French Second Empire drama, and were considered to be incomprehensible, even in passages where to-day we cannot detect any obscurity. By this time Norwegian drama had already made its mark on the theatres of all other countries, particularly in Germany. Not even England could withstand the flood tide of 'Ibsenism'. It made its way into Russia, where the Czarist regime was dying and the revolution looming, it broke all national boundaries, and reached the United States as soon as they were ready to consider seriously the problems of a literary theatre. The contribution of Norwegian drama was something unprecedented for a hundred years. The influence of Ibsen was at work in all the plays that circulated round the theatres of the world until the outbreak of the first world war. Authors often find it necessary to explain in a preface or an interview that this time they are presenting something fundamentally different from an Ibsen play. Closer examination usually shows that the ingredients, which have been skilfully compounded, come from the old master's laboratory.

Like Ireland thirty years later, Norway at the time of Ibsen and Björnson was engaged in creating—or rather re-creating—its literary independence. People were trying to throw off their cultural dependence on Denmark, as well as their connexions with Sweden.

Björnson and Ibsen were no more superficial than Yeats and Synge. They struggled against Norwegian particularism and the partisans of local dialects, with the same fervour as that which marked the resistance of the protagonists of the Anglo-Irish Renaissance to the excesses of Sinn Fein. Nevertheless, the feeling that they represented a young nation with a glorious history had a stimulating effect on both of them.

In their early days they were both busily engaged, as native-born Norwegian playwrights, in providing the Norwegian theatres in Bergen and Christiania with their own native plays instead of the traditional Danish works. They hunted for subjects in the legends and history of their own country with the same interest that Yeats showed in the legends of Ossian and Cuchulain. Later they turned to contemporary topics, but still attached importance to presenting them in a Norwegian setting. They spent a great part of their lives abroad, and after his journey in 1864 Ibsen never felt really at home on Norwegian soil. All the same, Björnson only wrote one play with a foreign theme, *Maria Stuart*, and Ibsen, after his first play *Catalina*, made only one more attempt at a historical play with a non-Norwegian theme, *Emperor and Galilean*; wherever he stayed, in Italian or Austrian or German hotels, he always wrote plays with a Norwegian setting.

Their plays usually had the same setting, a small town on the coast, and despite their different temperaments and attitudes to Norway, they conceived it in the same way, as closed in by high mountains, a community full of prejudice and hostility between various cliques. "Yes—up here in the North in our tiny communities, where everybody, friend and foe alike, goes to the same barber's shop—here it feels as if we were going round constantly stabbing at each other". These words are spoken by the raisonneur in Björnson's *The Editor*; they might so easily have come from a play by Ibsen. It is not surprising that, at first, foreign critics, and in particular foreign students of Ibsen, were convinced that the most remarkable quality of the Norwegian temperament was its capacity for devastating self-criticism.

Ideally, the dramatic works of Ibsen and Björnson should be studied together. Their interdependence makes it almost impossible to decide where the initiative lay. Björnson's *Leonarda* was the first of a series of great Scandinavian feminist plays. It was produced at the theatre in Christiania in April 1879, and the text was published in September of that year, three months before Ibsen's *A Doll's House* appeared. But it would be foolish to conclude from this that here Ibsen was Björnson's pupil. The first draft of *A Doll's House* is dated October 1878; the full version was written at Amalfi during the spring and summer of 1879. Ibsen may have read in the Norwegian press about the great success of *Leonarda* and the tremendous controversy to which it gave rise, but the idea of *A Doll's House* had been conceived long before—it was present, in embryo, in the Selma episode, from *The League of Youth* of 1869. It is however true, as Bull points out, that he did acknowledge his debt to Björnson. In 1878 he congratulated him, through an intermediary, on his story *Magnhild*, in which by an even more violent paradox than in *A Doll's House*, the moral is driven home that a woman whose marriage is not a real one should abandon it, rather than continue to countenance a false situation.

From this single example we may realize that the interplay of ideas between the two dramatists (though for long periods they exchanged no written word) is so complex that each must be studied separately. Björnson achieved world recognition as a playwright before Ibsen, but in spite of all their merits his plays are now hardly ever read or played outside Norway. It can hardly be assumed therefore that they are as widely known as those of Ibsen. Ibsen's work is the Rome of modern drama; all roads lead to it or from it.

BJÖRNSTERNE BJÖRNSON

WHILE Ibsen spent the greater part of his life in a world of darkness and mystery, Björnson loved the bright light of day. From the outset of his public career he was always in the thick of the fight, struggling, teaching, preaching and composing. Ibsen has left little material for his biographer, but for Björnson the sources of information are so rich that no one has yet been able to collect all the material. This also holds true of his work. Bull published an excellent nine volume edition of his "Collected Poetical Works", and this contains the greater part of his writings, though by no means all. Even in drama he wrote more than he ever bothered to publish. His centenary celebrations in 1932 occasioned the publication of a hitherto unknown play, *Kong Eystein* (*King Eystein*), which is considered one of his finest. In 1945 yet another hitherto unknown play by Björnson was published.

Björnson's political views have sometimes been misunderstood, particularly his activities and relations with Sweden. Fundamentally he was a warm friend of Sweden, and there was no malice or guile behind his savage outbursts, which were indeed received in Sweden with relative calm. There was no doubt at all where his heart lay. Björnson found it easy to make contact with people, both when addressing them in public and in private conversation. He had a natural and attractive eloquence, a trifle theatrical at times, and a readiness to tackle any problem, which almost savoured of meddling. Enthusiastic and eager as he was, he occasionally wounded people by his lack of tact. His intentions, however, were always chivalrous and helpful, his zest for life was keen and exuberant, and his naive charm was usually irresistible.

Every letter that Björnson wrote, every story that is told about him, confirms this impression of his character. He seemed to personify the spirit of Norway, to be in full harmony with his own people. Wherever he went abroad—and he travelled a great deal— Norway was always with him. His thoughts were always of home, and he was truly distressed if he was unable to find a compatriot to talk with, or at any rate somebody "of the same stock". The German papers in 1880 carried the story that Björnson was sick and tired of the conflicts in Norway, and was proposing to settle down in Munich as a literary *émigré* for the rest of his life. Then it was that he wrote to Georg Brandes the well-known lines: "I want to live in Norway, to strike and be struck in Norway, to sing and die in Norway. Be sure of that".

It is obvious that a life so full of intense activity in many fields did not provide breathing-space for the production of plays as polished and carefully thought out as those of Ibsen. Björnson often conceived the themes of his plays years before he actually wrote them, and he would discuss their implications with all and sundry. When he finally sat down at his desk, the characters he had originally conceived usually took a different shape. Albert Edelfelt wrote a letter from Paris, dated 4th February, 1883, in which he speaks of Björnson having discussed with him for the past fortnight nothing but the theme of *En hanske* (*A Gauntlet*): "Every time I met him he had some new notion. The main idea was of an educated woman, whose hand was being sought in marriage, insisting on premarital purity in her fiancé. His first conception of the play was so fantastic that for stage purposes it was useless. To-day, if what he said is true, he has modified it considerably and has even included some of the theatrical dodges, such as missing letters, handwriting recognized, etc., which give life to a play. Then, of course, he always has fire. No schoolboy talking about his first creative work could have been more enthusiastic. He shouted, he acted, he waved his arms about; no schoolboy could have produced a better blend of childishness and cleverness". Before *A Gauntlet* appeared in its first version, the third act had already been re-written twice, and Georg Brandes undertook to publish the piece and decide between the various readings. In the printed text the reader is given to suppose that there is hope of reconciliation between the two lovers. Björnson was attacked on all sides, by Garborg, by the Bohemian group in Christiania, and in Strindberg's *Married*, and in preparing the

stage version he took a further step, and closed the play with
Svava flinging a gauntlet at her fiancé. The play as performed
naturally roused even more opposition and criticism, which
infuriated Björnson, and during his great Scandinavian lecture
tour he proclaimed the rigorous code of morals for marriage
which became famous there as 'Gauntlet' morals. This incident
made him a bitter enemy of Georg Brandes, and—which was
worse—cast a slight shadow of ridicule over a play which was
one of the most skilful he ever wrote.

In *A Gauntlet*, indeed, the material for the plot remained the
same, though the treatment in the first version was fantastic, in
the second logical, and in the final version, paradoxical. Often,
however, a sudden idea produced by Björnson's uncontrollable
imagination might turn into something very different from his
original conception. Five years before producing his play,
Over aevne (*Beyond our Strength*), for instance, he wrote to his
friends saying that he was planning a comedy about a family
suffering from "that sort of sickness which makes one always
want something beyond one's strength". There was to be a big
party, and arguments about inheritance which each member of
the family would want to use in a different way. This idea
developed into a profoundly moving miracle-play—one of the
greatest of Björnson's works, and one of the greatest modern
dramas. How it happened is a problem which he tried to
explain in an article in 1902, but the metamorphosis remains
something of a mystery. What is clear, however, is that this
unmethodical approach to his writing played Björnson many a
trick. But occasionally it led him to surpass himself.

Björnson's dramatic work, like all his writings, belonged very
much to the period—far more so than Ibsen's, and it has therefore
been assumed by some that it was meant to portray an earlier
period than Ibsen's writings. Björnson's poetry was supposed to
represent the flowering of Norwegian national romanticism, and
Ibsen's work the progress of modern realism. Closer examination
will show that this distinction is untenable. As far as their relative
literary positions are concerned, Björnson was, throughout his
writing career, a good bit ahead of Ibsen. His wide reading and
lively interest in everything that went on in the world gave him
an advantage over the less adventurous Ibsen. During their early

years in particular Ibsen was usually a good length behind Björnson, and quite often his pupil.

It is obviously true that Björnson's youthful poems, his stories, and his first historical plays are romantic in tone. For us they seem to go with paintings by Tidemand and Gude, and the music of Kjerulf and Grieg. But Ibsen too had been caught up in the wake of Romanticism. Even a play like *Peer Gynt* owes a debt to the peasant writings of Björnson.

Scribe and Musset were at this time the two great names in the world of contemporary European drama. It is characteristic of Björnson, who was not, like Ibsen, too proud to acknowledge what he had learned from other writers, that he did not share the fashionable disdain for Scribe that was making itself felt even in Scandinavia in 1850—though he did once or twice speak rather slightingly about Scribe's "sugary trifles".

His letters show how impressed he was by the drama of the Second Empire, for he likes to compare his historic plays with those of the younger Dumas and Augier, even when the comparison seems pointless. The second play of his trilogy, *Sigurd Slembe* (*Sigurd the Bastard*), was, he felt, the closest to Dumas because of the "cold mathematics of suffering". His articles and reviews show that, much earlier than Ibsen, he realized how important this advance would be for modern drama.

Another great formative influence for modern drama, that of Friedrich Hebbel, was also appreciated by Björnson. He said that he wrote *Sigurd the Bastard* as a trilogy, after the style of Hebbel's *Dïe Nibelungen*, and when he first mentioned the project in 1858, he was conceiving it in the spirit of Hebbel. The hero's conflict with the established order was to represent the conflict that we experience daily in great things as well as in small. Björnson was right in his belief that his hero foreshadowed Skule in *The Pretenders*, which also presents the conflict between the individual and tradition.

Björnson was better acquainted than Ibsen with contemporary tendencies in literature. He was an early supporter of Zola's theories of heredity, and gave them expression in novels and plays, but he disapproved of Zola's frankness in sexual matters, and was revolted when he read Strindberg's *Miss Julie*. In his own way he managed to achieve a good many of the ideals which Zola had set for naturalistic drama. The first part of *Beyond our Strength* expresses most excellently Taine's theories of environment; there is very little action and the plot is really a 'case', an experiment, just as Zola would have wished. Björnson was particularly sensitive to all new ideas, and as early as 1883 he was displaying the interest in hypnotism and suggestion which everywhere marked the transition to symbolism. He visited Charcot in Paris, and his next publication contained a reference to a book written by Charcot and another French psychiatrist.

During the 1890's Björnson made one or two attempts at symbolism, as for instance in the revised stage version of *Geografi og Kjaerlighed* (*Geography and Love*) and in the second part of *Beyond our Strength*. He read Maeterlinck's plays and admired them greatly. This style, however, did not suit him and he returned to the realities of his own day.

The "fog-bound world of the present" had something of terror in it for Ibsen, even as late as the period when he was working on *Brand*; for Björnson, however, the contemporary play was to prove irresistibly attractive. Before he was twenty and while he was working at school for the university entrance examination, he wrote two contemporary plays which were accepted by the Christiania theatre. He withdrew them, however, and after a few months destroyed them because they did not answer to the times. This was also one of the reasons why he put his next plays into period dress.

For his first published play, *Mellem slagene* (*Between the Battles*) (1856), Björnson found his plot in an incident from real life which he at first intended to use for a contemporary drama, the story of a young daughter of a general, who shortly after her marriage ran home to her parents. He could not get his theme into shape until he turned it into a historical play, with King Sverre as a marriage broker. The theme is very similar to that of *De nygifte* (*The Newly-married Couple*, 1865). He had long been corresponding with friends about his ideas and plans for contemporary plays. In 1861, while he was still busy with *Sigurd the Bastard*, he wrote in a letter that this play and the others were only an introduction to something in the creation of which his whole being would participate—the bourgeois drama.

It was therefore a great relief to Björnson when he was at last able, in 1865, to write *The Newly-married Couple*, a modern play which he had been planning for two years. It won the greatest theatrical success that any Scandinavian play had ever achieved. It was presented simultaneously in Christiania, Stockholm and Copenhagen, a hitherto unheard-of event. Before Björnson was ready with his next great dramatic success, *En fallit* (*A Bankruptcy*), it had already been acclaimed in Germany, and moved on from there to Austria, Hungary, Russia and further still. If one reads this play, its success seems rather surprising, and the critics were not kind.

The Newly-married Couple consists of only two short acts, and is really a proverb in the style of Musset, as Brandes pointed out in a contemporary review, suggesting Musset's *Un Caprice* (*A Whim*) as its model. The play treats of a young man, and his wife who cannot disengage herself from her parents' influence. The husband first escapes from the uncomfortable position of a son-in-law living with his wife's people, and then succeeds in regaining his wife's affection and the respect of his old parents-in-law, this last by the help of a friend of himself and his wife, who performs the same function as in Musset's play. Modern Norwegian drama, which was to devote so much attention to the emancipation of married women, began here with a defence of man's rights. The play foreshadows Strindberg's work in the 1870's, in which husbands free themselves from feminine oppression.

Strindberg maintained that it was Nora who treated Helmer like a doll, and in *The Newly-married Couple* it is Axel who says to his wife's parents, "You let her treat me as the biggest of all the dolls you have given her". This significant riposte Björnson took from a play by Augier *Un beau Mariage* (*A Fine Marriage*, 1859), in which another young husband finally declares that he is no doll. The word 'doll' in Björnson's play seems to have stuck fast in Ibsen's memory, and as early as in *The League of Youth*, he makes Selma grumble at being treated like a doll. Let the final comment on the play be that of Georg Brandes, who said he took no pleasure in watching pale young lovers feeding on milk and water.

This is nevertheless the first instance of a modern marriage play in Scandinavian drama. Björnson himself felt that he had found his proper style, but it was ten years before he dared to repeat the venture and write the work which he had already conceived, and which was his first real success with a modern play, namely *A Bankruptcy*.

It was in Italy during the winter of 1873-4, that the two contemporary works, *Redaktören* (*The Editor*) and *A Bankruptcy* were written. Björnson himself was convinced that they would open new fields of conquest for Norwegian drama, and proposed to produce them first in Germany. It was, however, in Stockholm, in the spring of 1875, that both plays had their premières. *The Editor* was slashed to pieces by the critics, but *A Bankruptcy* proved a world-wide success, the greatest that Björnson ever achieved. Long after he died it was still in the regular repertoire of theatres all over Germany.

The Editor was actually the more original of the two plays, but in Sweden the critics of the day recognized the real characters on whose story the play was built, despite the public denials and explanations in the press which Björnson gave. In 1869 Ibsen had written the first modern political play—*The League of Youth*—which was hostile to Björnson and the Left Wing party. Björnson's reply was to portray the editor of the principal Right Wing paper, Morgenbladet, who was called Friele. When Björnson left on his foreign travels, Friele wrote that his writing had already brought him well within the reach of the law. In the play the Left Wing politician, Halvdan Rejn, who is seriously ill, has a stroke and dies when he reads a similar comment on his actions in the paper. Both in Sweden and Norway, Björnson's presentation of Friele as the Press Executioner was regarded as an outrage. His real intention was to show how publicity for political matters can ruin family life and human happiness. He did not succeed in this, however, until he wrote his best political play, *Paul Lange og Tora Parsberg*, using the same excellent device as before, but with himself not as the victim but as the criminal. Both the description of the editor, and the love-story were inspired by *Giboyer's Son*, a play which Björnson was to use again, even more skilfully, in *Det ny system* (*The New System*).

A Bankruptcy was more cut to pattern, and Sarcey considered it rather a tedious copy of French drama. As far as the plot is concerned this criticism is justified. As in French drama, particularly Sardou's *The Benoiton Family*, he presents a family financially ruined, compelled to abandon their luxurious life, and in the final act finding happiness in simple surroundings. When the disaster comes, the fiancé of one of the daughters, a lieutenant, deserts the sinking ship, but the kind-hearted book-keeper, Sannaes, his hands swollen with chilblains in the firm's service, stands fast, and his fidelity is rewarded when the younger daughter of the family, whom he has long adored, gives him her hand.

The chief merit of the play lies in its excellent descriptive passages. It is the first instance in drama where one is really aware of that strong 'home' atmosphere which has long been a strong feature of Scandinavian novels. This being so, it matters less that the characters are not profound psychological studies. The father of the family, a sanguine speculator called Tjelde, seems more of a poet than a jobber on the Stock Exchange. The financial transactions are no less mysterious than those in French plays. The big scene in the play is the great party which Tjelde gives at his country house. Abroad, however, audiences were more interested in the *scène à faire*, in which the emissaries of the banks compel Tjelde to become a bankrupt. "This is what we mean by 'good theatre' in France," writes the fastidious Sarcey.

Ibsen had, of course, *A Bankruptcy* in mind when he wrote his first social play, *Pillars of Society*. It is the least significant of his social plays, and the older generation of Norwegian scholars, such as Gerhard Gran, considered *A Bankruptcy* to be the better play. This, however, is only true from a purely technical point of view. Bernick is badly drawn, but he still has some of the stature of characters like Solness and John Gabriel Borkman. The setting and atmosphere are far inferior to Björnson's, and many of the characters are greatly exaggerated, but it is only in Ibsen's plays that we have the feeling of walking on a quicksand, of living in a community as rotten as the hulk of the 'Indian Girl' in the harbour. It is poetry and drama of quite a different calibre.

Björnson's next piece, *The New System*, was partly inspired by the attacks which had been made on his semi-symbolical play, *Kongen* (*The King*). In 1885, when *Beyond Our Strength* and *A Gauntlet* had already appeared, he wrote to Hegel, "I have never written better". Surprise has been expressed that Björnson copied, word for word, the great scene between Giboyer and his son Maximilien in *Giboyer's Son*. But he had himself produced Augier's play at the Christiania theatre; the dialogue had clearly remained fixed in his mind.

The subject of the play is the return from America of a young engineer, Hans Kampe, and his fearless struggle with the old director for reforms on the antiquated railway system. Gradually he gains more and more ground until the director is left quite alone, with nobody believing in his methods. Björnson was trying to present that conflict between authority and personal conviction which Ibsen had expressed in *Pillars of Society* a little while before. He succeeded fairly well. The action is lively, with no improbabilities, and characters are drawn with humour and gusto. In 1878, when it appeared, it was probably the most accomplished work in Scandinavian contemporary drama.

The chief weakness is that one is given no explanation of the advantages of the 'new system' over the director's system. Björnson had got his idea from an actual conflict which raged some years earlier between the director of the Norwegian Railways, who wanted narrow-gauge lines for the national system and a young engineer who opposed him. Björnson invited this young engineer to stay with him at Aulestad, but even so he did not succeed in making clear in the play exactly why the broad gauge was better. In the first version of the play, which appeared in German in 1878, he went so far as to end with an agreement that alternate sections of the system should have wide gauge and narrow gauge. This completely destroyed the basic argument of the play.

The already-printed Norwegian version was then withdrawn, and the end modified, to give complete victory to the young engineer. It needs a good deal of belief in authority to be convinced that belief in authority is wrong. The play should have shown how difficult it is to know the truth, but in fact it gives the impression that nothing is easier than to be the herald of a new age.

Ibsen was directly influenced by *The New System* when, after *Ghosts* had been boycotted, he wrote *An Enemy of the People*. But how much more clearly in his description of Dr. Stockman's campaign against the polluted water, which is the source of the community's prosperity, has he symbolized the struggle against corrupt social aims. Unlike Björnson, Ibsen allows his play to end with Dr. Stockman isolated, deserted by all, but with unshaken faith that the man who can stand alone is strongest. Not until he wrote *Paul Lange and Tora Parsberg* was Björnson to subscribe to this faith, when he made Tora say, "Man is not strongest because he wins: he is strongest when he is allied to the future—and stands by his principles".

A year earlier, in 1877, Björnson wrote a novel, *Magnhild* which started a debate on marriage problems, a debate which reached its peak with the publication of Ibsen's *A Doll's House*, and Björnson's *A Gauntlet*. The heroine of the novel is the forerunner of Nora in peasant dress. She despises her disagreeable husband, a saddler, and deserts him to escape to the freedom and unconventionality of America with a girl whom she knew as a child. America was of course also the haven to which Dina, oppressed by small town life, was escaping in Ibsen's *Pillars of Society*, which appeared at more or less the same time. There is one incident in *The New System* which suggests the thought that men and women are measured with a different yardstick, and this thought becomes the dominant one in Björnson's first feminist play, *Leonarda*. In this case Björnson was influenced by Dumas' campaign in favour of the same moral code for both sexes. Leonarda Falk is not received at the Bishop's house because she has been divorced, and because she goes about with General Rosen, whose aberrations are well known. But the General himself, despite his reputation, is very welcome. Björnson originally intended that Leonarda should triumph in the end by marrying the Bishop's nephew, who is in love with her. At the last moment, however, he changed his mind and made Leonarda give him up to her niece Ågåt and go abroad with the General, declaring him to be her divorced husband—a notion which in no way accords with their relationship at the beginnings of the play.

The result of this blow for women's rights and marriage based in spiritual affinity is that Leonarda, who had been freed, was enslaved again to her sinful husband, and that two young people who did not love one another were thrust into each other's arms. Björnson himself bitterly regretted this hastily composed ending, and planned another final act which was to put things right; but it was never written.

While he was writing this play, Björnson clearly fell in love with his young heroine, Ågåt, and she is the most vital character in the play. There is one scene where she comes in, warm and sunburnt, rucksack on her back, from a walking tour, and seeming like some premonition of Ibsen's Hilda Wangel, at once shy and bold, sober and ecstatic, imaginative and practical.

In his next play, *A Gauntlet*, Björnson once again scored a triumph with his female characters. It appeared four years later, that is in 1883, after *A Doll's House* and *Ghosts*, and was influenced by both these plays of Ibsen's. As with Oswald and Mrs. Alving, Svava, the heroine of the play, was brought up by her mother in ignorance of her father's misbehaviour. In contrast to Alving however, Svava's father is still alive, and depicted by Björnson as an agreeable 'bon viveur'. Svava throws her gauntlet in the face of her fiancé, Alf Christensen, when she hears that he has had relations with the society lady who lived, till her death, with his parents. Marriage, she thought, should not be a sort of superior washing-room where a man can cleanse himself. Her own home seems equally intolerable when she learns that the father whom her mother had taught her to venerate has just had an affair with a certain Mrs. North. In the final act Svava reproaches her mother with keeping secret the squalor in which she has lived, and allowing her daughter to demand the "strictest standards from a house like ours". It is with the feeling that she cannot escape the tangle of lies in which she has become involved that she finally, though hesitantly, gives her hand to her fiancé. In the revised version of 1886, she resolutely accepts the consequences, as does Nora, and a slap on the face with a gauntlet brings the play to a close.

The influence of Ibsen is also discernible in the fact that it is always the past, that which lies behind the play itself, which is decisive. But Björnson lacked Ibsen's gift of invoking the past as an all-powerful fate, and in the final, and more exacting, version of the play, we miss Ibsen's sure sense of logical consequences. The play was misunderstood by both Björnson's admirers and his opponents, and he was continually called upon for an explanation.

But while Ibsen does not succeed in fully reconciling the cheerful Nora of the first acts with the stern moralist of the second half of the play, Svava remains a lively young woman throughout. Her cheerfulness is inherited from her father, and theories of heredity are discussed a good deal in the play. From her mother she has inherited a lofty idealism. She broke off an earlier engagement because the young man did not conform to her standards of morality. Now suddenly she hears first of her fiancé's misconduct, and then of her father's, and all her illusions are shattered: "This is a whole mountain which I have been trying to push away with my bare hands". It compares with Mrs. Alving's attempt to drive away the Ghosts.

In the feminist campaign, Björnson was fighting a war on two fronts, in defence of equal moral standards for men and women, and against the exponents of 'free love', such as Garborg and the author of *Fra Christiania Bohemen*, Hans Jaeger. Strindberg was also included by Björnson in this camp.

At about this time he also came under fire from both sides in the current religious controversy. After much soul-searching he had left the company of his former Grundtvigian friends. The real reason why he became a freethinker was his belief that orthodox believers were disregarding too lightly the problems and discoveries of modern science. Unfortunately Björnson was not very particular in his choice of new leaders to follow, and to any American or German free-thinking journal which made a clean sweep of Christianity and the Bible, he immediately accorded the respect due to scientific authority of the highest rank. In vain he was warned by his new friends, Georg Brandes who had provided the initial impulse towards positivism, and Kielland, who laughed at his polemics against King David. In 1882 he translated two very elementary American Free Thought pamphlets, one of them composed by the famous Ingersoll. He also rewrote another pamphlet of the same calibre, "What is the origin of the miracles in the New Testament?" It was to attack faith in miracles that he wrote the first part of *Beyond our Strength*.

There is a remarkable contrast between Björnson's intentions with regard to this play, and the results he actually achieved. Most readers and audiences regard it as a work of religious edification. When it was produced in Paris Lemaître wrote, "The theme is

positivist, and worked out by an ardent mystic". The mistake
is understandable. Ibsen remained to some extent a mystic and
a pietist through all his various changes of belief. Björnson was
never a mystic, even in his Grundtvigian days. What gives an
impression of mysticism in the play derives from his understanding of the poetic value of religion, and his wish not to offend
any of his religious friends, with whom he had never broken off
personal relations. While writing the play he said in a letter that
he was trying to treat his subject in such a way that no genuine
Christian would be distressed by anything he saw on the stage.

From the naturalistic point of view, the play is a piece of real
life. Sang has hypnotic gifts which he himself ascribes to the
power of prayer. His wife, Klara, suffers from hysterical palsy,
and Sang can help her with his powers of suggestion far better
than the doctors, who only give her illness "a bad name". By
prayer and suggestion he induces Klara to get up out of bed—
and she falls, dying, into his arms. He dies in his turn, from
exhaustion. According to Björnson the play demonstrated that
miracles do not occur except when caused by auto-hypnosis, or
when hypnotism is exercised by others.

This outline does not indicate the poetic value of the play.
Without realizing it, Björnson has recreated a medieval miracle
in a modern setting. He protested violently when Christopher
Bruun, one of the people from whom the character of Sang had
been drawn, alleged that he had created a modern Christ-like
figure. This, however, is just the impression one does get from
Sang. He calls to mind the pictures of Fritz Von Uhde, who
painted the carpenter's Son in a modern setting, surrounded by
farm labourers and working men and women. A sense of the
miraculous pervaded this play, which was directed against the
belief in miracles.

None of Björnson's other plays has as slight a plot. In the two
short acts there is not a single conflict. In the first act Sang only
appears in a couple of scenes. In the second act he utters the final
words of the play, his dying words. But every word that is
spoken relates to his supernatural powers.

The first scene, in which the bedridden Klara and her sister,
Mrs. Roberts, just returned from America, appear, gives immediately the whole atmosphere of a house in the far north of Norway.

The windows of the little wooden cottage are open to the valley
and the mountains, and the soft scented air drifts into the room.
"How the sun shines on the birch leaves out there! And how
lovely they are, these leaves." These are the first lines of the play.
Then, as the sisters continue to talk, they relate Sang's miracles
to the workings of nature in this northern land. He would have
aroused a hundred times more interest elsewhere, maintains
Klara, who is normally more sceptical: "But there is something
in nature here which demands the unusual in us also. Nature
itself goes beyond all reasonable bounds here". All the winter it
is night, and all the summer there is daylight, and behind the sea
mists the sun looks four times its normal size. Curious colours
come and go in the sky: in the winter there are the Northern
Lights, and the great hosts of birds and fish. The mountains
stretch right into the sea; there are none like them elsewhere.
The tales the people tell are about incredible things, and Sang
seems himself to spring from them. The spectator may not be
aware of it, but Björnson has prepared for Sang's entrance
according to Taine's theory of environment.

When Sang does come in he is told that his children have left
their father's faith. He receives the news calmly with no word of
reproach, and his own faith is unshaken. Indeed, he now ventures
to attempt something he has feared to do before, to heal his wife,
and by his prayers enable her to leave her bed: "For faith, that is
to know that with faith nothing is impossible—and then to show
that faith".

In these conversations between Sang and his family, Björnson
only touches lightly on matters of religious controversy, which
he normally labours. Sang is "beyond our strength": "I believe
that the prophets must have been like this, both the Jewish and
the heathen. They knew more than we do in some ways,
though in all others they were a long way behind".

The act ends with an avalanche, which is expected to fall on
the church. Sang is there praying for the sick woman, who under
his influence has fallen quietly asleep. But the avalanche falls elsewhere, and she continues to sleep like a child in her bed.

The day after—in the second act—the rumour of the miracle
brings a great crowd to the little country church. The local
clergy, with the bishop at their head, leave a mission that they are

conducting and come over by steamer to see with their own eyes what will happen next.

The scene with the clergy, treated both with humour and pathos, is probably the most original that Björnson ever wrote. In a few brief sentences he conjures up a whole crowd of different personalities, from the simple village minister with his bleating voice to the grand old bishop. The latter is embarrassed by his clergy at this solemn moment, because they are most unsuitably hungry after being seasick, and continually exhorts them to keep an open mind about what they are going to see. From among the clergy who regard the day's events as a suitable topic for conversation, there suddenly emerges a passionate seeker after truth. For seven years Bratt has been proclaiming a faith in which he has not himself believed. He has visited every shrine in Europe to discover the thing that humanity must have if it is to believe—a miracle. This is his last attempt. If it fails there is only one way out, to abandon the Church and Christianity.

So at last we come to the incomprehensible: the stricken wife in her long white nightgown steps out of the bedroom, while the clergy and the congregation fall to their knees crying Hallelujah. With the evening sun shining on his face, Sang comes out of the church and enters the cottage, now crowded with people. He stretches out his hands to his wife, who falls dying into his arms, with the words "You were shining . . . when you came . . . my love". Sang looks up at the sky: "But this was not what I meant —or, . . . or—". He puts his hand to his heart and also falls down dead.

Was there a shadow of doubt clouding his last moments? His daughter asks what he meant by "or . . .", and Bratt answers, "I don't know exactly—but he died of it".

In this simple and great scene we are overcome by a sense of the supernatural, and scarcely stop to ask whether this is the act of a god who can work miracles, or the effect of nature's laws, no less mysterious. Men rise above themselves when they see the heavenly ones coming down to earth. They care nothing for risks: "One may not live so long this way—but one can't have everything". One of the priests says, "When a miracle has happened to a man, he gives out light himself". This light Björnson caught in his play. The characters are translucent, the atmosphere is mystical. This is what gives the play its special place in the world's literature.

Björnson's next two plays, *Geography and Love* (1885), and the second part of *Beyond Our Strength* (1895) were originally intended to complete the *Beyond our Strength* trilogy which he had planned. *Geography and Love*, in fact, developed into something quite different—one of the few comedies produced in Scandinavia in the latter part of the 19th century which were really amusing and could really be staged. It is difficult to imagine, when one reads or sees the play, that the irresistible Tygesen, a self-caricature or Björnson, was meant to be "beyond our strength". His eccentricity lies in a tendency, which Björnson certainly shares, to sacrifice everything for his work. He makes things intolerable for his relations by filling the whole house with maps, and destroys family life by incessantly talking about his geographical research. It is said of him that he can talk down ten ordinary mortals.

From Björnson's letters, it appears that the weaknesses we detect in the play are the last traces of the divorce theme that he originally intended to present. When he began to work on it in the summer of 1883 he intended to show a marriage foundering because the partners expected too much from it. Björnson was anxious to counteract the endless propaganda in favour of "a life of love"—"as if there were no life of work". In *Geography and Love*, however, it is just this life of work that he is mocking. But while he was writing the play, he was smarting from the attacks of the disciples of Free Love, who resented his play, *A Gauntlet*. He returned the compliment in the play by introducing the character Henning, a fascinating bohemian artist, who at one and the same moment succeeds in making fools of both Tygesen's wife and his daughter. Henning treats Björnson's 'one man, one woman' theory of marriage with the same contempt as Hans Jaeger used to do, and is shown the door. Tygesen is a comic figure, but Björnson uses him as a mouthpiece to express his moral indignation at recent immoral French literature. The uninitiated do not know here whether to take Tygesen seriously or not. The last act was revised some years later, but it is hardly an improvement. It does, however, indicate faintly the original idea of the play. Tygesen, the great and eccentric professor, turns into a hero of fantasy, and a martyr. Björnson was occupied at this time with writing the second part of *Beyond our Strength*.

Beyond Our Strength, Part II, appeared in 1895. It shows the dangers of excess in public life, with the theme of a modern strike which ends in disaster for both sides. Hauptmann had made the subject fashionable. In exactly the same way as in *The Weavers*, we are first introduced to the starving workmen, are then shown a scene with the employers, and in the final act are convinced of the folly of the whole dispute. Björnson put his plot in a modern setting, and related it to anarchist outrages of recent years which had greatly distressed him. He had much sympathy for the labour movement and regarded himself as a Socialist, but felt that strikes should be settled by arbitration. The third act, which is the best in the play, contains a meeting of the employers which foreshadows the parliamentary dinner in *Paul Lange and Tora Parsberg*. Here, too, representative Norwegian politicians, only slightly disguised, are given their say. It has been suggested that this act may have had some influence on the corresponding scene in Galsworthy's *Strife*. In 1890 Björnson's play had already been translated into German. But both Galsworthy and Hauptmann were concerned to preserve an unspoilt naturalism. So did Björnson in the first act, where, like Hauptmann, he indicates the misery and dumb revolt in the labour camp, and presents a colourful mixed group of workers and labour leaders. Later, his imagination got the better of him, and the scene—with theatrical effects—where Elias, the son of Sang, blows himself up and the employers with him, is worthy of Victor Hugo.

The play as a whole is somewhat disconnected. A few of the characters are familiar from the first part of *Beyond our Strength*, but they appear in rather a different guise. The symbolic scenes are positively unattractive, the chief person in them being Sang's daughter, Rachel, who here represents self-sacrificing human love. In complete contrast to her we find Holger, the factory manager, a type of Nietzsche's Superman. Björnson was rather critical of Nietzsche's theory of morals, but he seems to have been fascinated by the behaviour of his Superman.

Nowadays there are probably few people outside Norway who have read this play, but it is by no means insignificant. The social reforms which Björnson urged seem less Utopian than they did in 1895. The remedies he suggested for the solution of labour disputes have become everyday realities—at least in Sweden. He was also ahead of his time in presenting modern social problems in symbolic fashion. Andreev's plays on social problems, which were greatly admired in their day, have the same blending of realism and symbolism, but their literary quality is slighter, and they are marred by a false profundity from which Björnson is mercifully free.

Paul Lange and Tora Parsberg, the best play of Björnson's later years, aroused great resentment because it portrayed the actual person of Ole Richter, a Norwegian Minister of State who shot himself in Stockholm in June 1888. It was considered tactless of Björnson to have written a play about a suicide, particularly since his own fanaticism was held partly responsible. Björnson himself always liked it better than any of his other plays. It is also, except for *Geography and Love*, the drama that has best kept its place in theatrical repertory. This is partly because of a freshness in the dialogue, and a sharpness in characterization greater than Björnson achieved in any other non-historical play. It also has a relevance unaffected by the passing of time. In the rather pedantic last lines of the play, Tora Parsberg says, "Why must it be that the good are so often martyred? Will we never learn to take them as leaders?" Paul Lange did not seem built for a leader— any more than his prototype in real life. But, without in any way concealing Lange's weaknesses, Björnson has contrived to give the impression that he is head and shoulders above the other politicians in the play.

Less than a year after Ole Richter shot himself, Björnson was already contemplating the play, in the first instance perhaps to justify his own conduct. He had published in the press a condensed and sharper version of a private letter written to him by Richter, in which he accused his leader, Johan Sverdrup, of duplicity. Richter then telegraphed to Sverdrup, denying that he had made these charges. Björnson now wrote to Richter, threatening him with public exposure which would put an end to his career in Norwegian politics. Björnson's own defence was that Richter had promised him that he would cease to support Sverdrup.

An undated and unpublished draft, written at some time in

1889 or 1890, is said by Bull to give a rather undigested account of these events. In time, however, Björnson came to see things in rather a different light. He realized that in his anger he had used too strong weapons against an old friend. Above all, in 1897, when he went abroad after a new outburst of political fanaticism, he came to feel that distaste for party warfare which Paul Lange expresses. In his notes on the play he emphasizes expressly that not only did he make Arne Kraft (who acts a role in the play similar to his own in real life) a self-portrait, but that he recognized a spiritual affinity between himself and Paul Lange. With all his political passion, Björnson was something better than a thick-skinned prizefighter.

Bull pointed out that the theme of Ibsen's *Rosmersholm*, where the contrast is drawn between the noble but weak Rosmer and his fanatical son-in-law, the headmaster Kroll, is repeated in the contrast between Paul Lange and Arne Kraft. *Rosmersholm* was indeed composed under similar circumstances, for Ibsen had just visited Norway, had been drawn into the party war, and afterwards regretted it.

As a piece of literary composition, *Paul Lange and Tora Parsberg* cannot be compared with *Rosmersholm*, but as a stage play it is more acceptable. The second act is particularly effective; at Tora Parsberg's dinner for the members of the Norwegian Parliament the various figures come alive for us, sometimes through a single virulent remark. This representation of a political rabble is reminiscent of Shakespeare's *Julius Caesar*. Paul Lange treats the calumny of which he is fully aware with noble disdain until his best friend, Arne Kraft, joins in: "Now you have killed me. I didn't believe that you would be the one to do it". This is Caesar's farewell to Brutus rewritten in modern style.

The plays Björnson wrote after *Paul Lange and Tora Parsberg* are of minor importance. The best of them is the farewell play, *Naar den ny vin blomstrer* (*When the Vineyards are in Blossom*), which was written to contrast with Ibsen's *Naar vi döde vaagner* (*When we dead awaken*). Contemporary critics dismissed it as the work of an erotic old man, but it is written in a major key, and its cheerful confidence is infectious. It is fitting that Ibsen should end his career as a writer with an epilogue on his joyless life: but it was equally right that a man of Björnson's temperament should take his leave with a joyous song of praise to youth and life.

In his later dramatic work, Björnson took Ibsen as his model. He concentrated his attention on the chief character, and in the first part of *Beyond our Strength,* and in *Paul Lange and Tora Parsberg,* he began his play as near the catastrophe as possible. But Ibsen's great plays begin where Björnson's end—after the catastrophe. Oswald, Rosmer and John Gabriel Borkman have already been struck by the lightning-strokes of fate when the play opens. Broken by regrets over a wasted life, they have really nothing more to lose when Death reaps his harvest. Björnson's heroes sin and repent, but they are not tortured by having to endure a prolonged struggle with death. Sang is allowed to die at the very moment when into his highest exaltation creeps the first sign of doubt, while Paul Lange, ever sanguine, comforts himself only a short while before his suicide with the thought, "I will rise once again—of course I will".

Björnson realized that it was his happy outlook on life that prevented him from reaching those heights of world fame which Ibsen attained with his tragedies. But it was this very optimism that gave him the courage for which he was renowned, and enabled him to recreate modern drama. To his best plays, historical as well as modern, he can impart an epic and a lyric quality without causing the reader to resent them as irrelevant.

Indeed, it is his lyric poetry that has made Björnson the national poet, not merely of Norway but of all the Northern countries. The plays made his international reputation, but they also introduced to a wider public the poems which often come from the lips of his heroes and heroines. In 1870, when he was about to publish 'Songs and Poems', he proposed to his publisher that three lines from the trilogy, *Sigurd the Bastard,* should be printed on the cover. With a regal pride which was not unjustified, he considered that they described himself:

> "His ship with all her sails lay in the fjord;
> The waves were mirrored in the gleaming shields;
> His hand controlled the tiller".

HENRIK IBSEN

'Lord, make me rich in pain
And fearful of each tempting joy'.

SO Brand sings, in the epic version of the play, where the hero
sits and turns his back on the sun. Time and again this longing
for grief and pain appears in Ibsen's earlier work and in his letters:
"Believe me, it is not pleasant to see the world in an October
light, and yet there have been times, oddly enough, when I have
asked nothing better," he says in a passage from a letter of 1858.
"I have a burning desire for, almost prayed for, a great sorrow
which would really fill my existence and give meaning to life.
It was foolish—I have fought my way out of that stage, and yet
the memory of it is always with me".

All his life, Ibsen was indeed to bear the marks of that sickness.
When in *Gengangere* (*Ghosts*) Oswald and Mrs. Alving proclaim
that life is a thing of joy and not of duty alone, it is in a spirit of
dogged defiance that they do so, and in the plays of Ibsen's old
age the atmosphere has become even more hopeless. At this
period he was no longer moved by a longing to experience grief,
but by regret that life had passed him by, and that he had not
enjoyed its riches.

Ibsen in his youth was convinced that he could only become a
great tragedian if he received the gift which Jatgejr in *Kongsemnerne*
(*The Pretenders*) claimed had made him a bard: "I sought sorrow;
others there may be who seek faith, or joy, or doubt". In later
days he felt bitterly that human happiness was too high a price to
pay for his life's work. At the same time he was convinced that
this change of attitude was due to deeper causes, and not to his
platonic passion for young girls, about which so much was
heard. In a manuscript version of *Lille Eyolf* (*Little Eyolf*) Ibsen
puts the following words into the mouth of the author, Allmers
—"Something has happened which has changed me. Something

has happened inside me. It's nothing in the outside world that I have experienced".

Ibsen's life was not eventful, and he was not usually communicative about his affairs. His dramatic works, however, provide a continuous flow of self-expression. He wrote in a letter in 1870 that all his work was inspired by a mood or a crisis in life, and that he was never tempted to write simply because he had found a good subject. After that date there were very few exceptions to this rule. The different stages in Ibsen's dramatic development were on the whole determined by developments in his own attitude to writing and life in general.

Anyone attempting to analyse Ibsen's growth as a dramatist should have regard to the advice he himself gave his readers in the preface to the popular edition of his works in 1898, namely to study them in the order in which they were written. It was, however, with *Brand* and *Peer Gynt* that he began to influence world drama, and his earlier work must be treated here in a more summary fashion.

The most important fact about Ibsen in his youth was that he was influenced by various predecessors. Occasionally he imitated them rather slavishly, but his own temperament was usually dominant. In his first play, *Catalina* (1850), written in the rhetorical and flamboyant Shakespearean style beloved of the age, the hero displays certain characteristics which are unmistakably Ibsen's. Catalina, a rough sketch of what Skule was to be, is obsessed with ambition and the desire for greatness, but is also gnawed by doubts about his vocation. He has also to choose between two women, makes the wrong choice, is ensnared by his past and is ruined.

From 1852 to 1857, Ibsen was the director of the Bergen National Theatre, and the following five years he spent in the same position in the National Theatre at Christiania. By the end of this period he was no longer a journeyman; he was a master craftsman.

At first he was not sure which way to follow. The repertory he built up at Christiania contained such lightweight material that the theatre was mockingly dubbed The Vaudeville. Scribe and Heiberg were the playwrights he cultivated most, and they were his first teachers of stage technique.

His first significant play, *Fru Inger til Östråt* (*Lady Inger of Östråt*), was produced in 1855 without any success. The theme was taken from Norwegian history; the style was Scribe's. Ibsen's taste for mystery prevented him from seeing that the charm of a Scribe plot lay in its intelligibility. The characters overreach themselves and the audience become completely confused by monologues, secret confidences, and theatrical asides. The usual conspiratorial dialogue, in which Scribe delighted, is present, with metaphors taken from fashionable games. "God help me, to-night we play dominoes for the whole Kingdom of Norway", cries Lady Inger.

We also see for the first time the Ibsen mists descending on the stage, and, rising up through the gloom, the striking figure of Lady Inger. Long after all else is forgotten can be heard her mournful lament for one called to play a great part in life but lacking the strength to sustain it.

The young poet has here created his first heroine, and he has already accepted the fact that his vocation will cut him off from his friends and relations, and will raise a wall between him and life.

The next two plays, *Gildet paa Solhaug* (*The Feast at Solhaug*) and *Haermaendene paa Helgeland* (*The Vikings at Helgeland*), are concerned with vocation and marriage. *The Feast at Solhaug* is a folk play in the style of Hertz, a style which was very popular everywhere in Scandinavia at this time. Here it is the woman who deserts her childhood friend for the tedious but rich Bengt, the first instance of the Helmer type in Ibsen. Unfortunately the play is neatly rounded off with a happy ending. In *The Vikings* the plot moves relentlessly on to a tragic end, and Sigurd has to pay with his life for the unpardonable sin of sacrificing his love for Hjördis to his friend Gunnar. Her words, only slightly adapted, would serve as a motto for a whole series of Ibsen's plays, including *John Gabriel Borkman*: "All good gifts a man may give to a faithful friend, all—but never the woman he loves; for if he does that he breaks the secret thread spun by the Norns, and two lives will be lost".

There was an affinity between Ibsen and the reserved men and women of the Icelandic Sagas, which he was now reading for the first time. His contemporaries disapproved of the note of hardness in his treatment of these legendary tales, though in our day they seem too mild; and his writing was such that, particularly in the final scenes, the play appeared to be a modern tragedy of marriage in Old Norse dress. All the same, one can hardly read an Icelandic saga now without thinking of *The Vikings at Helgeland*.

In an essay on the Ballad written at this period, Ibsen maintained that stories from the Icelandic Sagas would be better dramatized in the classical Greek tradition than in the modern romantic style. He introduced the oracular prophesies of Greek tragedy, and also, like Sophocles, moved the significant action to the past, so that as it was gradually revealed it became the Nemesis which destroys the hero.

Hjördis in particular is a Medea in Amazon's dress. In the dusk she dreams of the dead returning to Valhalla: "They are the brave men who have fallen in battle, the strong women who have not spent their life tamely, as you and I have done; in the storm and tempest they hurtle through the air with their black horses to the sound of bells". She is a sea of seething passions, exacting, unscrupulous, terrifying and yet irresistible.

Even when Ibsen actually borrowed material for his play, it sounds as if it might have been written for Hjördis. There is one passage from the Saga of Njal which he adapted particularly well. Hjördis dreams that Sigurd is coming to burn down the house with herself and her husband in it, and that Gunnar is begging her to make a bowstring with the strands of her hair; their lives are at stake; "But I laugh and say 'Let it burn, let it burn, life is not worth a handful of hair to me' ".

Hjördis becomes the outlet for Ibsen's ideas about vocation, love and marriage, but she never loses the spirit of the saga; she remains one of the wild Valkyries from the realms of Asgard.

The Pretenders (1864) is a finer work of art than *The Vikings*, but lacks somewhat its unity of style. There are touches from Shakespeare's chronicle plays, and Bishop Nicholas is a conspirator after the style of Scribe. Above all, it is the last great example of the drama of historical principles, which was so popular in the 19th century. The conflict of ideas was to be transferred to Ibsen's social plays.

The conflict here is between a number of minor kingdoms,

and a single united realm. In the background we can discern the notion of a united Scandinavia, which was in the minds of the Northern Kingdoms at this period. This symbolic significance is, however, kept in the background by the contrast between the fortunate 'Sunday's child', Håkon, and God's stepchild here on Earth, Jarl Skule, Ibsen's first great tragic hero.

Much of *The Pretenders* now seems out of date, and one may well agree with Vedel's dictum that the play is three times more unhistorical than Oehlenschlaeger's *Haakon Jarl (Earl Hakon)*, but Skule, anxious, wondering whether he will be the chosen one or not, reaches depths which Oehlenschlaeger never could. In the scenes where Skule and the Icelandic bard, Jatgejr, talk together they raise problems which were of such vital and intense importance to Ibsen that they re-appear constantly in his work. We over-simplify if we regard the drama as merely an instance of the rivalry between Ibsen and the much more famous Björnson. Ibsen is both Skule and Håkon; he combines the inner certainty of greatness with a fear that he will not be the one chosen.

"Yes, I have heard the call, but never for long. The moon waxes only to wane again". These are Brand's words in the epic version. Hakon and Skule represent the two poles between which Ibsen moves at this period; confidence at having had the call, and fear that he lacks the ability to respond, and will throw away his life for a dream. There is something of Ibsen too in the bard, Jatgejr. He says that he has a shyness of soul, and will not unclothe it when there are many people in the hall. Ibsen later used these phrases about himself. Jatgejr also resembled Ibsen in his belief that 'unsung poems' are the sweetest, and in his firm refusal to give up poetry, whatever the cost. When he was living in Rome and at his poorest, Ibsen always said it would be better, like Chatterton, to swallow one's door-key if one was hungry than to go and work in an office.

As soon as he had finished *The Pretenders*, Ibsen wanted to write a new historical play about Magnus Heinison. This was never written. Instead, he began his last historical play, *Kejser o Galilaeer (Emperor and Galilean)*, which was not completed until nine years later and pleased neither the public nor its author.

The chief character, Julian the Apostate, was to reflect Ibsen's own personality, but he was also more than ever concerned to preserve historical accuracy. The difficulty of matching action and idea proved insuperable, and the play never achieved unity. Its principal value now is as a source of information about Ibsen's own ideas.

In historical plays Ibsen had devoted much attention to realism and historical accuracy. In his contemporary plays he at first did the exact opposite, indulging his imagination and sense of romance, and letting prose give way to verse.

Naturally Ibsen was still unaccustomed to writing modern dialogue, and in reviews of this date he criticizes contemporary French drama which, for all its perfect technique, completely lacked poetry. From Heiberg he had drawn the conclusion that vaudeville, with its neo-romantic irony, was really the finest form of art.

In a review as early as 1851, he took up the cudgels to defend a student vaudeville production which had been damned by the critics, and a year later he wrote *Sankthansnatt* (*Midsummer Night*) in the style of Heiberg's *Elverhöj* (*The Hill of the Elves*). It was produced at the Bergen Theatre, but was shouted down. It was not till ten years later, in 1862, that he dared to try his hand again with *Kjaerlighedens Komedie* (*Love's Comedy*), really a student vaudeville in construction. According to Ibsen's recipe in the review mentioned above, such a play should present a student, standing for spiritual values, in his conflict with the philistines. Falk is therefore a student, living in lodgings where there are various sentimental young couples, rather of the kind seen in Heiberg's *De uadskillelige* (*The Inseparables*). They become the victims of his stringent satire in the well-known teacup scene, and the play ends when he hands over his fiancée to Guldstad, a wordly-wise grocer.

This subject is taken further in the prose version of *Valborg* in 1860, where it is treated as a tragi-comedy. The heroine is a silly girl, and Guldstad is dull and narrow in his outlook.

In *Love's Comedy* there is a different tone. This is the first play Ibsen wrote after his marriage with Susannah Thoresen, and he explained in a letter that he took her as the model of his heroine, whom he called Svanhild. She rebukes Falk for being a self-centred poet, and they agree to fight together against falsehood. But their struggle ends in the same kind of defeat as befell Gregers

Werle in *Vildanden* (*The Wild Duck*). So that their love shall not
be spoiled by everyday life, they separate, Svanhild happy because
she has been able to fill Falk's soul with light and poetry. He goes
off to "the future and its possibilities", and the play ends with
his joining in the chorus of a student song:

> "And if at last I sailed my ship aground,
>   Yet sweet it was to sail".

The idea that love should be ended in the greatest heat of
passion so as to leave the sweetest memories, love "freed from
longing and from wild desire" was derived, it has often been
pointed out, from Kirkegaard's *The Devil's Journal*. By him
Ibsen was also inspired to attack casual love-affairs.

There is another personal touch in this play; Falk and Ibsen
alike can never forget, even in their passion, that poetry is their
vocation in life, and the beloved one only a means to that end.
Even in his love-letters to Susannah Thoresen, written in verse,
Ibsen hailed her as "Bride of my thoughts", and describes how
she will inspire him to poetic creativeness.

This thought is also expressed in *The Vikings* by Hjördis whom,
incidentally, Ibsen also conceived with Susannah Thoresen in
mind. She rejoices at her approaching death with Sigurd before
she has ever belonged to him: "Oh yes—it is better so than if you
had married me here in this life, better than sitting in your house
weaving linen and wool, and bearing children to you".

In *Brand*, which was written in Rome, this thought of vocation
returns in tragic form. The hero wants to force his dying mother
to give away her property. He refuses to allow his wife to take
his child away to a milder climate in order to save its life. When
the child dies and his wife clings to its clothes as her only remaining link with life, he compels her to give them away to a gipsy.
"Brand is myself in my finest moments", Ibsen declared in a
letter. He admired the granite-like and inhuman quality in his
creation, which indeed took the Scandinavian public by storm.
While he was writing the play, it was gradually borne in upon
him that his passion for sacrifice contained an element of ascetic
gluttony, that he was tormenting himself and enjoying the
process. In the final scene, Brand feels the ice in his heart melting,

and begins to realize that his superhuman efforts of will have not brought him an inch nearer to God. His last words, ambiguous though they are, suggest that the God who has buried him under the avalanche is "Deus caritatis". In spite of well-meant efforts by Scandinavian scholars to fathom Ibsen's meaning, it is not easy to see this ending as an absolution. The God whom Brand worshipped showed few signs of the 'caritas' which Ibsen, replying to Brandes' criticism, defined as divine love and mercy.

Brand was a success and marked the climacteric of Ibsen's fortunes as a writer. In Rome he had not been far from starvation: it was significant that when writing to Björnson at this time he accepted the latter's offer to send his letters unstamped, "though it is against my will".

With one stroke, Ibsen became a prophet of the Judgment, and a fashionable author. *Brand* was published in 1866, and was reprinted four times before the year was out. The rewards of his labours which he had long and vainly sought were now granted, and also a travel grant which he had not even asked for. 'God's stepchild on Earth' also had two wins in the Danish Lottery.

Ibsen's external appearance also changed. In Christiania, and during his early days in Rome, he looked like a bohemian artist when he wore his long black cloak and a great wide-brimmed hat. Snoilsky immortalized him in this garb in a poem called *Il Capellone*. His face was concealed behind a forest of hair and beard.

Ibsen had made a virtue of necessity. As soon as his means permitted, he laid aside this artistic attire, and appeared, to the disappointment of the admirers of *Brand*, as a very elegant gentleman with mutton-chop whiskers, a velvet jacket, light waistcoat, check trousers and patent-leather shoes. Ibsen, the drunken student of Christiania days, vanished, and in his place appeared a respectable citizen, who wrote a fine upright hand, kept his admirers at a respectful distance, was careful on points of etiquette and punctilious about titles and honours. When in the fourth act of *Peer Gynt* Ibsen transforms the Norwegian peasant boy into the wealthy cad, 'Sir Peter Gynt', he is probably laughing somewhat at himself.

It was during those first happy days of independence that Ibsen wrote *Peer Gynt*. He began to write the play in an old palace at Frascati, 'glittering and cheap'. He felt the capacity for work so strong within him that he could move mountains. "This was all intoxication", he wrote later about this period of creative activity.

Brand attracts by its mixture of inhumanity and weakness. It has the beauty of ice and hoarfrost. Peer Gynt has an exuberance and poetic richness not apparent in any other play by Ibsen. On the stage it is sure to survive his other work. Ibsen wrote, rather mysteriously, that it seemed to follow Brand "almost of its own accord." There may be various explanations for this. Peer Gynt is the exact antithesis of Brand, and Bull suggested in his excellent book on Peer Gynt that Ibsen liked to work with such contrasts. Having created that seeker after truth, Dr. Stockman, Ibsen then conceived the embodiment of the life-lie, Hjalmar Ekdal.

People sometimes relate these words to the political satire on the desertion of Denmark by Norway and Sweden in her hour of need. There are also two verses in Brand which point to the essence of the Peer Gynt theme:

'Who goes too far in the greatest thing,
Not all the rest shall lighten his doom'.

To read this autobiographical letter which Ibsen wrote to P. Hansen, and in which this oracular passage appears, is to get the impression that Ibsen felt he had given free rein to his imagination, and allowed the play to create itself, without too much careful planning. He says that Peer Gynt was written in Southern Italy, at Ischia and Sorrento: "So remote from one's potential readers that one becomes insensitive". He goes on to say that the play contains much that springs from his own youthful experiences, and that his own mother was the original Åse, "with the necessary exaggerations". From the word 'insensitive' it appears that he had in mind the caricatures which contemporary critics quickly recognized—Ole Bull, Manderström, Vinje, Lieblein and others. It is also obvious that here Ibsen, who was normally very careful to cover his traces, had borrowed freely. There is Asbjörnsen, from whom the whole story of Peer Gynt was borrowed; there is Oehlenschlaeger's Aladdin, The Hill of the Elves, and the stories of H. C. Andersen, Adam Homo by Paludan

Mueller, *En Sjael efter Döden* (*A Soul after Death*) by J. L. Heiberg, and *The Phantasts* by Schack; there are occasional echoes from Wergeland, Björnson, Tegnér and Runeberg; and last but not least, there is the remarkable similarity between the last scene of *Peer Gynt* and *Faust*. And then, in the two last acts, as Bull points out, the hero fairly revels in quotations. Such methods are so different from Ibsen's usual ones and the preliminary drafts so slight that it is difficult to avoid Bull's conclusion that in writing this play Ibsen was very sure of his own originality. Nowhere else does it show through so splendidly.

The main reason for this lies in Peer Gynt himself. Ibsen's gallery of characters is more varied and comprehensive than his contemporaries would acknowledge, but he never created another character comparable with Peer Gynt. He is Ibsen's whipping-boy, but whom we chastise we love. In his heart of hearts Ibsen cherished an unquenchable affection for the go-ahead and yet dreamy country lad of the first two acts. Never was Ibsen so attracted by the cheerful vigour and straightforwardness of his countrymen as in this satire on the Norwegian temperament. Peer Gynt is humanity personified and a follower of that most deceptive calling, the poet's, with the saving humour of a man who knows himself to be "a rascally poet", and is, in spite of everything, proud and glad to be one.

Ibsen said in 1874 that he had "by self-analysis . . .brought to light many of the qualities of Peer Gynt and Stensgård". It sounds strange, because neither character displays any resemblance to Ibsen as he appeared at that time. But since he himself refers to his youthful experiences, we must assume that behind the mask which was put on for the benefit of the outside world, there was a face which he had succeeded in concealing. Björnson had some notion of this, for he wrote in 1871, "Not till Peer Gynt did Ibsen become himself; for Peer Gynt was himself". To draw the conclusion from this remark, as Sigurd Höst did, that Ibsen throughout his life was an imaginative dreamer who abdicated in favour of a sober scribe when he sat down to write, is to over-simplify the problem. To become a tragedian it is not enough to write tragedies, nor does one become dry and sober by sheer determination. A man's imagination may sometimes cause him to cut a caper, without marking his features. One may look

repeatedly and searchingly at the long row of Ibsen portraits
without a glimpse of that spirit of youthful mischief which
caused him at the age of thirty-nine to surprise his age with Peer
Gynt.

Just as the hero of the play differs from all other Ibsen characters,
so the world in which he moves differs from any setting that
Ibsen created either before or later. In *Peer Gynt* we find the
high fell country of Norway, with sun and cloud over the peaks.
Most of his characters move in a historical or domestic setting,
but in the Haegstad wedding scene the country folk are drawn
with greater comic force and with more clarity and precision
than in Björnson's *Synnove Solbakken*. In the Dovre scenes,
where the tone is one of burlesque and fantasy and of demoniac
savagery, Grieg's music seems refined and conventional.

The Danish critic, Clemens Petersen (whom Ibsen unjustly
accused of being prompted by Björnson) denied that *Peer Gynt*
was poetry, thereby kindling Ibsen's wrath. "My book is poetry,
and if it isn't, it will be. The idea of poetry in our country, in
Norway, will take its shape from this". They were bold words,
but Ibsen has been proved right, and not merely about Norway.
While realism and symbolism were the words of the day, *Peer
Gynt* remained a Scandinavian speciality, but at the threshold of
the present century the perspective widened. Tolstoy created
the realistic play of the people, but the imaginative peasant
dramas that followed would have been unthinkable without
Peer Gynt. Synge was sometimes critical of Ibsen, but would he
have written *The Playboy of the Western World* if he had not been
deeply influenced by *Peer Gynt*? O'Neill never hesitated to
include Ibsen among the great masters, and used the *Peer Gynt*
theme, with variations, several times.

Anger at Björnson's supposed failure to appreciate *Peer Gynt*
drove Ibsen to include a caricature of him in his first realistic
drama, *De unges forbund* (*The League of Youth*, 1869). From the
correspondence that passed between Ibsen, Brandes and his
publisher, it is clear that Ibsen only released *The League of Youth*
after a certain amount of hesitation. This was not merely because
he was putting contemporary Norway, only thinly disguised,
on the stage for the first time, but also because domestic drama
was a step down from the poetic drama of ideas with which he

had previously been concerned. As has been already indicated, in France domestic drama had already achieved literary status, thanks to the efforts of the younger Dumas and Augier, but in Scandinavia it was still despised. To write domestic drama as did Jolin and Frans Hedberg, was considered an honourable trade but in no way connected with literature. Frequently in his letters Ibsen emphasized that this time he was writing solely for the stage, and in his fear of being labelled a domestic dramatist he made a great feature of the farcical elements in the play. When writing to Brandes he expresses considerable doubt whether he will be at all interested in a play of this kind. He emphasizes also that he did not want to portray anything except ordinary every-day life.

At the same time, Ibsen felt that he was approaching a new stage in his writing. "It is written in prose", he says of the play in a letter to Brandes, "and therefore it has a strongly realistic tone. I have handled the form of the play with great care, and among other things succeeded in completing my play without a single monologue, and even without a single aside".

At the première, the play was received with boos by the Left Wing elements who were attacked in it, and though the critics of the Right were satisfied by the political satire, they found that the comedy was unpoetical and they could see no promise for the future in the new form. Brandes was the only person who realized the advance implicit in the play.

It is actually not difficult to understand why *The League of Youth* did not succeed in opening the way for modern Scandinavian drama. The dialogue is sparkling and the characters remarkably lifelike, with the result that the play has held its own on the stage longer than many of Ibsen's later social dramas, but the plot and the psychological motivation are conventional, and in the final acts far too many concessions are made to the technique of Scribe.

The opening scene is quite enchanting, throwing us as it does right into the heart of a Norwegian 17th of May celebration, with all its politics, its chatter and its toasts. From the very first words the characters come alive for us; there is Bratsberg, a gentleman of the Royal Household, senile but aristocratic, Monsen with his parvenu manners, Daniel Hejre with his endless gossip, Lundestad with his peasant shrewdness and Aslaksen the printer, with his tipsy speeches. In the midst of the confusion we see young Stensgård, the lawyer who has come to this out-of-the-way corner to stir it to life. He is all afire with liberal ideas; he is straining for action; he is drunk with desire to make himself heard. He has been restrained with difficulty while the first speeches were made; now he leaps on to a table and bursts out with a flood of grand phrases which mean nothing in particular.

From all directions applause reaches the happy speaker, who is now basking in blissful self-approval. Over in the tent the crowd are cheering and founding the League of Youth, as Stensgård has been exhorting them to do, and overcome as he is with excitement, he bursts out, "Listen, listen! They're drinking to me! Something that can grip them like that—by Almighty God, there must be truth in it!" With an almost imperceptible smile, Ibsen reveals to us at this early stage that same opinion of the applause of a majority which he is to show us again in *En folke-fiende* (*An Enemy of the People*).

In this opening act, which alone is worth more than the whole of the rest of the play, there are signs of some of the new tendencies which were to be prominent in modern Norwegian drama.

The setting of a play was a point barely considered by Dumas and Augier, and even Sardou was only beginning to pay attention to it. The little town on the coast of Norway in *The League of Youth* is alive with political activity, gossip and intrigue. The horizon is darkened by mountains, there is not much space, and quarrels always tend to grow bitter. "The damnable part of small communities is that they make small souls", wrote Ibsen from Sorrento in 1867 to his mother-in-law. Characters are determined by environment, but among the stunted dwellers in little places we find an occasional wild bird who longs to spread his wings and fly far afield.

Gran has said that when Ibsen wrote *The League of Youth* he created Norwegian prose dialogue. One might go further and say that he created a new dialogue style for modern European drama. The first act of the play represents Ibsen's most realistic everyday style. When in later plays he allows the turn of the dialogue to conform too closely to the changes in the plot, the tone seems more forced. Here, however, there seems no ulterior motive behind the remarks that are let fall; they are intended simply to give the atmosphere of a popular celebration, and also to indicate the various characters. This result is partly achieved by one of the simplest conventions of farce—to give each character a single phrase which he constantly repeats; there is Daniel Hejre's "enough said", and Aslaksen's "local conditions". This was a device that Ibsen continued to use in all his plays. Moreover, Ibsen had early acquired the capacity so to modify the style oi speaking of each character, without involving him in any dialect, that his character became easily distinguishable. How easily discernible is the countryman's dialect behind the slow and almost drawling speech of Lundestad, and how clearly the somewhat stilted speech of Bratsberg reflects the inborn nobility and simplicity of the man.

It was also from farce that Ibsen got the notion of plunging the audience straight into action, without any preparation whatever. Indeed, the play begins in the middle of a speech—Lundestad is just uttering the final phrases of his oration—and it continues without any of the sentences usually inserted for the information of the audience. We are not told why Stensgård has come. Who he is and how he has become what he is, is only divulged by the raisonneur, the doctor, in the final act when he clears up the mystery of his parents and his upbringing. Nevertheless, Stensgård and the other characters are very clearly drawn for the spectator.

Unfortunately there are also disadvantages arising from the farcical element in *The League of Youth*. On the debit side must be put the very complicated and improbable plot, which contrives in subsequent acts to spoil the excellent effect of the opening scenes.

A contemporary German critic immediately pointed out the similarity between Stensgård and the ambitious politician Vernouillet in Augier's *The Impertinents*. Like Stensgård, Vernouillet makes his way by his unequalled audacity and by frankly making use of the press. He uses the journalist Giboyer just as Stensgård uses Aslaksen. Towards the end of *The Impertinents* someone prophesies that Vernouillet will one day be a cabinet minister; in the same way Lundestad at the end of *The*

I

League of Youth says, "Yes, mark my words, gentlemen. In ten or fifteen years' time Stensgård will be sitting in the people's council, or the King's, or maybe both at once". The similarities are not great, but at this time Augier's political plays were circulating round Europe. Björnson was of course also indebted to them when he later wrote his first political plays, *The Editor* and *The New System*.

Meanwhile Ibsen had not yet grasped the significance of the simplified plot used by Dumas and Augier. For this reason, and because he wanted to stress farcical humour in his play, he makes Stensgård engage in three separate courtships, all for money, and all brought to nothing by the familiar stage device borrowed from Molière, that the suitor imagines his loved one, or her parents, to be ruined.

In this light and airy plot there is one strand which is later woven into the main fabric and which has considerable interest though it does not lead to anything. The old courtier, Bratsberg, the counterpart of the Marquis of French drama, has a son who has forged his father's signature. He refuses to acknowledge it as his own because that would involve him in moral guilt. When the son confesses to his family that he is ruined, Selma Bratsberg, the daughter-in-law, refuses to share his misfortunes: "How I used to long for a drop of your sorrow! But if I had asked you, you would only have made a joke of it and laughed me away. You dressed me up like a doll; you played with me as one plays with a child. And yet I would have exulted if I had had a burden to bear. I was in earnest, and I longed for everything that meant storm and jubilation and the heights of exaltation". This Selma is akin to Dumas' young women, impulsive, and, despite all their elegance, rather masculine. But what an Ibsen character she is! She foreshadows not only Nora but also Hilde Wangel, an impetuous child who sees herself as a fairy princess with magic castles and a prince who frees her from the witch's spell. Suddenly she discovers that she belongs to a man to whom money, his house and his heritage matter. At a stroke she becomes a mature woman, and to the surprise of those around her she wishes to leave the husband who has never understood her: "I must leave you. I'd sooner sing and play in the streets". In the final act, however, this kinswoman of Brand regains her calm and speaks a good word for her father-in-law. Young Brandes, in the review he wrote at the time of *The League of Youth,* was alone in his realization that this character of a young woman, who did not achieve her rightful place in this play, contained the germ of a completely new and original and more profound type of drama.

It is not only the Selma episode which indicates the beginning of a real social drama in *The League of Youth.* The character of Stensgård is intended both as a caricature of the national temperament, and as a typical representative of contemporary society. In the final paragraphs of the play, when Dr. Fjeldbo, the raisonneur, sums up its conclusions, he passes judgment on the educational system of the day. The object of this system seems to be learning rather than being; it lets loose hundreds of half-ready persons who are one thing in feeling and quite another when making and doing. People are building on insecure foundations. Here *The League of Youth* leads on to *Samfundets stötter (Pillars of Society)* and the plays that followed it, but unfortunately the Doctor's words come too late to remedy the situation they describe.

It has long been known from Ibsen's correspondence that he meant to write another contemporary play when he had finished *The League of Youth,* but it was not until 1933 that two drafts of the projected play were found by Ibsen's daughter-in-law among her family papers. They were written in 1870, and published by Koht as drafts for *Pillars of Society* (which was not completed till seven years later). They were entitled 'Sketches for the Comedy' and bear very little resemblance to *Pillars of Society.* The hero is a naval officer who has been away for ten years in foreign service because he was afraid of accepting too many commitments and obligations. In this he shows an attitude which Ibsen shared, for at this time he also had been abroad for ten years and on returning to Stockholm in 1869, with the intention of proceeding to Norway, had instead turned back and gone to Dresden. The officer, however, does return to his home town, where he stirs up a good deal of excitement and interest, but also resentment among 'the respectable citizens'. He is compared, to his detriment, with his brother, a shipowner and a good business man, who despises ideals. We find here the same contrast between the conventional supporter of the community and the free man which is characteristic of Ibsen's early social plays.

In the drafts, the shipowner is much concerned about the gossip which is current about his family. His wife is dissatisfied with life and with her marriage: she is distressed by her husband's lack of poetry and idealism. He falls in love with his sister-in-law: "He overcomes prejudices; the woman is freed; but he conquers himself". The emancipation of woman is already the main theme, and we also have an instance of a situation which constantly recurs in Ibsen's plays, and in *John Gabriel Borkman* in particular, where a man falls in love with his wife's sister.

These *Sketches for the Comedy* contain suggestions for themes which occur again in Ibsen's writings. Clearly at this time Ibsen had more on his mind than could find an outlet in a single play.

When Ibsen, in 1875, began to work on his first proper social play, *Pillars of Society*, circumstances were in many ways different from what they had been when he wrote *The League of Youth* eight years earlier. Brandes, with whom he had been corresponding vigorously, had published the first part of 'Main Streams.' Ibsen immediately grasped its fundamental point: "In our age, every new poetical composition must accomplish its task of shifting frontier posts."

In this context Brandes also urges the debate of current problems in literature, giving contemporary French drama as an instance of what can be done. There is a frequently quoted passage in the first part of 'Main Streams'—"If you give an inhabitant of Sirius, who has only read our classical poetry, one or two modern European plays to read, for instance Alexandre Dumas' *The Natural Son* and Augier's *Giboyer's Son* and *The Impertinents*, he will then become acquainted with numerous social problems and practices, which he did not know of before, because though they exist in our community they do not exist in our literature."

Modern French drama is here very emphatically proclaimed as a model for modern literature. In the early part of 1875 Björnson broke the ice with his *A Bankruptcy* and *The Editor*, and Ibsen appears to have sat down promptly that summer and begun to write his first modern problem play, *Pillars of Society*.

The younger Dumas and Augier were the first dramatists to
draw attention to social problems in a realistic modern drama,
and to use the stage as a pulpit from which to preach sermons.
The conflict between social and individual morality, which is the
core of Ibsen's dramatic work, had been initiated by Dumas. As
regards dramatic form, the debt which Ibsen owed to his masters
is equally apparent. It was Dumas and Augier who raised the
level of the bourgeois drama and gave it artistic standing in the
theatre; their plays had carefully constructed plots, the psychology
was subtle, and the dialogue sparkling, sometimes even too
witty. In the first play of this category, *Pillars of Society*, Ibsen
lagged behind his masters; he was still dealing too much in the
traditional devices of the domestic drama. With *A Doll's House*,
where his technique is reminiscent of Dumas, he drew level with
the Frenchmen. In *Ghosts* he left them far behind, and it is not
surprising that in Scandinavia and the Germanic countries the
French dramatists were swept completely off the stage. The
difference in poetic stature between them and him was too great
not to make itself felt.

In so far as Ibsen surpassed the Frenchmen, he also naturally
learned, as he says in a letter to Brandes in 1896, to avoid their
grossest errors and misconceptions. But this should certainly not
be taken to mean that he disregarded their technique. In stating
a problem, working out a plot, drawing a character, or writing
dialogue Ibsen was developing the technique of French drama.

Once this point had been made, it may seem of purely secondary
importance to discover how much Ibsen learned, either directly
or indirectly, from the French playwrights. Ibsen's first steps in
the theatre were taken in company with Dumas and Augier.
He reviewed their plays, he produced them as a theatre manager,
and in his own first dramatic work he transmitted impulses
received from the younger Dumas, and above all from Augier.
By 1880, Dumas and Augier had disciples all over Europe and
their plays could be seen all over the world.

The link with French social drama must clearly not be forgotten, but it is possible to see why Ibsen declared in 1896 that
he preferred to stand outside its domain. It was not merely that
his drama signified a higher artistic standpoint; it was because it
was different in kind. The social play by Ibsen is not purely

realistic, as are the plays of Dumas and Augier, nor is it really intended to be. Dumas' plays illustrated the conflict between the legal and the natural code of morals, but in Ibsen these two concepts are personified in the chief characters. In *Pillars of Society* the community and the individual are opposed to each other in the persons of Bernick and Lona Hessel. Helmer and Nora in *A Doll's House*, Mrs. Alving and Pastor Manders in *Ghosts*, the official—Stockman—and the Doctor in *An Enemy of the People*, are other instances of this opposition, for though the actual occasion and issue vary, the fundamental cleavage recurs in all Ibsen's later social dramas.

Dumas the younger was campaigning against specific social injustices, and Ibsen was naturally more concerned with current problems than he was ready to admit towards the end of his life. He created something of a sensation when, at a dinner arranged in his honour in 1898 by the Norwegian Feminist Association, he declared firmly that he had never consciously worked for the women's cause, indeed that he did not really know what the women's cause was. At the time he wrote *A Doll's House* he was an extremely violent supporter of the controversial demands made by the women's movement. But Ibsen was right, in so far as he explained in his speech that he was looking for something greater than the emancipation of women, that he was concerned with the "cause of mankind," not the "cause of women" alone. In his modern plays Ibsen also presents a conflict of ideas, and thereby invests them with a universal and tragic quality which is lacking in French drama of the period. They deal with eternal issues no less than do the historical plays.

Many German scholars have pointed out that in this respect Ibsen was developing Hebbel's concepts in *Maria Magdalena*. Resistance on this point by their Scandinavian colleagues is not justified. Through Hettner's *Das Moderne Drama* Ibsen knew of Hebbel's domestic tragedy, and is supposed on some occasion to have expressed his admiration for it. Björnson, as has been said earlier, was quite familiar with Hebbel's dramatic work. It should not, however, be forgotten that Ibsen's social plays were dreceded by his historical tragedies, which also dealt with conflicts of idea and principle, and that shortly before he composed

Pillars of Society he was engaged on just such a tragedy, with a wide historical sweep.

Ibsen's contemporary dramas contain a good deal more of the 19th century Norwegian and German historical drama than Hebbel with his special theories succeeded in infusing into *Maria Magdalena*. The fact that it was possible for Ibsen to combine this historical drama with a fully developed realistic modern technique gave it artistic completeness. Historical drama had by this time disappeared almost entirely from the repertory lists, and had become purely literary. When Hebbel enlarged its scope with his philosophical approach to history, it began to be read in quite exclusive circles. Ibsen with his contemporary plays succeeded in writing dramas which could be read and expounded by a literary *élite*, and also enjoyed on the stage. It may be that in this welding together of the historical play with literary value and the domestic drama of the stage lies Ibsen's main contribution to literature.

The first social plays show very clearly Ibsen's efforts to achieve a semblance of realism. These efforts culminate in *Ghosts*, the play which also had the greatest significance for the development of naturalistic drama. "My intention was to give the reader the impression that while he was reading he was experiencing a fragment of real life," wrote Ibsen to Sophus Schandorph after the play was published in 1881.

In the next two plays of the series a distinct change of direction is noticeable. *The Wild Duck* and *Rosmersholm* (1886) attach less importance to the propagation of ideas, and pay more attention to psychology. In *Rosmersholm* this concern for psychological accuracy is carried so far that the continuity of thought becomes obscured, and the dramatic force of the play is considerably diminished. Ibsen was also anxious that his interpreters should understand that the play was first and foremost a "poetical composition about human beings," a conception which he continued to maintain.

At the same time, though the characters before the audience lead a richer life and display themselves more clearly, the symbolism in the plays brings with it certain romantic traits. These were present in the earlier plays, in much the same way as in the historical plays. The rotting ships in *Pillars of Society*, the burning

asylum in *Ghosts,* the polluted water in *An Enemy of the People*—
all these only serve to illustrate the main theme of each play.
They are illustrations of a thought of Ibsen's contained in a
rhyming letter which he wrote in 1875, "I believe we are sailing
with a corpse in our cargo." But they do not force themselves
on the reader and they do not affect the real content of the play.
In *The Wild Duck* we find Ibsen's attitude to symbolism at a
transitional stage. The duck with a broken wing from which the
play takes its title, the symbol of shattered illusions, is actually on
the stage, though the audience cannot see it in its basket. Indeed,
we have the whole menagerie which old Ekdal collected up in
his attic as a compensation for the open-air existence which he
used to lead in the days when he was a mighty hunter. The whole
incident of the wild duck, that it was injured by a shot from old
Werle, and then given by him to the Ekdal family, with whom it
throve in captivity—all this has an allegorical significance and
relevance. On the other hand, there is the seduction of Gine by
old Werle, who then handed her over to Hjalmar Ekdal, and the
fact that his family was content to live on the charity of the
wealthy merchant. The allegory and the main theme move on
parallel lines. This notion of giving the symbol a kind of half-
real existence has of course been frequently developed by modern
dramatists. One of the greatest of them, Chekhov, used *Chaika*
(*The Seagull*) in exactly the same way. Ibsen, however, was
clearly not satisfied with what he had done. In the next play,
Rosmersholm, he allows the symbol, the white horses which
traditionally appear at the house on the occasion of a death, to
remain in the background. It does, however, set its mark on the
play, giving it a somewhat dreamlike quality.

The next two plays, *Fruen fra havet* (*The Lady from the Sea*), and
Hedda Gabler show Ibsen unsure of his way. With *Bygmester
Solness* (*The Master Builder*), Ibsen's plays begin to be autobiographical in character, and now the action is symbolical as it
was in the plays of his youth. The symbolical technique also
comes into use again. When Solness builds churches he is fulfilling his vocation no less than Brand was when he wrote poetry.
John Gabriel Borkman, in the same way, echoes the symbolism of
a youthful poem, *The Man of the Mountains.* One can take
practically the whole story literally without being really disturbed

by anything, except that all the events seem to be thoughts.

Often, in these later plays, Ibsen becomes so absorbed in his art for its own sake that a realistic stage production shows up gaps here and there. This weakness is apparent even in *The Master Builder*, where the question whether Solness is to climb the tower of his own building seems rather meaningless unless it is interpreted symbolically.

In *Little Eyolf*, Ibsen for the first time since *Brand* and *Peer Gynt* introduces a figure of fantasy into a play. She is the Rat-wife, and with her flowery skirt, her cloak, her big umbrella and her disagreeable dog Mopseman, she goes round to all the houses to ask, with a curtsy, if they have anything gnawing there, and then coaxes the rats with her pipes to follow her boat until they drown. It was from old legends like that of the Pied Piper of Hamelin that Ibsen drew this figure.

When the play was published in 1894 these episodes were laughed at, while people studied with dutiful respect its simple and familiar philosophy of life. In fact it is the fantastic sections of the play which give it its value. Ibsen had a natural gift for creating grotesque and terrifying characters; one has only to remember the horrid ghost stories of his childhood reminiscences from Skien. Little Eyolf with the evil, unnaturally large eyes and the deformed body gives a much more real picture of the unhappy marriage which gave him birth than does the somewhat laboured dialogue of husband and wife.

The Master Builder, Little Eyolf and *John Gabriel Borkman* all contain some of the ideas which are later found in *When We Dead Awaken*. It was mainly because he saw it as concluding this series of plays that Ibsen called it "a dramatic epilogue." Years after it was published in 1899 he wrote to his French translator that he was hoping to produce more work if the state of his physical and mental health allowed it. His long decline did not, however, make it possible, and *When We Dead Awaken* remains the epilogue of all his poetry, one might almost say its funeral song.

The idea which gave him this title is already present at the end of *John Gabriel Borkman*. After Borkman's death in the cold of a winter's night, his wife declares that the cold killed him long ago. And in the draft version, her sister replies, "Us too. We three are dead, we three here." When Rubek in *When We Dead Awaken* meets his old model, Irene, they discover that they are both dead and have risen again, only to discover that they have never lived.

John Gabriel Borkman, which only refers symbolically to the fatal risks of the artist's calling, became a realistic play whose message is clear. *When We Dead Awaken*, on the other hand, with its sculptor hero, became more and more difficult and remote from reality, though Ibsen in the opening act was unusually careful to get the setting right, with a Norwegian seaside hotel, guests, waiters and an elegant inspector of bathing establishments. Outwardly, the play runs its normal course in realistic style right to the very end, when Rubek and Irene disappear in the avalanche, while Maria's freedom-song can be heard echoing through the valley and the ghostly Deaconess makes the sign of the cross, crying "Pax vobiscum." But this conclusion, clearly intended to serve as a counterpart to that of Brand, was not in the original draft.

The preliminary studies for the play contain a number of everyday characters and scenes which were rejected. It looks as if Ibsen, while he was working at the play, gradually allowed the dream atmosphere to gain control. The minor characters become unimportant, almost stylized types like the deaconess and Ulfheim, the bear-killer, a faun in modern shooting costume who pursues every kind of game, "eagle and wolf, woman and elk and deer, if only it is fresh and juicy and has plenty of blood in it." Even Maia Rubek, the last of the series of ill-treated women who were sold into matrimony or lured into it with promises of being taken to a high mountain and shown all the beauties of the world, cannot retain our interest. All our interest is concentrated on the two dead who have risen again and who talk about their past, without our ever being quite sure whether they really mean what they say. With Irene in particular we never know which of her memories relate to real experience, and which belong to her period of madness. Up at the sanatorium they stand one on each side of the stream, and drop leaves and petals into it, pretending that they are the white swans from the Taunitzer See where the little cottage used to stand, and where they lived their short and interrupted love-story. In the final act, high up on the mountains, the dark mists sweep everywhere, and neither of the two can really distinguish between dream and reality.

The play reminds one of Strindberg's *Damascus* series, and may indeed have contributed something to it. On the 23rd October, 1898, Strindberg had sent Ibsen a copy of the first two parts of *Till Damaskus* (*To Damascus*) with a message apologizing for his failure to attend the seventieth birthday celebrations of the master of modern drama. But even if this influence could have made itself felt, it is certain that Ibsen came nowhere near Strindberg in his ability to suggest that dream atmosphere which fills *To Damascus*, in spite of—or perhaps even because of—the complete clarity of the realistic elements in the play.

When We Dead Awaken seems to mark the beginning of a new stage which illness prevented Ibsen from completing. The realist and writer of problem plays had been for many years a symbolist, hailed by Maeterlinck and other poets of the Nineties as the great model. With his last plays he had come back, full circle, to the point from which he started in 1860, with symbolic idea drama. *When We Dead Awaken* shows that he was well on the way to abandoning the realistic stage-setting, which he had adhered to for so long, in favour of the dream play.

Together with this development towards symbolism in Ibsen's contemporary drama, we find a change in the content of ideas. At first it was the feminist cause that dominated them. In *Pillars of Society* Lona Hessel declares that the community in her day is "a society of old bachelors; you don't see women". As late as 1877 he was distressing Camilla Collett by his old-fashioned attitude about woman's place in the community; but in the following year he signified his support for the cause by proposing to the Scandinavian Society at Rome that women members should have the same voting rights as men. In his speech he maintained that if women lacked business sense, they had instead "a brilliant instinct which unconsciously found the right answer." The contrast between masculine and feminine morality, the one reasoning, the other instinctive, was, as we have already seen, indicated in the first three contemporary plays. In the first series of sketches for *A Doll's House* these words may be found: "There are two kinds of spiritual love, two kinds of conscience, a man's and—very different—a woman's. They do not understand one another, but woman is judged in actual life according to the laws of man, as if she were not a woman but a man."

These lines also explain a radicalism which grew stronger from play to play. In the manuscript of *Pillars of Society* Ibsen wanted to strike a blow for free love. Johan Tönnesen and Dina were to go to America without benefit of clergy. Lona Hessel comments triumphantly, "There's a blow in the face for your community, just as I once . . ." In the printed version this revolt against the community is toned down a good deal. Bernick comforts the agitated schoolmaster, Rörlund, with the news that Dina has gone to America and will be married as soon as she arrives.

By the time he wrote *Ghosts* Ibsen had freed himself from such considerations. To Pastor Manders' horror, Oswald is allowed to praise the free associations of the artists in Paris, and Mrs. Alving proposes to him a marriage between Oswald and his half-sister Regine, with the justification that away in the country there are many married couples who are quite as closely related. One can also compare the veiled reference to hereditary disease in the case of Dr. Rank in *A Doll's House*, while in *Ghosts* it constitutes the actual catastrophe of the play.

Of the heroines in the three plays, Lona Hessel in *Pillars of Society*, despite her mannish ways, is the most moderate. According to the original plan, Nora was to commit suicide because her blind faith in authority had led her to lose belief in her moral rights. In the play as it was finally published she does the exact opposite, becoming more assured and clear sighted, until she comes to consider it a sacred duty to leave her husband and children. In *Ghosts*, even the word 'duty' has become hateful to Mrs. Alving. Man has a right to happiness, and she reproaches herself for having made her home intolerable for her husband by preaching the obligations of duty which she learned from Pastor Manders.

Mrs. Alving's revolt against the slavery of duty represents a renunciation of the stern code to which Ibsen had been faithful ever since his youth, and to which he still adhered in *Pillars of Society* and *A Doll's House*, though he gave it a different twist in the latter play. Like Mrs. Alving, Ibsen felt the puritan cloak constricting his throat, and knew how difficult it was to escape from one's ghosts.

Year in and year out, Mrs. Alving has lied to her son. Pastor Manders believes that she has confirmed a happy illusion which has helped him, and says it would be criminal to shatter this illusion. "But what about truth?" asks Mrs. Alving, and Manders answers with another question, "What about ideals?" Here, Ibsen is hinting at a point of view which he is to adopt in *The Wild Duck*, when Relling urges Gregers Werle not to use the foreign word 'ideals,' but the good old native word 'lies.'

But when Mrs. Alving speaks the truth it does not prevent a tragedy. In the final scene she stands face to face with an even more merciless speaker of the truth, her son Oswald, who shatters her last illusion, that by her sacrifices she has assured herself of his love. During the debate on *Ghosts*, Ibsen's conceptions of truth were modified and became less absolute, thus preparing the way for the conception of a 'life-lie' in *The Wild Duck*.

Dr. Stockman in *An Enemy of the People* declares that a conventional truth holds good for twenty years at the most, and that no community can live a sound life on the basis of hollow and worn-out truths. Ten years earlier, Strindberg in *Mäster Olof* (*Master Olof*) had taught the doctrine of the relativity of truth as he had learned it from Buckle. Ibsen kept the notion at a distance, and even Dr. Stockman shows a certain zeal for truth which appears rather pointless if truths are to become out of date in less than twenty years.

When Brandes was reviewing *Peer Gynt* he argued against Ibsen that illusions are inevitable for mankind, and a source of comfort and beauty. It is the same case that Relling argues in *The Wild Duck*. Here Ibsen changed his views so completely that his contemporaries stood questioning. To show that it was his own past that he was attacking, Ibsen included among the objects of his satire an institution which he had wished to transform, the state of marriage. It was not, as had been suggested, Björnson's *A Gauntlet* which Ibsen was attacking when he made Gregers Werle campaign so eagerly for a true marriage in the Ekdal home. After Hjalmar, like a masculine caricature of Nora, has rushed out of the house, and returned home later hopelessly drunk, Relling says to Werle, in words which recall the final words in *A Doll's House*, that he is wrong about "these infernal duns" and that he has come to the wrong place with his claim of the 'ideal': "There are no solvent people living in this house." In the original sketches for *The Wild Duck*, Ibsen conceived Gregers Werle as a spiritual sybarite who took an unhealthy pleasure in meddling in Ekdal's life. In the final version he appeared as the ascetic moralist that young Ibsen himself had been. He wants a cure for his uneasy conscience and suffers, as Relling tells him, from an inflammation of conscience. From now on, Ibsen's heroes all have some sore point, some wound that will not heal and of which they try in vain to rid themselves.

Happiness is the most important thing in *The Wild Duck*. In a letter written to a Norwegian poet at this time, Ibsen explains that he is no longer concerned with the formulation of universal principles, because he no longer believes it possible to lay down any such: "I believe there is nothing else, nothing better, that any of us can do than to realize ourselves in truth and in spirit." In *An Enemy of the People* the idea had already crept in that we must cease to be evangelists and first of all educate ourselves, for only in this way can we create a truly noble race.

This hope, however, seems to fade in *Rosmersholm*. Rosmer comes to realize that people cannot have nobility thrust upon them from outside. He himself is too much hampered by certain finer qualities of character and by his old family traditions to feel really at home in the modern world of ideas. It is this which is expressed by the symbol of the play, the white horses: "All the people I have known who have liberated themselves, or have believed they have done so—all have kept such a white horse in which they have never lost faith." These were Rebecca West's words in an early version of the play. Instead of finding happiness together, she and Rosmer seek death in the mill race.

Even in *Ghosts* it was the memory of the dead which stood in the way of the happiness of the living. There too, there are traditions—a dead faith and a dead sense of duty, which are walking the earth again. "They are not living in us," says Mrs. Alving of the ghosts, "but they are there all the same, and we cannot get rid of them." In *Rosmersholm* the past is not dead but living, and somehow connected with the finest and most sensitive aspects of personality.

Rosmersholm to some extent marks Ibsen's farewell to the social play; it is the last of the series which began with *Pillars of Society*, but it is also the first of the series which he was to write in his later years. *The Lady from the Sea* might also be reckoned among the problem plays, though its cryptic message about man not being really born for dry land but for the sea and the air was already discussed in early versions of *Rosmersholm*. Akin to the problem plays is the treatment of the marriage conflict, and Ellida's feelings for the 'stranger,' the sailor whose affection she forfeited when she sold herself to the widower, Wangel. The problem is solved by the magic formula, freedom with responsibility. There is always trouble when Ibsen breaks his own rule: "I prefer to ask questions: it is not for me to answer them." He can give surprisingly feeble answers to profound questions.

When Ibsen sent *Hedda Gabler* to his French translator he wrote that he had not intended in this play to treat "problems": "My main purpose has been to draw human beings, their moods and characters, in the light of certain current attitudes and circumstances." It is plain that Ibsen did not want to lose touch entirely with social conditions, but wanted to shift the emphasis to psychology, an intention of which he had already spoken when asked about *Rosmersholm*.

Contemporary critics used to blame Ibsen for starting with abstract ideas, and then freely creating characters to sustain them. To-day critics go to the opposite—and equally superficial—extreme and look for the real-life original of every Ibsen character.

In this issue one must look for a middle way. In the most skilfully constructed of Ibsen's plays, *Ghosts*, it is not easy to see Mrs. Alving or Pastor Manders as psychologically convincing. His portraits of pillars of society, constricted by authority, were regarded as stereotyped in his own day, and they have not become any more life-like with the years. This holds good of figures such as Helmer, Manders, the Magistrate, Stockman, Kroll the headmaster and various others. In the female characters one can sometimes hear the rough tone of Ibsen's own voice, even when they ceased to be mouthpieces for the women's cause. Mrs. Borkman, and also her fair twin sister, Ella Rentheim, are exacting, unforgiving and implacable, despite their self-sacrificing ways. To some extent this is also true of Irene in *When We Dead Awaken*. Ibsen's greatest failures are young women, eager for life, such as Rita in *Little Eyolf* or Maia Rubek, whom he depicts as positive gluttons in their greed for happiness. The real Ibsen heroes are the tragic dreamers like Rosmer or Solness, obstinate builders of castles in the air, who are tortured by qualms of conscience which they are forever trying to suppress. Even Rubek in *When We Dead Awaken* is one of these *Einsamme Menschen* (*Lonely Men*), if we may borrow the title of one of Hauptmann's plays which was greatly influenced by Ibsen. They are examples of a hero-type which reappears, with variations, in plays by not only Hauptmann, but Maeterlinck, Strindberg, Chekhov, and other contemporary and later dramatists. That they are pictures of their creator no one doubts, but only very rarely has Ibsen produced an authentic self-portrait such as John Gabriel Borkman, irritable and cold, and yet with an inner uncertainty behind a façade of superiority. In his room he hears a knock on the door, looks at a mirror, waits for another knock, poses himself with the left hand on the table and the right across his breast, resting in the folds of his coat, and calls sternly, "Come in."

With comic characters Ibsen fails when he draws them too emphatically. He is generally at his best when creating characteristic Norwegian types. Stensgård represents Norwegian impetuosity and self-preoccupation, Stockman Norwegian frankness and cheerful talk. In both cases Björnson, seen from two different angles, was the original figure. When Ibsen presses his satire too far, as with Jörgen Tesman in *Hedda Gabler*, he loses effect. It is almost more difficult to believe in the bovine stupidity of this scholar than in the genius of Eilert Lövborg.

Even the best known of Ibsen's comic characters, Hjalmar Ekdal, who has been more imitated in drama and novel than any other, suffers from this weakness. Ibsen noticed it himself, and when *The Wild Duck* was to be performed for the first time at Christiania Theatre he asked that the role should not be played "with any trace of parody in expression, or any sign that the actor sees anything comic in his lines." These directions are difficult to follow, for Hjalmar Ekdal is a cheerful Dickensian figure, with all the exaggerated qualities which this description implies. He has been

compared with Micawber, and also with Harold Skimpole of
Bleak House, for his fluttering artist's bow and his naive egoism.
He has a tendency to parody himself when he speaks, and is really
best understood through references to him by other characters.
Gregers Werle maintains that there is something of the Wild
Duck in him, but when Hjalmar Ekdal is worried about having
been one of thirteen guests at Werle's dinner party, Relling says
tersely, "Take it easy Ekdal; heaven knows it won't affect you."

The comedy of Hjalmar Ekdal, and his tragedy—for as Ibsen
indicates in the letter mentioned above, he has his darker moments
—is just that he is not the thirteenth guest, but one of the twelve
ordinary guests, no wild duck, but the most inoffensive of farm
ducks swimming round the community pond. The 'life lie' by
which he exists is that he is an exceptional person, and his real
talent is for dramatizing his own existence. A trifle is enough to
cast him down from the heights of bliss to the depths of sorrow,
but throughout he retains his expansive gestures and his complacency. When old Ekdal was sentenced to imprisonment for
swindling, Hjalmar held a pistol to his own breast—but he never
pulled the trigger: "No. At the decisive moment I conquered
myself. You can imagine—it needs courage to choose life under
such circumstances." Hjalmar Ekdal is not Ibsen's greatest
character, but apart from Peer Gynt he is the most universal.

In Ibsen's last plays it is the women characters who are most
memorable, though the woman's cause was no longer in his
mind.

Hedda Gabler's character, as Sten Linder pointed out, resembles
that of the General's daughter in one of the stories from
"Married," Volume II—"For Payment." But she bears the
stamp of her period, the turn of the century, more obviously than
Strindberg's harridan of the Eighties, or the eccentric women of
Dumas' later plays with whom she has been compared. Ibsen had
none of the misogyny of these two contemporaries, which is
apparent from the fact that Koht in his first monograph interpreted Hedda Gabler as another Nora, an ill-fated woman, who
had not been educated according to her talents. The wealth of
material in notes and drafts of plays that was produced from
Bergliot Ibsen's personal papers, caused him to change his ideas
in the centenary edition. Even in the first draft the picture is of a

K

married woman pretending to be a person of importance, and anxious to create a sensational story about herself. Without a scrap of love for him, she has married an innocent lecturer, Tesman, and even his rival, Eilert Lövborg, she only treats as a plaything. In the final scene all her illusions are shattered: "The ridiculous and the sordid lie like a curse on everything I touch." After playing a wild dance tune on the piano she shoots herself; she has even discarded her last hope—of a beautiful death.

By his fumbling efforts to create a new type of character, the hysterical, self-centred, destructive type of woman, Ibsen has shown the way to a number of modern heroines. Hedda Gabler is no longer one of those outstanding roles that every actress is anxious to play, but her ghost continues to walk the boards in many a drama.

Hilda Wangel is based to some extent on the same model as Hedda Gabler, the eighteen-year-old Viennese girl Emilie Bardach, who once charmed Ibsen and scared him by saying that she wanted to steal men from their wives. This is a taste shared by Hilda Wangel. In the second act of *The Master Builder* she says that she is a bird of prey that seizes what she wants, "as soon as I can get my claws into it." It is not until after the moving meeting with Mrs. Solness that she renounces her intention of using her claws against the rather reserved master builder. Hedda Gabler is delighted at the thought of the race for promotion between her husband and Eilert Lövborg: "It will be almost like some sort of game—I am really very excited about the result." Hilda Wangel is also 'very excited' when Solness risks his life to climb the tower. What makes her Ibsen's most enchanting heroine is that she has her world in the same place as Solness himself, in a castle in the air. When she first knocks on the door of the old master builder's house, she corresponds exactly to Gran's admirable description of her as a sporting young Norwegian who brings fresh air into a room with her, and seems herself like a breath of fresh air. This quality she retains, but in other respects she changes —and the play with her—not all at once, like Nora in *A Doll's House*, but gradually. One's first impression is that the spirit of youth and joyful love has come to bring Solness back to that life which he once rejected for the sake of an imagined vocation, but the feelings of the couple grow cooler, until there is no more than a flirtation between them, half mischievous, half mocking. They dream of building a castle in the air together, and of other things which might make them happy. Words begin to acquire a hidden significance. Hilda's description of her past life acquires a symbolic content, as do Solness's accounts of his building activities. Finally it seems quite natural that she should obstinately insist on the fairy prince of her childhood days climbing the church tower at the celebrations marking the completion of the building, as he did ten years earlier in Lysanger. When the others mourn because he has fallen, Hilde is triumphant: "But he got right to the very top. And I heard the harp in the sky." She swings her shawl up in the air and cries, with passionate intensity "My—My Master Builder."

The connexion with *Hedda Gabler* is plain; but the atmosphere of *When We Dead Awaken* is also anticipated. A character from the past is restored to life for one purpose only, to remind the hero, Rubek, a sculptor, that he sacrificed her for his art and used her as model without remembering that she was a warm-blooded human being. This notion of sacrificing life for art, one's life's happiness for one's work, is always present with Ibsen, though in such works as *The Vikings,* and *Love's Comedy* the sacrifice seems more like a release. By the time of the last plays it has become a crime of which the hero is guilty, and so Solness feels when he contemplates his life's work and finds it meaningless.

This sculptor whose group of statuary, *The Day of Resurrection,* included the figure of a young girl rising from the sleep of death is reminiscent of Walter Runeberg, who actually did produce a sculpture called *Resurrection.* Thea Bruun, the original of Agnes in *Brand,* had been the object of Walter Runeberg's devotion in Rome (an incident recalled in the scene between Agnes and Einar), and he had made a bust of her. A year or so later she died of consumption. Her fleeting visit to life was celebrated in Ibsen's wonderful poem *Borte* (*Away*) and Bull maintains that the poem *En Svane* (*A Swan*) was also composed at the news of her death. Ibsen had promised to commemorate her in his poetry, but *Brand* was not published till after her death.

If we realize that Ibsen was remembering the days of his youth and the poems he wrote then, it becomes easier to understand *When We Dead Awaken*, particularly the dreamlike scene where Rubek and Irene stand by the stream and throw leaves into it pretending that they are swans. The merry Thea Bruun has, however, been transformed into a disappointed woman, a merciless judge, condemning Rubek for having regarded her merely as a model, for having been an artist, merely an artist, not a man. Behind a calm exterior her heart is aching, and some of her utterances are coloured by passion.

Among the notes for *When We Dead Awaken,* one line sounds reminiscent of poetry: "Great white swans dipping their heads in the waters." Can this be a half-remembered quotation from Snoilsky's poem, "Black Swans," the final verse of which runs—

> White swans serenely glide in and out among the reeds,
> Looking for titbits and for bread;
> Away, away to the deeper waters, you black swans,
> Children of night and fire.

It is the fateful journeying of the black swans to the deep of which Ibsen dreamt in *Hedda Gabler, The Master Builder,* and *When We Dead Awaken.* In *Hedda Gabler* it is merely a sense of foreboding; in *The Master Builder* and *When We Dead Awaken*, it has the fascination of the unknown, but in both plays it brings about the death of the hero.

It is above all as a technician that Ibsen has influenced the course of modern drama. To those who feel he has greater merits in other fields this may seem unjust, but he was, to a truly remarkable degree, the master of dramatic form, and he devoted himself to its development with a care which has hardly been equalled. The result has been a faultless, clockwork precision. When the plays were published, this well-devised and ingenious mechanism was highly praised, but at a later period it has been condemned as too artificial.

Ibsen's first aim was to surpass technically the *pièce bien faite* of the Second Empire. He succeeded in further reducing the number of characters, and in maintaining the three unities, particularly that of time.

In *A Doll's House* the duration of the action has not yet been reduced to a single day, but the audience are kept well informed of the passing of time. In the second act, when Nora has determined to seek death, she looks at the time to see how many hours she has still to live. When Krogstad's letter appears to the unsuspecting Helmer to put an end to her anxiety, he bursts out, "These must have been three terrible days for you." But Nora again looks at the clock. "It is not as late as that yet" she says. "Sit down here, Torwald. We have a lot to talk about, we two."

With *Ghosts*, Ibsen succeeded in keeping within the permitted twenty-four hours, and praised the performance in Berlin, because Mrs. Alving's clock in the sitting room struck the right time throughout the play. How closely the acts followed each other may be seen from the following details. The second act ends with Mrs. Alving telling Regine to fetch a bottle of champagne and three glasses. The idea is that Oswald and Regine are to learn that they have the same mother. But the asylum is set on fire, and she never has a chance to tell her story. During the final act, the still unopened champagne bottle remains on the table as a symbol of the secret which has not yet been revealed.

This observation of the unities sometimes produces for Ibsen the same sort of unreasonable situation as for the French classical playwrights. Mrs. Linde, Nora's confidante, has sent Krogstad a message that he is to meet her at midnight in the Helmers' sitting-room. "Must it really be in this house?" Krogstad asks on arrival. One is reminded of the *antichambre* of French classical drama, in which couples arrange to meet so freely.

The unities may have caused complications in *A Doll's House*, but in *Ghosts* they are used in masterly fashion. The play lasts from just before midday to sunrise, and each act ends just as an important statement is about to be made. As Mrs. Alving is telling Manders the real story about her husband and Regine's birth, the conversation is interrupted to show Oswald flirting with Regine in the conservatory, a scene which stirs ghostlike memories. The fire in the second act prevents Mrs. Alving from completing her explanation of their position to the half-brother and sister, and in the final act the curtain goes down before Mrs. Alving has decided whether she will give her son poison or not. Ibsen refused consistently to tell his English translator, William Archer, how he imagined the play to end.

The real action in *Ghosts* occurs in the scene where Oswald is struck by madness. Otherwise the plot consists entirely of the gradual piecemeal revelation of the past. The technique of *Oedipus Rex* has never been used so wholeheartedly as here. What is characteristic of Ibsen is that he makes his tragic revelation at the very moment when everything has apparently been put right. All the ghosts seem to have been swept aside, and mother and son dream about the happy time that is coming when Oswald will be able to work again and cease to brood over the past: "Soon you will see the sun." At the very moment when the sun shines through, Nemesis strikes her last shattering blow; Oswald suffers his onset of madness and cries out for the sun.

Oedipus Rex begins after the actual catastrophe and allows us to see its consequences. Ibsen goes a step further with *Ghosts*. Oswald is a broken man before he comes on the stage. Instead, Nemesis strikes at Mrs. Alving, who has known everything but did not wish to spoil her son's memory of his father: "It seemed to me that the child would be poisoned if he breathed the air of this polluted house. That was why I sent him away." Is it pure coincidence that the words chosen to express her meaning resemble those in the *Oedipus*?

The method of retrospective analysis ensures the unity of *Ghosts*, but it detracts from the effectiveness of the plot. In his first review not even Georg Brandes grasped its full beauty, and Edward Brandes considered it far inferior to *A Doll's House*. One wonders how effective it would seem to a modern spectator who had no previous knowledge of the plot.

The dialogue in *Ghosts* conforms to the principle of unity as much as does its general construction. It is always relevant, not merely to the personality of each character, but also to the conception of the whole play. Every line, however prosaic it may seem, is there for a purpose; a rejoinder missed may mean that the whole continuity of thought is lost.

The dialogue in Ibsen's plays shows him at his strongest and his weakest. When *Ghosts* was to be translated into Swedish, Ibsen was very anxious to ensure that the different characters' ways of speaking should be distinguished, "For after all, one person does not express himself in the same way as his neighbour." All digressions in the dialogue were ruthlessly excised in the final version.

If Ibsen thus succeeded in escaping from the long speeches beloved of French dramatists and their audiences, yet his dialogue also lacked something of the spontaneity to be found in them, in Björnson, and, in a different form, in Strindberg. The characters remain at arm's length from each other, and seldom indulge in sudden interjections or unexpected bursts of feeling. Ibsen cut out all asides and monologues, and in the later plays he even fought shy of the sententious remarks for which he used to have a liking. He often has a weakness for catchwords, frequently repeated in various contexts. In *Ghosts,* not only does the title recur in several places, with varying significance, but so does the phrase 'joy of life.' Oswald considers that the joy of life is lacking in Norway, and is only to be found abroad. Everything that he himself has painted deals with the joy of life. By the final act he has converted his mother; speaking of his father as a young lieutenant, " 'The joy of life' was strong in him, you see," she says. There was not much room for the joy of life in the little township which made Oswald's father what he was, and Mrs. Alving blames herself for not having brought any "Sunday weather" into his home. Sometimes the keyword takes on the character of a universal elixir, such as 'freedom with responsibility' in *The Lady from the Sea,* and 'the law of change' in *Little Eyolf.*

In the plays of his old age, Ibsen relaxed the rigid composition which marked *Ghosts,* occasionally introducing scenes which were not absolutely essential to the plot but possessed considerable poetic beauty. Landscapes also acquired more significance. *Ghosts* and *Rosmersholm* are set entirely indoors, though the constant rain and mist of *Ghosts* accords well with the story of the play. In *Rosmersholm* the old manor, with the sound of the mill-race in the background, where the children never smile, is inextricably bound up with the Rosmer attitude to life, a noble attitude, but fatal to happiness.

After *The Lady from the Sea,* all Ibsen's plays included scenes out of doors, many of them by the sea. As the years passed, he became steadily fonder of his cottage fireside, but he always retained his love of the open sea. Actually, the sea scenes are rather stilted; as time passed, Ibsen—like John Gabriel Borkman a son of the mountains—could no longer endure the keen wind. However, the heroes and heroines he now created belong to a younger, more sporting, generation, figures such as Hilde Wangel and Erhart Borkman. Allmers, in *Little Eyolf,* wants to bring up his child as an open-air lad and Borkman, in the final act of the play, says he wants to be an open-air man. *When We Dead Awaken*, which of all Ibsen's plays is most remote from the world, is played entirely out of doors, ending up on top of the high fells, which Ibsen, as a dramatist, had not visited since the days of *Brand* and *Peer Gynt*.

It is both a return and a good-bye to the Norwegian countryside that we witness in these plays, morbid and heavy with dreams as they are. We note a longing for nature, the nature in which the poet has never lived—for a way of life which has never been his.

While Ibsen still lived, his followers had already begun to range themselves with the two principal schools of thought among modern dramatists, the Symbolists and the Naturalists. In January 1882, Per Staaff wrote to Strindberg, "Ibsen, with *A Doll's House* probably, certainly with *Ghosts,* has joined the Naturalists". Indeed, naturalistic drama was more profoundly influenced by *Ghosts* than by Zola and his faithful disciples. In the same way, Ibsen was ten years later proclaimed by the Symbolists as a pioneer and a master. Maeterlinck greeted *The Master Builder* with enthusiasm, as a sleep-walking play in which unknown powers bear sway. The same growth in appreciation can also be observed by studying the *premières* of Ibsen plays at independent foreign theatres. In France it was the naturalistic Théâtre Libre of Antoine which first took up *Ghosts,* but a few years later the home of symbolic drama, Lugne-Poë's Théâtre de L'Oeuvre, became the real centre of Ibsen drama in France, with *The Master Builder* in its regular repertory. Plays such as *The Wild Duck* and *Rosmersholm* have exercised an influence on both naturalism and symbolism. Here it may suffice to mention Björnson and Lie, Strindberg in Sweden and J. P. Jacobsen in Denmark. It may even be suggested that *When We Dead Awaken* was partly inspired by Zola's artist novel, '*L'Oeuvre*', which Ibsen knew of from newspaper articles. This, however, does not mean that anything of significance in Ibsen's work can be explained entirely by reference to the theory or practice of either school.

Modern Norwegian scholars have sought to trace the combination of realism and symbolism in Ibsen's contemporary drama to Zola's novels, and have paid particular attention to the interest shown by Ibsen in a certain essay by Brandes. This was published in 1887, and called *"Realism and Temperament in Emile Zola"*; it treats of Zola's concern with symbols.

But ten years earlier, in *Pillars of Society*, before Zola had become known outside France, Ibsen had written a realistic modern play dominated by a symbol, though perhaps not so completely as are *Ghosts* or *The Wild Duck*—and even these are earlier than Brandes' essay.

Ibsen's first modern plays deal with questions of heredity and the survival of the fittest. In one of the manuscript versions of *A Doll's House* there is a lecture by Dr. Rank on the struggle for existence as exemplified in the human world. There are already signs that Ibsen was thinking about eugenics on lines which Dr. Stockman makes familiar in another play. This interest in heredity and the theories of Darwin is not derived from Zola. It is an echo of the eager discussions which went on in the Scandinavian Colony in Rome during the winter of 1878—79. Darwin was the principal subject of conversation, mainly because J. P. Jacobsen, who had translated his works, took a regular part in the debates.

Ibsen accepted these ideas about heredity and progress only in so far as they fitted in with his moral philosophy. The identification of might and right which Rank expounded in the earlier versions of *A Doll's House*, was strongly disapproved of by Ibsen, who also disliked the idea expressed by John Gabriel Borkman, that strong, exceptional people are entitled to everything they want. In this matter Ibsen was opposed to Nietzsche. The noble creatures of whom Ibsen dreams in *An Enemy of the People* and *Rosmersholm* never become the mouthpieces of any doctrine of that kind.

His tendency to deal in symbols Ibsen took over from the neo-classical and romantic schools. Symbols are more significant in his later work than in the plays of the Eighties, but this can only be partly ascribed to the fact that he made contact with the new symbolism through Scandinavian authors.

Ibsen was the starting-point from which dramatists set out

at the end of the 19th and the beginning of the 20th centuries, and his influence is still felt to-day. He did not wish himself to be associated with any particular literary group, and in this he was right. He was affected by ideas and tendencies current in his day, but his work is an artistic whole in itself. When one reads the works of his numerous followers, one realizes how inimitable and individual his plays are. He has become the great classic of modern drama.

AUGUST STRINDBERG

STRINDBERG is the boldest and most poetic experimenter in modern drama. He was in much closer contact than Ibsen with new developments, and he gave out more impulses than he received. His work must therefore be considered before we turn to the spread of naturalism in France.

In the development of modern drama Strindberg made himself felt on two occasions. His naturalistic plays were included in the repertoire of such theatres as the Théâtre Libre, and later in other theatres in different countries. He became internationally famous and cherished hopes of a future as a French or a German writer. In literary circles his plays were appreciated and imitated, but these experimental theatres did not bring him into contact with a wide public.

After the production of "Inferno" the situation changed. During the years immediately before and after the first world war Strindberg was constantly played and read everywhere, and *Ett drömspel* (*A Dream Play*) and the chamber plays, when produced by Reinhardt, were world-wide successes. The critics considered that Strindberg's posthumous reputation depended largely on the fact that his later plays reflected faithfully the disturbed and chaotic conditions of the world. It was prophesied that his plays would disappear from the stage when Europe's wounds were healed. However, the Strindberg fever did not abate even during the quieter years between the wars, and it seems quite probable that it will flare up again when theatres recover after this last war. In any case it does not seem to be merely a passing symptom.

While Reinhardt's fame as a producer was at its height, a good deal of Strindberg's success with his later plays, and especially the chamber plays, was ascribed to him. But without decrying his admirable work one must oppose the suggestion that he could have accomplished miracles with ill-constructed or incomprehensible plays. Both in Sweden and elsewhere later producers have scored equally great successes with the same plays, and sometimes adhered much more faithfully to the original stage directions.

In this connexion a protest must be made against the commonly held opinion that Strindberg's plays lack interest when read and can only be fully appreciated on the stage. To some extent this is true of all plays. A good stage production can make even a poor play enjoyable, but it cannot create great poetry where none exists in the play as written.

These attempts to explain away the enduring quality of Strindberg's popularity may primarily be due to the absence of any message in his work as a whole, such as marked that of Ibsen and Shaw. For a hundred years now people have been accustomed to regard the stage as a pulpit for the lay preacher, and it is not merely in the social problem play that authors from Dumas onwards have been anxious to present their gospel. Maeterlinck and the Symbolic dramatists had their own mystical wisdom to offer their listeners.

Strindberg's drama does not lack purpose. Hatred of the emancipated woman is as characteristic of the plays of the Eighties as is the theme of expiation in the series of plays which begins with *Till Damaskus* (*To Damascus*). Often, however, the purpose simply appears as a disturbing element which the play might well do without. The denigration of woman in *Fadren* (*The Father*) has very little to do with the strong impression created by the play as a whole, and *Gustav Vasa* is not a play which one reads for religious edification.

In contrast to most contemporary dramatists, Strindberg made no attempt to conceal his indebtedness to the various schools of literature. In 1880 he proclaimed boldly that he was aiming at realizing Zola's ambitions for naturalistic drama. In the same way he declared himself early in the 20th century to be a pupil of Maeterlinck. Jolivet considered that he overstressed his dependence on him. Ultimately he always went his own way, and at heart he was aware of this.

Among Strindberg's naturalistic plays *The Father* appeared in a French translation with a charming introduction by Zola, and it was performed at the Théâtre Libre which was under his patronage. Strindberg also wrote *Fröken Julie* (*Miss Julie*) and *Fordringsägare* (*Creditors*) for this theatre. The preface to *Miss Julie* is a piece of propaganda on behalf of Antoine's new ideas for theatrical reform. At one time Strindberg proposed to publish *Creditors* in French only. The plays which followed these were one-act single-scene pieces of the kind called 'quarts d'heure' by Antoine and 'the type of play for modern people' by Strindberg. He had read Zola's *Le Naturalisme au Théâtre* with great care, and had also secured copies of all the published plays of the Théâtre Libre repertory. Resemblances that are more than just superficial are, however, hard to find. Zola's introduction to *The Father* shows that he did not regard the play as conforming completely to the requirements of naturalism. An American scholar has recently published two works, designed to show that *The Father* and the plays which immediately followed it are not naturalistic but expressionistic. However one may regard this attempt to place Strindberg's plays in a category which was unknown at the time, it is evidence that those of his works which are best known abroad are not considered properly naturalistic in style. On the other hand it is generally acknowledged that the expressionistic playwrights of the German school, which later spread its influence to other lands, were directly or indirectly inspired by Strindberg.

Strindberg differs from naturalistic playwrights in most countries in that he is not concerned with peasants or workers, and does not allow social problems to occupy the foreground of his plays. *Miss Julie* conscientiously states the preoccupation of naturalism with 'rising and falling in society,' as the preface has it. The play deals with heredity and degeneracy, and is supposed to prove the Darwinian theory of the survival of the fittest; but its value as drama has very little to do with these topics or with the fact that Strindberg met Nietzsche while actually writing the play—or at any rate before he wrote the preface. In *The Father* and *Creditors* there are no social problems at all.

All three of these plays deal with the struggle between the sexes and owe some of their colour and material to Strindberg's personal experiences. *The Father* may be regarded as a study for

A Lunatic's Defence, a book which he began to write six months later; *Miss Julie* and *Creditors* were written at the same mtie as this book.

The lawsuit which followed the publication of *Married* had ended with Strindberg's acquittal, but it left him in great financial difficulties, with his nerves badly shaken and a renewed fear of persecution which finally led him to turn against his wife. It would be interesting to know who was really responsible for opening legal proceedings about the first part of *Married*, a collection of short stories which Strindberg during the campaign against him prophesied would one day be read in girls' schools. He actually believed in the existence of an international league of women throughout the whole of Europe who had persuaded his wife to join them against her husband.

By the end of 1886 his wife, Siri von Essen, had asked a Swiss doctor for advice about her husband's state of mind, and at the same time Strindberg had read a newspaper article by the Frenchman, Paul Lafargue, describing the dreadful battles between the sexes which preceded the introduction of patriarchy, and which might break out again if people tried to return to matriarchy. Siri von Essen's action inspired him to make Laura in *The Father* try every means of inducing the Captain to betray his deranged state of mind so that he could be secured in a strait jacket and put away. The article which Strindberg read made him see the incident as part of an eternal war between the sexes. Of all the plays which have been written with madness as their theme none has been composed in such a state of tension. Every moment Strindberg was expecting the doors of the asylum to close implacably behind him, or the final death struggle between the sexes to begin.

It is this tension which gives *The Father* both its greatness and its absurdity. 'You see, all boilers explode when the pressure gauge shows 100; but 100 is not the same for all boilers,' says the Captain to the Doctor in the second act. From the very beginning he is at odds with his wife, a struggle which he interprets as an inevitable war of hatred between the sexes. From the very beginning he is prepared to suspect her of anything.

That Laura is intended to be the incarnation of all feminine evil is not doubted by any one. There is, however, considerable doubt about the Captain, and how Strindberg conceived him. When the play was to be performed at Copenhagen he wrote about the title part to Lundegård, 'to me personally he represents a masculinity which people have tried to undervalue, deprive us of, and transfer to a third sex. It is only in front of the woman that he appears unmanly, because she wants him so, and the laws of the game compel a man to play the part that his lady commands.' In the play the impression created is of the Captain's kinship with 'the great,' the clumsy giants who become the helpless victims of the poisonous intrigues of 'small men.' Perhaps it was this that led Strindberg later to explain to Nietzsche that he had anticipated his Superman in the Captain.

Paul Lafargue had found in the *Oresteia* a reflection of the struggles which preceded the introducion of patriarchy. His interpretation of Aeschylus was commented upon by Strindberg in an article optimistically entitled *The Last Word on the Woman Question*. It was clearly his intention in *The Father* to achieve a counterpart to the *Oresteia* before the threatened return of matriarchy. Lundegård describes the play—very probably according to Strindberg's directions—at its première at Copenhagen in 1887 as 'a modern life-story presented with a touch of the inexorable solemnity of classical tragedy.' This classical quality has indeed always been noted and emphasized, and it gives to *The Father* a primitive grandeur which was not attained by subsequent naturalistic plays.

It might be supposed that *The Father* was sufficiently one-sided —but it does end with the defeat of the man. The Captain is not even given the opportunity to tell Laura the whole truth about herself. It was therefore necessary for Strindberg to restore the balance in *Creditors*. This play was even more successful abroad than *The Father* and *Miss Julie*, because people felt that they were on more familiar ground. This tragi-comedy, as *Creditors* is called—though the ending is pure tragedy—presents a theme common in French drama, the triumph of the original husband over his wife's lover or second husband. That Strindberg himself was possessed by feelings both of jealousy and fear towards Siri von Essen's first husband was not generally known until *A Lunatic's Defence* was published. Strindberg held that the play was even better than *Miss Julie*, 'with three characters, a table and two chairs, and no sunrise.' In *Miss Julie* he had been tempted to imitate *Ghosts* by allowing the rising of the sun to contrast with the tragic ending of the play. The title, *Creditors*, reflects the main idea. Both Tekla's present and first husbands are exacting creditors who have provided her with the spiritual food by which she lives: "she is nothing more than a gramophone which reproduces rather colourlessly your words and those of others." Everything she possesses has been stolen from the two men; "she has consumed your soul, this woman, your courage, your knowledge."

What makes *Creditors* such good theatre is its sure composition and its absorbing presentation of a struggle of personalities, using suggestion as a weapon. The ending, when the new husband Adolf falls dying in an epileptic fit after receiving proof of his wife's unfaithfulness, is more melodramatic than the naturalistic canon really permits. Strindberg's dramatic naturalism sometimes includes rather improbable characters and situations. This is also noticeable, though to a less extent, in *Miss Julie*. If one tries to interpret the play according to the preface which was written afterwards, one may easily exaggerate the significance of problems and new stage devices which were not Strindberg's own, and which now seem very much out of date. Even Edward Brandes doubted when he read the play whether it had really been written with so much conscious theory in mind.

The reason why *Miss Julie* still holds its place as one of the great modern works of drama is above all because of the drawing of the heroine's character. One may detect traces of Siri von Essen, as Strindberg saw her before the days of *A Lunatic's Defence* but she is, for all that, a free creation, his finest female character. She explains her own character, the combination of haughtiness and an urge to lower herself, in a passage which was horribly garbled by the publisher, and though Strindberg was furious at his intervention he never remembered to correct it in subsequent editions. Julie's mother was of humble origin and first came to the estate as the Count's mistress. Because of this alliance he was excluded from society and practically confined to his estates, but she left him to become the mistress of a brick manufacturer in the neighbourhood. Apart from the three characters who appear on the stage, Julie's mother is the most significant figure in the play.

Her head was full of feminist ideas but she could never maintain her dignity, for in some things, as Jean said, she was too proud, and in others not proud enough. "She was happiest in the kitchen and the farmyard, but would never drive one horse alone; her cuffs might be soiled, but there was always a crest on her buttons."

In *The Father* Strindberg expressed his irritation at Mrs. Alving and her speeches about her dead husband, but in *Miss Julie* he created a counterpart in the person of the dead Countess. Naturally, Strindberg did not fail to maintain that the ideas of feminine emancipation which Julie inherited from her mother were the cause of her yielding to temptation, and first allowing herself to be seduced by the groom and then being so furious that she could find no words to express her loathing.

Miss Julie is the last member of an old family whose blood has run thin. In the preface Strindberg tries to convince the reader that her fall serves a purpose. She is "a relic of the old order of fighting nobility" who must make way for Jean, "the creator of the new order", and it is all to the good that the royal park should "be cleared of the dark, overgrown trees which have stood in the way of others." Strindberg was only theoretically satisfied by this mixture of Darwin and Nietzsche which his best pupil, O'Neill, inherited from him. He was himself a hypersensitive, nervous creature, with an instinctive dislike of the masses. Julie, despite her erotic passions, her tactlessness and her caprices, is head and shoulders above Jean the servant and Kristin the cook, who rejoice at her downfall. As Strindberg originally conceived the ending, Julie was to snatch the razor from Jean and open her veins, with the taunt, "you see, servant, you cannot die." In the final version she lacks the courage to commit suicide, and submits to Jean's suggestions. But her steps are firm as she follows him, razor in hand, to the door. Strindberg says in the preface that it is her inherited sense of honour that leads her to prefer death to disgrace. "And so Jean, the servant, lives, while Miss Julie cannot endure life without honour. The slave has this advantage over the master, that he does not hold any fatal notions of honour; all we Aryans have in us something aristocratic, something of Don Quixote." In spite of the Nietzschean cast of the sentence, the thought is the same as in *The Father*—the fate of the great is to be fettered and subdued, while the small shall possess the earth.

The classical unities which Zola preached, but could not practise in his own plays, were carefully observed by Strindberg both in *Miss Julie* and *Creditors,* as also in Germany by Hauptmann and his friends in the plays by which they made their name. He determined to make his characters "feeble and exhausted, blends of the old and the new, of tradition and modernity, snippets from books and newspapers, fragments of men, the tattered remnants of fine clothes." There are attempts in *Miss Julie* to escape from the "simple stage characters" condemned by Strindberg in the preface, but it was in the chamber plays that he first achieved the desired result. It was in them that he also succeeded in presenting the wandering, purposeless dialogue described in the preface, and in allowing "brains to work irregularly, as they do in real life, where no topic is ever exhausted in a single conversation, but one brain engages at random into the cog provided by another." He tried to write in this way in *Miss Julie,* but the technique was too obvious, and the characters too anxious to present Strindberg's own theories of evolution.

In his *Open Letters to the Intimate Theatre* Strindberg described the preface to *Miss Julie* as an expression of "the materialistic strivings of the age towards realism." He must have been thinking at the time of his own desire for theatrical reform and greater realism, and also of the theories of Darwin which he admired. He retained and developed the dream-like quality in his characters and also the unexpected turns in the dialogue. Thus it was that when, in his last period, he was writing plays of pure fantasy he was at the same time composing drama such as the first part of *Dödsdansen* (*The Dance of Death*), in the style of the naturalistic tragedy of 1880 and onwards.

In considering Strindberg's dramatic work after the Inferno crisis it must not be forgotten that his great cycle of historical plays was appreciated outside Sweden only when audiences who were not familiar with Swedish history could understand them. It is therefore not surprising that *Gustav Vasa,* which Swedes have gradually come to consider as their national play, was rejected in favour of *Eric XIV*, with its psychological problems, and that a play such as *Kristina* was more successful abroad than in Sweden. In the preface to *Caesar and Cleopatra* (1899) Shaw

described Strindberg as the only living dramatist of Shakespearean
calibre, referring to the Shakespearean qualities of *The Father*
which no one can fail to notice. It was a prophetic remark.
Thanks to Strindberg, historical drama in other countries took on
a new lease of life. *Cyrano de Bergerac* was a masterpiece which
Rostand himself could not repeat. Shaw's own recipe, which he
followed in *Caesar and Cleopatra*, was to pour new life into old
historical characters by means of deliberately shocking
anachronisms; but this was not Strindberg's method. In *Saint
Joan*, however, Shaw adopted the technique that Strindberg used
in his best historical plays. On the whole, he avoided the temptations of modern parody and tried to keep closely to original
sources. He did, however, give the characters a modern psychological outlook, and made the dialogue contemporary in
style as Strindberg had done. No small part of the strong impression made by *Saint Joan* is due to the carefully inserted anachronisms of emotion and speech. This is also true of O'Neill's
Mourning becomes Electra, which is placed in a period fifty years
earlier, during the American Civil War. The events are those of
days gone by; the characters are sometimes simplified as in
Strindberg—carved in solid stone. But they are drawn with a
modern outlook and the dialogue is contemporary in tone, with
an occasional dash of archaism. When one sees the play, one has
the same feeling of moving simultaneously in the present and the
past as one has when watching Strindberg's historical plays.

Strindberg's greatest contribution to modern drama consisted,
however, in the series of autobiographical plays which began with
To Damascus and ended with *Stora landsvägen* (*The Great Highway*)
and the dream plays, among which must be reckoned such pieces
as *Advent* and *Spöksonaten* (*The Ghost Sonata*).

All these plays are very closely connected with his own
experiences and attitudes, and are purely personal in their form.
With these plays Strindberg opened up whole new fields for
drama. Often they are contemporary in setting, dealing with people, events and circles which Swedish readers can partly recognize
from Strindberg's other writings and letters without further aid.
With the help of *Inferno*, *Legends*, and the *Quarantine Officer's
Second Story* in *Fagervik and Skamsund* it is easy to follow the
main threads in the first two parts of *To Damascus*. But already

reality is seen veiled in a dream. This is partly confirmed by Strindberg's description of *To Damascus* (in a postscript to the preface of *A Dream Play*) as "my earlier dream play." In both plays the characters "are split, duplicated, evaporate, coalesce, flow away and are gathered together." The Beggar is a duplicate of the Stranger; like him, he bears a scar on his forehead received at the hands of a near relation. In the home of the Doctor there is a madman nicknamed Caesar, as was the Stranger during his school days. In *A Dream Play* Strindberg tried to imitate "the incoherent but apparently logical form of a dream," but he did not quite succeed in his purpose. He created a greater work of art, one more liberated from his own experiences, but it lacks that sense of "near reality" which makes the first part of *To Damascus* so remarkably moving. Never before in the history of drama has the inner struggle of a soul been so graphically, one might almost say so tangibly, exposed to an audience. After *To Damascus* a new function of drama was revealed; to present a state of mind, but not primarily through the words of the character or by the introduction of allegorical figures. What the Stranger is thinking takes bodily form; his unexpressed longing brings the Lady to him, but everything that they subsequently experience together is a repetition of something that has happened before. Even the words that they exchange seem like an echo from the past. Even the scenery in the first half of the play is used again in the second half, but in reverse order, with the exception of the asylum scene in the middle, where all the characters resemble people from the Stranger's life though he does not recognize them exactly. "I see them as in a mirror," he says. In *Peer Gynt* the fantastic elements come from Asbjörnsen's saga, though others in the same vein have been added. It is the underworld of the myths and of the romantics, brilliantly reconstructed. Hauptmann in *Die Versunkene Glocke* (*The Sunken Bell*) and Maeterlinck in *L'Oiseau Bleu* (*The Blue Bird*) are working with familiar clichés, not original ideas. In *Kronbruden* (*The Bridal Crown*) Strindberg was also to build a play round Swedish legend and superstition, and go further than Hauptmann and Maeterlinck. But in *To Damascus* he was entirely on his own ground, dramatizing in a half-visionary, half-realistic way the strange and dreadful experiences of *Inferno*. When Pirandello and O'Neill try to follow him into this unreal world the intellectual and artistic effort is all too obvious. The nightmare of *The Emperor Jones* and the horrible experience of *Six Characters* are, in spite of everything, no more than the imaginings of a writer at his desk.

Strindberg is different. As early as 1884 he told Jonas Lie that he was no realist: 'my best writing comes when I am suffering from hallucinations.' What Strindberg meant was that he wrote best when his imagination was free to work creatively on all the most mysterious experiences of his life. Then he achieved work which seemed to its author to hover between poetry and reality. When he was watching the final rehearsals of *The Father* at Copenhagen he wrote to Lundegård: "I feel as if I were walking in my sleep, as if my life and my writing had become confused. I don't know if *The Father* is just a poem, or my very life . . . "

A Dream Play can literally be called a 'desk fantasy,' for a good many of the scenes are day dreams inspired by what Strindberg saw from his window while he was composing the play. Figuratively speaking, however, it is very different from the product of a writer at his desk. "And the children of men believe that we poets only play . . . making things up and inventing them." Those are the words of the Poet to Indra's daughter in Fingal's Cave. From the carefully preserved drafts and notes one can see that originally the play was not planned as a complete dream sequence, nor was the heroine intended to be the daughter of the god Indra. Notes in Strindberg's *Occult Diary* also show that it was not until after he had finished the play that he re-read the legend of Maya and Brahma, and perceived "the explanation of my dream play, the significance of Indra's daughter, and the secret of what lies behind the door—nothing."

Commentators are still busily trying to discover a single dreamer to give coherence to the shifting visions, and a consistent philosophy running through *A Dream Play*. Strindberg himself never had the opportunity to read these commentaries, which appeared after his death, but there is no doubt what he would have thought about them. In a letter written the night after its first performance he said of *A Dream Play* that it was "my most dearly loved play, the child of my greatest sorrows." At this stage, too, he was uncertain of the boundary between life and poetry, a doubt which is explicitly stated in the drama.

It was during the worst crisis of his third venture into married life that Strindberg wrote *A Dream Play*. In his journal he writes that the dissolution of this love-story into mere mockery has convinced him that life is an illusion: "We do not belong here; we are too good for such a wretched existence." He had had the same idea earlier, when he wrote the scenes in the corridor of the Opera, with the eternally waiting Officer whose story forms a little play within the main play. Now wholly or half-forgotten thoughts from the past come back to his mind, all confirming him in his belief that "the loveliest tales, which dissolve like bubbles of dish-water, are conceived to make us loathe life." Is mankind or its Creator responsible?

> The earth is not clean;
> Life is not good;
> Man is not evil,
> Nor good, either.
>
> Men were given feet to trudge,
> Not wings to fly.
> Dusty they are;
> Is the fault theirs,
> Or Thine?

The author of *A Dream Play* did not see life, as Kafka did, entirely as a nightmare; that conception did not occur until he wrote *The Ghost Sonata*. The atmosphere of *A Dream Play* is best expressed in the snow-covered summer landscape of Fagervik. Even the greatest imaginable happiness, love, is a harbinger of ruin: "for in the midst of joy, a seed of ill is growing; it consumes itself as a flame of fire."

With a subtlety which Strindberg never before or later exhibited so richly, he describes how illusions are created only to be dispelled. In the preface he explains that dreams are often so painful that the act of waking up reconciles the dreamer to disagreeable reality. The oppressive dream of our earthly life cannot be expiated until death; "Suffering is release, and death freedom." So the Poet proclaims, but when he has been nearly drowned in Fingal's Cave and Indra's daughter asks him if he desires freedom, he replies in terror, "Yes, yes, of course I do—but not now, and not by drowning!" Our misguided will to live forces us to wish to continue our existence, though we realize that we shall continually meet with new disappointments.

Although *A Dream Play* was rewritten several times, it gives the impression of free inspiration. Its purpose is at one and the same time to present the world of dreams and the dream which is our life in this world. His experiences of real life have given the author most of his raw material, but the play has taken its form from dreams, with their incongruous associations and the grotesque but often moving situations which arise in them.

This play has often been put forward as an instance of modern drama's taste for logic. It is to be found in the Frenchmen and Ibsen, and even a naturalist like Galsworthy constructs his plays and characters with strict regard to logic. Shaw's paradoxes are logical somersaults, and despite all their fantasy and irrationalism both Pirandello and O'Neill are concerned with logical construction and thought-processes.

In Strindberg's earlier plays, such as *Miss Julie*, this logic was also apparent. In the first part of *To Damascus* the scenes at least followed each other symmetrically, and the Stranger became the central figure in spite of the ghosts who met him.

In *A Dream Play* Strindberg also tried to arrange the scenes from the first half of the play to come in reverse order in the second half, but he only succeeded with the opening scenes in front of the growing castle, and those which follow in the corridor of the Opera. For the rest, the scenes come in any order, following the random movements of the dream. Indra's daughter appears in a different guise in almost every episode. First she is the Glazier's daughter, then the Portress's deputy at the Opera, then she marries the Lawyer, and at last takes her place by the side of the Poet. In the prologue specially written for the stage performance an explanation of these changes is provided.

The Martyr, who in most of Strindberg's other plays speaks with his own voice and pleads his case, as in *To Damascus*, has here been replaced by three different characters, the Officer, the Lawyer and the Poet. They are rivals who constantly wrangle, but except in a few isolated passages they do not speak with that passionate desire for self-justification which Strindberg's dramatic mouthpieces so often display.

Strindberg was not inclined to self-caricature, but—precisely because they are dream figures—the Officer, the Lawyer and the Poet have been allowed to become deliberate parodies of a self-portrait.

It would be presumptuous to single out one play by Strindberg as his best: that is something about which every admirer of Strindberg has his own opinion. It is, however, fairly safe to say that *To Damascus* displays the greatest wealth of poetic feeling. It is a peculiarly personal work, but it has also achieved a universality not often attained by Strindberg. The world's literature is full of plays depicting dreams, or with a dreamlike atmosphere. Strindberg himself, in one of the *Open Letters to the Intimate Theatre*, described Shakespeare's *The Tempest* as a dream play, but his own *Dream Play* has two functions to fulfil: it is both a distorted image and also a symbol of our reality. We find ourselves listening to situations and dialogue that seem perfectly familiar and matter-of-fact, until suddenly with a start we realize that we have moved beyond the bounds of our ordinary existence. In the most fascinating way the play rings the changes on reality, poetry, and dreams, whose mysteries are discussed by the Poet and Indra's daughter. When it first appeared *A Dream Play* was not very clearly understood, but in the fifty years that have passed since then it has come to take its place as one of Strindberg's chief works. It would not be surprising if ultimately it came to rank as his greatest contribution to world drama.

The chamber plays that he wrote in 1907 were Strindberg's last considerable dramatic work. They are still being performed, and are considered to be his most original writing, second only to *A Dream Play*. This may seem surprising as they are difficult to understand without reference to the writer's experience and recollections, but they have a violent dramatic force which the spectator finds irresistible, and it is really only in reading that one notices the absence of logic.

The earliest of these plays, *Oväder* (*Storm*), is the best example of Strindberg's own definition of a chamber play as "the idea of chamber music translated into drama." It is a fine, gentle play about "old age and its quiet peace." When he had written *Brända tomten* (*After the Fire*) and *The Ghost Sonata*, Strindberg came to despise *Storm;* he called it "an excellent potboiler, which can be discarded." He felt that in it he had depicted a "lower," "full" reality.

After the Fire, The Ghost Sonata and *Pelikanen* (*The Pelican*) try to afford us glimpses of the reality which lies behind our daily life. Just as the burnt house in *After the Fire* reveals its inmost recesses, so Strindberg tries in these three plays to show us the inner mind of the characters he presents on the stage. We all move like sleepwalkers through our world—at one time Strindberg thought of calling *The Pelican* 'The Sleepwalker'—and we need someone to wake us.

Strindberg shared with the Stranger in *After the Fire* and the Student in *The Ghost Sonata* the consciousness of being able to see life without a veil over his eyes. In the *Blue Book* he tells how at a party he would often wake up and see all the guests naked with all their bodily blemishes, and would also hear the thoughts behind their words. While he was writing these chamber plays he was also revising the manuscript of *Black Banners* for the printers, and preparing for the production of *A Dream Play*. *The Ghost Sonata* combines the brutal naturalism of *Black Banners* with the lyrical mood of *A Dream Play*.

Even when one has access to the draft, notes and entries in the journal of this period, *The Ghost Sonata* is extremely difficult to understand. "It is a world of allusion", wrote Strindberg to Schering, "where people talk in semitones, with their voices muted, and one is ashamed of being human." The great revelation occurs in the second act; "it is the usual 'ghost-supper,' as we call it. They drink tea, and do not say a word, or else the Colonel does all the talking; suddenly they all nibble at their biscuits and it sounds like rats in an attic . . . and they have been going on like this for twenty years, always the same people saying the same thing, or saying nothing at all for fear of being found out." The word 'ghost-supper,' which was the original title of the play, is said to have been suggested by the appearance of the guests. They are ghosts bound together by common crimes and secrets, and a shared guilt, and they only long for death: "O God, if only we might die! If we could only die!" The feverish visions from the asylum scenes of *To Damascus* have become reality.

This ghost-supper is the most bizarre episode in all Strindberg's drama, but it is also one of the most moving. Strindberg had already given expression to the misery of life on earth by showing the monotony and the grind of everyday life. He did it in *The Dance of Death* and in the marriage scene in *A Dream Play*, and he repeated the theme in the final act of *The Ghost Sonata*, where the Colonel and his wife sit in silence, 'because they have nothing to say to each other, because neither believes what the other says.' He can also achieve the same effect by a shrill cacophony, as in the ghost-supper, where all are equally anxious to unmask each other, to remove each other's wigs and false teeth, their false titles and their imaginary benefactions. Ultimately the result is the same, that our world is one of "villas and debts, a world of suffering and death, a world of eternal change, miscalculation and pain." This is the spirit of the final act, which takes place in the Hyacinth Room. The Student kills the young girl by his brusque outspokenness. She falls down dead, but the golden harp, hitherto silent, begins to sound and the room is filled with a white light. "O Buddha, wise and gentle, who sittest waiting for heaven to grow on earth, grant us patience in our trials, and purity of will, that our hopes may not come to shame." Strangely enough, the Buddhism of *The Ghost Sonata* is less pessimistic than in *A Dream Play*. There is at least the fleeting hope that the world of villas may one day resemble the heavenly world, in whose image it was created.

What distinguishes Strindberg from his great contemporaries in the world of drama is his originality. There is much that is false alongside the real profundity in Ibsen, and even more in O'Neill. Pirandello can spoil his effects by casuistry, Shaw by his passion for paradox. From all these faults Strindberg is free. Maeterlinck infected him, but only for a short time; *Svanevit* (*Swanwhite*), his most elaborate attempt in Maeterlinck's style, seems thin and sickly. Strindberg was hypersensitive, but he was not subtle.

Even in his finest work Strindberg could not help dwelling on personal grievances of a kind which later generations find trivial. In general, however, these private echoes, which are also perceived by foreigners, have only caused the plays to be admired the more. Though the themes are often drawn from Strindberg's own life, his dramatic works seem to cover a wider range than those of any other contemporary. One need only compare *Creditors,* with its naturalistic limitations and simplicity, with the apparently chaotic confusion of *A Dream Play* or the witchery of *The Ghost Sonata.* Strindberg's dialogue shows the same wide range, changing from the vigorous style of the Eighties to the almost musical diction of the plays written after the *Inferno* crisis, when the change to free verse was made so imperceptibly that it was not even indicated typographically. During all these changes, however, Strindberg's dialogue retained its inner rhythm. It has not even been ruined by bad translations, in which the tendency usually is to treat Strindberg's expressions with greater solemnity than he ever intended. All the skill which psychiatrists have devoted to analysing Strindberg's personality has not been able to conceal the man from us. In the plays he reveals himself with elemental force. He is not a 'case'—to use the word which occurs so often in the preface to *Miss Julie;* with all his merits and his faults, he is a remarkable personality. To read or see his plays is to know Strindberg himself.

It is difficult to determine the relative merits of the great dramatists who wrote at the same time as Strindberg. Let it suffice to say that he is the most modern. Thus, too, he has been regarded by those who followed him. It was no empty compliment that O'Neill paid to Strindberg when he was receiving his Nobel Prize and hailed him as "the greatest dramatic genius of modern times," the man from whom he had received a vision of what drama could be, and an urge to write for the stage.

THE FIRST SYMBOLISTS

THE first representatives of the Symbolist school of drama to have their plays performed were the Belgian, Maeterlinck, and the Frenchman, Claudel. Both acknowledged the same master, the curious Villiers de L'Isle Adam, but he died at the age of fifty in 1889, before his dramatic masterpiece, *Axel*, had been published. It appeared in 1890, the year after Maeterlinck's début on the stage, and its performance in 1894 was chiefly due to the reputation it had gained as the bible of symbolism. Villiers de L'Isle Adam was a friend and admirer of Wagner, and he formed the link which connected opera and symbolistic drama. Maeterlinck also, and other dramatists of the same school, such as Hofmannsthal, wrote plays which were intended as opera libretti.

Villiers de L'Isle Adam himself was content to give his words a musical, almost a religious tone, a tendency which was later followed by Claudel. Otherwise it is difficult to find the similarities between *Axel* and Wagner's *Tristan und Isolde*, which are commonly suggested. The plot of *Axel* is extremely complex and occasionally melodramatic. The Restoration period is the setting for the play, but it is deliberately presented in such a fantastic way that a spectator has rather the impression of the Middle Ages. Maeterlinck, Claudel and several of their followers went the whole way back, and wrote fairy plays in a medieval setting. This was the Middle Ages as the 1890's saw them, a more delicate conception than that of the Romantics, with young maidens in white flitting to and fro along the ruined castle walls, and sighs of anguish heard under the arches.

To describe the contents of the plot in *Axel* would be to defeat the author's intentions, for the fateful events that take place on the stage are to be interpreted symbolically. When Sara refuses to take her vows and forces the Abbess with her axe to step down into a grave, and when Count Axel of Auersberg kills his cousin in a duel, they are both obsessed with the idea of acquiring the great treasure which the soothsayers declare to be lying under the walls of Auersberg Castle. They meet for the first time in the hidden vault where the treasure lies. But their enmity turns so suddenly to love that they forget the treasure, and decide to seek death together; to live on would only mean disgrace. 'Live? Our servants can do that for us.' These well-known words mark the extent of Villiers de L'Isle Adam's contempt for reality. Such an attitude is also common in Maeterlinck and Claudel, and is to be found in various forms in Hofmannsthal and Yeats.

To give a comprehensive definition of symbolist drama is hardly possible. Some plays of this type have been produced by authors who are buried in a dream-world of poetry, others by writers like Strindberg and Hauptmann who also wrote plays in a naturalistic style. With the advent of Yeats and Synge in Ireland and Lorca in Spain a type of peasant drama began to appear which was poetic and sometimes legendary in character, contrasting strongly with the realist peasant drama as exemplified by Tolstoy's *Power of Darkness*.

In fully developed symbolist drama the clear daylight of naturalism, the exact contours and the precise language, are replaced by a feeling of vagueness and an atmosphere of uncertainty. One chooses to live in half-darkness, in order to reach the soul of things, not just their surface. The characters are mere shadows, and events have no significance in themselves, for the real action takes place off stage beyond the horizon, where the Divine and the Infinite, Fate and Death have their being.

Maeterlinck and Claudel are still alive, and differ greatly. Maeterlinck was born in 1862 and educated at a Jesuit school in Ghent, but he moved so far from Catholicism that his works were placed on the Index. Paul Claudel, six years younger, became a fervent Catholic in 1886 and painted an idealistic picture of the faith and the Papacy in his plays. He had a brilliant diplomatic career, a fact that is reflected in the various exotic settings of his plays. He has acquired a considerable following of admirers from among his fellow-Catholics, while Maeterlinck's home-brewed mysticism is no longer so popular. Claudel also has the advantage of never having made any concessions to gain popularity on the stage. That his last masterpiece, *Le Soulier de Satin* (*The Satin Slipper*), ever came to be performed, as it was in 1943, seems like a miracle when one reads the play; not, of course, that it will ever be in regular demand.

Maeterlinck seemed to be lowering his standards as early as 1902, when he wrote *Monna Vanna,* and the fairy play, *L'Oiseau Bleu* (*The Blue Bird*), confirmed this impression. They were world successes in their day, but no one dreams of reviving them now, and they are only read for historical interest.

In the light of this development, writers on literature, particularly in France, have reconsidered the merits of these two playwrights. Maeterlinck is declared to be artificial, and charged with always borrowing his ideas from others, while Claudel is praised as the greatest Christian playwright of modern times— as a new Calderon.

There is no need to take sides in this contest, and it is perfectly possible to admire Claudel without prejudice to Maeterlinck. In the pages that follow, more attention is given to Maeterlinck than to Claudel, and for a simple reason: he has had much greater significance for modern drama, not merely through *Pelléas et Mélisande*—immortalized in Debussy's music—but also through his one-act plays. Works such as *L'intruse* (*The Intruder*) and *L'interieur* (*The Interior*) continue to fascinate, and must surely be due for revival. They possess undoubted originality, and are written by a great poet—who has since lost his way in the mazes of poetry. One may also ask of Claudel, with all his steadfastness, whether he has ever written anything to compare with the masterpiece of his youth, *L'Annonce faite à Marie* (*The Tidings brought to Mary*).

Maurice Maeterlinck was compelled by his father to enter the legal profession, and he practised for a while at the courts in Ghent, but soon proved his unsuitability by losing a series of cases. He had long been writing verse and prose poems, and belonged to a group of young Belgian poets, school friends, who had come under the influence of the French symbolists. It is said that he himself, with the help of a friend, printed the first edition of twenty-five copies of his play, *La Princesse Maleine,* in a stable which had been fitted up with a press. An article by Mirbeau, who was loud in his praise, made him famous overnight. The roars of laughter with which his enemies greeted the play only spread its fame. The way for symbolist drama lay wide open.

In appearance Maeterlinck fails to conform to the impression given by his plays. He is a broad-shouldered Fleming, but by nature he is subtle and sensitive, with a dislike of noise and fame and so taciturn that not even his nearest friends have much to tell about him. Once he had achieved financial independence he retired to a deserted monastery, which he purchased and turned into a home.

Maeterlinck's objective as a mature playwright has been excellently expressed in the essay dealing with the tragic element in everyday life, in *Le Trésor des Humbles* (*The Treasure of the Humble*). He complains that tragedians are only aware of life's violent and primitive elements, and that this is the reason why our theatres and dramatic art are as out of touch with reality as sculpture: "When I go to the theatre I feel as if I weres pending a few hours with my ancestors and their incoherent, prosaic and brutal outlook on life. I watch a deceived husband murdering his wife, a woman poisoning her lover, a son avenging his father, a father sacrificing his children, children killing their father; I see kings murdered, maidens seduced and honest men thrown into prison, all those themes traditionally regarded as sublime, but whose sublimity—so superficial and so materialistic—shows itself only in the shedding of blood, tears and death."

In contrast to this traditional conception of tragedy, Maeterlinck advocates an everyday tragedy which is more real, more profound and more in keeping with our true existence: "Is it not quietness that is terrifying when one thinks about it, and when the stars look down on it? I have come to think that an old man, seated in his armchair, simply waiting beside the lamp, listening, without knowing it, to all the eternal laws that reign about him, interpreting, without understanding it, what there is in the silence of the doors and windows and in the small voice of the light, undergoing the presence of his soul and of his destiny, leaning a little his head, without suspecting that all the powers of this world are intervening and watching in his room like attentive servants, not knowing that the sun itself sustains the little table on which he rests his elbows and that there is not a planet in heaven nor a power of the soul which is indifferent to the dropping of an eyelid or the disclosure of a thought—I have come to think that this motionless old man was living in reality a deeper, more human and more general life than the lover who strangles his mistress, the captain who wins a victory, or the husband who avenges his honour."

In his critical attitude to pathetic and heroic tragedy, Maeterlinck stood close to the naturalist school, for both were concerned with the tragedy of everyday life, and both came to the same conception of a static play without action. There was a good deal of naturalism in Maeterlinck, above all in his technique. Like the Flemish painters of the 15th century he had a capacity for depicting minute and realistic detail, but he also set his figures against a background of gold, and the main impression they leave is not one of naturalism. It was natural that Maeterlinck should place many of his plays in a world which reminds one of the Breton novels. Even when he allows his characters to wear contemporary dress he is not concerned, as the Naturalists were, with external settings but with an inner atmosphere. By describing a piece of real life he does not wish to tempt the spectator to believe that he is witnessing something real. He is anxious to give an impression of the inner reality, the infinity that lies behind every event in real life.

Maeterlinck considers that our souls can apprehend each other without help from the senses, and that we gradually learn to communicate with each other in this inner way: "There must be something other than the dialogue which by external standards is necessary. It is really only those words which at first seem unnecessary that mean anything in a play. They contain the soul of the play. Alongside the inevitable dialogue there is nearly always a second dialogue which is apparently unnecessary. Watch carefully, and you will realize that this is the only dialogue to which the soul is attentive, for only in it is the soul discussed. You will also find that it is the purport and range of this unnecessary dialogue which finally determine the value of the play and its influence."

Behind all this there appears a philosophy akin to that of Swedenborg, namely that beyond this visible universe there is another invisible one, and that even our most ordinary words contain a hidden symbolical meaning. It is also founded on observation, in so far as words, apparently uttered about the most trifling and ordinary matter, acquire an added significance for us according to the context and atmosphere in which they are spoken.

During the period when *The Treasure of the Humble* was being written, the play which Maeterlinck felt most fully met these demands for the spiritualization of the stage was Ibsen's *The Master Builder*. At this time his own plays also conformed to his theories. But Maeterlinck had begun to write plays before the book was written, and before he had become acquainted with various types of mysticism.

Maeterlinck's first play, *Princess Maleine* (1889), does not entirely conform to the canons he was later to lay down. It is full of action and has a large cast. The story was taken from a tale by the brothers Grimm, about a wicked stepmother, Jungfrau Malene, and is set in a Holland of fantasy not unlike Hamlet's Denmark. Princess Maleine has fallen in love with young Prince Hjalmar, but his stepmother separates them and Hjalmar is betrothed to her daughter, Uglyane. Finally Maleine is strangled by her stepmother, and as the play ends the Prince kills first his stepmother and then himself, leaving only the infirm old king.

The drama is a chronicle play, like those of Shakespeare, and is constructed in the same way. The scenery is changed with every scene, almost all the action takes place on the stage, and the play ends with a general blood-bath, as in Hamlet. People act without discernible motives, and the characterization is even slighter than in Elizabethan drama. Sometimes the characters seem no more than puppets, helpless, unperceiving and awkward in their speech. In this deliberately naive setting we find elements of modern symbolism, and characters whose normal style of speech is awkward, almost childish, occasionally utter lines indicating the over-sensitiveness of an artist.

In the final act there is a man in the castle who says "All the walls are trembling, as if in fever." This feverish tremor is also typical of the inhabitants of the castle. They often repeat the same word four or five times. In their quieter moments they make subtle comments, or let fall cryptic remarks.

By now Maeterlinck had developed to the full the stylized

characters and the inconsequential dialogue, with its pauses for silence and its many repetitions, sometimes rising in anguish, sometimes dying away in melancholy. One feels as if one had landed, not in an unreal past peopled with shadowy heroes, but among a group of symbolist poets posing in artificial light and uttering the most commonplace remarks with profound solemnity to the accompaniment of affected gestures.

The play was much parodied, and Maeterlinck himself admitted later that the characters seemed like sleep-walkers continually dragged away from a nightmare. Obviously he was not really satisfied with the melodramatic content of the play.

The next two dramas, in 1890, were one-act plays, *The Intruder* and *Les aveugles* (*The Blind*, or *The Sightless*), set in an indeterminate period, probably contemporary. In both, Death is the uninvited guest. They contain practically no action, are concerned primarily with atmosphere, and both express the same philosophy of life. In *The Intruder* the members of a family are all assembled one night in the dark hall of a castle. In a neighbouring room lies a mother suffering from puerperal fever. Her husband and her brother try to persuade each other and the rest of the family that all will be well. The sick woman was delivered of her child with much difficulty, but that afternoon she was looking better. A greater cause of concern should be the new-born child, which has not uttered a single cry. But her father, aged and blind, hears what the others do not hear, that the nightingales have stopped singing, that someone is sharpening a scythe; it is the gardener, who is mowing the grass on the eve of the Sabbath. He believes he hears someone coming in—but there is no one there. The others shake their heads and think him strange. He replies that he considers them to be more blind than he is himself. Anxiety increases, and finally what the old man has foreseen from the beginning occurs. A nurse comes in from the other room, makes the sign of the Cross, and in silence the rest of the family go into the dead woman's room, while the old man is left to close the play with the despairing cry, 'Where are you going? Where are you going? They have left me all alone.'

The same theme is treated in *The Blind* a play inspired by Pieter Breughel's well-known picture. A group of blind folk are sitting in a forest, waiting for their leader to return. He is an old half-blind priest who has taken them from their hospital for a walk, and has now gone to fetch water for them. He does not return, and they feel the approach of night and the snow beginning to fall. Then the hospital dog joins them, the only creature who can see in the group. One blind man catches hold of the dog, who leads him to the tree where the old priest has fallen dead. They try to revive him, but he is already cold and has been dead all through the play. The little child of a blind and mad woman begins to cry, and they wonder if there is anyone in the neighbourhood who can save them in their distress. The child continues to cry with ever-increasing misery, and the blind call for mercy; but no answer comes.

Here, as in *The Intruder*, is shown Maeterlinck's pessimistic conception of mankind wandering blindly and aimlessly through mist and darkness with nothing but death as their ultimate goal.

The death theme is handled in various ways in Maeterlinck's later plays. The setting of *La Mort de Tintagiles* (*The Death of Tintagiles*) is outside and inside the so-called "sick castle," and here death is a nightmare which causes the hoarse voice of the old porter to falter, passes through closed doors and in the darkness seizes on little Tintagiles, guarded though he is by his two sisters.

Moving and perfect of its kind is a short one-act play of 1894, *The Interior*. Here also Death is the chief character, but he has done his work before the play begins: a young girl has drowned herself. Her relations utter no word that we can hear, but we see them through the window of the house at the back of the stage. When we first see them they are sitting happily in the living-room in the light of the lamp—father, mother, two daughters and a baby sleeping in its mother's lap.

At the front of the stage an old man of eighty and two of his grandchildren are talking to the Stranger who found the dead girl. Yesterday she was sitting in the lamplight with her sisters; now she has gone. Why? "Nobody knows," says the old man, "And what does anyone know? Perhaps she was one of those who don't want to say anything, and everyone of us has in his heart at least one reason for not wanting to live. One can't look into a soul as one can look into a room."

He feels the deepest sympathy for the unfortunate family:

"They are too confident in this world . . . They are separated
from the enemy only by defenceless windows. They believe
that nothing will happen to them because they have shut the door,
and they don't know that things also happen in their souls, and
that the world does not stop short at the door of a house."

Gradually a group of villagers approaches, bearing the dead
girl on a litter of branches. The old man is compelled to disturb
the evening peace in the lamplight. We see him enter the room,
where he is invited to sit down. His manner creates uneasiness,
and we watch the mother rise trembling to her feet. She asks the
old man a question and he nods assent. They all rush to the door,
and the room empties, except for the baby, left lying in the chair.
The Stranger brings the play to an end with the words "The child
has not awakened." It is only the newly-born who fail to realize
the anguish of death. All the rest of us live lives of misery.
Sometimes we believe we are happy and secure, and do not know
that fate is always deceiving us, and that it ruthlessly pursues its
way.

The same idea of fate dominates Maeterlinck's earliest plays.
The first of these is *Pelléas and Mélisande* (1892).

Mélisande is married to the elderly Golaud, but falls in love
with his younger brother, Pelléas. The story somewhat resembles
that of Tristan, or the Paolo and Francesca episode in Dante. But
Mélisande's love for Pelléas does not in Maeterlinck lead to any
closer relationship. On her deathbed she affirms that she and
Pelléas have never committed any sin together.

The basic idea of the play is that love—like life and death—
is governed by fate. Pelléas is killed by his brother, and Mélisande
withers like a flower. The doctor's comment is, "She was born,
without reason, to die—and she dies without reason." King
Arkel, the grandfather of Pelléas, and the wise old man beloved
of Maeterlinck who sees further than anyone else, says of her:
"She was a poor little creature of mystery, as we all are." In words
that recall Strindberg's *A Dream Play* he says, "If I were God I
would have pity on the human heart."

What Maeterlinck makes plain in this play, as in several that
follow it, is the irresistible, fateful and innocent quality of the
love which binds the two lovers. When Pelléas realizes his love
for Mélisande he avows it to her, and says that he is resolved to

go away. She replies that she has loved him from the first moment that she saw him. There are never any long explanations between them. "Men's souls are very silent," says wise King Arkel.

Compared with the burning passion of the Tristan story, that of Maeterlinck seems remarkably cool, almost as cool as the well where the two lovers liked to sit and carry on their leisurely conversation. The castle is old and mossy, its inhabitants remote from the world, and there are no sharp contrasts between light and shade.

Maeterlinck himself seems already to have realized that his brittle romantic poetry was becoming monotonous when in 1895 he met the beautiful opera singer, Georgette Leblanc, later to be his wife. According to her, he was already saying then that he was tired of his fairy princes and princesses, and was proposing to give up his work on puppet plays, which led nowhere.

Nevertheless, he continued for some years to write plays in the same style, though he did adopt a more conciliatory attitude to life. Georgette Leblanc was a revelation in the luxuriant fin-de-siècle style, and created a sensation in the streets when she appeared dressed as a woman from a Rubens picture. In the first play which Maeterlinck wrote under her influence he tried to contrive that the new ideal woman should triumph over the fairy-tale world, but was unsuccessful.

Aglavaine et Sélysette is really a variation on the same theme as *Pelléas and Melisande*, but here there are two women, who are rivals for one man. Méléandre is living happily with little Sélysette, but the lovely Aglavaine comes to visit them. Méléandre and Aglavaine fall in love at first sight. To avoid standing in the way of their love Sélysette throws herself from the old tower, in the hope that they will believe it was an accident. They discover her plan and, to judge by the mood of the final scene, the shock kills their love. The tragic ending is supposed to resemble Goethe's *Die Wahlverwandschaften*, but really it is more like Musset's *No Trifling with Love*.

Both Goethe and Musset, however, conceive of the triangle relationship as a tragic one, whereas Maeterlinck, as one can see in both his plays and his letters, tried his best to make the play end in harmony. Why should such trifles as jealousy and selfishness come between three people who love each other? Aglavaine asks Sélysette, "Isn't it strange, Sélysette—I love you, I love Méléandre, Méléandre loves me and he loves you, too; we all love each other, and yet we cannot live happily together, because the time has not yet come when human beings may achieve such a relationship." Against his will, Maeterlinck was driven to the tragic conclusion, "My characters do as they choose. I can no longer guide them."

In the preface to a collection of his early plays which Maeterlinck published in 1902 he explained that in Aglavaine and Sélysette he wanted death to surrender some of its power to love, wisdom or happiness, but death refused. In this preface he is dreaming about a new kind of play, which without losing any of its beauty can proclaim a happier truth than the one he used to preach, about death being always with us.

In his next plays, which he himself describes as texts for opera composers (and they were so used), he tried in various ways to escape from his earlier outlook. In *Ariane et Barbe-bleue ou la Délivrance Inutile* (*Ariane and Bluebeard, or Useless Deliverance*) he introduces all the fairy princesses of his earlier plays, such as Mélisande, Sélysette and others, as prisoners in Bluebeard's dungeons. The heroine, Ariane, a new incarnation of Georgette Leblanc, goes down to release them. But though Bluebeard is wounded and the gates to freedom are open, not a single one of the captives will avail herself of the new-found freedom. This trifling piece reflects accurately Maeterlinck's half-conscious realization that his delicate dramatic technique would never survive the bright sunlight to which he was proposing to expose it. What Maeterlinck needed was a more powerful and logically constructed plot than he had hitherto taken the trouble to work out. His imaginative powers were actually not very great, and the half-developed plots of his early plays suited him best. From now on he began, more and more deliberately, to work with borrowed themes.

His very next play, *Sœur Béatrice* (*Sister Beatrice*, 1901), is an instance of this—a rather uninspired dramatization of a so-called *conte dévot*. The author was a 13th century monk, Gautier de Coincy, who wrote a number of similar Mary legends. This is a story of a nun who ran away from her convent. When she returned, destitute and penitent, she found that nobody had noticed her absence, because the Holy Virgin had stepped down from her niche and donned her habit while she was away. Maeterlinck could have turned this legend into a moving drama about the power of faith, or treated it half-ironically, as Anatole France did so well in his remarkable story, *Le jongleur de Notre-Dame*, which retells another legend from the same collection. But he seems to have been uncertain which method to adopt.

In his first great stage success in 1902, *Monna Vanna*, Maeterlinck definitely returned to the conventional, more romantic type of drama. Nowadays we are so certain that this brilliant success marked the beginning of Maeterlinck's poetic downfall that Georgette Leblanc was very careful, when she wrote her *Souvenirs* in 1934, to deny that he wrote the play to provide her with a great part. It is true that it was her first straight part, and that she played it on several European tours, but obviously Maeterlinck was influenced by other considerations also. It must indeed have been depressing to spend year after year writing plays which could only be performed at the rather exclusive Théâtre de L'Oeuvre, and of which the critics always said that they were wonderful poetry but really rather too delicate for the limelight of the stage. When he was over thirty Maeterlinck still had no income of his own, and lived with his very prosperous, but quite uneducated parents. In 1897 Rostand achieved his greatest success of the century with *Cyrano de Bergerac*. It must have been a temptation to present a historical theme in that way. Moreover, Maeterlinck, who had been studying natural history and producing theories about the life of the bee, had come to adopt the Darwinian faith in progress which did not accord well with his earlier pessimism.

The main theme in *Monna Vanna* is that in order to save the beleaguered city of Pisa from starvation Monna Vanna agrees to the conditions of the Condottiere captain, Prinzivalle, that she shall spend a night in his tent, naked except for her cloak. The contemporary world was familiar with the legend of Lady Godiva, who saved the city of Coventry from the cruel taxation which her husband had imposed on it by complying with his wish that she should ride across the market-place, covered only by her flowing hair. This legend was retold in Tennyson's famous poem. Maeterlinck apparently took the idea from an old painting by a Dutch master.

Maeterlinck combines the medieval legend with an idea from Flaubert's *Salammbo*, where the heroine, to save her native city Carthage, makes her way to the enemy commander's tent and gives herself to him. This piece of borrowing did not escape the notice of his contemporaries.

While Flaubert allowed his heroine to lose her heart to that grim warrior, Matho, Maeterlinck conceived the story in a more idealistic way. Prinzivalle and Monna Vanna used to play together as children when he was only twelve and she was eight, and he has preserved such an imperishable memory of her beauty that when she arrives in his tent he does not even allow her to open her cloak, but immediately orders provisions to be sent to Pisa.

When she returns to Pisa with Prinzivalle neither her husband nor the inhabitants of the city are willing to believe that she has not been seduced. To save Prinzivalle from torture and death she is obliged to declare, untruthfully, that he did ravish her, and that she has therefore a claim to him as her prisoner. The play ends with her being given the keys of Prinzivalle's prison. Her secret intention is to elope with him.

Maeterlinck's intention is not to create the counterpart of *A Doll's House*, as some critics have supposed. His purpose is rather to emphasize that human life is worth sacrifice, even the sacrifice of such duties as might be held sacred. "Believe me," says Marco, Monna Vanna's father-in-law, and a new version of the wise old man, "There is nothing comparable in value to the saving of a life; all the ideals of men, all that we call honour, faith and the like, are mere playthings when set beside that."

Monna Vanna is an effective play, but lacks the artistic distinction that marked Maeterlinck's early puppet plays. The characters have lost their capacity for silence and swell the dialogue with eloquent speeches that sometimes last for a page. The half-light has gone and everything is bathed in bright sunshine.

Maeterlinck is not at home in such strong light. Rostand came from the south of France and was a childlike enthusiast by temperament. *Cyrano* sounds no great depths, but it is transparently clear, graceful and witty. Maeterlinck was incomparably the

greater poet and above all the more original writer. But mist
and melancholy were his proper element. Like the people of
Pisa, we find it rather difficult really to believe in Monna Vanna.

Maeterlinck the symbolist now began to adopt the universal
language of romanticism, and taking subjects from any quarter,
the Bible, the Renaissance and the Fairy Tale, he turned them
into plays. His first great success was the fairy play, *The Blue
Bird,* which was written in 1908, was given its very first performance at the Moscow Theatre, and was then performed all
over the world. It is much more allegorical than Atterbom's
play of the same name. The Woodcutter's young children,
Tyltyl and Mytyl, learn in a dream that they are to go and fetch
the blue bird, that is happiness, for a friend who is ill. They go
off to the 'pays bleu,' where they see all sorts of wonders. The
conclusion is that complete happiness, the real blue bird, does not
exist. When they wake up in their own beds they see life with
new eyes, while their little friend has identified the blue bird
with a dove which they had had in a cage when the play began
but did not think was blue enough. The moral of the play is that
such happiness as we can achieve is always near us, and that we
only lack the ability to recognize it.

When Maeterlinck ceased to be a poet, and became instead an
author of poetry books for grown-up children, all the world's
honours were showered upon him. He received the Nobel
Prize, was made a Belgian Count, and continued to write dis-
quisitions on philosophy which seemed to say less and less, as
well as scientific articles and plays. From having been a pioneer
of symbolism he became a mere echo of other men's opinions.
Other authors studied his early plays and developed his ideas in
new ways, but the real founder of symbolistic drama had said
what he had to say, and the plays which he continued to write
were no more than drudgery.

Despite the inglorious end of his career, Maeterlinck was
undoubtedly an original writer. His first three volumes of
puppet plays started a poetic revolution, in much the same way as
MacPherson did with Ossian in the 18th century. He created a
peculiar poetic setting, half medieval, half modern, which was to
reappear in many forms in the works of his successors all over the
world. Like MacPherson, he also created a new poetic prose

which influenced the style of his followers, whether they chose prose or verse as their medium of expression.

Paul Claudel developed independently of Maeterlinck, and the similarities that can be traced between them result from the fact that they had the same masters, the lyrical poets of the symbolist school and Villiers de L'Isle Adam the playwright. Some of Claudel's plays had already been drafted in the Eighties, he tells us. His finest work, *The Tidings brought to Mary* was completed, in its first but still imperfect form, in 1892. Though it was not until after Maeterlinck's appearance that his own works received any attention from literary circles, Claudel actually began to write plays at the same time.

His style is very different from that of Maeterlinck, who during his great period was very sparing with dialogue, sometimes contenting himself with the barest indication of his meaning. Claudel, on the other hand, is notable for his wealth of words. His characters do not speak—they chant in a language which seems biblically inspired. This seems reasonable in *The Tidings brought to Mary*, which is called a mystery, but it recurs in all Claudel's plays, even those which have a present-day setting, such as *L'Échange* (*Exchange*), a marriage play.

Another peculiarity of Claudel is that in one and the same play he can both ignore and over-emphasize the demands of style. A recent play, *The Satin Slipper*, is set in 16th century Spain, and ends at the time of the loss of the Armada. The characters, the situations and the stage directions have become allegorical and didactic.

Claudel's best plays were performed at L'Oeuvre, but except for *The Tidings brought to Mary* have hardly ever been performed outside France. It is really only in this play, and particularly in the decisive scene, that Claudel's stature is equal to that of the great masters of drama. This is the scene where young Violaine, a leper who has been deserted and abandoned by everyone, restores to life her sister's dead child, and takes him under her cloak. The play much resembles Hartmann von der Aue's *Der Arme Heinrich* which Hauptmann dramatized in Germany. In both plays leprosy is regarded as a trial sent by God, which can be cured by human love. Violaine sees life opening out before her and is about to marry Jacques Hury when, moved by pity for a leper, Pierre de Craon, she kisses him. This cures him of the disease, but Violaine herself catches it. Her sister, Mara, is in love with Jacques and tells him about the kiss. When Violaine discovers the first symptoms in herself she tells Jacques about them. He then deserts her and marries her sister, Mara. Mara conceals the fact that Violaine restored her dead child to life, and even tries to kill her. Though Violaine is blind and her body is consumed with leprosy, Mara notices that Jacques cannot forget her. In the rather weak final act Violaine, dying, is confronted with Jacques, who now at last learns the truth.

In this dramatized legend of a saint, the plot, as often in Claudel, is unnecessarily complicated and the play is over-weighted with long liturgical passages. What gives the drama a higher place than Maeterlinck's *Sister Beatrice*, which is also a modern miracle play, is the fact that Claudel really believes in a possibility of a miracle, and communicates his faith to the audience. He has drawn an excellent picture of the young heroine, Violaine, particularly in the first scenes where she is an ordinary happy woman ready to share her happiness with the sick Pierre de Craon. He was smitten with leprosy as a punishment for having once tried to assault Violaine.

No one around her understands her sacrifice, and even on her deathbed when she tells her story she is not moved by any sense of self; she has only been God's tool.

Claudel might have put most of his plays into medieval dress; they belong to the world of pious legend and to his self-sacrificing Catholic faith. In *Exchange*, written in 1893—the year after the first version of *The Tidings brought to Mary*—Claudel tried for a change to place his heroine in a modern American setting; at that time he was serving as a diplomat in the United States. The play is a curious mixture of primitive religion and a very lightly sketched American background. There is the American multi-millionaire, Thomas Pollock Nageoir, who sings paeans of praise to the dollar, industrial enterprize and his mistress. She is Léchy Elbernon, an intoxicating and intoxicated actress, and both might well have come from the pages of a popular magazine. In the French girl, Martha, the faithful wife of a good-for-nothing Louis Laine, Claudel has created another character of the type of Violaine. The plot is highly melodramatic.

Claudel's best known play in his later period is *L'Otage* (*The Hostage*), which is set in 1812 and ends with the fall of Napoleon and the return to the throne of the rightful king. In the castle of Coufontaine, or rather in the monastery which is all that remains of it after the Revolution, there lives Sygne de Coufontaine. She has just promised her hand to her cousin, and they are the only surviving members of the family.

Without his cousin's knowledge, her fiancé has installed in the house an elderly stranger who turns out to be none other than the Pope, whom Napoleon has been hunting. Meanwhile, Toussaint-Turelure, a product of the Revolution and a son of a local forest warden, has been made Prefect of the surrounding area and has learnt that the Pope lies concealed at Coufontaine. As the price of silence he demands that Sygne marry him. She is appalled at the thought, for Turelure caused her parents to be guillotined. After a long conversation with her Father Confessor she is convinced that it is her duty to sacrifice herself not merely for Christ but also for His Regent here on earth. She therefore marries the detestable Turelure, who at the fall of Napoleon hastily joins the Royalists.

When one reads the plays which followed *The Hostage*, *Le Pain dur* (*Hard Bread*) and *Le Père humilié* (*The Father Humiliated*), it is difficult to see what purpose was served by her sacrifice. Louis, the son of Sygne and Turelure, kills his father, whom he hates. In the final play he is the French Ambassador to the Vatican and responsible for the withdrawal of the French troops from Rome, which occasions the collapse of the Papal State. Louis, who has inherited his father's weathercock temperament, seeks his fortune in the Third Republic.

Claudel believed that he had written a trilogy of the Aeschylean type; he also translated the *Oresteia*, though his version is said to be a very free one. But it is difficult to find any point of similarity between the *Oresteia* and this chronicle play which presents the history of the Papacy from 1812 until the fall of the Papal State, together with a condensed version of French history during this period. Claudel does not seem particularly interested in the revolutionary changes occurring in the wider world, but he is profoundly moved by the fate of the Papacy: "The world can do without a king, but not without a Pope," says the exiled Pope in *The Hostage*.

As in all Claudel's plays, it is the heroines who come out best. This is true both of Sygne de Coufontaine and her blind grand-daughter, Pensée, whose spiritual life and world of ideas have been drawn with sensitiveness and understanding. Claudel's heroines always allow their fate to be governed by the Church, and, following the advice of the wise Pope, Pensée is betrothed to the one of the two brothers whom she does not love.

In Claudel's latest great work, *The Satin Slipper*, the heroine, Prouhèze, takes the advice of her guardian angel. At the beginning of the great dramatic sequence she is married to the elderly Don Pélage. After his death, and to preserve his life's work, she marries the detestable Don Camille, a renegade who has become a Mohammedan. The man she really loves is Don Rodrigue, but she is never united with him. Her virtue consists in remaining utterly faithful to the two men whom she has married against her will. Claudel's admirers consider this to be the finest play he has ever written, and the noblest expression of his religous faith.

The Satin Slipper is an imaginative chronicle play in the Elizabethan or Spanish style. It is divided into four 'days,' and perhaps includes more experiments in stage technique than any other play of the period. So far it has only been possible to produce an abbreviated version. It is interesting to note, however, that Claudel, who is thoroughly conventional in his morals and whose religious attitude borders on the bigoted, has allowed himself complete freedom in his treatment of style and character and all the problems of the stage.

The introductions to his plays usually promise more than the continuations can perform. The opening scene of *The Satin Slipper*, which explains the title, gives us a delightful picture of the young heroine. As the play continues, Claudel's evangelistic zeal gets the better of him, and one's interest is dissipated among the many unnecessary characters and passages. He is a significant writer, but less as a dramatist than as a preacher. His plays have had very little influence on the development of modern stage drama.

While Maeterlinck and Claudel had difficulty in gaining stage success with their plays another writer of the same school, but of incomparably lower calibre, Edmond Rostand, succeeded in winning the heart of the great public. *Cyrano de Bergerac* was the theatrical triumph of the century, quantitatively perhaps the greatest that the history of the theatre has ever known. For some years the young author was universally acclaimed as the king of modern drama. This enthusiasm, however, began to wane even during his lifetime, and in histories of literature Rostand is now dismissed with a lack of appreciation which is as unjustified as the earlier excessive praise.

Rostand was an exact contemporary of Claudel but he came from the south, like his master Victor Hugo, and like Daudet and his Tartarin. The passionate troubadour and the boastful Gascon are the two standard types from the South of France. Rostand achieved the feat of combining them in Cyrano, a character with the bravado of a Gascon and the heart of a troubadour.

Before Rostand achieved this tremendous success he had spent his apprentice years in the Symbolist school as a writer of lyric poetry, and later of plays which did not meet with much appreciation and did not deserve to do so.

Rostand's first play, *Les Romanesques* (*The Romancers*, 1894), was an attempt to dramatize the world of Watteau. There was in his nature an element of affectation, and it was precisely in periods characterized by affectation that he found his themes, the period of the troubadour for *La Princesse lointaine*, (*The Faraway Princess*), the period of supreme affectation in which Cyrano is set, and the age of Rococo for *The Romancers*.

The plot of this play, in which two fathers pretend to be enemies in order to tempt their children to fall in love with each other, has also been used in a comedy by Otto Ludwig. It is not certain whether Rostand knew this work, but there is a similar situation in Musset's *A quoi rêvent les jeunes filles* (*What do young girls dream of?*).

It is of Musset and Marivaux that the play reminds us, though it lacks their psychological subtlety. The meaning is not that the young people will be cured of their romantic fancies when they have discovered how they have been puppets in their fathers' hands. The epilogue explains that they have only been deceived about the outer and unimportant appearance of things; in their hearts they have known the truth.

In his next play, *The Faraway Princess*, Rostand throws himself headlong into the most ethereal of romances. The real hero of the play, who does not appear very often on the stage, is the troubadour, Rudel. In character and style he is the perfect expression of the courtly, platonic affections of the Middle Ages. He is a character who has been treated by all the world's romantic writers, Heine, Browning, Swinburne and Carducci.

Like *Pelléas and Mélisande* the story is a variation on the Tristan theme. Rudel is at death's door, but before he dies he wishes to see Princess Mélissinde, for whom he has conceived a lofty passion through the songs of wandering minstrels. When at last he reaches Tripolis he is too weak to go ashore, and sends his friend Bertrand in his place. When the Princess catches sight of Bertrand she takes him for Rudel, and when he reads out the love poem that Rudel composed for the distant Princess she falls in love with him.

Meanwhile Rudel is still alive, though his last hour is near. During his final struggle with death the Princess and Bertrand come aboard, but the chaplain forbids Bertrand to cloud his friend's last hours by telling him of his intended deception. In a scene that is reminiscent of the end of *Hernani*, Rudel dies with his lips pressed against those of the Princess.

The plot anticipates that of *Cyrano*. Roxane is in love with the handsome face of Christian, but at the same time, and without realizing it, she loves the noble soul of Cyrano, for it was he who under the cloak of darkness made a declaration of love in Christian's name and wrote his letters for him.

Rostand's idealism is not profound, but it is genuine. The superficiality of his characterization is plainly apparent here, as well as his liking for startling stage effects. The plot is unnecessarily complicated, and the dialogue tediously wordy.

None of Rostand's early plays was particularly successful, least of all *La Samaritaine* (*The Woman of Samaria*), with its New Testament subject and the figure of Christ as an actor in the play.

Cyrano de Bergerac made him world-famous at once, and the morning after the première on 28th December, 1897, the French critics were prophesying that this date would mark a new epoch in drama as clearly as *Le Cid* and *Hernani* had done. This exaggeration was disproved by events. *Cyrano* did not turn out to be the beginning of a revolution, not even in France. The play is a vigorous and faithful revival of the great heroic drama of the French classical and romantic periods; it is in no sense a new creation.

Subject to these reservations, however, it cannot be denied that *Cyrano* exercised an influence on modern drama. Its remarkable success was convincing proof that the day of historical drama was not yet past, as critics tended to assert. The increase in the popularity of historical plays in all countries around the turn of the century is not unrelated to *Cyrano de Bergerac,* and it was never really dropped from the repertory lists of French theatres. Even in Sweden it is constantly revived, and always with success. It is unjust, too, to complain of the public's bad taste. The play is remarkable neither for its merits nor its faults. It has no unusual artistic merit, nor does it make greater concessions to the public's liking for stage effects than plays usually do.

Cyrano's struggle against a cruel fate, his ability to stand fast by his ideals in the face of opposition and defeat, his determination to put a brave face on humiliation and poverty, and finally, when all else fails, to go down with a brave gesture—all this is not something particularly French or 18th century; it is universal in its appeal. This play resembles too painstaking a copy of an old master, a typical, average piece of Dutch painting, with a few bold strokes of the brush added by Franz Hals.

Cyrano de Bergerac was a lucky shot. Rostand had found a period which perfectly matched his temperament. The early 17th century was an age of affectation, of idealism and sensibility, of gallant and elaborately turned phrases. When Rostand endowed Cyrano with his own exalted passions and his too brilliant vocabulary he gave the play its natural period flavour.

The beginning of the 17th century was also an age of military bravado, of the *Fronde* and *The Three Musketeers.* When Rostand makes D'Artagnan wish Cyrano luck and shake his hand, he clearly indicates that we are in a period where no act is too heroic to be believed. Cyrano is allowed to vanquish a hundred men and to tell the tale with his characteristic gallows humour. His long nose prevents his being taken really seriously by the audience, even when he is carrying out deeds of incredible heroism or showing a superhuman capacity for selfless resignation and exalted idealism. He has a half-mocking, half-tragic way of looking at himself, but Rostand does not allow us to witness any real soul-searching in him, and he does not even give us the impression that such a thing has ever happened.

Cyrano quickly selects the attitude which he feels honour compels him to adopt, and then abides by it stubbornly to the end. He is perfectly aware that such quixotic behaviour will not earn him esteem, but he is incapable of acting otherwise. The moral rectitude of the hero, which has been emphasized by modern dramatists from Schiller to Ibsen, practically reached its climax with Cyrano, the poet and long-nosed braggart. The effect was smaller and less convincing in him than in many of his predecessors, because he is so completely lacking in any sense of doubt. Cyrano belonged to an age when men acted more from impulse than reflection. He was created by an author who was in complete sympathy with him. This is why Rostand was able to work on audiences to whom the heroes of Kleist, Hebbel and Ibsen, with all their introspection, will always remain incomprehensible.

Nearest to Cyrano probably come Victor Hugo's heroes, for they are based on a similar antithesis. Just as Hernani and Ruy Blas bear noble souls under their robber cloaks or servants' uniforms, so Cyrano's sensitive and poetic soul contrasts with his robust exterior and his extravagant boastfulness. The two sides of his character drive him from one deed to another, each more heroic, more wildly idealistic than the last. He resembles Hugo's heroes in their unceasing desire to excel themselves. The knowledge that Roxane loves the stupid Christian causes him to do something more positive than merely to renounce his claims nobly; he wants Roxane to have Christian and to owe her happiness to him. To do this he determines that Roxane must not realize the extent of Christian's stupidity, so he composes letters for Christian, and takes his place in the dark to make that grand avowal of love which she has demanded. These tactics make it even more certain that he will lose Roxane, but they also give him the bitter-sweet satisfaction of knowing that it is really his soul, as expressed in letters and declarations of passion, that Roxane loves. Cyrano abides by his intention even when, sorely wounded, he visits Roxane in the final act. When he reads Christian's last letter, which he himself has written, his voice betrays his feelings. But when Roxane asks him if he loved her he steadfastly denies it, whispering at the end, "No, no, my love, I did not love you." Two lives have been destroyed for a dream; in the hour of Cyrano's death they both realize this. But Cyrano also knows that this struggle for a dream has been worth while just because it was a struggle, just because more than any other struggle it has demanded courage and sacrifice. In Rudel's song in *The Faraway Princess* Rostand praised that same love, noble because of its hopelessness, "plus noble d'être vaine."

Apart from Cyrano the characters in the play are insignificant. Fair without and hollow within, Christian is the antithesis of Cyrano, in the Victor Hugo style. Roxane says in the final act of the play that she has only loved one person but has lost him twice, a thought which Hugo might have expressed in the same way.   Rostand and he both revel in grand period pictures which still retain a festive quality.

Our own generation does not, however, find the play as poetic as did the audiences which filled the Théâtre Porte Saint Martin for six hundred performances, or the reading public which bought more than a million copies. What remains most firmly in the memory is probably the final act, with its autumn mood of falling leaves; the sonorous Gascon song is an imitation of a poem which was wrongly ascribed to the real Cyrano.

The play is like a rich brocade which on close examination is found to contain crudities of colour and gems which are not real, but this is less disturbing because it contains an undertone of burlesque. Less easy to forgive are the hackneyed situations of the Scribe type which occasionally occur in it.

In *L'Aiglon* (*The Eaglet*), which Rostand wrote three years later, we get an impression of the actor anxious to gain the applause of his audience. Here we have a loud-voiced patriotism, sentimental and full of speeches but lacking the ability to laugh at oneself that is to be found in Cyrano.

The play was written for Sarah Bernhardt, then no longer young, and was one of the attractions of the Paris Exhibition of

1900. To read it now is like being confronted in some out-of-the-way place by a vast and pretentious exhibition building, hastily constructed of shoddy material. It may be splendidly painted and equipped to please the eye during the short summer months, but seems frighteningly empty and dismal if put to longer use.

Why Rostand really failed was because he selected a profoundly tragic subject. Napoleon's unfortunate son, Frans of Reichstadt, assumed a burden that was too heavy for him when he tried to win again for France the glory that had been Napoleon's. Rostand did the same when he chose a theme that was too great for his poetic talent. One might almost believe that he realized this better than his critics when one reads his last play, *Chantecler*, where he writes with charming irony of the henhouse and its chief singer, the cock, who believes that his throat can rival that of the nightingale.

The Emperor's son, obsessed by Napoleon's dream, but lacking the power to realize it—this was the essence of the plot, but Rostand could not bring it out without resorting to theatrical devices.

Napoleon himself could not be brought on to the stage, so instead Rostand, in an unlucky moment, introduced a veteran of the Old Guard whose name was Flambeau, and who was a sort of travelling museum of Napoleon's relics. From various corners and pockets of his clothes he produces a snuff-box, a pipe and a glass, all bearing Napoleon's picture or his monogram. The tragic death of the Duke on the stage is also embellished with Napoleonic souvenirs. The cradle which the City of Paris presented at his birth is carried in, and the Grand Cross of the Legion of Honour is hung over his night-shirt. There is a statue of Napoleon in the room, and he hums the tunes of his father's day while he is receiving the sacrament.

The Eaglet is set in Scribe's period; a performance of a Scribe play is announced at a fancy-dress ball at Schönbrunn. This may explain the deliberate Scribe touches in the play, the manoeuvres and counter-manoeuvres and the endless disguises. Flambeau says somewhere that he is never satisfied simply with providing the basic needs, but has a crazy passion to 'faire du luxe.' It is this southern French characteristic which has got the better of Rostand in *The Eaglet*.

Although the faint protests against *The Eaglet* were drowned in shouts of approval, Rostand seems to have realized the validity of the criticisms. He wanted to be a poet, not just a stage technician. After *The Eaglet,* to the surprise of the public and the critics, he retired to the country, taking his family with him, and settled for ten years in a quiet corner of the Pyrenees. Rumours were rife about the great stories that he was going to dramatize, such as Faust and Don Quixote, and there was much disappointment when it was learned that he was actually writing a play about hens in a farmyard, with a cock as the hero. The idea came quite soon after *The Eaglet*, but Rostand had trouble in expressing it. In any case, he was ill at the time and was not confident about his subject. The play was not completed until 1909.

A work which had met so many obstacles and taken so long to write was awaited by public and critics alike with understandable suspicion, and the première did not dispel all doubts. Maeterlinck and his *The Blue Bird* were to triumph three years later, and *Chantecler* did not meet with the recognition it merited. In it Rostand took his revenge for *The Eaglet*. He spent ten years of his life on a play which he must have known the ordinary public would never approve, for *Chantecler* is more of a literary drama and actually a more original piece of work than *Cyrano*.

In most European countries there is a legend to the effect that a cock believes that he causes the sun to rise because he predicts it with his crowing. This notion is elaborated by Rostand in the style of a fable. Chantecler, the name of the cock in *Roman du Renard*, is convinced that without him all would be darkness and nature sunk in eternal sleep. The jeers of envious rivals cannot shake his faith. A golden hen pheasant lures him into the forest away from all his hens, but she cannot accomplish alone her wish to make him forget his mission. She therefore summons to her aid the songster of the night, the nightingale, and at his first note Chantecler feels himself finally defeated. It is the same for him as for all who hear the song of the nightingale; they believe that they are only listening for a minute, but when the singing is ended they find they have been listening all night. The sun has risen, but Chantecler has not summoned it with his crowing. Chantecler suddenly sees that he has lost his throne. When the dog from the farmyard comes to greet him and tell

him that everyone wants him back to bring up the sun, he answers
in a moment of gloom, "Now they have the faith which I have
lost." But his depression only lasts a moment and then he lets fly
a full-throated crow. When the pheasant asks in surprise why he
has done this he replies that it is his calling. The sun may have
risen without his help, but it remains for him to awaken all to
life, to open all eyes. "Who sees that his dream has died must die
at once, or else rise up in greater strength."

This simple story has sometimes been taken to be an allegory
on the fate of mankind, or in praise of the value of daily toil, or
as an exhortation to all men to do their duty without too great
illusions about its importance. This is a fairly widely held point
of view, but we grasp the purport of the play better if we consider what the poet's function is. He cannot give life to nature,
but he can open men's eyes to it, and he is most faithful to his
calling when he regards himself as a worker among fellow-
workers. "If I sing clearly and truthfully, and if every farm has a
cock who sings in his place, then there will be no more night,"
says Chantecler.

Rostand explained that the cock expressed his own dreams,
and indeed embodied something of himself. During this ten-year
period while he was working on the play he had come to realize
that his merits were overrated both by himself and by others.
Both in the troubadour of Rudel and in Cyrano he had shown
something of himself. Cyrano's self-sacrificing idealism becomes
little less than a desperate gamble, a desire to make all the noblest
and most extravagant gestures himself. Chantecler is less brilliant
and more natural. He is the hero of domestic virtues, the citizen and father of the family, the faithful guardian. But as with all
his fellow-countrymen, there is a touch of romance in his blood,
and he believes that really he is something quite different.
Rostand has brought out the sunny and frankly naive qualities of
this Tartarin of a cock in a very human way. He is 'un brave
meridional' like Tartarin, who finds it hard to see reality except
through the veil of romance. Daudet blames this trait of the
southern French on the burning sunshine which seems to shroud
everything in a haze. So it is with Chantecler. His imagination is
always a stage ahead of reality, and his sensitive soul is often
wounded.

In his posthumous play, *La dernière nuit de Don Juan* (*Don Juan's Last Night*), Rostand writes a sequel to the Don Juan legend which leaves that most famous of all heroes morally naked. The play was not published until 1921, and it consists of a prologue and two acts which were already complete when the first world war broke out. The best scene is the one where Don Juan, released from hell, is confronted by shades of the thousand and three women whom he has seduced. He has to remember their names, but is always guessing wrong, and the shades mock him as they turn away. Finally they say that he has never known them, never possessed them—it is they who have possessed him, just to pass the time away. Romeo and Tristan are the two real lovers who have left behind something of themselves in those they loved. Don Juan is a mere intruder who has struck down those who are already wounded. He appears to have possessed all women, but in fact has possessed none. There is one single shade whom he has occasionally met but who is not on this list of conquests, the white one, the Ideal. At last the unhappy Don Juan begins to long for hell, but the cruel Devil tells him that a hell of a special sort is reserved for him. He is not destined for eternal fire but eternal theatre; he is to be one of the puppets in the Devil's collection. The play is slightly influenced by the Button-moulder episode in *Peer Gynt*, but the thought is typical of Rostand, namely that only love that is unselfish and idealistic is real.

RUSSIAN DRAMA

IN the 19th century, long before Tolstoy and Chekhov became
world-famous, Russian dramatists had been preoccupied with
the social problems of their country; serfdom, corruption among
officials, luxury and idleness in the upper classes. The classical
example is Gogol's *Revizor* (*The Inspector-General*, 1836), which
soon became known outside Russia. The plays of Ostrovski
and Pisemski, on the other hand, written between 1850 and 1870,
were only rarely translated or played abroad and it was in Russia
round about the turn of the century, during the hey-day of the
Russian theatre, that they met with their warmest reception.
Sometimes their merit was exaggerated. In many books on the
theatre one may read that Tolstoy imitated, but did not surpass,
Pisemski's *Gorkaia sudbina* (*Bitter Destiny*) when he wrote *The
Power of Darkness.*

Bitter Destiny was written before the ending of serfdom. The
chief character is a serf who returns to his home after two years'
absence in St. Petersburg, to find that his wife has borne a child
to the young landowner. He kills the child, gives himself up, and
is deported to Siberia. The husband is a proud man and his
attitude is heroic when compared with the weakness of the
landowner. That he did not kill his wife can be explained by the
fact that as they were serfs their marriage was none of their own
making. What is more difficult to understand is why he kills the
child and not its father, since he is certain to be condemned in
either case. The plot may have been turned this way out of
deference to the censor. In spite of this rather mysterious point
the play is effective because of its closely-knit form. It is probably
the best Russian peasant play written before *The Power of Darkness*, but it certainly does not stand comparison with that masterpiece by Tolstoy. The fact that a man kills a child and gives

himself up to justice in Tolstoy's play also is not significant, for
Tolstoy's source was the report of a criminal trial, not *Bitter
Destiny*. Pisemski did not bring out the psychological implications of a bad conscience as effectively as Tolstoy, and he lacked
the deep human feeling and the religious awareness of *The
Power of Darkness*. It is doing an injustice to *Bitter Destiny* to
judge it in the same class.

The plays of Turgenev were somewhat neglected by his
contemporaries, but they came to occupy a firm position in
classical Russian repertory, and in our own day he is played all
over Europe and America. Turgenev wrote them round about
1840, when he was still uncertain whether to become a novelist or
a dramatist. Ultimately he came to the same conclusion as
Musset, whose *Proverbes* he often used as a model, that his plays
were only meant to be read, and was surprised to find towards
the end of his life that *Mesiats v derevne* (*A Month in the Country*)
had achieved great success in the theatre.

In this play Turgenev deliberately borrowed the plot and some
of the situations from a melodrama by Balzac, *La marâtre,* (*The
Stepmother*), which deals with the rivalry between a step-mother
and her step-daughter for a young man who had been the step-
mother's lover. To prevent the young people from being united
she poisons the girl, but the young man also takes poison and
follows her to death.

Turgenev was apparently trying to show that he could handle
such a story without introducing any crude effects. The twenty-
nine-year-old Natalia is not happy in her marriage, but cannot
quite make up her mind to leave her husband and run away with
the faithful friend who is always dancing attendance on her. A
newly engaged tutor then sets her heart on fire but her ward,
Vera, also falls in love with him. Both Natalia and Vera dislike
this state of rivalry, and Vera accepts the hand of a fat country
gentleman in order to escape from the house. Meanwhile Natalia
has been making her feelings all too plain, and her husband
suspects that something is going on behind his back. In order
to save the situation, the faithful friend confesses to Natalia's
husband that he has long been nursing a guilty passion for
Natalia which she has not returned, and that he is going away
for ever. He takes with him the twenty-year-old tutor, who was

at first flattered at being the object of two women's adoration but has by now become so entangled that he can see no way out. This tutor is a character rather like one of Musset's novices in the art of love, but more confused and bewildered. So Natalia has to return to her dull husband and live on alone with him.

A Month in the Country anticipates Chekhov in its attention to psychological detail, and also in the way the story returns full circle to its starting-point. *Leshii* (*The Wood Demon*), a study for *Diadia Vania* (*Uncle Vania*), resembles Turgenev's play in its general structure. Chekhov is supposed to have said that he tried to develop his technique on the lines of Turgenev's subtle analysis of everyday happenings. A letter to his wife shows that in his later years he no longer admired *A Month in the Country*. What he did praise at that time was *The Bread of others*, a moving play about an impoverished but proud old nobleman who is compelled to live as a dependant with a rich couple in the country. There is no trace of Chekhov's originality in Turgenev's graceful plays written in the French style.

Not until *The Power of Darkness* appeared did Russia take the lead in modern drama, or begin to produce work more significant than that of the French dramatists. One of the reasons for this advance was that the Russians were less bound by theories than the Romance playwrights.

LEO TOLSTOY

DURING his lifetime Tolstoy was only known as a play-wright through *Vlast tmi* (*The Power of Darkness*). *Plodi prosveshcheniya* (*The Fruits of Enlightenment*) was supposed to contrast with it as a satire on the upper classes and the current craze for spiritualism, but it is a weak play. The works which were published after his death, however, and which were much more frequently performed, serve to confirm his reputation as a dramatist.

The Power of Darkness was written in 1886, but permission was not given for its performance in Russia until after the death of Alexander III in 1894, though a printed version was widely read. It was first performed at the Théâtre Libre in 1888, where it was warmly applauded by Zola, and then a year later at the Freie Bühne in Berlin. Everywhere, with Ibsen's *Ghosts* and Strindberg's *Miss Julie*, it sponsored the growth of naturalistic drama. Actually it pointed the way to a wholly different sort of naturalism from that which Zola and Strindberg had fostered. *The Power of Darkness* is a dramatized story from the life of the people, and has therefore directly inspired both modern peasant drama and the sort of play about the proletariat of which Hauptmann's *Die Weber* (*The Weavers*) is the first masterpiece. Although the play is no longer performed, one is continually seeing new plays which are imitations of it.

The Power of Darkness has as its second title a Russian proverb, "If the claw has caught in the net, the bird will not escape." The play is partly a picture of life in the Russian countryside, and partly a study in the psychology of crime.

Zola demanded that the stuff of naturalistic drama should be taken direct from real life, and should be an actual 'case,' but in practice he tended to make plays out of his novels. Tolstoy, who did not consider himself to be a Naturalist, set about his task more thoroughly. He studied the reports of a case heard before the court in whose jurisdiction Yasnaya Polyana lay. At first he proposed to treat his material as a novel, but the wish to hear his characters speak was too much for him. Without departing from the spirit of the records, he wrote a play in which there was no padding and no mention of irrelevant incidents.

The main story, probably by coincidence, is not unlike that of *Thérèse Raquin*. The Don Juan of the village, a peasant called Nikita, has become the lover of his master's wife, Anysha, and has persuaded her to poison her old and ailing husband so that he can marry her and get hold of her money. Then Nikita becomes involved with Anysha's step-daughter, a sixteen year old half-wit, Akulina, and has a child by her. Then, in order to be able to marry her off, Nikita kills their child in a most barbarous fashion. The final act of the play includes Akulina's wedding. Under the influence of his pious father Nikita is seized with revulsion at his crimes, confesses them openly, and is dragged away by the gaolers.

Nikita is the black sheep of his family but he is no cold and calculating villain. His first crime was committed when he deserted his real love, an orphan girl, for the wanton farmer's wife and the prospect of becoming lord of the farm. Then one crime leads to another. He is fond of pleasure, over-confident, and inconsiderate, but not really cruel. With all his crudeness and violence he has the typical Russian sentimentality and unbalanced emotional life.

In Nikita's parents Tolstoy has created representatives of the two forces which, in his belief, struggle for mastery in the human soul, the mind that only seeks its own advantage and the heart that inclines instinctively to goodness. The contrast is the same one that Rousseau found in mankind, and which Tolstoy had already presented in Anna Karenina. In *The Power of Darkness* the spirit of selfishness is represented by Nikita's mother, Matriona, who is the most disagreeable character in the play and the real force behind the various crimes that are committed. She is a bustling old woman, quite unscrupulous in her desire to make her son's fortune, and perfectly ready to serve as a procuress or a blender of poisons. Her husband is the exact opposite, for Akim is a genuinely good man, a typical example of the illiterate saint

so common in Russian literature. When he first appears on the
stage the old man seems half crazy; he is a shy, stammering little
man, whose job is to empty the cesspits in the village. Whenever
he speaks he becomes confused, his sentences get entangled, he
stutters and repeats himself and can only utter the most commonplace remarks. Nevertheless, he is the only disinterested character
in the play, and every good action is the result of some impulse of
his. In the end his son, who has treated him in an impudent and
hectoring manner and yet with a consideration which he has
shown to nobody else, is finally persuaded by him freely to confess his crimes. When this has been done Akim is carried away by
a typically Russian ecstasy of expiation and joyfully embraces
Nikita, his own dear child, promising him God's protection. The
play was written after Tolstoy's conversion in 1879.

Besides these two there are several other excellently drawn
characters. There is Anysha, the energetic farmer's wife, covetous
and heartless. Her punishment, the faithlessness of Nikita, is
swift, but she retains to the end her bitter and vengeful cast of
mind. Akulina, an ugly, over-grown child, is at first completely
under her mother's thumb but later on, with the help of Nikita
and after her father's death, she learns to browbeat her in her
turn. Then there is Peter, always ill and whining, and a group of
gossiping old peasants and their wives who run in and out in
their stockinged feet.

Though Tolstoy did not attach as much importance to realistic
environment as his successors, Chekhov and Gorki, there is a
genuine flavour of the *mujik's* hovel in this play. The very
tone of the dialogue goes a long way to give an impression of the
setting. In contrast to Zola, Tolstoy does not write a single line
of rhetoric and very few which are faultless in logic or construction. Most of the dialogue is in peasant dialect which can
only be faintly conveyed in translation, but even so the absence
of elegant phrases is apparent. Everything, even scenes of
horror, seems to happen and be discussed as if it were quite
natural, with the result that the audience is doubly moved.

Nikita is neither thin-skinned nor soft-hearted; his conscience
is too robust for that. At first we hardly realize that he is reacting
against the crimes in which he has been involved, but when we
do, it only shows in onsets of bad temper which he tries to cure

with brandy. By this use of detail Tolstoy achieves much more dramatic effects. Nikita's attacks of conscience find their sole expression in his habit of throwing his concertina into a corner, or bursting into tears, or grumbling that he is bored. His conversion is introduced with equal suddenness as the outcome of his ever-growing disgust at his own crimes, and his distaste for the farmer's widow, who is drunk with most of her guests at Akulina's wedding. Nikita is the only sober man there, for alcohol no longer has any effect on him. He is always musing about his crimes, partly because his conscience is uneasy but partly also because they have served no purpose. When he meets his childhood love, Marina, who is now married to a drunken peasant, he is in despair because he has wasted his life for nothing. It only needs a word from his father—and this incident occurs offstage—to cause him, just when he is expected to bless the bride whose guardian he is, to pour out instead the tearful confession which will bring him to prison.

The Power of Darkness has the sure balance of classical drama, and its creative calm. Our world, with all its rottenness and crime, is presented with a sober and confident realism. The whole conception is treated on a tremendous scale, but Tolstoy never gives the impression of having to struggle to achieve it.

The mists roll thickly over Tolstoy's world of peasants, and the air is hard to breathe and yet there is no sense of black pessimism. Akim's apostolic gentleness, and the remorseful confession of Nikita which earns for him the same pardon that the thief on the Cross received, bear witness to Tolstoy's faith in the essential goodness of the Russian people, as indeed of any other people.

At the turn of the century Tolstoy took up playwriting again and seems partly to have worked on earlier ideas. His last three plays were not published until after his death in 1910, because he was anxious to avoid the constant quarrels between his wife and those fanatical adherents who were trying to persuade him to vest the copyright of his works in the people.

The Root of All Evil or *The Cause of it all*, which is dated spring 1900—though there may well have been earlier drafts—is based on the same theme as *The Power of Darkness,* the ineradicable wildness of the Russian spirit and its equally ineradicable goodness. The treatment, however, is lighter and more graceful. The chief part in the play is that of the nameless Stranger, but the real hero is the *mujik* Michael, who is typical of every Russian peasant. In the detailed list of characters he is described as "impulsive, self-centred, vain, strong." It might be added that when drunk he is a man of bloodthirsty violence, but when sober he is the most kindhearted of giants. "The root of all evil," the title of the play, refers to brandy.

The opening scene of the play shows us the women of the household, mother, wife and little daughter, worrying about the state in which the father of the family will return from his visit to the town. They are roused from their gloomy speculations by the patriarchal village constable, who introduces a stranger seeking lodgings for the night. He is a lean, under-nourished man, some forty years old, dressed in a threadbare frock-coat. With his foreign words and technical expressions he seems to the women to be a man of vast learning. He is a highway philosopher of the kind so often to be described by Gorki.

While the vagabond is delighting the ladies of the house with his store of wisdom, the husband returns in company with a good friend. They are both reeling drunk and boast that they have spent all their money on drink. This is too much for Marfa, the patient wife, who has not a scrap of food in the house, and she refuses to serve any more brandy for her husband and the guests. The husband is furious and, roundly abusing his wife, he clouts her over the head and grabs her shawl. In his drunken rage he is nearly killing her when the vagabond, almost drunk himself but retaining some instinct of chivalry and a faint echo of modern ideas of emancipation, rushes forward exclaiming, "You have no right at all to insult the female sex." The peasant is completely taken aback by this extraordinary remark, but afterwards threatens the wretched knight of the road with a box on the ears that will send him flying over the roof-tops. The stranger's only reply is to put forward his face courteously and invite him to strike, whereat Michael drops his hands, shakes his head and says, "That's an odd body."

His fit of rage over, the peasant tells his wife good-humouredly that she ought to light a candle for the stranger, "for had it not been for him I would have smashed you into little bits." He even pulls out a few kopeks, the last remains of his money, and a packet of tea and sugar which are the only material gains from his journey to town. The scene of drunken fury gradually becomes one of friendliness and sentimentality. With admirable speed, the stranger catches up with his friends and makes a speech in praise of brandy; the play ends with him embracing the others and singing a revolutionary song.

In the space of two scenes Tolstoy has given us a cross-section of the soul of the Russian people, with its fantastic paradoxes, and in the short final act the picture is completed. In the morning the *mujik* gets up, feeling out of sorts after his drinking-bout on the previous day, to discover that the stranger has made off while the household was still asleep. The packet of tea and sugar is also discovered to be missing. It is impossible not to connect the two events, and Michael sets out to catch the thief. With the help of his neighbours he drags home the vagabond, having found the packet in his pocket. The unhappy thief sees his last hour coming and, almost beside himself with fear, says that he is no thief but an expropriator, "a living force who can suffer for his convictions. If you were cultured people, you would understand . . ." Once again one may observe the magic effect of these learned and unfamiliar words on the hearers. The wife pleads that the poor fellow be allowed to go, since the packet has been recovered, but the husband repeats time after time, "So you're teaching me. Don't you think I know what to do without your help?" Finally he addresses himself to the stranger, reproaching him for his meanness. He becomes so moved by his own words that, anxious to outdo his wife in generosity, he hands over to the thief, to refresh him on his way, the stolen packet which is the only food in the house. Triumphantly he turns to his wife and says, "So you're going to teach me, are you?"

Such a noble gesture melts even the calculating heart of the vagabond, and with trembling voice he replies, "If you had beaten me like a dog I should have felt better. Don't you think I know what I am? I am a poor wretch—a degenerate subject, I should say. For Christ's sake forgive me." With a sob he drops the packet on the table and slinks quickly away, while the peasant is still muttering his stock reply, "So you're going to teach me, are you?" His more practical wife thanks God that he did not take the tea, and the old grandmother adds thoughtfully, "After all, he is a man too."

The drama is a realistic picture of peasant life, of the kind which is so fashionable in every country nowadays. What makes it stand out is, curiously enough, its light touch. It lacks entirely that heaviness and clumsiness which often seem inherent in dramatic presentations of the life of the people. The comedy is never forced and the manifestations of human feeling never degenerate into sentimentality.

Tolstoy naturally shared the opinion that alcohol was the root of all evil. He had once written a kind of dramatic sketch about the Devil sending one of his emissaries to teach the peasants how to distil vodka from grain. But Tolstoy had also, as Gorki tells us, an abiding sympathy for drunkards. He held that intoxication endowed people who were dull when sober with originality and wit, "with beauty of thought and a wealth of expression. At such times I am ready to sing the praises of wine." It is this freedom from prejudice which makes a slight peasant comedy into an impeccable work of art.

The two remaining plays, *Zhivoi trup* (*The Living Corpse* or *Redemption*) and *I svet vo tme tsvetit* (*The Light Shines in the Darkness*), are both profoundly serious and deal with Tolstoy's own tragedy in disguised form. The deep impression they make is increased by the fact that they are the frankest of his autobiographical works.

Tolstoy had handed over his property and the copyright of his early works to his wife, and had gone to live as a labourer at Yasnya Polyana. But this was only a compromise, and he was unhappy because he was not living according to his own principles. In the end, of course, he left his home in 1910, to die of exhaustion on a railway station in a Russian village.

Tolstoy took the original for *The Living Corpse* (1900) from real life—the story of a woman who believed her husband was dead, married again, and, when her original husband was shown to be alive, was arrested and condemned for bigamy. Combined with this story were incidents from his own life.

Protasov, who sees life in a different way from his wife, has become a burden to her, to his family and to his fine friends. He gives her his property, and goes off to lead a bohemian life of wine and song with the gipsies. His hope is that his wife will get her divorce and then be able to marry Karenin, a dull and respectable official whom she loved before she met Protasov. She, however, is a faithful wife with a high conception of her duty, and she will hardly admit to herself her love for Karenin, much less think of deserting her husband.

The knowledge of this constraint in his wife and the ill-success of their marriage has driven Protasov, not entirely against his will, on the downward path to drink and doubtful companions. Unfortunately, it is not enough to provide grounds for divorce to enable his wife to marry Karenin, for his family are ultra-conservative, and insist that he have the blessing of the Church on his marriage. Protasov therefore pretends to commit suicide, and allows his clothes to be found on a river bank. This notion, which is not exactly an original one, Protasov claims to have taken from Chernichevski's "What's to do." Happily, a few days later a body is found which the wife identifies as that of her husband. She is now a widow, and agrees to marry Karenin.

Protasov continues his anonymous existence in various drinking dens, but one evening in his cups he tells the whole story to a companion. His words are overheard by a police spy, he is arrested, and the Karenins are brought before the court. When Protasov hears that the most they can hope for is that his former wife will be separated from her present husband and reunited with him, he shoots himself at the door of the court-room, to allow them both to continue their lives in peace.

The chief interest in the play lies in the character of Protasov. At times he is an ascetic, renouncing the world; at others he is a man without principle, living only for pleasure, a nihilist like so many of his class. In one conversation with a friend he says, "For all of us in the circle in which I was born there are only three things to choose between, only three. The first is to have a career, make money and continue to add to the filth in which we live. This did not appeal to me. It may be that I did not know how to do it, but the main reason was that I did not want to do it. The second is to start to sweep away the filth, but to do that one has to be a hero—and I have never been a hero. The third is to forget everything, to drink, to roam, to sing; that is what I have done. And now I have finished my song."

In reality Protasov, though fallen from his own class, represents in a slightly different form the same fundamental ideas in the Russian soul that Tolstoy had already treated in *The Power of Darkness* and in *The Root of All Evil*. The conflict is still between bestial passion and the inexhaustible goodness of the human heart. But even at a higher level of culture there is no question of any internal conflict; we are not dealing with 'either-or' but with 'both-and.' Tolstoy believes that he is presenting universal human qualities. We are all a combination of beast and angel, of thief and saint.

The play is written with real pathos, and our indignation is directed primarily at the senseless laws which prevent the dissolution of an unhappy marriage such as that of the Protasovs, and also at the heartless conventions of social life in Russias. There is one scene, for instance, where a high-ranking friend of Karenin urges Protasov to commit suicide to make it possible for his wife to have a church wedding.

The Light Shines in the Darkness, which Shaw called "Tolstoy's greatest dramatic work," was begun just before 1890 and continued between 1900 and 1902, but was never completed. For the last act only rough drafts exist. It depicts Tolstoy's struggle with his own conscience, and the consequences for him and his dependants, and there are actually in this play forebodings of the tragic end which he foresaw more clearly than others. Like the hero of his play, he had thought more than once of running away, but had always stopped himself.

The poetic disguise is very thin, and we continually perceive through it the circumstances of Tolstoy's own life. In its autobiographical form it is often reminiscent of Strindberg's *Damascus* plays, but it is less compressed than these. Sentences from the dialogue are often to be found almost word for word in Tolstoy's writings, letters and journals. But he succeeded in making the play an independent work of art, attracting and absorbing even the reader who knows nothing of Tolstoy's personal life. He has not fallen into the usual trap that awaits the painter of self-portraits, the temptation to beautify his model. The hero of the play, Nicolai Ivanovitch Saryntsov, is no impressive prophet. Any contemporary of Tolstoy who wanted to describe him would have made him a much more heroic figure.

All the half-heartedness which Tolstoy found in his own life he has painted in his hero.

In the completed parts of the play it is not Nicolai Ivanovitch but his disciples who become the martyrs for his ideas. He himself continues to live in the luxurious home which he has bequeathed to his wife, so that he may escape the sense of living on other people's toil and suffering. In the fourth act there is a ball at Nicolai's house during which he makes the attempt to leave home, but has not the strength to carry it through.

Tolstoy's chief object in this play was to convince people of the truth of his ideas, even if the characters who presented them did not seem admirable. His concern, therefore, was to show that these ideas were greater and more significant than the frail vessels whose task it was to proclaim them. To see Nicolai Ivanovitch moving about in his usual setting is to realize that he is regarded as an unpractical dreamer. Tolstoy even allowed him to play in scenes in which he appeared in a more or less comic light.

On his first entry he shakes hands with the embarrassed servant. At a later stage he installs a carpenter's workshop in his Moscow house and tries, unsuccessfully, to use a plane because he feels that it is shameful to live in idleness. The carpenter wonders why His Excellency has to pick on his trade, in which there are already so many workers that it is hard to earn a living. Later still the carpenter asks him why he does not give away his possessions and he answers, abashed, "I wanted to, but I did not succeed. I gave them to my wife."

Until the period in the Seventies when he was troubled by problems of religious faith, Tolstoy had been a believer in the Orthodox Russian Church. After this period, when he came under the influence of the Bible critics, he preached undenominational Christianity with the Sermon on the Mount as its core, exactly as Nicolai Ivanovitch did. Like his hero, he was mainly concerned with ethical problems, and like him he suffered from being a parasite. According to his gospel it was above all important to avoid sharing in the guilt of evil-doing, to avoid offering resistance in any way, to act as little as possible according to previously determined principles, and to allow impulses to determine one's actions. "Not to act according to any made up plan," says Nicolai Ivanovitch, "but only when one's whole being craves action." The illogical attitudes which the hero adopts in the play are due simply to this fear on Tolstoy's part of doing too much. "It is worse to do too much than too little" is Nicolai Ivanovitch's motto. At other times he reproaches himself for continuing in this way to acquiesce in situations of which he disapproves. "Anyone is entitled to say . . . that I am a traitor, that I speak but do not act, that I preach the gospel of poverty but in practice I live in luxury, under the pretext that I have given everything away—to my wife . . . O God, it is Thy manifest will that I should live as a labourer in Thy vineyard, that I should be humbled, that all men should point the finger of scorn at me and say 'He preaches what he does not practise.' Well, so be it. He knows best what He desires."

Everywhere in Russia sects were being formed to follow the tenets of Tolstoy's faith; eager adherents defied the laws, endured prison, and underwent more grievous punishment as martyrs for his teachings; men gave up their lands and estates because they believed his words. And all the while the Master himself, protected by his European reputation from censorship or any legal or official action, lived comfortably on his great estate which was nominally owned by his wife. Many of his contemporaries held that Tolstoy practised what he preached less than any of his followers, and the play shows that he reproached himself in the same way. In the later part of the play Nicolai Ivanovitch gives place to young Prince Boris, who refuses to take the soldier's oath of allegiance and is imprisoned in an asylum.

From Tolstoy's draft for the final act it can be seen that he originally meant Nicolai Ivanovitch to meet a tragic end. He remembers how he brought Boris to ruin and that another of his followers has renounced his teaching: "I am weakness personified. Clearly God does not wish me to be His servant. He has many other servants, and His work can be done without me. When I realize this clearly I feel calm." At the very moment when he is bowed in prayer the mother of Boris forces her way in and kills him. In the hour of death he has the satisfaction of receiving a deputation of Dychobors, the Russian sect to which Tolstoy stood closest. "He dies rejoicing that the deceits of the Church are revealed. He has found the meaning of life."

Even the very modest part, however, that Tolstoy allowed the hero, his mouthpiece, to play seemed to him false. In a later version he omitted the murder and made Nicolai Ivanovitch end the play with some reflections to the effect that it would be a hundred years before his ideas could be realized. This, indeed, is the real significance of the title, '*The Light shines in the darkness,*' which is taken from St. John's Gospel. St. John's text continues, "And the darkness comprehendeth it not." It is still the Power of Darkness against which Tolstoy is fighting.

ANTON CHEKHOV

WITH all his admiration for Tolstoy, Anton Pavlovitch Chekhov was his exact opposite. Tolstoy was a member of a noble family, a Count with princely blood in his veins and the bearer of a name which had already won fame in Russian literature. But for the greater part of his life he went about barefoot, in the dress of a *mujik*, doing manual work of the hardest kind. Chekhov was the grandson of a serf. By sheer hard work his grandfather had succeeded in saving enough money to purchase freedom for himself and his family at a cost of 700 roubles a head. Chekhov's father was then nine years old, and he never succeeded in acquiring enough education even to be interested in his son's writings. After a short period in which he ran a general store with but slight success, he and the whole family relied for their support on Anton Chekhov's earnings as a doctor and an author. For the greater part of his short life Chekhov had to support his parents, four brothers and one sister. The father was an intolerable tyrant, and two of his brothers were unhappily married and drunkards.

With such a background, Chekhov could not share Tolstoy's adoration of the *mujik*: "There is *mujik* blood in my veins, and *mujik* virtues do not surprise me."

Chekhov was no prophet like Tolstoy; he was not even a man with firm roots. He was a sceptic who was to some extent justified in denying that he was a pessimist, though at heart he was uncertain whether life had any meaning. All the things that Tolstoy rejected Chekhov appreciated, as only a genius who has grown up in poverty can. He loved art and beauty and even the small amount of luxury that he could afford. It was not his principles but his kindness of heart that made him submit to the depredations of his family, his author friends and poor patients.

There was tuberculosis in the family; one of his brothers had died of consumption. The first symptoms revealed themselves in Chekhov just as he achieved his first success. As the illness advanced, the dual nature of Chekhov's temperament, which had always been present, showed itself more and more clearly. He was both indolent and restlessly energetic, and blamed himself equally for both. While he was staying at Melichovo, outside Moscow, it became vital for him to entertain all the time, and to take part in every kind of social or philanthropic enterprise. At the same time he felt happiest when he could be quite alone with his dreams. There was a pond on his land, and Bunin tells how he used to spend hours there every day with his rod. A visitor stated that there was never a single fish in it. At other times he was seized by a tremendous urge to travel. The long journey to Sakhalin to examine conditions there, together with his other exertions, probably played a big part in shortening his life. The last years of his life he spent—on doctor's orders—in his "warm Siberia," at Yalta in the Crimea. He loathed the town, partly because it was like a market, and also because it was both European and provincial in character. What he longed for was the cold and noise of Moscow. When Trigorin, in *Chaika* (*The Seagull*), complains that he cannot escape from himself, he is expressing a thought to which Chekhov often gave expression.

These contrasts in Chekhov have been discussed in some detail because they recur, though in exaggerated or even caricatured form, in the characters of his plays. Chekhov's plays are admired, as are his novels, not least because they present such a vivid picture of Russian life. This they certainly do. But one would not find them so moving if they did not also give us a strangely distorted reflection of the author himself.

Chekhov felt that he belonged both to the proletariat, so recently released from serfdom, and to a dying intelligentsia. He had had to struggle hard to reach his goal, and he complains in his letters that as a dramatist he lacked that sense of freedom which authors born into the nobility are naturally endowed with, while those who work their way up from lower levels acquire it at the cost of their youth. It is Turgenev and Tolstoy that he has in mind when he refers to literary noblemen, and it must have been with a certain amount of envy in his heart that, speaking of Tolstoy as a misanthrope, he once said, "I do not think he can ever have been unhappy."

If Chekhov had been granted a longer life—he died in 1904 at the age of 44, just before the ill-fated revolution—he would have seen the old privileges of class disappear, to be replaced by new ones. At the time when he became prominent, in the Eighties, Russia was undergoing a period of reaction. Ten years earlier people had been indulging in optimistic day-dreams, but when these came to nothing the intellectuals relaxed into a passive fatalism. Though he did not believe in a brighter future, Chekhov, like many of his contemporaries, felt the ground tremble beneath him. He never proclaimed any political message, but Soviet Russia has never tired of maintaining that he would have been a Marxist if he had lived longer. This conviction has had the happy result that Chekhov is not only eagerly read and played at the present time in Russia, but has also been the subject of much indefatigable research. The most remarkable outcome of this as far as his dramatic work is concerned is that a copy of his first play has been found.

According to his brother Michael's account, Anton Chekhov was still at school when he wrote his first play, a serious piece entitled *Fatherless*, but after leaving school he tore it up. In 1923 the manuscript of a Chekhov play without a title was found and given the name *Fatherless*, though the content bears no relation to such a title. The chief character is the twenty-seven-year old schoolmaster, Platonov, who believes himself to have rotted away internally: "My soul has long been a skeleton, and it is too late to re-awaken me." Like Turgenev's Rudin, Platonov poses as a philosopher and makes many lofty speeches about work and freedom, without in fact achieving anything. He is always drunk, and always falling in love with new women. He can see that in thirty years' time he will still be the same, leading the same dissolute life. This prophesy is not fulfilled, however: Platonov is shot by a married woman whom he has seduced.

The plot is completely insignificant, but the chief character is of interest mainly because he is the first of a series of similar characters in Chekhov, people who have come to the wrong place and feel that they are superfluous in life. With all his grand words that have nothing substantial behind them, Platonov reminds us of Hjalmar Ekdal. But this play is earlier than *The Wild Duck*, and in any case Platonov has many predecessors in the Russian novel.

After writing several one-act plays, of which *Medved* (*The Bear*) is most frequently staged, Chekhov tried in his four-act play of 1887, *Ivanov*, to create another character of the same kind as Platonov. It was mutilated by the censor and performed that same year at Korsh's theatre in Moscow, the Russian counterpart of the Théâtre Libre, but two years later it was revised and performed with much greater success at the Imperial Theatre in St. Petersburg.

Both actors and critics interpreted the characters in this play in so many different ways that Chekhov had to explain his conception of it in a series of letters. To his good friend Suvorin, the journalist, he admitted that the letters are clearer than the play, which is analysed by students to-day in very different ways.

In order to understand Chekhov's comments it is necessary to know something of the play. Ivanov, an educated country gentleman, has married a Jewess. Because she marries a Gentile and is baptized her parents disown her, and Ivanov's relations will not accept her either, with the consequence that he is forced to live in complete isolation and on the brink of ruin. He no longer loves his consumptive wife but is attracted by a young Russian girl, Sasha, who falls in love with him. Then the wife dies and the doctor leaves the impression with Ivanov that his heartlessness was the cause of her death. In the final act he is committed to marrying Sasha, but a sense of guilt torments him and to escape the new marriage he shoots himself shortly before the wedding.

In his letters Chekhov denies Suvorin's suggestion that he meant Ivanov to be conceived as a rogue. He is a nobleman with a university education, in no way remarkable, though he himself believes that he has done great things. "Never, or hardly ever, do we find in Russia a gentleman or a university man who does not boast of his past. The present is always worse than the past. Why? Because Russian irritability has this peculiar quality, that it is quickly followed by exhaustion." Chekhov goes on to describe how the Russian is hardly out of school before he takes up burdens beyond his strength. He founds schools, educates the peasants, fights against social evils of all kinds, but by the age of thirty-five he is tired and worn out. "At this stage people without vision or scruple blame their circumstances, call themselves superfluous, see themselves as Hamlets and leave it at that. But Ivanov is a straightforward man who admits openly to his doctor and the public that he does not understand himself . . . the change which has taken place in him offends his sense of decency. He seeks the cause outside himself and cannot find it. He looks inside himself, and can only detect a vague feeling of guilt. It is a typical Russian feeling. A Russian always feels that he is to blame when anyone has died in his house, when he possesses money, or when he lends it . . . People such as Ivanov do not solve problems; they only sink under the weight of them. They lose themselves, do not know what they ought to do, become fidgety, quarrel, behave stupidly and give way to their nerves. They lose the ground under their feet and join the ranks of the downtrodden and misunderstood." Later on in the letter Chekhov emphasizes that what he was anxious to bring out in the play were the typically Russian qualities. "This excessive sensibility, a feeling of guilt, weariness, are all purely Russian characteristics. Germans are never moved in this way and therefore Germany has no disillusioned, superfluous or weary people."

It is clear that in these criticisms Chekhov was thinking of the contemporary Russian intelligentsia. It was a section of the community with which all his plays were to deal. He felt that he belonged to it, though he was not exactly of it, and there are traces of him in Ivanov, whose character is therefore slightly blurred. In later plays Chekhov presented so many varieties of intellectuals that one easily forgets that peculiar quality which they all have in common, and which Chekhov pointed out in his letter, the easily aroused enthusiasm quickly followed by apathy and hatred of the world. Chekhov had only one remedy for this disease, hard work for some end which cannot be perceived. This idea is most plain to see in *Diadia Vania* (*Uncle Vanya*), but it is also present, though not fully worked out, in a study for *Uncle Vanya, Leshii* (*The Wood Demon*).

The Wood Demon, which was completed in 1889, takes its title from a nature-loving estate owner who is also a doctor, and who is so zealous in his care and nurture of the forests on his land that he is dubbed The Wood Demon by his friends, and indeed claims that there is a wood demon within him. It is Russia's misfortune that her forests are being swept away. Only if they are replaced can the beauty of Russia be restored, and the living conditions of her people be improved. From the earlier versions of the play, which have now been printed, we see that this wood demon was intended to play a more important part than he ultimately did. In *Uncle Vanya* he has receded even further into the background, and has been replaced by Doctor Astrov, who continues to complain that the forests of Russia hear too much of the woodman's axe. He considers that if he can save one peasant's woodland from being cut down this will be his humble reward, if men a thousand years ahead are made happier thereby. His soul swells with pride when he plants a young birch tree and watches it sway in the wind. Chekhov was a town child with a real passion for nature, and when he acquired his little estate at Melichovo he became completely absorbed in planting trees. With his inexhaustible capacity for laughing at himself he allowed the Demon of the Woods to be charged with being a *poseur*, and Doctor Astrov with being a drunkard.

Otherwise *The Wood Demon* contains the same characters as *Uncle Vanya*, and some of the lines could be transferred without alteration from one play to the other. The vain and petulant professor and his eager second wife, with her love of flirting and her hunger for life, are drawn with a skill which only Ibsen at this period could have equalled. The ambitious Voinitski is no less intensely alive than the hero of *Uncle Vanya*. In his despair at finding his life ruined he shoots himself. The final act, which was omitted from *Uncle Vanya*, brings reconciliation and general harmony. The play was probably written in a desperate attempt to win popular approval, but it was not successful, and seven years passed before Chekhov again tried his luck as a playwright. A draft for a play about King Solomon, whose weariness of the world resembled Chekhov's own, was never completed.

Of the plays which Chekhov wrote between 1880 and 1890 it was the farces and the vaudevilles which were most successful. This may be the reason why during his great creative period after 1890 he persisted in calling his plays comedies. His more serious plays were described by contemporary critics as dramatized novels, though they had considerably more plot than his

last masterpieces. In these plots, however, there is no compelling
logic; it is already clear that Chekhov was destined to be a master
of the static drama. He admitted freely that as drama his plays
were weak, but "the characters are alive and real, not just
invented."

From both Chekhov's letters and the stage directions of his
plays it is plain that he believed them to be lyrical. They also
contain lyrical passages, but these are really extraneous to the
main theme. Beginning with *The Seagull* Chekhov succeeded
in giving his plays a basic melody. There is a symbolism which
runs throughout each play, a sustaining theme.

Chekhov's decision in 1895 to return to his hitherto un-
profitable dramatic work was partly due to the fact that his friend
Suvorin, always interested in drama both as a writer and as a critic,
founded the Little Theatre in St. Petersburg in that year. Tolstoy's *The Power of Darkness* was performed there and also plays
by Ibsen and Hauptmann. Chekhov's letters to Suvorin show how
interested he was in the project. He was anxious that Maeterlinck
should be included in the repertory list, and that 'decadent,'
i.e., symbolistic, drama should feature largely. Clearly Chekhov
regarded himself as partly a symbolist, and a number of his
novels had an undercurrent of symbolism. In his next play,
The Seagull, young Konstantin Treplev speaks of the theatre of
the day as all repetition and routine, and says that it presents
nothing but people "eating and drinking, flirting, strolling and
wearing fine clothes." New forms are needed which will "show
life, not as it is or ought to be, but as one sees it in a dream." The
atmosphere of *The Seagull* is dreamlike throughout, and not only
in Treplev's play which is to be produced at an amateur theatre
in the park, but is abandoned when Arkadina, an actress of the
old school, finds it decadent and begins to parody it.

Chekhov's own play combines the symbolic and the real.
When it was first produced, at the Imperial Theatre in Moscow,
the effect was so bewildering that the audience laughed in the
wrong places and Chekhov, who had built great hopes on this
play, suffered his greatest disappointment. Nowadays *The Seagull*,
particularly to a Scandinavian reader, appears the most straightforward of the four plays which made Chekhov one of the most
outstanding figures in modern drama.

The setting of the play is an estate on the shores of a lake. Nina, a young amateur actress, says as she comes on the stage that she is irresistibly attracted to this lake, like a seagull. Konstantin, who is hopelessly in love with her, comes on carrying a seagull which he has just shot, and lays it at her feet. "Soon I shall be shooting myself like that," he says. Nina complains that he is talking in obscure symbols. "This seagull is, I am sure, a symbol, but you must excuse me for I do not understand it." As *The Wild Duck* was for Ibsen, so *The Seagull* is for Chekhov a symbol of shattered illusions, and its fate is woven into the real plot. The conceited author, Trigorin, who is the lover of Konstantin's mother, orders the seagull to be stuffed. He is going to introduce it into a story about a young girl who grows up free and happy as a seagull by the shores of a lake. "Then someone happens to pass, sees the seagull and shoots it just to pass the time, and for lack of anything better to do—exactly the fate that befell that gull there."

The story is never written, but Nina suffers the same fate and is the victim of a man's desire "just to pass the time." As if she were acting in his story, she is seduced by Trigorin, who then deserts her for his old mistress. As she travels on her tour she dreams that she is a seagull. Konstantin has been unable to forget her, though she refuses to see him and will only communicate by letters which she signs 'the seagull.' Two years pass and she returns to the estate, still in love with Trigorin, though she knows that he regarded her merely as a character for a story. Trigorin also arrives and is shown the seagull which has been stuffed at his expense, but he has forgotten the incident. At that moment a shot is heard off stage. Konstantin has committed suicide.

There is little point in following the example of certain Russian scholars and others in denying the influence of Ibsen. Chekhov is supposed to have found the idea for his play during a hunting-trip with his friend, the painter Levitan, when the latter injured a seagull with one shot (Chekhov's own letter describing the incident mentions a woodcock). There is no mention in the letter of Levitan's subsequent behaviour, but even if it did resemble that of Konstantin in *The Seagull*, that only explains the scene at the beginning of the play, not the link between the seagull and the girl—which is similar to that between the wild duck and Hedvig. The contrast between the characters is also typical of Ibsen: Arkadina, self-centred and affected, is opposed to the naive and natural Nina, and there is an equally vivid contrast between the selfish, fashionable author Trigorin and young Konstantin, who is fighting for new forms and a new content in literature.

Tolstoy did not fail to notice the influence of Ibsen in *The Seagull* when speaking to Suvorin after the publication of the play: "It is worthless nonsense, written as Ibsen writes. Words are piled on each other, and one does not know why. And Europe cries 'Wonderful!' Chekhov is probably very talented, but *The Seagull* is very poor." Tolstoy appreciated Chekhov's stories to the full but he could not appreciate his plays, which seemed to him artificial. He is supposed to have said later to Chekhov, "You know that I don't like Shakespeare, but your plays, my dear Anton Pavlovitch, are even worse than his."

In *The Seagull* Chekhov was not satisfied, as he was in his later plays, with a static plot and tried to introduce action. Compared with *The Wild Duck*, *The Seagull* seems to be very casually constructed. Its charm lies in the details, in the admirable picture of everyday life on a Russian estate, and in the magnificent characterization. For the first time Chekhov succeeded in imbuing a play with the dreamlike quality which we know from his stories, and also in bringing out the same pessimism, often touched with poetry. Arkadina's brother, Sorin, grumbles, "I have served for twenty-eight years as an administrative judge, but I have never yet lived, never drained anything to the dregs, and now I really want to live." But for him life only holds in store the aches and pains of old age. In the same way both Nina and Konstantin end by being bitterly disappointed. Nina's acting has become coarse and vulgar since Trigorin deserted her, and Konstantin's first story is damned by the critics. He loathes Trigorin's sugary style and clever tricks, but he has become convinced that the problem is not one of new or old forms: "The whole secret is that a man must write without thinking of form at all—let it all flow freely from the soul." Arkadina and Trigorin alone survive as conquerors in the struggle for life. She, at the age of 44, is still able to play the *ingénue* and score successes everywhere. Trigorin is successful; from his pen flows ·

an unending stream of works. He is a coward and a liar, but lucky at cards and lucky in love. He is probably the best-drawn character in the play. With his usual habit of poking fun at himself Chekhov has endowed Trigorin with several of his own traits. He can sit and fish in a pond for hours without catching anything, and in the middle of a conversation he is quite likely to pull out a book and note down amusing anecdotes and sayings for future use, a practice which Chekhov also followed. It is possible, as Russian scholars suggest, that Chekhov took as his model his friend Potapenko, an author now practically forgotten, but if so—as Nils Åke Nilsson says—it can only have been in respect of Trigorin's relations with Nina. In any case, the similarity does not appear to have been so great as to be observed by Potapenko himself. Chekhov sent him the manuscript of *The Seagull*, and was very anxious to learn his opinion of the play. Later Potapenko accompanied Chekhov daily to the rehearsals. At the *première*, when the play was badly received, Chekhov, in great distress at the hostility of the audience, sought refuge behind the scenes after the second act and returned to Moscow the following day. Potapenko, however, sent him a consolatory telegram, "Colossal success." Chekhov describes him in a letter to Suvorin in 1895 as a simple soul, and expresses regret that he has not yet found his true vein as an author. This does not fit in with the picture of Trigorin in *The Seagull*.

After the fiasco of *The Seagull* Chekhov ordered the printing of his plays to cease: "Never again shall I write plays or have them performed." He soon, however, resumed the printing of *Ivanov, The Seagull* and *The Wood Demon* in its new form with the title *Uncle Vanya*. His determination to carry on with his literary work, irrespective of its reception by the public and the critics, is probably reflected in the new last scene of *Uncle Vanya*. The professor and his wife go away and leave Vanya and his niece Sonia, who turn sadly to their tedious book-keeping duties; "We must go on living, Uncle Vanya. We shall live on through a long, long line of days, of endless evenings; we shall patiently endure the trials that Fate brings us; we shall toil for others, now and when we are old, without rest; and when our time comes we shall die without complaint, and there beyond the grave . . . we shall rejoice and look back tenderly at our troubles with a smile, and we shall be allowed to rest. I believe, Uncle, I believe with all my heart, with glowing faith . . . there we shall be allowed to rest." There is slow music from a guitar, and Sonia tells how heaven is sparkling with diamonds, and how all earthly evils are drowned "in the great mercy which fills the whole world." Tears come into Uncle Vanya's eyes, sceptic as he is, and then the night watchman knocks on the door, the old nurse picks up her knitting, and the guitar begins to play a different tune. It is one of Chekhov's most unforgettable scenes. He himself has summarized its content in these words: "The whole purpose and drama of man lies in the workings of his soul, not in his external actions."

Chekhov would probably have crowned his dramatic work with those masterpieces, *Tri sestri* (*The Three Sisters*) and *Vishnevii sad* (*The Cherry Orchard*), even if he had met with the same lack of understanding which greeted the very first performance of *The Seagull*. But he was naturally profoundly influenced by the fact that two years after the failure in St. Petersburg *The Seagull* achieved a resounding success at the Arts Theatre in Moscow— so much so that a seagull is still the emblem on the stage curtain there. This theatre, which had only been in operation for two months, was to achieve greater fame and a longer existence than the experimental theatres founded elsewhere on the Continent and in England. Chekhov proved a true prophet of Russia's future when he wrote, as early as 1899, that when a history of modern Russian drama was written this theatre would give it its finest pages.

The Moscow Arts Theatre was founded by an amateur actor of noble family called Stanislavski, and a playwright and teacher of dramatic art called Nemirovitch-Danchenko. The former of these two was a brilliant producer, and came to have a great influence on modern acting. Nemirovitch-Danchenko's plays did not penetrate beyond Russia, but his vision was amazingly wide and his literary taste sure. It was thanks to him that the plays of Ibsen and Maeterlinck came to occupy such a prominent place on the repertory lists. With Chekhov he had already made contact, and in 1889 had suggested certain alterations in *The Wood Demon*. When the first performance of *The Seagull* proved a fiasco Chekhov blamed Nemirovitch-Danchenko for having tempted him to write a play. Nemirovitch-Danchenko, however, remained steadfast in his admiration. In 1897 he was awarded the Gribojedov Prize for the best play of the year, but wrote to the Committee refusing to accept it because they had passed over *The Seagull*—a play which wholly and indisputably deserved it: "Here you have a real gem, here Russian drama celebrates a new triumph." These generous words were written at a time when *The Seagull* had been completely cut to pieces by the critics while his own play, *Life's Value,* was proving most successful. It was also Nemirovitch-Danchenko who insisted that *The Seagull* should be included in the repertory of the Arts Theatre. Stanislavski himself admitted that at first he had not understood the play.

The naturalistic conventions, as laid down by Zola and Antoine, were carried out by Stanislavski in an almost eccentric way. To mark the fourth wall of a salon, the imaginary one between the stage and the audience, chairs were placed along the footlights with their backs to the auditorium. The actors were to act as if no audience existed, and to add to the illusion of reality a distant sound of hooves and carriages was introduced. In *The Seagull* one could hear the croaking of frogs and the chirrup of crickets. At first Chekhov was exasperated by this ultra-realism, but when the Moscow Theatre toured Europe with his play its value was realized. It was this naturalism, carried almost into symbolism, that enabled a foreign audience, unfamiliar with the language and sometimes with Chekhov's plays, to appreciate the presentation. It gave the play atmosphere and something of a feeling of Russian life. In his two last plays, *The Three Sisters* and *The Cherry Orchard,* Chekhov took even more trouble than usual to bring out to the full the tedious monotony of everyday life in Russia. There are no uproarious scenes. Chekhov's earlier serious plays had often included a murder or a suicide, either on or off the stage. In *The Three Sisters* one of the characters is shot dead in a duel off stage, but when Chekhov was working on *The Cherry Orchard* he wrote in a letter that there was not a single shot in the whole play.

This sparing use of external action should not lead us, as it has some critics, to regard Chekhov's plays as 'tranches de la vie', the phrase used by Zola to describe the ideal which he himself

P

never achieved for naturalistic plays. Chekhov never became
as ardent a follower of naturalism as Gorki. He had in 1895
proposed to Suvorin that he should try out some of Zola's plays,
notably *Thérèse Raquin*, "a fine play," but the playwright whom, he
said, he admired without any of his usual reserve was Maeterlinck,
whom he was then reading. He found that his plays were "strange
and remarkable things, but they create an overpowering impression, and if I had a theatre I would assuredly perform *The Blind*."
Maeterlinck's contemporary plays and the last works of Chekhov
have this in common, that the symbolic undercurrent of meaning
never takes concrete form as in Ibsen, but is blended into an
actionless plot. But while the characters in Maeterlinck's best
plays are stylized and have very little to say, Chekhov's are
always talking restlessly, and are as tense and nervous as he was
himself. As far as one can tell from his letters, he began his last
plays without any clear conception of anything but the outline
of the plot. This makes them difficult to analyse, but at the same
time contributes to the unequalled impression of reality that
they give. In *The Three Sisters* and *The Cherry Orchard* a spectator
from the West is introduced to a setting that is unfamiliar to
him. Yet it seems more alive and less artificial than plays of our
own day dealing with our own problems.

Chekhov had been thinking about *The Three Sisters* at the end
of 1899 and it was completed a year later, but when he first began
to work at it he wrote to the actress, Olga Knipper—later to be
his wife—"This is not a play but a sort of a skein. There are
many parts; I may get entangled in them and have to give it all
up." When the play was finished and had been dispatched to the
theatre at Moscow he grumbled: "It is as complicated as a novel,
and people say that the atmosphere is suicidal." It was not until
two years after the first performance that *The Three Sisters* was
properly appreciated.

The government town where the story takes place is modelled
on a provincial town not far from Moscow, where one of
Chekhov's brothers had been a school-teacher. He himself had
practised as a doctor in a place some miles away, and had often
visited his brother. Stationed in the town was a battery of
artillery, and it was the memory of its officers that enabled
Chekhov to produce his excellent characterization of military

types. The passionate longing of the sisters for Moscow, and
their final disappointment, reflect Chekhov's own feelings. When
he was writing the play, down in Yalta, he felt cut off from everything, his beloved Olga, the theatre which staged his plays, and
his circle of literary friends. His correspondence at this period
contains constant complaints that his health prevented him from
living in Moscow.

   The play begins with one of the sisters describing how wonderful life was before their father got his brigade eleven years ago
in this provincial town; he has now been dead for a year. "In
Moscow everything was bright and warm in the sunshine and
gay with flowers . . . this morning I woke up and saw the great
flood of spring light, and there was joy in my soul; but I was
seized by such a terrible longing for our home over there." The
second act closes with a passionate cry from the youngest sister,
Irina, "We must go to Moscow—to Moscow! To Moscow!"
At first the sisters build their hopes around their brother, Andrei,
who is to be a professor there. When he marries and accepts a
place on the local government board that hope is lost. Irina
accepts an offer of marriage from the ugly Baron Tusenbach
because he will bring her to Moscow: "Nothing in the world is
like Moscow! We must go there! Olga, we must go there!"
These are the last words of Act III. But in the fourth act
Tusenbach is killed in a senseless duel and the regiment is moving
away. "We are left alone to begin our life anew, and we must
live, we must live . . ."

   Like Ibsen, Chekhov hated small town life because it made
people petty. In a letter from Yalta he asks one of the foremost
actors at the Moscow Arts Theatre to reserve a seat for him at a
performance of *Pillars of Society*: "I want to see the wonderful
Norwegian played . . . You know that Ibsen is my favourite
author." There are plenty of stunted small town eccentrics in
The Three Sisters. The middle sister, Masha, is married to an
incredibly dry and tedious schoolmaster, who might well have
been taken as he stands from an Ibsen play, as might also Andrei's
wife, with her tasteless clothes and her eternal chatter about her
children and her household. One or two of the officers have also
ceased to have any interest in higher things, and are entirely
absorbed in everyday trivialities. We also have the drunken army

doctor, who is always reading the paper and finds it so remarkable that Balzac was married in Berdichev that he records the fact in his notebook. Then there is the dutiful second lieutenant, who runs errands for the sisters. He displays with pride his latest purchase, a knife with scissors, ear-cleaner and nail-cleaner. One discusses a meat dish, writes down a recipe for a hair lotion, plays patience, all with the same air of bored indifference. In the first act there are celebrations for a Name Day; in the second there is a supper-party; in the third act our interest is aroused for a time by a fire in the town. But this leads the Colonel into a disquisition on philosophy—until he interrupts himself with the words, "But they all look as if they were asleep." The final act gives us the death of Tusenbach and the departure of the regiment. More than ever, the town has become an empty prison.

In the Prosorov family we have been observing small town life for a period of five years, and received the impression that it will not change in another hundred. Occasionally one of the characters shows a faint conception of the coming revolution. Tusenbach, for instance, in the first act says, "The time is coming, an earthquake is approaching, a great and cleansing storm is gathering and will soon be upon us. It is not far off and it will soon come and sweep away idleness and indifference from our community, the dislike of work, and all that is rotten and tedious . . . I am going to work, and in twenty-five or thirty years every-one will have to work." The brother of the three sisters, Andrei, turns for a moment to dreams of a golden future, "The present is beastly, but when I think of the future, how good it is! I feel so light, so free. A new light is shining in the distance. I see freedom approaching. I see myself and my children freeing ourselves from vanities, from *kvass*, from goose baked with cabbage, from the after-dinner nap and from base idleness." Chekhov had a pre-monition of the coming storm, but he did not allow his characters from the intelligentsia to do more than exercise their imaginations about a glorious future. Andrei pushes his perambulator patiently, and pretends not to see how his wife is deceiving him with the chairman of the local government board, without even the hope that his children will lead a happier life than he has done: "And wives deceive their husbands, and the husbands lie, and look as if they neither saw nor heard anything, and the bad influence irresistibly oppresses their children. The divine spark is quenched within them and they become just as pitiful corpses and just as much like one another as their fathers and mothers." Tusenbach himself declares, contradicting his own prophecy of a coming revolution, "And in a million years life will be exactly the same as it was before. Life does not change; it remains inexorably itself, obeying its own laws which do not concern us, or which at any rate we can never learn to understand." We are birds of passage like the cranes, flying, flying without knowing whither or why. It means nothing; "The chief thing is that they fly."

We are forced back, therefore, to what the youngest sister, Irina, said in the first act: "Man must make the effort and toil by the sweat of his brow, whoever he may be. In that alone lies the meaning and purpose of life, all happiness and exaltation." That is the theme of *Uncle Vanya*, repeated here in more intensive form. Irina has never been in love: "Oh, I have dreamed so much about love. I have been doing it for a long time, both by day and by night. My soul is like a wonderful piano, but it is locked, and the key is lost."

Would it have been better if the sisters' dreams of going to Moscow had been realized? The Colonel, whose life has been full of trials, has his doubts. He speaks of a French Cabinet Minister who was imprisoned and rejoiced to see the birds through the bars of his window. He had paid no attention to them when he belonged to the Cabinet, "But now that he is free, of course he cares no more for the birds than he did before. In the same way you would no longer notice Moscow once you were there. There is no happiness for us anywhere; we only wish for it."

The plot of *The Three Sisters*, if indeed one can speak of one, peters out into nothing. And yet dramatically the play is loaded with explosive material. Chekhov was right when he protested against Stanislavski's suggestion that in the final act Tusenbach's body should be carried across the stage. Existence would have been equally comfortless if he had survived. The tragedy does not lie on the surface. Both those who grumble at the shabbiness of small town life and those who have settled down in it are equally passive, almost paralysed. But this town, which has existed for two hundred years, and in which not one person of note has ever lived, where people only eat and drink, sleep and die—to make way for another generation which will do exactly the same—this town becomes a symbol of the senselessness of life, more comprehensible than the symbol in a play of Maeterlinck or in Strindberg's *A Dream Play*, because it is never commented upon or emphasized. The cheerless repetitions of life are presented in full detail; there is no need of a schoolmaster with a pointer. Only an unobservant reader or spectator could find the play boring, as Chekhov himself complained that it was when he had finished it. Without arriving at any conclusion, it surveys the whole of our earthly existence and our vain dreams of a happier future. There is a suppressed pathos in it, and this drama of everyday trivialities has a poetry all its own, at which Chekhov was aiming in his apprentice work, but never succeeded in creating as finely as in this masterpiece. Music has come from the wonderful piano, even though it is locked.

The Cherry Orchard, Chekhov's last play, is easier to grasp than *The Three Sisters*. When at the end of the play we hear a note that sounds "as if it came from heaven, the sound of a breaking harp-string" and then, after a moment's silence, the blows of an axe cutting into wood, it is not only an ancient orchard that is falling to destruction; a whole section of the community is falling to the axe. Chekhov was not to know that the new owner of the estate, Lopachin, the son of a serf, would in his turn be liquidated as a Kulak. This development, however, fits in with his general conception of existence as a process of continuous repetition of the past.

No play, with the exception of Gorki's *Na dne* (*The Lower Depths*), has been as popular in Russia since the Revolution as *The Cherry Orchard*. It is played every year at the Moscow Arts Theatre, and with a steadily increasing number of performances each year; in 1930 there were seventy-one. It has also been performed in many other theatres in the Soviet Union. Modern Russia has of course produced many plays in which the glories of the Revolution and the new State are conscientiously presented, but *The Cherry Orchard* appears to a present-day Russian as a prophecy, written during the last years of the Czarist regime, of what was to come. The raisonneur in the play is the old tutor, Trofimov, bald and bespectacled and always wearing a shabby old student's uniform. The family are surprised that in spite of his advanced years he is still only a student. His reply is that he is surely destined to be the eternal student. In a letter to his wife Chekhov complained that he had not been able to include all the relevant facts to explain his character: "You see, Trofimov has had to go into exile on several occasions; he was continually sent down from the University. But how can one explain all this?" Chekhov finally ventured to insert into the dialogue the information that Trofimov had twice been sent down from the University, but he made no mention of his exile. After the failure of the revolution in 1905 The Czarist censor nevertheless forbade any public performance of the play.

Chekhov had visited France and Italy in the winter of 1897-98, and there made the acquaintance of Russian émigrés. At Nice he lived in a Russian boarding-house, and at Beaulieu he became good friends with Maxim Kovalevski, the brother-in-law of Sonia Kovalevski, who fell in love with him during the last years of her life. Kovalevski had been a professor at Moscow University, but was dismissed for his "free political views," as Chekhov says in a letter. "He is head and shoulders above our advanced Petersburg intelligentsia who celebrate their triumphs every day." How 'advanced' Kovalevski was can be seen from the fact that in 1901, when Chekhov was working on the first stages of The Cherry Orchard, he was founding in Paris a Sociological Institute at which Lenin, among others, was to serve as a teacher. It was while Chekhov was seeing Kovalevski and revising The Three Sisters that the prophecy about the coming revolution was put into the mouth of Baron Tusenbach. In The Cherry Orchard we find the same prophecy in more symbolic form expressed by the student Trofimov: "All Russia is our orchard . . . Think, Ana, your grandfather, your great-grandfather and all your ancestors were owners of serfs, holders of living souls—and can you fail to see tortured human souls looking at you from every cherry, from every leaf, from every stem? Don't you hear voices there? Oh, this orchard is terrible; and when in the evening or at night you walk through it, and the old bark on the trees glows dimly, then the old cherry trees seem to be dreaming of all that was, a hundred, two hundred years ago, and their visions weigh them down. But how can words

help? We are at least a century behind in our development. We
have to begin everything from the beginning. We are not even
sure of our relationship to the past, we can only philosophize,
complain of boredom or drink vodka. And yet it's so clear; in
order to begin to live in the present, we must first pay for the
past, make our peace with the past, and that payment can only
be made through suffering, in hard and patient work." Elsewhere
Trofimov explains that the work that is needed for man's progress cannot be performed by the Russian intellectuals: "They
call themselves intellectuals, but they are too familiar with their
servants and treat the peasants like animals. Their studies are
quite superficial, their reading is never serious—in short, they do
nothing. They prattle about the sciences, and of art they understand hardly anything. They are all so self-important; they look
solemn, walk about and philosophize, and talk of nothing but
the biggest of life's problems. And all the time most of us
Russians, ninety-nine out of a hundred, are living like savages;
at the merest trifle we knock each other's teeth out, swear and
curse. They eat miserably, sleep in filthy conditions and breathe
polluted air. There are lice, stenches, damp and vice . . . All our
fine words have only combined to distort our vision, and that of
others. Show me our famous crèches and libraries; they can be
found in novels, but not in real life; in life there is only dirt,
vulgarity and an Asiatic lack of culture . . . I hate all these self-
important faces; I am afraid of all these profound conversations."
But Trofimov does not like Lopachin either; "My feeling about
you, Yermolai Alexeivitch, is this; you are a rich man, you will
soon be a millionaire. As long as there are in existence beasts of
prey who devour all that crosses their path, so long will there be
a place for you."

Trofimov's remarks, full of spleen as they are, show us the
attitude of a radical revolutionary to existing conditions. He
loathes the intellectuals, and quite as much the nouveau riche
plebeians who are to succeed them. Chekhov has allowed him to
have his say, but has not used him to express his own opinions.
Despite Chekhov's eager association with Kovalevski in Italy
and Gorki in Yalta, he could not quite share their passionate faith
in the future, or their unhesitating satisfaction that the old
patriarchal character of Russia was disappearing. In an almost

disconcerting way his sympathies are divided between the old cherry orchard and its owner, and the new day which is dawning. Lubov Andreievna, the mistress of the estate, is incurably extravagant but good-hearted and attractive. She is torn between her love for the old manor where she was born, and where her eldest son was drowned, and her longing to return to Paris, where waits the lover who robbed and deserted her. Her brother, Gaiev, with all the haughty manner he has inherited, is equally attached to the old traditions, and Lopachin is both proud and distressed at being the one who drives out his old master's family. He has done everything to try to persuade the owner to sell off pieces of land for villas, but his suggestions have been rejected as incompatible with the family honour. He and Lubov Andreievna's foster-child, Varya, are slightly in love with one another, and he readily agrees to propose to her if her mother will help. But when they are left in a room alone together they are too shy to reveal their feelings, and the proposal is never made. The last chance is now gone of enabling the former owners to return to their cherry orchard, and when the woodmen begin to work on it only the faithful but sick old servant, Firs, is left: "Closed! They have gone . . . left me here . . . doesn't matter . . . I can stay here . . . Life has gone, just as if one had never lived." The old servant had grown up before the emancipation of the serfs, but had never wanted his freedom. He grieves that his old master is no longer living; he used to cure all illnesses with sealing-wax. He also grumbles at the guests who have come to the ball in the third act: "In the old days at our balls we used to have generals, and admirals, and barons to dance, but now we send for the postmaster, and the station master, and even they hardly bother to come." Things move so fast that people can hardly keep up with events, and the individual, whether he belongs to the new rich or the old, feels himself without roots. Lopachin walks about in his white waistcoat and yellow shoes with his pockets full of money: "But getting right down to the root of the matter, I am heart and soul a *mujik*. I have been trying to read this book, but I understand nothing."

The Cherry Orchard is interpreted in Russia as a prophecy of the Revolution, but in Western Europe it has been taken to be the swan-song of the Russian intellectual. With all its simplicity, it is far too complicated to fit neatly into either category. Chekhov's directions to the actors show how anxious he was to do justice to both sides. His wife was to play the part of Lubov Andreievna, and he describes the role thus: "She dresses with good taste, not ostentatiously, and is talented. She is very good-hearted, absent-minded, friendly and kindly to all, and there is always a smile on her lips." He begged Stanislavski to see that Lopachin was not allowed to become a caricature of a financial shark: "Lopachin is a business man, but a thoroughly decent fellow. He must behave like an educated man, with perfect manners and no petty mean-nesses."

By sketching his characters in such a light but extraordinarily vivid manner, Chekhov has really succeeded in dividing our sympathies as he wished. He was not, however, successful in producing the cheerful atmosphere at which he was aiming. Not only did he call the play a comedy, but in various letters he spoke of it as farcical. When Nemirovitch-Danchenko read the manu-script he commented to Chekhov that it was full of people weeping. Chekhov replied that they were happy and lively though there were tears in their eyes, and that their tears need cause no depression in an audience. He held that such changes of mood were inseparable from the volatile Russian temperament.

Chekhov was annoyed when *The Cherry Orchard* was regarded as a churchyard, but it does have a sad and mournful atmosphere. The excellent description of the setting gives the play its peculiar atmosphere. Even in the first act the old manor shows signs of having known better days. It is a repository both of precious traditions and gloomy memories. When the cherry trees are finally cut down it is only the student Trofimov who sees that the last traces of the Russia of the serfs are being swept away. One has the feeling that the little houses to be built on the cleared ground will also rest on uneasy foundations. Chekhov was no profound political philosopher, but he had a poet's awareness of a shifting wind. It is not only *The Cherry Orchard* but our whole culture, with its thousand years of tradition, that has been hollowed out at the roots; a single storm can lay it low now. That is why *The Cherry Orchard* is still played and admired as a warning of an uncertain and threatening future.

When *The Cherry Orchard* was completed Chekhov wrote to

his wife: "The worst thing about the play is that I did not write it in one stretch, but over a long, a very long period, so that sometimes it must appear too drawn out." Similar complaints appear in his letters about *The Three Sisters*, but it is just because these plays are the result of so many sleepless nights and of lonely days of meditation that they rise to the topmost heights of modern drama. They realize its ideal of giving symbolical significance to descriptions of everyday life, of blending realism and poetry, more comprehensively than any earlier work. It says a good deal that a playwright so utterly different from Chekhov as Shaw proclaimed him as his master in *Heartbreak House* and, with a modesty that was rare in him, once admitted "Every time I see a play by Chekhov I want to throw my own work on the fire."

MAXIM GORKI

MAXIM GORKI was nine years younger than Chekhov, and was not the son of a labourer; his father was first a carpenter and then a shipping agent. Gorki was only four years old when his father died, and he endured all the hardships which he was later to describe in his autobiographical works, which are indeed his best. He became a shoemaker's errand-boy, a steward on a Volga boat where a drunkard of a cook taught him to read and write, a baker's apprentice, a railway worker and many other things. Most important of all, he was out of work for long periods, and wandered everywhere in Russia. It was during this time that he began to write and to have his first efforts at composition printed. He came to earn a good part of his living by writing short stories for the provincial press; but when in 1898 his collected tales appeared in two volumes he achieved world fame overnight. A contributory factor to this reputation was also his well-known play, *Na dne* (*The Lower Depths*).

Gorki began by holding vaguely revolutionary notions, but he later became a faithful adherent of Marxism and an early supporter of the Bolsheviks. When they came to power he felt it his duty to try to preserve cultural values, and above all to save writers from death by starvation. He came into contact with Tolstoy during the latter's last years, but Tolstoy could not approve his thorough-going naturalism. His real teacher as a dramatist was Chekhov. It was Chekhov who urged him in 1900 to write a play for the Moscow Arts Theatre. His first play, *The Smug Citizen*, or *The Middle Class* (1902), was not particularly successful, as it was found to be a mere copy of Chekhov. In the same year he wrote *The Lower Depths*, which was a brilliant success in Moscow, and in the following year was even more warmly received in Berlin, where it had a run of 500 performances. Equal success attended it in other countries. Other plays which Gorki wrote later achieved nothing like the same success outside Russia, in spite of his great reputation. Even after the première of *The Lower Depths* there were some critics who doubted whether the play deserved such praise, pointing out that it lacked originality and was influenced by Tolstoy's *The Power of Darkness* and Hauptmann's *The Weavers*. Gorki shows us a cross-section of the life of the town proletariat, as Tolstoy had done with the peasant class. The form of the play, however, is Chekhov's; there is no action, no conflict, and no leading characters in *The Lower Depths*.

The dismal basement room is really the chief character in the play, and the players are merely accessories. When the curtain goes up we see a number of people crawling about over each other in a dirty cellar. When it drops at the end of the third act we have seen one die of neglect and one killed on the stage, while another has hanged himself. A young girl has had her legs scalded and a boy has been imprisoned for theft and murder. It is easy to see that the others may well go the same way unless their wretched existence is terminated first. One cannot even say that the play consists of a series of dialogues, for one of the characteristics of the people in it is that they have to some extent lost the capacity to talk rationally to each other. They talk to themselves without listening to what other people have to say, indeed without showing any interest in what is happening to them. Chekhov has already shown us characters who have some difficulty in understanding each other, and are inclined to talk in monologues. In Gorki this is the rule, not the exception. We have the decayed actor, who almost mechanically repeats the doctor's words that his constitution has been completely undermined by alcohol, until, unnoticed by his companions, he hangs himself. Then there is the common street girl, Nasha, who feeds her imagination with third-rate tales in tattered novels. Her protector, the Baron, who has been in gaol for fraud and appears to have lost every trace of his education, mutters something now and then about his wealthy ancestors and relations. The old locksmith, Kletsch, works away at his trade, entirely unaffected by the fact that his wife is dying of consumption behind a curtain. The most lively character is Pepel, the thief. He has been having an affaire with Vassilissa, the cruel and dissolute wife of the lodging-house keeper. Unfortunately he falls in love with her young sister, Natasha, and is about to leave the house with her when Vassilissa deliberately pours boiling tea from a samovar on to her legs. In his fury Pepel kills the landlord and is arrested by a policeman, who is always on hand because he is Vassilissa's uncle and daily drinks himself drunk at the inn. Into this bestial setting, where people commit crimes and murders without any particular reason, comes a sixty-year-old pilgrim, Luka. His white beard makes an impression on the others, and they call him 'Little Father,' though that does not prevent them from pushing him out of the way occasionally. Luka shows sympathy for the others' sufferings; he tells them that when he was younger he was no different from them. Age has brought him calm and resignation, joy in the midst of wretchedness and a philosophy of life which is probably Gorki's own. It is based on mutual respect between men. Man ought to believe in something, it does not matter what; it does not even matter if it is true. He wants to save his fellow-beings for a better life. The actor is to return to the stage and Pepel, the pickpocket, is to begin a new life in Siberia. But when Luka goes away in the third act his clients have already shown themselves to be incurable, and have relapsed into their bad old ways. In the final act one of the basement-dwellers, Satin, takes the lead, sometimes quoting Luka as his authority. Men must go on living, because Superman is coming, perhaps in a hundred years: "So we must respect all human beings, and children most of all." This Nietzschean teaching has no effect on life in the basement, but towards the end Satin and the Baron drink a toast to the nobility and freedom of man. He is not to be degraded by pity, but exalted by respect. The actor's suicide at this point comes as a cold shock: "The fool has spoiled our song."

In *The Lower Depths* Gorki is not yet writing positive propaganda. The Baron calls Luka a charlatan, and Satin says that he has made all the lodgers feel rebellious. What has enabled the play to retain its hold on the stage for nearly half a century is its excellent portrayal of characters and setting. Gorki lacks the pathos of which Tolstoy was a master, and, compared with Akim in *The Power of Darkness*, the pilgrim Luka is not precisely drawn.

Neither then nor later did Gorki achieve the object of which he spoke in a letter to Chekhov while he was writing *The Lower Depths*, to bring out a hidden music. He could admire, but not imitate, the strange twilight in Chekhov's plays.

The Lower Depths is a significant play, but it is no faultless masterpiece. Even Chekhov, who was a friend and admirer of Gorki, wrote to him that he found the last act dull and unnecessary. This was not the first appearance in modern drama of the world which Gorki describes. The lowest class in the community had already provided the setting thirty years earlier for Zola's *Thérèse Raquin*. But Gorki contrives to give us an impression of horrifying reality, perhaps because one instinctively feels that the writer has himself lived in the appalling conditions which he describes.

In his later plays, however, Gorki presented with tiresome obstinacy caricatures from classes of the community with which he was not really familiar, but which he regarded with a real frenzy of hatred, the Russian aristocracy and the middle-class intellectuals.

As far as one can tell from translations and reviews, Gorki has not written any further plays which are really about the working class. In *Vragi* (*Enemies* 1906) he described the class war, as illustrated in a strike, but whereas Hauptmann in *The Weavers* and Galsworthy in *Strife* give us pictures from both camps, Gorki is content to show us the prejudices which dominate the factory-owner's family, and the stupid brutality of the soldiers who have been called in. The work-people only appear when they are summoned before their employers or arrested, and display invincible nobility and readiness to sacrifice themselves. In the play they are defeated, but a woman in the factory-owner's family proclaims her certainty that ultimately they will triumph.

It is as a critic of bourgeois society that Gorki is most admired in Russia to-day, but it is not easy to find any significant sequence of thought in his plays. During the Czarist regime Gorki's dramatic writing suffered because he had to consider the censorship. It was realized that his plays made dangerous propaganda. *The Lower Depths* could only be performed after many of its lines had been cut, and the unexpurgated edition was not available to the Russian public until after the Revolution. Other plays, such as *Enemies*, were not allowed to be performed at all. When the revolution of 1905 failed, Gorki was arrested and imprisoned in the fortress of St. Peter and St. Paul, where he contracted the tuberculosis with which he had to struggle for the rest of his life. After his release he had such great difficulties with the censors that his plays had to be toned down.

After the Revolution, of course, his position became very different. His was the great literary name of the Soviet Union, and in 1918 he founded a theatre in Leningrad which in 1932, on the thirtieth anniversary of *The Lower Depths*, was renamed after him, as was also his birthplace, Nijny Novgorod. Even the Moscow Arts Theatre was by official decree associated with his name. But the ideas which he had been one of the first to proclaim in the days when authority tried to suppress them were now official doctrine, and no longer inspiring.

It was significant that Gorki ended his life as a dramatist with a trilogy about the Russian Revolution. The first part, *Egor Bulichov i drugie* (*Egor Bulichov and Others*), contains a hero who is powerfully drawn, a business man whose lust and passions are as violent as those of animals. He dies of cancer, unreconciled to God or Social Reform, to the sound of a Revolutionary song that is heard through the window. In the second part, which takes its title from the name of Bulichov's companion, Dostigaev, we hear something about the story of the Revolution, but the play lacks coherence. The last part of the trilogy, which deals with life in Soviet Russia, was not printed or performed during Gorki's lifetime. By this time he had become very critical of his dramatic work. While he was writing *The Lower Depths* Gorki wrote to Chekhov, saying that if this play failed he would write ten more, until he achieved the perfect expression for what he wanted. The remarkable success of *The Lower Depths* seems to have caused his ambition to weaken. He was himself conscious that the twenty or so plays which he produced had no particular literary merit: "I wrote plays because I had to; that is why they are so bad. But if I had studied the theory of drama they would have been even worse." This last point may be doubted. Chekhov had with considerable difficulty acquired an intimate knowledge of foreign drama, a knowledge which Gorki seems to have lacked. Through its bold choice of subject and its rank realism

The Lower Depths came to be regarded by the contemporary world as something of a miracle. But Gorki never again fulfilled the expectations which this play had aroused, and which were also justified by his outstanding talent. His gift for creating living human beings is admirable, but he had difficulty in setting his characters in motion. His plays do not merely lack plot, as Chekhov's do; they lack any sort of inner life. The political purpose—at any rate in the plays read by the present writer—is never integrated with the action.

With all its obvious weaknesses, Gorki's trilogy of the early Thirties remains the last manifestations of that great period in Russian drama which began with Tolstoy and Chekhov, and which had an inspiring influence on so many Western playwrights.

GERMAN DRAMA

THE introduction to this book made it plain that German drama had a big part to play in the growth of modern drama. This holds good not only of the works of the neo-classical and romantic periods, but also of the later stage, when Hebbel was the greatest exponent of German drama. In 1852 Hettner wrote *Das Moderne Drama*, referring, quite correctly, to German drama. After Hebbel's death in 1863 there was a sad dearth of great names in Germany: Gerhart Hauptmann, who lived until 1946 and wrote both symbolical and naturalistic dramas, is the only really great figure. The modernistic experimental plays in which German dramatists have since excelled have proved to have only ephemeral value.

Nevertheless it is difficult to imagine how modern European drama between 1870 and 1940 could have developed without the co-operation of Germany.

Ten years before the Théâtre Libre was founded, the Scandinavian writers had already been having their plays performed on German stages, and had achieved their first great successes there. After 1870 Björnson and Ibsen won a European reputation with their contemporary plays as performed in Germany, and they used to publish a German version simultaneously with the original. Strindberg and the great Russian writers followed them. Ibsen, after all, spent a number of years abroad, and many of them in Germany, and in 1892 Strindberg made an attempt to acclimatize himself as an author in Germany. None of these displayed any great enthusiasm for contemporary German drama, but in Germany they could count on a sympathetic public such as they failed to find at home. The Freie Bühne was founded in 1889 by Otto Brahms on the model of the Théâtre Libre, but this was only one expression of the desire to foster modern drama irrespective of its national origin.

The Théâtre Libre and its imitators never quite succeeded in breaking down the barriers that cause national isolation. But just because Germany lacked native playwrights of high calibre, her experimental theatres afforded more opportunity for dramatic writers to earn world reputations.

As this book is not intended to be a history of the theatre the details of this story cannot be described here. One name, however, must be mentioned, that of Max Rheinhardt, who died in 1943. By his choice of plays to be performed and his many brilliant productions he made immense contributions to the development of modern drama. He did not limit his support to the work of any one school, as is occasionally the case with great directors. Rheinhardt was responsible for the production of Gorki's ultra-naturalistic *The Lower Depths* which made that play a world-success, but he achieved an equally harmonious co-operation with the Austrian symbolist playwright, Hofmannsthal. By his production of *Jedermann* (*Everyman*) and *Das Grosse Welttheater* (*The Great Theatre of the World*) at the Salzburg Festival he achieved a greater success than these plays had ever met with before. Rheinhardt was also instrumental in winning for Strindberg's later dramatic writings the reputation they deserved. If it had not been for his productions, it would have taken a long time for people to appreciate the poetic qualities of *To Damascus, A Dream Play* and, above all, the chamber plays. Apart from working in his own theatres, Rheinhardt was invited to produce abroad, often with his own company but sometimes with foreign actors. He was in close contact with every theatre which had a progressive policy, and, though he did not settle down to live in the United States until his last years, he had long been an influence in American stage production.

The influence of Germany on Scandinavian drama has been particularly important. In a letter to Schering, Strindberg said that for a time he was living almost entirely on German royalties, for his plays were only rarely performed in Sweden, and during the ten years after his death he was the most popular playwright in Germany.

This keen interest in the works of foreign dramatists naturally produced a considerable amount of critical literature on the subject. The commentaries on Ibsen produced by Dresdner and Roman Woerner are better than anything written in Norway at the time, while critical studies of Strindberg were much more advanced in Germany than in Sweden.

Hans Johst, in whose play, *Schlageter,* appears the notorious line, "When I hear the word 'culture' I reach for my gun," said in a happier moment that the theatre "provides the last pedagogical opportunity of saving the people from the total materialism of a wholly realistic world." This opportunity has now, it seems, been lost, but we should not forget the contribution made by Germany before the first world war, and between the wars, towards establishing contact between dramatists of different countries.

GERHART HAUPTMANN

GERMAN naturalism had some difficulty in finding a wind to fill its sails. Both audiences and critics long remained content with historical plays and imitations of French comedies. Even as late as 1890 Hermann Sudermann scored great triumphs with plays in the Augier and Sardou style, with a modest admixture of naturalistic traits and parts, suitable for the great foreign primadonnas.

A naturalistic pamphlet of 1886 by Bleibtreu, called *Die Revolution der Litteratur*, caused a group of German authors led by Gerhart Hauptmann, Arno Holz and Johannes Schlaf to form an association called Durch. Three years later, in 1889, the Freie Bühne was founded in Berlin. Here performances were given of such plays as Zola's *Thérèse Raquin* and *L'Assommoir*, Tolstoy's *The Power of Darkness*, Ibsen's *Ghosts* and Strindberg's *The Father*. In close relationship with these foreign models there grew up a collection of naturalistic German plays.

Gerhart Hauptmann was born in 1862, the same year as Maeterlinck, and like him he was destined never to satisfy the high expectations created by his youthful achievements. He was a richly talented artist, but he lacked the single-mindedness of genius, and its capacity for finding new ways of advance. He frequently felt the need of linking himself with some earlier writer. During his early years he worked so closely with Holz and Schlaf that their plays sometimes seem to parody one another. Of foreign writers it was mostly Ibsen and Tolstoy who influenced his work, and it was directly under the inspiration of Tolstoy that he wrote his great masterpiece, *Die Weber* (*The Weavers*). Later he wrote plays both in the naturalistic and the symbolical vein, without ever being able, like Strindberg or Chekhov, to weld the two styles into one by the force of his personality. He is always at his best when he draws his material from his native region, Silesia.

In this part of Germany the life of the country people had been transformed in Hauptmann's boyhood by the discovery of coal. It was round this revolution that Hauptmann's first play, *Vor Sonnenaufgang* (*Before Sunrise*), was built, and it appeared just as the Freie Bühne was being opened. From the most abject poverty many of the coal-owning peasants were suddenly pitched headlong into a state of affluence which they were ill equipped to support. There must have been many farms like the one which Hauptmann describes, where people lived on oysters, lobsters and champagne while the cattle munched their hay from marble cribs. Both the farm people and their servants lived a life which was little better than that of the beasts, and in a state of spiritual poverty which Hauptmann described in colours borrowed from Tolstoy. The master of the farm is a monster of drunkenness and depravity. His second wife is having an *affaire* with her cousin, whom she is anxious to marry off to her step-daughter, Helene, to conceal the existence of this relationship. There are scenes in which drunkenness, seduction and the cries of childbirth are represented with the utmost crudity, and they aroused a good deal of indignation at the first performance.

What disturbs a modern reader is not so much this crude portrayal of the setting, for in many respects it is milder than Tolstoy's, but rather the plot, which indicates a positively doc-trinaire adherence to the theories of heredity.

Helene, who has been away at boarding-school, has managed to grow up pure and innocent in spite of her home. An eager social reformer, Alfred Loth, arrives and falls in love with her. They become engaged. Then the family doctor, whose name is Schimmelpfennig and who is akin to Ibsen's Dr. Relling, tells Loth that Helene is a hereditary drunkard. Her elder, married sister is a helpless victim of the craving for drink, and she has had a son who died at the age of three years after injuring himself with a bottle of vinegar which he grasped by mistake instead of his beloved bottle of brandy. When Loth asks if there is no chance of his fiancée and their future children escaping the taint of drunkenness the doctor replies doubtfully that cases have been known where such hereditary weaknesses have been overcome.

At this news Loth immediately leaves the house without even daring to bid farewell to Helene, who then in her despair commits suicide.

Hauptmann at this period was a fervent teetotaller, and was undoubtedly as sincere a believer in the possibility of hereditary alcoholism as he made Dr. Schimmelpfennig appear to be. It is, however, still possible to agree with German scholars that he was not on the side of Loth either, whom he conceived as a narrow-minded idealist of the same sort as Gregers Werle, and whose prejudices he laid bare by allowing him to despise Zola and Ibsen. In this play Hauptmann has tried to follow the naturalistic pattern, eschewing monologues and asides, and conforming as closely as possible to the unities of place and time. The greater part of the action takes place before sunrise, as in *Ghosts*—hence the title.

Some months after *Before Sunrise* Holz and Schlaf secured the performance at the Freie Bühne of their first play, *Die Familie Selicke* (*The Selicke Family*). This repeats the story of Hauptmann's drama, but it is set in the home of a poor town family, living on the borders of starvation with a drunkard of a book-keeper as its head. The unities of time and place have been more strictly observed than in Hauptmann's play.

In his next play, *Das Friedenfest* (*The Feast of Reconciliation*, or *The Reconciliation*), Hauptmann took a further step and concentrated the whole action of the play into one Christmas Eve. The story concerns a family whose hereditary disease is a nervous complaint. The fiancée of the youngest son is a figure of light, like Helene in *Before Sunrise*, who has prevailed on all the members of the family, normally at odds with each other, to agree to meet on this particular evening. But though for the first time the house has a Christmas tree alight with candles, the family cannot suppress their quarrelsome instincts. The play culminates in a scene of violence between the engaged son, Wilhelm, and his father, in which both men are quite unable to control themselves. The father then has a stroke and dies, and Wilhelm tries to break off his engagement, as he is certain that he will cause his wife much unhappiness. The young girl, however, believes in the power of their love to overcome the curse of hereditary weakness.

With its rather weird family quarrels this play reminds one of

Strindberg. But it is also the first play in which we meet the highly-strung and over-sensitive characters who are to become so typical of Hauptmann, and with whom he felt himself closely related.

The personal element is also very strong in *Einsame Menschen* (*LonelyMen*, or *Lonely Lives*), which has a hero of Hauptmann's own age, twenty-eight. He dedicated it thus: "I place this drama in the hands of those who have experienced it." The title also refers to people in the plural, though in fact it is really only the hero, Johannes Vockerat, who lives in spiritual isolation. Hauptmann tried to make him typical of a whole generation, that which at the end of one century hopes for better understanding in the next.

Johannes Vockerat is a scientist, who puts up pictures of Darwin and Haeckel on his walls and is writing a great work on psychophysiology. His conventional and narrow-minded parents are appalled at his modern ideas. Hauptmann himself was brought up, after his father had lost his fortune, by relations who were of the Moravian persuasion, and they served as models for the well-meaning but stubbornly conservative Vockerat couple.

The plot of the play was constructed with *Rosmersholm* in mind. Johannes is married to Käthe, who has the patience of an angel, but is completely lacking in personality and is a creature of convention. As a guest in the family there suddenly appears a young student, by name Anna Mahr, with advanced ideas, a mysterious past, and plans for the future that are equally uncertain. When he is with her Johannes feels that he is understood, and that she can inspire him in his scientific work. Both of them believe that it is only a spiritual friendship that unites them. Poor Käthe, however, feels humiliated, and the parents compel Anna Mahr to leave the house. When she goes, Johannes realizes the true nature of his feelings for her, and commits suicide in the very boat where they used to sit and carry on their philosophical discussions.

Lonely Men was Hauptmann's first great success, and it was played both in Germany and in other countries. In contrast to *Rosmersholm* it is a purely psychological play, with no suggestion of symbolism. As in Scandinavia the title of Bang's novel, *Hopeless Generations*, so likewise in Germany *Einsame Menschen* became a generic term for describing the younger generation which felt that its modern ideas were irreconcilably opposed to the conservatism of its elders. Maurice Gravier put the question in a recent article whether Hauptmann was influenced, not only by *Rosmersholm,* but also by the *Married* stories of Strindberg, in his analysis of the neurasthenic young social reformer and the emancipated young girl student.

It is significant of the reputation which the play won in Germany that when *The Master Builder* first appeared, and Ibsen made Solness express his fear that Ragnar Brovik would put him in the shade, everyone assumed that Ibsen was referring to Hauptmann. It is known that he was thinking of Hamsun.

Incomparably the greatest play that Hauptmann wrote, *The Weavers*, was composed in 1891-92, at first in a pure Silesian dialect, and was performed in 1893 at the Freie Bühne. To some extent in this play Hauptmann was feeling back to the setting of his first play, *Before Sunrise*. He took the story from the country near his own home, although the events and conditions he describes actually come from a period fifty years earlier, a weavers' rising in the 1840's in Silesia.

Hauptmann had personal reasons for choosing this subject, as he indicates in the dedication of the play to his father. He did in fact come from a family of weavers, and his ancestors had taken part in the events described in his play. His great-grandfather had migrated from Bohemia to Silesia and earned his living there by weaving. His grandfather had also started life as a weaver, and when he later became a prosperous hotel proprietor he used often to tell his son, Hauptmann's father, about the horrors of his life when he was a workman. Hauptmann himself says in the dedication to his father that it was these tales of how his grandfather used to sit at the loom that gave him his first idea for the play.

Apart from these family traditions, Hauptmann had also studied historical sources. An economic study by Zimmerman of the rise and fall of the linen industry in Silesia was published in 1885. It described the amount of work done at home in the various villages of the region, how the system had lasted ever since the Thirty Years War, and how much it had contributed to the existence of an under-nourished rural proletariat. Silesia had been transferred from Austria to Prussia, prices and taxes had changed, but nothing had effected any permanent improvement for the weavers. Only once during these hundreds of years had the weavers dared to take up arms against their oppressors. In the summer of 1844 the weavers of Eulengebirge were seized by an irresistible desire for a breath of freedom. A weavers' song of unknown origin, called the Judgment of Blood, spread from house to house and acted as the spark which sets all aflame. The men rose and plundered the homes of the manufacturers. For a moment it looked as if they would triumph, but they lacked any organization, and their courage waned as quickly as it had risen. Two weavers were shot down by the hastily summoned soldiers and the remainder returned to work, to resign themselves once again to their wretchedness.

Hauptmann's play is a faithful account of this incident in all its detail. The savage song of the weavers is a constantly recurring refrain, which also brings the play to a close.

The Weavers is really a historical play, but the subject made it seem modern and topical. The Police Censor in Berlin refused to allow it to be performed in public, but only at the private theatre of the Freie Bühne. Since then also there have been some German historians of literature who have sought to delete the play from the list of Hauptmann's works. Adolf Bartels, who was otherwise an admirer of Hauptmann, complained in 1905 that he was "obsessed by these enervating modern ideas of humaneness," and that in The Weavers "he had allowed himself to be deceived by phrases about international democracy." This is rather the sort of stern sermon that Dreissiger, the manufacturer, and Pastor Kittelhaus give to the young tutor, Weinhold, in the fourth act. He is never allowed to say more than that the weavers are hungry and ignorant, and are trying to express their discontent in the only way they know. Having got so far he is dismissed without ceremony by Dreissiger, who loathes all "sentimental humanitarians." In his socialist sympathies Hauptmann did not go much further than Weinhold. He regarded the weavers' rising as an enterprise that was hopeless from the start, and his real hero is the weaver, Hilse, a Tolstoyan character who first appears in the final act, and who remains at his loom when all the rest join in the acts of violence.

But the consciousness that he himself sprang from this community of weavers enabled Hauptmann to give this picture an undertone of warmth, and the play loses none of its freshness and topicality. It is the only one of Hauptmann's plays which seems as modern to-day as it must have done when it was first performed. It is a masterpiece unsurpassed by any other naturalist playwright, and not again equalled by Hauptmann himself.

The leader of the weavers' rising is unknown, and in *The Weavers*, likewise, there are no prominent characters. There are a number of excellently delineated characters, but no one is allowed to push himself forward at the expense of another; they are all voices rising from the crowd, the suffering, grumbling, rebellious crowd. Zola's account of the miners' strike in Germinal may to some extent have inspired Hauptmann, but he treats the subject much more soberly and realistically, and without any of Zola's exaggerations. It is significant that Hauptmann's historical sources give a more unflattering picture of the original of his character, the manufacturer Dreissiger.

In the original version of the play there is a fresh list of characters for every act; new people are continually being introduced, and the final act takes place in the home of old Hilse who has not hitherto been mentioned, and whose meaningless death from a stray bullet brings the play to a close.

Of action in the ordinary sense of the word there is none in *The Weavers*. The rising is about to start when the play begins, and the play ends before it has been finally put down. The soldiers have attacked, but been repulsed by the weavers, and it is only Hilse's prophecies in the final act which show us that an inglorious defeat is inevitable.

Similarly, there is no one scene round which the play can be said to be built. The weavers' storming of Dreissiger's villa is only an incident. The wretched workmen feel clumsy and embarrassed in the deserted salons, and only after a time do they hit on the idea of destroying the furniture in order to impoverish Dreissiger.

Yet in spite of the lack of plot the play does not feel like a dramatized novel or a series of unrelated tableaux. The sequence of events is depicted with an inner logic which makes plain the development from low murmurings to open revolt. We hear of

the short-lived bliss of the poor weavers when they empty the
manufacturer's wine-cellar and make merry with his stores of
food. From the first moment the revolt is hopeless, for the mob
does not know how to use its freedom.

One is already convinced of this in the first act, where the
weavers, their wives and children bring forward the pieces which
they have been weaving during the week, to receive their payment. It says in the stage directions that they look as if they
are standing at the bar of a court, awaiting a verdict of life or
death. They make themselves as small and humble as possible,
in the hope of getting a little on account, and of escaping criticism
of their work from the inspecting officials. There is one exception
—Bäcker, a sturdy young man with rough manners. He is
already infected with the spirit of revolt. When he receives
payment for his piece of cloth he calls it filthy charity, and
Dreissiger is summoned. He accuses Bäcker of inciting the people
and making them sing the shameful weavers' song. Dreissiger
dismisses him; he waits with threatening gestures while his
wages are being counted out, and then takes his leave.

Not until the second act do we hear the weavers' song, pain-
fully spelt out from a piece of paper by one of the rioters who can
read—Jäger, a veteran returned from the wars. The words about
the court which slowly drains away the blood of the workers
carry a ring of literal truth. Even old Ansorge, who has just said
that he will never leave his cottage, where every nail marks a
night without sleep, and every beam a year of living on dry
bread, flares up and cries, "There must be a change . . . we'll
endure it no longer, come what may."

In the fourth act, which is set in Dreissiger's home, Hauptmann
reveals for the first time his capacity for humour. The sudden
change of mood when the manufacturer and his uneducated wife
realize that the matter is serious and their lives are at stake is
conveyed in a passage of brilliant comedy. After their hasty
flight the much-feared army of rioters enters, apparently still in a
state of bewilderment. The weaving girls stand before the great
mirrors and gaze at the reflections of their pinched faces and
ragged clothes.

The last act is a play in itself, but is perfectly connected with
what has gone before. The violence of the rising and its useless-

ness are both reflected in Hilse's little hut, where his son's wife is seized by the spirit of revolt and succeeds at last in dragging her husband with her, and to which the little seven-year-old grand-daughter returns carrying a silver spoon from the Dreissigers. But Hilse and his blind and deaf wife are immovable. Hilse will not even listen to those who warn him to go away from the loom by the window lest he be hit by a bullet: "Listen, mother, here we are going to sit and do our duty, even if all the snow burns away." A new salvo is heard. Hilse rises up at his loom and drops down dead. The curtain falls while the weavers' song is heard off stage. It is a bitter irony of fate that the one man who, in the face of all insults, stayed at his work should be the blind bullets' first victim.

When dedicating the play to his father, Hauptmann wrote that his play was the best which "a poor man like Hamlet" had to offer. The expression contained more truth than Hauptmann realized. He was never again to create anything comparable to *The Weavers*. And yet this masterpiece has in some respects shown the way for some of his subsequent plays. It convinced him that Silesia was the right world for his compositions, and that peasant drama lay nearest his heart. He also discovered that he possessed a comic vein, which had never come to light in his earlier, grimly serious plays.

After *The Weavers* Hauptmann wrote two comedies, *Kollege Crampton (Colleague Crampton)*, and *Der Biberpelz (The Beaver Coat)*. In *Colleague Crampton* the chief character is a drunken professor of the Academy of Art, a bohemian type modelled on one of Hauptmann's own teachers from the days when he was learning to be a sculptor. With his wide-brimmed hat, his Italian cloak and his mandolin, he seems a typical German, and one hardly gets the impression that he has been a great artist with liberal ideas. He is an amusing and eccentric character, set in a very ordinary plot.

Hauptmann had no particular gift for invention when he had to construct plots. *The Beaver Coat* has links with the best German comedy of the 19th century, Kleist's *Der Zerbrochene Krug (The Broken Jug)*. In that play a judge has to discover who has broken a jug, and it turns out to be himself. In Hauptmann's play the thoroughly Prussian 'President of the Court,' von

Wehrhahn, has the thief of the beavercoat, the cunning washer-woman, Frau Wolff, in his own house. Yet he pats her amiably on the shoulder and praises her honesty. The victim of the robbery has a lodger, who is suspected of being a political agitator, and is therefore treated by von Wehrhahn as a criminal. The task of protecting the nation's highest interests he regards as his life duty; to discover who stole the fur coat seems to him the merest trifle. This typical Prussian official with his monocle, his military terseness of speech, and his untiring zeal "to reform, introduce drill and discipline, review, purge and regulate," has so often since been the subject of caricature in comic papers and books, that one forgets that it was Hauptmann who first painted a full-length portrait of him. German literary historians have maintained that there is nothing in real life to correspond to this picture, but posterity has agreed with Hauptmann.

In the same year, 1893, in which Hauptmann wrote this amusing and still playable comedy, he made his first and best attempt at a symbolistic drama with *Hanneles Himmelfahrt* (*The Assumption of Hannele*). It deals with a poor little Silesian girl and her death after an attempted suicide. We share the last visions that she sees in her fever, and witness scenes from the dismal reality that surrounds her.

The resemblance to Andersen's story about the girl with the matches, which every reader notices, is not fortuitous. Already in 1885 Hauptmann had written a descriptive poem, *Die Mondbraut*, in which the influence of the Danish story is quite unmistakable. Hauptmann has not succeeded in producing such a graceful and polished little work of art as H. C. Andersen. But he has treated a subject of the same kind as is found in Maeterlinck's plays, with their innocent fairy princesses who are rescued from death, and has transferred it to his own Silesian peasant setting. In so far as he constructed a peasant drama in symbolistic style, he is a fore-runner of later dramatists; the Irishman Synge in particular is considered to have been directly inspired by him.

Hauptmann is less original in *Die Versunkene Glocke* (*The Sunken Bell*, 1896), which at that time was the most popular of his plays, and went into more than twice as many editions as *The Weavers*. This attempt to recreate the elfin beauty of romanticism in the character of the nature spirit, Rautendelein, and her husband, Nickelmann, is no longer of interest. The rather obscure symbolism of the play has an autobiographical content. The bell-founder, Heinrich, a cross between Brand and Solness, never succeeds in realizing his dream of creating his great masterpiece, a bell for the church on the top of the mountain. He is torn between his earthly wife, a very ordinary and colourless person, and Rautendelein, the bewitching but unreal creature of fantasy. He feels himself "a stranger though at home down below; at home though a stranger up here in the mountains." This may seem to be merely a reference to the way in which Hauptmann hovers between naturalism and airy symbolism. But an old witch, Die Wittichen, expresses the fundamental idea when she says of Heinrich, "You were one of the called, but not one of the chosen." In a much later play, *Michael Kramer*, Hauptmann repeated this theme in a modern setting. Here he shows us an idealistic artist who is hampered in his development, and never allowed to complete his great work, a picture of Christ.

The Sunken Bell has some beautiful poetic passages, but has to bear a heavy load of neo-romantic fairy nonsense. The Irishman Yeats can paint the fairy world with a light and airy touch worthy of Shakespeare. In Hauptmann it seems heavy and lifeless.

Next to *The Assumption of Hannele* and *The Sunken Bell*, *Und Pippa Tanzt (And Pippa Dances!)* is the most original of Hauptmann's symbolistic plays. The name and some of the atmosphere is reminiscent of Robert Browning's beautiful *Pippa Passes*. In Hauptmann's play the chief character is the daughter of an Italian glass-blower. She has lost her way up in the Silesian mountains, and drives all men crazy by her bewitching dance. She is a wood nymph disguised in earthly rags. But Hauptmann lacks the graceful fantasy of his contemporary, Hofmannsthal. He has himself written a note on this play: "Pippa is meant to be beauty, fantasy, the blue flower which everyone longs to find."

Along with his symbolistic plays Hauptmann also wrote naturalistic peasant dramas from Silesia. The best of these is *Fuhrmann Henschel (Drayman Henschel)*. It was written in 1898, but the plot is taken from a real life incident which Hauptmann had treated in a novel as early as 1887, *Bahnwärter Thiel*.

In *Drayman Henschel*, however, there is a new theme. The

worthy driver has broken the promise he made to his wife on her death-bed by marrying his housemaid. She treats him badly and neglects his child, who dies. Shattered by this final blow he goes and sits in the inn, where he hears that she is deceiving him, and that she is suspected of having murdered both the first wife and the child. Pangs of conscience and shame drive Henschel to hang himself with his own whip. It is the theme of *Rosmersholm* which we find once again in Hauptmann's dramatic writing.

The last play of Hauptmann to achieve world fame was *Vor Sonnenuntergang (Before Sunset)*, written when he was seventy years old. The title is chosen to contrast with his first work, *Before Sunrise*, but the play, which describes an unhappy late-summer love affair, reminds one rather of *Lonely Men*. As in that play, the hero is the same age as the author. When his relations try to prevent him from marrying quite a young girl, and look like succeeding in having him put away, he takes poison. As in *Lonely Men*, and in another earlier play, *Gabriel Schillings Flucht (Gabriel Schilling's Flight)*, we find here a faint echo of the main theme in *Rosmersholm*.

Hauptmann in his dramatic writing has a natural preference for large canvases and large problems. Only in one work, however, *The Weavers*, has he fully succeeded in realizing his intentions. His symbolistic plays lack clarity in their ideas, and the poetic power to support them; his naturalistic, bourgeois plays lack psychological depth. His heroes tend to be all alike, nervous, irritable and easily swayed. Even *Drayman Henschel* seems brittle and fragile. Hauptmann's ambition was to become the greatest dramatist of his day, but from the beginning he suffered from the fear that he would not reach his goal. This is the burden of a whole series of his plays, and has been best expressed in the phrase used by the old witch in *The Sunken Bell*; he was 'called, but not chosen.'

AUSTRIAN DRAMA

IN Germany naturalistic drama had developed into a heavy and oppressive presentation of everyday life as lived by the lower middle classes and the social strata below them. Symbolism had sailed hastily into the wake of romanticism and adopted its well-worn fairy-tale themes, its pretensions to profound philosophy, and its inability to create real characters. In Germany there was an instinctive opposition to these lines of development, and this may partly explain why dramatists there never felt at home for long in either of these schools. It was felt that the German temperament did not possess that realistic power of psychological observation demanded by naturalistic drama, or the light fantasy needed by symbolism. The result was that constant and ever more frantic attempts were made to create something else. Some authors reverted to neo-classicism and the great days of German drama, but did not succeed in producing anything but pale imitations. Others sought inspiration in modernism, and of these Wedekind was the pioneer. Yet others approached the films, and imitated the new tendencies of painters, with but poor artistic results.

In Austria conditions were different. Even if dramatists there were not unaffected by the prevailing confusion of ideas in Germany, there was a living force, both in symbolism and naturalism, which they could develop creatively in a way that had not been possible in Germany.

During the last quarter of the 19th century Vienna was a ghost of the Paris of the Second Empire. In the old city on the Danube reigned Europe's oldest and probably most degenerate dynasty. There was a distinguished aristocracy which had known better days, but which continued to live in the style of the 'ancien régime,' and a middle class which must have resembled that of

Germany in the days of the Little States. The patriotic, social, and industrial interests which had prevented the free growth of Germany's art and culture did not exist in Austria. Life was a more gracious and pleasant affair, and there was little interest in politics, social problems, or even the more fundamental issues of life. There was no unrestrained carnival atmosphere, as in the Second Empire, and the pace was slower. Vienna was the city of music and dancing, and many composers, of whom Strauss was the latest, chose to live there. It had also become the home of operetta when the misfortunes of 1871 drove it out of Paris into exile. Right up to the outbreak of the first world war Vienna presented the appearance of a city which was in some way a generation behind the times. As in the Paris of the Second Empire, there was a revival of rococo, but it was less pompous and more graceful than the Parisian version, and more middle-class in character.

It was a gay period, with a streak of melancholy running through it. A thirst for pleasure, alternating with a longing for death, are characteristics of the rococo Vienna of both the 19th and the 18th centuries. Love and death are the two motive forces of Austrian drama, but love is not a shattering, tearing passion; it is a graceful, butterfly emotion, a rococo conception usually accompanied by weariness of life and melancholy—not "Liebe" but "Liebelei," not love but lovemaking, to use Schnitzler's own terms. In the same way, death is no terrifying skeleton but rather the sad ending of life's happiness, the corruption which is always to be found at the bottom of the cup of joy. In one of Schnitzler's plays somebody asks, "Then why are you talking about death?" The reply comes, "What decent man in his inmost soul thinks of anything else in his happy moments?"

This trait of Viennese rococo in both the Austrian writers Schnitzler and Hofmannsthal must be stressed if we are to do them justice. If one takes too lofty and tragic a view of the problems which they treat, they seem trivial, and in the same way the authors themselves can easily appear to strike a false note directly they try to go outside the range of their soft voices. When Schnitzler attempts to present a picture of the world of the professions, as in *Professor Bernhardi*, where the setting is a medical one, or the world of journalism in *Fink und Fliederbusch*, all he achieves is caricature. He has the hand of an artist, but it was not meant to paint with a big brush. When, however, he describes the somewhat unreal life which is lived by his *alter ego*, the pleasure-seeking but disillusioned Anatol, he is on his own ground. This is also true when he portrays actors, who are never quite sure on which side of the curtain they are, or when he disguises his characters as marionettes who are human beings at one moment, and pure puppets at the next. His characters have perhaps never existed anywhere except in his own imagination. At the same time there is something typically Viennese about them. Fritz in *Liebelei*, (*Light o' Love*), no less than Schnitzler's characters from the French Revolution in *Der Grüne Kakadu*, (*The Green Cockatoo*), is fundamentally Viennese, not observed in harsh daylight but in the soft light cast by pink lamp-shades. Schnitzler's pretty girls speak with the confiding accents of the real Viennese, but they are as remote from prosaic reality as Watteau's shepherdesses are from the peasant girls of his day.

As in Schnitzler the illusion of realism is never complete, so in the symbolism of Hofmannsthal the imagination is never quite free. Maeterlinck's princes and princesses have no national associations, but those of Hofmannsthal speak with a Viennese accent, however elaborate and colourful their Oriental disguise may be, and however exotic their setting. The heroine of his verse play, *Hochzeit der Sobeide* (*The Marriage of Sobeide*), is an excellent example. Even in the early play, *Der Tor und Der Tod*, (*The Fool and Death*), Claudio is a sophisticated young Viennese, and in Hofmannsthal's version of the old morality play, *Everyman*, the hero—who represents all mankind—is drawn from a young Viennese gallant. It is Anatol in medieval dress who is being torn between love and death.

Between the first plays of these two authors there are only a couple of years, but the difference in age was quite considerable. Arthur Schnitzler was born in 1862; Hofmannsthal twelve years later. But while Hofmannsthal had already made his début at the age of 17, and by 19 had written his best play, Schnitzler was brought up to be a doctor and did not devote himself entirely to literature until later in life.

Much has been made of his profession and professional training

as factors which may throw light on his dramatic work. But
the cold inhumanity of vivisection and the ruthlessness of the
surgeon's knife which are ascribed to him are hardly his most
important qualities. His great medical play, *Professor Bernhardi*,
is not as great as it was once thought to be, and is not even a
typical Schnitzler play. It is what Schnitzler saw outside the
clinics and the operating-theatre which has provided the material
for his work.

Schnitzler began his career as a dramatist with a series of seven
one-act plays called *Anatol*. These are the most frequently
performed of his works, and it is in the short one-act play with
only a few characters that Schnitzler really comes into his own.

The sort of situation which suited him best as a subject, and
which he chose by preference, was not usually capable of expansion
into a full-length play. Schnitzler is not a great tragic or a great
comic writer. He lacks the pathos of the tragedian and the fertile
invention of the comedian. He has no ability to reveal the more
profound qualities of his characters. They are as they seem to us
at first sight, and they can easily become uninteresting if we have
to listen to them too long. His proper field is the quick, confident
sketch, not the careful painting. There is a collection of his
one-act plays which is entitled *Lebendige Stunden* (*Living Hours*).
In the first of them the hero says, "Living hours! And yet they
live no longer than the last of those who remember them. It's
no bad trade to prolong the life of such hours." Such living hours,
living minutes, are what Schnitzler describes best, the moments
when one soul reveals itself to another, when one man's fate
suddenly appears in a totally new light. This is not the usual
method of naturalism, whereby the audience are given the
illusion of participating in ordinary life, in all the dreary repetitions of our everyday existence. Schnitzler's dramatic writing
was still sufficiently close to that of the Second Empire for the
characters to be shown in their moments of excitement. It
follows that his dialogue is not that of ordinary naturalism. It is
lively and sensitive, matching the situation. Exactly as in the
French playwrights, the action must be affected by every line
that is spoken; there are practically no static periods. Indeed,
Schnitzler called one of his last trios of one-act plays *Komödie
der Worte* (Comedy of Words).

In the *Anatol* series Schnitzler took his technique from the Frenchman Lavedan, who also wrote a number of short sketches dealing with groups of people who are usually concerned with the problems and conflicts of love. In the *Anatol* series the love-interest is also predominant. But while the merit of the French sketches is the wit and humour with which the situations are presented, the Austrian author goes deeper. This is already made clear in the exquisite introductory sketch which is called *Questioning the Irrevocable*. Anatol, who describes himself as a light-hearted melancholic, is discussing with his more jovial and humorous friend Max his experiments in hypnotism. They agree that he is to hypnotize his mistress, and then to ask her if she has been faithful; he strongly suspects the contrary. The girl comes, is hypnotized, and Anatol puts a number of questions, all of which she answers correctly. But, despite Max's reminders, he cannot bring himself to ask her whether she is faithful to him. He finds excuse after excuse, and finally drives his friend out of the room so that he shall not hear the answer. Now Anatol can put the fateful question, but instead he goes up to the girl and wakes her out of her sleep. At the decisive moment he prefers to live in uncertainty, rather than to know the truth. We have the thesis about the need for a 'life-lie' all over again, but in miniature form.

This miniature form is the one which suits Schnitzler best. The more trifling the plot, the better it seems to bring out his philosophy of life; the briefer his statement, the more clearly he expresses his meaning, and the better he can establish and maintain an atmosphere which is easily lost in longer plays. There are, however, one or two of these which have the same exquisite atmosphere and the same elegant execution. The best of these is probably his early play, *Light o' Love*, which was written five years after the *Anatol* series and which was Schnitzler's first real success. It is not a great play, but within its three short acts we find a refinement, a gentle and assured technique, which make it the equal of the best of Maupassant's tales.

It is actually a subject akin to that treated by Maupassant in his novel, *Notre Cœur*, that Schnitzler has chosen for this play. Young Fritz is having an affair with a noble lady, who torments him with her hysterical accusations and her continual hallucinations. He lives in constant fear of scenes, and is harassed by her constant anxiety that her husband will discover something. Fritz has a friend, Theodore, who is trying to distract his attention from this affair by introducing him to a young girl of the middle class. She is the daughter of an orchestra player, a naive and sensitive Viennese, who falls head over heels in love with him. She has no hopes of marrying Fritz, but she believes that at least she might fill his life for a time, and then die when life is no longer worth living. In her company Fritz feels a calm and a warmth which make him realize that here happiness is to be found. At that moment, however, his past catches up with him again. The husband of his noble mistress has discovered their letters and challenged him to a duel. Fritz accepts, and is killed. Not until after he is buried does any one tell Christine what has really happened, for she has been told that he was away with his family. She is utterly prostrated, not only because of his death, or his death for another woman's sake, but because he went to the duel without telling her about it, without leaving word for her, because he was buried and she was not allowed to be there. "I have only served to pass the time for him: it was for another that he died . . . He could leave me with a smile, leave this room and let himself be killed for another."

With her childish eyes and her confiding voice the little bourgeois girl, Christine, is the greatest heroine that Schnitzler created. Perhaps this is the clearest expression in Schnitzler of the distinction between real love, which so seldom comes out in his plays, and the lighter and more frivolous love-making, or "liebelei." It is of "liebelei" that Fritz's cynical friend, Theodore, speaks when he reproves him for taking his love affairs too tragically. Women are there to pass the time and, he continues, "You must seek your fortune where I have sought mine hitherto, where there are no great scenes, no dangers, no tragic developments, where there are no particular difficulties in the opening stages and no final agony at the end. The first kiss is received with a smile, and one breaks away with the slightest of gestures."

On the surface, Fritz's relations with Christine follow this peaceful course. But what is only an incident to him means her whole life to Christine, and that is why she seeks death when she realizes that she meant no more to him.

There is the same contrast of character between Fritz and Theodore as there is between Anatol and Max. Theodore is a humorist and a cynic, while Fritz is a modern creature of moods, melancholy despite his gay bachelor existence, and sensitive though too spoilt to sustain an emotion and allow it to grow deeper. Fritz may to some extent be a self-portrait of the author, still no more than thirty-two years old. Unfortunately he was all too soon to lose the more gentle and tractable side of his character, and his attitude to life was to approach the sober and controlled cynicism of Theodore.

Between the Anatol series and Schnitzler's next collection of one-act plays, *Reigen* (*Hands Around*), which was written during the winter of 1896-7 and published in 1900, there exists the same difference as between Anatol and Max and between Fritz and Theodore. Love is still the theme, delicate situations are still the plot, but there are no more young dreamers like Anatol or Fritz, no more innocent girls like Christine. The "Süsse Mädel" that we find in *Hands Around* are more coarse and more vulgar. The comic element is stronger than in the earlier plays, which may have treated the slender love theme too seriously. On the other hand, the atmosphere is less poetic. Schnitzler is still describing the blind-man's-buff game of love, but he is no longer concerned to show its idealistic aspects in relation to a sober reality, to allow the joy of love and the fear of death to meet in opposition. In *Hands Around,* love is described with merciless candour and in its ugliest aspects. The series has been called *Reigen,* or Ring-dance, because it consists of a number of love relationships between various couples; in each new situation we find one member of the earlier couple reappearing, but linked with a new partner. Despite the terrible pessimism of the author's attitude to love in this play, there is a trace of the suppressed pathos which has grown into hard cynicism.

In later years Schnitzler turned to other subjects for his one-act plays. In *Grosse Scene* (*Great Scenes*), we find a character-study of the modern actor, who is at heart a spoilt child but whose emotions have been so falsified, who is so completely accustomed to acting other mens' lives in front of the footlights that he can no longer distinguish between truth and falsehood. We realize that Schnitzler means something more than this, and that in creating this character it was not only the actor's profession that he was attacking. "We are always acting; it is a wise man who realizes this," someone says in another of his plays.

As a pure artist, Schnitzler has certain qualities which Hauptmann lacked. He has calm and restraint, and a certainty of form. Without being in the highest sense of the word a poet he has succeeded in giving his plays a most convincing atmosphere, characterization which without being excessively realistic is accurate enough to give us our bearings, and finally dialogue which though a trifle artificial is yet straightforward and lively. An English writer has compared his plays with Mozart's music. This may be a little too generous: it would have been enough to say Strauss.

Schnitzler has no social reforms to his credit, but his plays will surely have the same enduring vitality as the waltzes of Strauss. People do not dance to these as much as they did but they listen to them readily, as to ghosts of a bygone age. In the same way, when Schnitzler's plays become out of date they will acquire a value as period pieces. Some day they will be performed, as Marivaux is played to-day, not because he gives us realistic pictures of 18th century life, but because he has captured the very essence of the rococo and illuminated it with the magic light in which we love to see bygone ages.

The conception of Schnitzler as a late rococo artist was already expressed in poetic form as early as 1892, in an introductory poem written for *Anatol* by his eighteen-year old friend and brother poet, Hugo von Hofmannsthal. In a magical way Hofmannsthal here conjures up for us in a few smoothly running verses the Vienna of 1760, Canaletto's Vienna, as the proper setting for Schnitzler's art. It is the Vienna of cascades, of tritons who have overslept, of gay ladies and Watteau shepherdesses, of Monsignore, Abbés and cavaliers.

This poem is already typical of Hofmannsthal. From it we learn in a flash the difference between him and Schnitzler. Schnitzler believes he is a Naturalist. He believes he is describing reality as he sees it around him, but all unconsciously he gives it an aura of its own, something of the light and airy magic of rococo. Hofmannsthal, on the other hand, is an avowed symbolist who sees everything through the eye of the past. For him reality is merely a piece of translated poetry. But though he himself is conscious that he can only reach life indirectly, through books and art, yet his poetry—even more than he realizes—is an expression of his own time, of his own Vienna setting.

Hofmannsthal set up a record for poetic precocity which had never been equalled in the 19th century. Already in 1891, at the early age of 17, he had written his first play, an artistically perfect piece, called *Gestern* (*Yesterday*). It treated a problem in which he was always to be interested, the relation between to-day and yesterday, and the feeling that the past is as important a factor in our lives as the present, that it is still active and retains its hold on us, however much we believe that we are absorbed by the present. The play is set in the Renaissance, and presents this thought in a way that reminds us of Schnitzler. Andrea praises the present and despises the past. But when he discovers that his loved one has once deceived him he cannot forget it: "What has once been, must live on for ever." Historians of literature have assumed that Hofmannsthal's little play, *The Fool and Death,* which was not published until two years later, was actually written at the same time as *Yesterday.* A collection of youthful letters which has since been published shows, however, that it was written in 1893, when Hofmannsthal was nineteen. But it is still a very remarkable work. With this play Hofmannsthal has assured himself of a place in world literature which he will not lose, though he was himself fully aware that none of his later work reached the same high level. He has expressed in this play just those weaknesses of temperament which were to cause his precocious genius to dry up before long, and to lose all inspiration.

In his letters Hofmannsthal speaks of *The Fool and Death* as a "tragedy-proverb," and it has since been called a miniature *Faust.* In its form, which is a monologue interrupted by conversations between the chief character and a number of dreamlike figures, it is more like *Manfred.* And yet one is anxious to retain the appellation, Faust play, because it does deal with one of the basic problems in *Faust,* and in particular the *Ur-Faust* which Goethe wrote when he was only a few years older than Hofmannsthal, namely the relation between art and life. When the curtain goes up we find ourselves in a room furnished in the style of the Empire, and advancing to meet us is a young man of

the 1820's, by name Claudio. His very first monologue gives us
Hofmannsthal's theme, a theme which is clearly related to the
innermost core of his own being. Claudio complains bitterly
that life is something quite unfamiliar to him, and that he has
never drunk its true wine. The works of art on the walls, the old
chest and its carvings, speak a plainer language to him than
human beings; it all seems more real to him than life itself.

> "So much have I lost myself in the world of Art
>   That I saw the sun only with dead eyes
>   And heard no more than dead ears can hear."

This was a personal confession, the truth of which Hofmannsthal
was to prove only too well in subsequent work. His relations
with life were so indirect, so dependent on the medium of books
and art, that towards the end of his life he had to seek his inspiration almost entirely from foreign works. It was no accident but
the psychological result of his literary bent, of his lack of an
immediate awareness of reality, that during his last twenty years,
the flowering period of a man's life, he wrote principally modern
paraphrases of older works.

In the continuation of this charming play of youth we see how
the melancholy music of a violin, which is heard outside the
window, leads Claudio to sad reflections on the sunny days of his
youth. Then suddenly, anxious to know who is playing, he
throws open the door, only to meet Death. And to Death he
makes the same complaint that he has expressed before: the days
of his youth are gone, and life has vanished without his even
having known what it was. He has never felt himself really
aglow, never been lifted on the crest of the highest waves.

Death replies that what has been given to all has also been given
to him, and that he is now ripe for harvest. But Claudio protests.
He explains that now for the first time he is really longing for
life. All that he has hitherto experienced, all that he has loved
and hated, all of this he has failed to understand in its full meaning.
Death is now to show him the life which was once his, and which
he has wasted. In a series of scenes of extraordinary beauty appear
those who have been nearest to him, his mother, the young
girl he loved and left, the friend whose loved one he stole and

whose confidence he forfeited. The dream characters disappear, and Claudio is again alone with Death. Now he is seized by infinite grief that it is not until life's end that he has learned to see life whole and clear, when before he saw it through a veil.

"First when I die, do I see that I am."

Here in this little play by a poet who had just left school we find all that the author of *The Sunken Bell* was vainly trying to achieve, a modern treatment of the age-old theme—how the poet is torn between reality and poetry.

For the generation of the Nineties the contrast seemed different to the one which faced the Romantics. It was a conflict between the desire for pleasure, which was so often proclaimed in their poetry, and a sense of remoteness from real life. The aesthetic finery in which they loved to clothe their enjoyment of life ruined the effect. Such importance was attached to the drinking of wine from wonderfully cut and coloured glass that one tended to forget its bouquet; one was so disposed to see in the loved one the lineaments of Mona Lisa that in the end one forgot that she was not a picture, but a creature of flesh and blood. It is to this disharmony between the aesthetic joys of looking at beauty and the actual enjoyment of life itself that young Hofmannsthal gave such perfect poetic expression. It is hardly right, as has sometimes been done, to interpret this play as a criticism of the aesthetic approach, but it is equally erroneous to consider it as an expression of decadence. The play sets out to show the inner conflict.

This little play seems more like an epilogue to a lifetime of poetry than a prologue, and this in fact it was to be. Hofmannsthal's later dramas resemble the literary experiments of an author who is well read in Keats, the English Pre-Raphaelites, the French symbolists and D'Annunzio. They are set in strange and exotic places, from the distant Orient and the world of the medieval legend to Renaissance Florence and the Venice of Casanova. Such are the settings of his most popular play, *Der Abenteurer und Die Sängerin* (*The Adventurer and the Singing-girl*), and the comedy, *Christinas Heimreise* (*Christina's Journey Home*), with themes taken from the memoirs of Casanova.

They are skilfully and tastefully constructed, with an excellent sense of period and local colour and interesting characterization. Moreover, most of them are written in a verse as melodious as a mandolin, and one forgets that it is this same German verse which proved such a recalcitrant tool in the hands of Hauptmann. Their weakness is a certain preciousness, both of form and content. "You talk like a book," is a comment in one of his plays, and up to a point it holds good of all Hofmannsthal's characters. They talk like books, they talk of books, they talk of aesthetic values and of beautiful *objets d'art*, they talk of vague ideas and fleeting impressions. In *Der weisse Fächer* (*The White Fan*) the hero, Fortunio, says "This adventure is almost nothing and yet it confuses me. One must be on one's guard, for 'almost nothing' is the stuff of all existence—words, an eyebrow raised, an eyebrow lowered, a meeting at the cross-roads, a face which resembles another, three memories that melt together, the scent of flowers borne by the wind, a dream we thought we had forgotten . . . there is nothing else. Such a shadow-play is our life and death."

This is Maeterlinck's thesis about small, unnoticed incidents and thoughts being the most important. But in him they are invested with a mystical content which incidents and impressions in Hofmannsthal seem entirely to lack. Maeterlinck convinces us that life is composed of just such small things, of "almost nothing," to use Hofmannsthal's expression; Hofmannsthal only succeeds in convincing us that his play is almost nothing. A play such as *The White Fan* is indeed almost nothing, and is so intended. Not until the epilogue are we given an explanation of the title, that its theme is no more than a motto painted on a fan.

Such are most of Hofmannsthal's plays, lovely soap-bubbles that glitter and disappear. He lacked the power to make a character or a conflict really moving. This lack is particularly evident when occasionally he tries to portray heroic or attractive women. It is remarkable how quickly one forgets any play of his that one reads.

As long as symbolism was in fashion, Hofmannsthal was regarded as one of the great hopes of modern drama. But as the movement gradually lost impetus, so his work appeared less significant, and he himself became clearly aware of his own lack of inspiration. The poor reception given to his plays on the stage he first interpreted as a sign that they were too poetic, and too far ahead of their time. Later it began to worry him. He began to write libretti for Richard Strauss's music, *Der Rosenkavalier* for instance, and achieved thereby the satisfaction of seeing his name rather more often on the theatre boards. The second remedy that he found is, however, more important. It was to rewrite older plays, or to write a modern paraphrase of material already produced in dramatic form. As he had read widely, had a considerable knowledge of the history of literature, and possessed a sense of style he managed in this way to produce several excellent plays for the stage.

As is well known, Hofmannsthal achieved his first success of this kind with his modernized version of the 15th century English morality play, *Everyman*. This play had been revived in London in 1902, and by the following year Hofmannsthal was working on his own version, which was complete by 1911. In this picture of a gay young man who is taken away by death before he has had his fill of pleasure, Hofmannsthal found something which struck a chord in his own nature, a chord on which he had already played in *The Fool and Death*. This enabled him in a remarkable way to put new life into the old morality play and, though retaining the simplicity of the original, yet to put a note into the hero's anguish which moved a modern audience. In *Das grosse Welttheater* (*The Great Theatre of the World*) Hofmannsthal succeeded even better in paraphrasing one of Calderón's *Autos,* and finally he wrote *Der Turm* (*The Tower*), based on Calderón's *La vida es Sueño* (*Life's a Dream*).

It is interesting to compare Hofmannsthal with that most precocious of 18th century geniuses, Thomas Chatterton, who was famous by the age of fifteen and died at eighteen. Chatterton achieved some remarkably beautiful poetry when he wrote poems about the cathedral in Bristol, in a 14th century style of English which he invented himself. He pretended that the poems had been written by a monk called Thomas Rowley. Poems written by him in a contemporary style were much more commonplace. It was not, however, the archaic language which had inspired him. He wrote the poems in contemporary English and then, with the help of a dictionary, translated them into medieval language. He was inspired by the subject itself, and by his readings of Chaucer.

Hofmannsthal differs from Chatterton in that his ordinary writing cannot be described as banal. He was a polished writer, but except in *The Fool and Death* he cannot be said to have handled the essential issues. He could treat them, however, when he was recreating dramas from classical, medieval or renaissance literature. Then he escaped from the artificiality which troubled him when he was dealing with more primitive subjects and writing in a simpler style. His plots took on bold lines and became dramatically effective. The characters were no longer shadow figures but real people, even when, as in *Everyman* and *The Great Theatre of the World*, they are allegorical figures. When one reads his plays now, about twenty years after his death in 1929, these are the two which seem to have lasted best. The relations of Everyman with Death are not so personal as those of Claudio in *The Fool and Death*, but they are more universal. In the Beggar in *The Great Theatre of the World*, who is taken against his will to a high place, to look down in derision at the rich and the powerful, and who finally greets death, at which the others tremble, as a deliverance, Hofmannsthal created his only really convincing hero. Many symbolists before him and after him have tried to turn old masterpieces into modern plays, but he was the most successful in pouring new life into old forms.

GEORGE BERNARD SHAW

ENGLAND was the last European country to produce modern stage drama, and this was largely the result of a lack of native tradition on which to build. In the 18th century the reaction against the immorality of Restoration comedy had left drama with but a languishing existence, in spite of such excellent authors as Sheridan and Goldsmith. The Romantic movement produced only literary plays and the intellectual public had ceased to attend theatres, where they took no satisfaction in a repertory of melodrama, farces and spectacle plays. The great authors of the day took no further part in drama than to allow their novels to be dramatized. The influence of French drama of the Second Empire resulted in England mainly in a sort of mechanistic drama. With this must be included the greater part of Wilde's work, which was old-fashioned in structure and unoriginal in idea. What did, however, make him a forerunner of Shaw was his sparkling dialogue, which even in Wilde tended to be an end in itself, a means by which the author could give playful expression to his ideas. His characters, too, eccentric and nonchalant like all men of the world, remind one of Shaw.

The new movements reached England later than other countries. In 1899, that is ten years after it first appeared, *A Doll's House* was played in the original version, and provoked violent discussion: the drama of Ibsen had arrived. The Independent Theatre, an offshoot of the Théâtre Libre, was opened in 1891 with *Ghosts,* the play which everywhere paved the way for modern drama. Here were performed many of the modern plays which were already familiar to Continental audiences, but which were as yet unknown to the British public. From the production in 1892 of Shaw's first and rather immature comedy,

Widowers' Houses, we date the beginning of modern English drama.

It is already apparent that Shaw's work has been of immense importance, and not least, negatively speaking, because it broke down many of the barriers and conventions which guarded dramatic art. This may not be so true, however, as regards the plot. Although Shaw campaigned vigorously against *la pièce bien faite* and claimed to have begun his dramatic career for the very reason that he wanted to protest against this form, yet one cannot say that he made a clean sweep of the ordinary dramatic plot, in the same way as the French and Russian Naturalists had done.

Shaw offers us a long gallery of varied characters whose superficial and deeper qualities he reveals to us with the precision of an etcher. But a good deal of his characterization is to be found in the exhaustive and witty stage directions which precede the entry of every new character, not to say almost every significant line or gesture. It is hardly possible for an actor to carry out all these directions, and Shaw's plays have to be read if full justice is to be done to his characterization.

The same is true of Shaw's dialogue. It sounds easy and spontaneous, and many have tried but few have succeeded in imitating it. In some ways this dialogue appears to be extraordinarily natural, but the impression of a real-life conversation which one gets from Chekhov's dialogue is lacking in Shaw. It is strikingly easy, too dazzlingly witty, too close to the brilliant discursive style of the long prefaces with which every play is provided.

Shaw gives his characters a spark of his own vitality, of his own astounding candour. His characters all belong to the same brilliant family. But they captivate, both by their nature, and by what they have to say. All this means that one can hardly count Shaw among the Naturalists, not even as a member of that moderate school of naturalism which he strongly influenced, and to which belonged his younger contemporaries, Granville-Barker and Galsworthy. The dramatist whom he most resembled and most admired was Ibsen, in spite of the fact that he opposed his attitude on several points. Before Shaw had published any play, he had already written *The Quintessence of Ibsenism* (1891), in which he shows how well he understood, and how greatly he admired, all Ibsen's work to date.

Like Ibsen, Shaw was a writer of problem plays who used the stage as a pulpit from which to expound his opinions. His characters represent various social and moral points of view, and the action often takes the form of a debate. At first he used to present this discussion through the actions of the characters on the stage, as Ibsen did, but in his later works the discussion often forms the whole play.

Shaw was not content, as Ibsen was, to ask a question; he also wanted to give the answer. Shaw is a playwright with a strongly marked sense of purpose, even though in the interests of dramatic tension he does not always allow this purpose to become too obvious, or at any rate not until the end of the play. He likes to allow the speakers on all sides to have their say, and to show that there is something to be said for each. But no one can fail to realize that Shaw has his own well marked point of view, and if by any chance this should not be made clear in the play, it certainly will be in the preface.

There is naturally a great difference between the deadly serious Ibsen and Shaw, whose greatest sorrow it is that no one will take him seriously, because he himself does not ever appear to do so. In reality Shaw is not the amusing and superficial inventor of paradoxes that he appears to be. He is neither a moral anarchist nor a dandy. This author, who seems to wish to overturn every moral concept, is a non-smoker, a vegetarian and a faithful Marxist. Next to Ibsen he most admires Tolstoy.

Shaw is an Irishman, born in Dublin in 1856 and belonging to what he himself called "Ireland's Protestant garrison," the puritanically Protestant section of the population. He was of the same origin as Swift, whom he frequently quotes. Like Swift he does not feel himself to be either a real Englishman, or a real Irishman. In the preface to his witty study of national psychology, *John Bull's Other Island,* he writes, "Personally, I prefer Englishmen to Irishmen, but I never think of Englishmen as my own countrymen. I would as soon use the term about a German." From this we see that Shaw does not suffer from any sense of patriotism, either Irish or English, and he has taken some hard knocks from both sides.

Shaw is a protestant in the literal sense of the word, and the Puritan strain in him was to become ever stronger as he grew older. He certainly denied Chesterton's suggestion, in a monograph of 1910, that if he had been born in another age he would have been a saint. But it was no accident that thirteen years later Shaw wrote the masterpiece of his life in *Saint Joan*, a play about a saint. In the preface to *Three Plays for Puritans*, he explains that he has always been a Puritan in his attitude to art. There are also early hints of the modernized, socialist-coloured Christianity, which he proclaims as the remedy for our world of misery in the preface to *Androcles and the Lion*, and the mystic faith which he acknowledged in the preface to *Saint Joan*. When material for a biography becomes available it will be an urgent task for scholars to trace this development from a starting-point of almost paradoxical rationalism and a ruthless desire worthy of Swift himself to reveal the truth. The rest of this chapter can only indicate some of the main stages.

★   ★   ★

It took a remarkably long time for Shaw to discover his true vocation. His first play was not performed until he was thirty-six, and it took a long time after that before he was acknowledged as a real author.

This was the result partly of the very difficult conditions in which he grew up, and partly of his inability to fit into English society.

Shaw has described his childhood and youth in his own inimitable way in two of the prefaces to collections of his writings (one of which contains an early novel, *Immaturity*), and has also given a good deal of information to would-be biographers. It does not all have to be believed—Shaw is never one to spoil a good story—but on the whole this account seems reasonable.

Shaw sprang from a proud and ancient English family in Ireland. For two generations, however, it had been coming down in the world. His father was at one time a modest clerk in the Dublin Courts, but the office was abolished in 1850, six years before his son's birth. After this he tried with very little success to earn a living as a grain dealer. At the age of forty he married, and George Bernard Shaw was the only son of the marriage. The first moral lesson that his father taught him was to loathe

spirits, and the lesson was so convincingly delivered that his son
decided to become a total abstainer. "But one evening, when I
was no taller than the top of his boots, he took me out for a walk.
As we went along I began to have the most incredible and
dreadful suspicion. When we reached home I crept to my mother,
and in terror whispered to her, 'Mother, I believe Father is
drunk.' She turned away with impatient distaste and said, 'Is
he ever anything else?" Since then I have never believed in
anything."

When his father was invited out to dinner he was never quite
sober when he arrived, and was shockingly drunk by the time
he left for home. Shaw lamented that his father belonged neither
to the happy nor to the quarrelsome class of drunkard. He was
an abstainer in theory, and just a pitiable creature.

The family therefore was soon cut off from all society: "If
my parents had been invited out their child would have been
more surprised than if the house had caught fire!" The only
way the children could treat the situation was to take it as a joke.
The mother, however, had no sense of humour at all. She shut
herself off from the outer world, ignored her husband and neglected her children. A music teacher who lived in a neighbouring
street discovered that she had a very beautiful voice, and wanted
to train it. She never became a great singer, but she was impressed
by the teacher's methods, and agreed to become a sort of factotum
in his house. The family moved in with her, and life became a
little easier. George Bernard Shaw grew up with music in his
ears; his mother and her teacher were always practising, while
his father played the bassoon. At that time the son hoped to
become an opera singer, and almost his first successful occupation
was as a music critic.

It took him sometime, however, to get so far. After having
attended a Methodist school without any great success until he
was thirteen he was found a job as a clerk, but was not happy.
Meanwhile the fortunes of the family had become worse again,
and the mother moved to London where she hoped to earn her
living by giving music lessons. In 1876, when Shaw was twenty,
he followed his mother to London, and became yet another
burden for her to bear. For thirty years he never saw Ireland,
and he declared once that as long as St. Helena was available he

would never settle in his native island. How he managed to support himself during the next ten years is something of a mystery. He wrote novels of which very little notice was taken, and joined one or two debating-societies. It was at this time that he was advised to read Marx, a piece of advice which changed his whole life.

Now he had a mission, something to work for, and he preached Marx wherever he was allowed to do so. For the next twelve years Shaw spoke on an average three times a week, at street corners, in the market-place, to societies, in public halls, wherever he was given the opportunity: "I first caught the ear of the English public in Hyde Park, through the blare of brass bands." It was not until after a serious illness at the age of forty that he ceased to speak regularly every week, though he still held himself to be available for special occasions. At first he was, of course, a relatively unknown and indeed a very nervous speaker. It was some years before any speech of his was reported, but later his name sufficed to fill the largest hall.

This speaking in public compelled Shaw to educate himself for the first time. He maintains that he knew the whole Encyclopædia Britannica by heart, except for the scientific articles. He now came into contact with England's Left-Wing intellectuals, joined the Fabian Society, and found many good friends among the Socialists and more or less utopian anarchists. He was one of the agitators who helped to bring about the important strike of the unemployed in 1887, and he also took part in the bloody encounters in Trafalgar Square which followed.

His plays also show signs of being written with the verve which is characteristic of a public speaker. The composition is often very careless, and sometimes Shaw goes down a side-track to follow up some problem that has aroused his interest. The wealth of words is enormous. Speaking of Saint Joan, Shaw tells us that he had to cut the play to the bone; and yet the present cut-down version still takes four hours to play.

That Shaw became a dramatist rather than a professional speaker was the result of his strictly refusing, on principle, to accept payment for his lectures, other than the price of a third-class train ticket if they were to be delivered outside London. Sometimes he would go round with a hat and take a collection, but never on his own behalf. When one regards him as a 'parlour-socialist,' which he is to some extent, it must not be forgotten that he was poorer than the working-class people to whom he spoke. He had only one lounge suit, and that not respectable enough to appear in public, and used therefore only to go out in the evenings, when he could wear an old tail coat, "that blessed shield of literary shabbiness."

William Archer, well-known as a critic and the translator of Ibsen, took a fancy to the red-bearded Irishman who used to sit at the next table in the British Museum, reading alternately Wagner and Marx's *Das Kapital*. He made his acquaintance, and secured him occasional work as a reviewer. Archer was later urged to take the job of art critic by his editor, but since he knew nothing about art, and was too tired to go to the exhibitions, Shaw went in his place and dictated suitable art notices to Archer. He refused, however, to let Archer pay him, saying, "One can't be paid for ideas; or else I should have to pay the artists for the ideas they give me." Archer then went to the editor and told him that the articles were really by Shaw, whereupon he was paid a modest salary. It was not until he became the music critic of the paper, however, that he achieved a really secure position.

Archer was also a playwright, but he believed that his dialogue was weak. As Shaw, with reason, considered that this was his strong point, they decided in 1885, when they were working side by side in the British Museum, to write a play together. Archer produced a scenario, and Shaw wrote the first act, without even using the beginning of Archer's plot. Then, after Archer had talked seriously to him, he used up the whole plot in the beginning of the next act. Archer did not approve, and the two acts were put away for seven years, until in 1892 the Independent Theatre began to cast round for modern English plays. Shaw then took out his two old acts, added a third, and the resulting play, *Widowers' Houses*, was the first of his works to be performed.

Archer has told us what his plan for the play was. A young man wishes to marry a girl whom he believes to be the poor niece of a rich man. This man lets out slum tenement rooms to poor people at exorbitant rents. It is subsequently revealed that she is the landlord's daughter, and not his niece. The noble young man refuses to accept money earned in this way. Archer admits himself that he took the idea from Augier's *La ceinture dorée* (*The Golden Belt*), which treats of a similar theme. Zola had condemned the plot as being extremely improbable. He points out that in real life it seldom, if ever, happens that sons or sons-in-law refuse to accept money because they do not think it has been honourably acquired, nor do they usually have scruples about marrying wealthy heiresses.

Shaw reacted just like Zola against the heroic gesture of the young man, not because he considered it to be psychologically improbable, but because he considered it to be illogical. All capitalists live on the exploitation of the poor proletariat, whether directly or indirectly. When the young man, Dr. Trench, learns the source from which his future father-in-law's money comes he rejects the offer of a dowry, and says that he and his wife will live on his own private income of seven hundred pounds. The girl refuses to agree and the engagement is broken off. When he later explains the position to her father he learns that his own income comes from a mortgage on some of the property which her father owns. He is, therefore, quite simply his prospective father-in-law's employer, and the latter is compelled to extract rents in order to pay the interest on the mortgage. This is the situation at the end of the second act.

Shaw does not in any way make the plot more probable; he only gives it a wider application than it had before. He is no longer concerned with glorifying a young man who refuses to accept advancement at the cost of accepting tainted money, but with illustrating Proudhon's thesis that all capital income is theft. In the final act the owner of the slum property, who is having trouble with the authorities, is anxious to dispose of it in return for shares in a company, which will then be able to claim handsome compensation when the area is taken over by the London County Council. Dr. Trench at first refuses to take part in this deal, but when the others threaten to pay back his mortgage, thereby reducing his income by more than half, he gives way and resumes his engagement with the daughter. The result is a good piece of business for him, and ruin for the unfortunate tenants. It is these poor working-people and their homes to which the title of the play refers, though none of them ever appears on the stage. This rather badly constructed play is a socialist attack on society, despite its playful tone. The drily ironic conclusion, which is reminiscent of Becque, made the play a failure.

Shaw's next play, *The Philanderer,* was equally unsuccessful. It was an attack on the Ibsen cult and feminine emancipation, not unlike those which we met in Strindberg's plays of the previous decade. This satire on Ibsen's women left Shaw the victim of cross-fire. The opponents of Ibsen knew that Shaw was really a supporter of Ibsen's ideas, while his friends were distressed that he, Ibsen's foremost interpreter in England, should mock him. This rather dated play need not be considered further.

Shaw's third play, *Mrs. Warren's Profession,* was a highly significant work. The idea for the plot Shaw took from a story by Maupassant, which a woman friend had told him. An intelligent and charming girl, Vivie, is about to become engaged to a young man, Frank, when she discovers that her mother has been a prostitute, and at the age of 45 is still the proprietor of several brothels, with a principal establishment in Brussels and branches in various capitals. Thanks to the profits from this flourishing business she has been able to give her daughter a first-class education, including a full university course, and to bestow a fine dowry on her. When the young girl learns the whole story she resolutely refuses all further financial support, and takes a job in an office.

Vivie is very reminiscent of an Ibsen heroine with her clear intelligence and her strong will. The technique of construction is also borrowed from Ibsen. The whole action is determined by past events which are gradually revealed to the characters. It is Mrs. Warren's mysterious past, her profession, which is the Nemesis of the play. Vivie has only on rare occasions met her mother, who has been abroad a good deal, and whom she only knows as a wealthy widow. When for the first time she really learns to know her, she is surprised at her vulgarity, and her strange circle of friends. She then learns that her mother has been a prostitute, and after a long conversation between mother and daughter, Vivie finds herself half moved by her mother's misfortunes and her naively practical way of looking at them. She regards her more as the victim of circumstances than as a bad woman, and decides to stand by this mother of hers, who is at least better than those who have abused her poverty. But her attitude changes when she comes to realize that her mother is the proprietor of several brothels. She also learns that Frank's father, a hypocritical clergyman, had in his youth been her mother's lover. It is suggested that he may be Vivie's father, and that she may therefore be Frank's step-sister. This suggestion is denied by Mrs. Warren and neither of the young people believes it. Shaw touches here on the same problem as is found in *Ghosts*. But although in "The Quintessence of Ibsenism" he praised Ibsen's courage in allowing Mrs. Alving deliberately to approve such a relationship, he evades the issue himself. He wants above all to drive home his main contention, that it is dishonourable to receive tainted money.

The real plot then, lies in the past. What we see on the stage is Vivie's meeting with her mother, and separation from her, the engagement with Frank and the breaking of it. But, thanks to the use of Ibsen's technique, the plot becomes so exciting as to bewilder the audience.

Some of the situations and characters resemble those of French comedy. But Mrs. Warren shows how much Shaw had learned from Ibsen's characterization. She is a practical woman, but her character has not been strong enough to keep her in a decent occupation, while her intelligence has not sufficed to raise her above her own class when she had earned enough money so to rise. In the second act she tells her whole story. She was brought up by her mother, who owned a fish-and-chip shop, and, after spending some miserable years as a waitress, was tempted by her sister to become a prostitute, and to set up a brothel: "The only way for a young woman to provide for herself is for her to be good to some man that can afford to be good to her." This is true in all classes of the community: "What is any respectable girl brought up to do but to catch some rich man's fancy and get the benefit of his money by marrying him?—as if a marriage ceremony could make any difference in the right and wrong of the thing." In this matter Mrs. Warren is a supporter of the feminist case, though in her own simple way: "It can't be right, Vivie, that there shouldn't be better opportunities for women."

In order to secure her daughter's future she has provided her with the best education that England can give. Vivie, who

began by reproaching her mother for her way of life, becomes
gradually impressed by her energy and ability, and touched by
the sacrifices she has made for her. But when she learns that her
mother is still continuing to follow the same profession, her
mood changes and in the final scene they face each other as
enemies. Mrs. Warren is unable to see that she has really done
anything wrong: "I always wanted to be a good woman. I tried
honest work; and I was slave-driven until I cursed the day I
ever heard of honest work. I was a good mother; and because I
made my daughter a good woman she turns me out as if I was
a leper." There is something bourgeois in the way she regards
her profession, and Vivie indeed tells her that at heart she is a
conventional woman, and that that is why she is leaving her.
One can imagine Shaw's delight when he allows Vivie to charge
the woman of the brothel with being conventional.

It was not his intention to allow the figures of Vivie and her
mother to appear as completely contrasted characters. Time and
again Vivie emphasizes her relationship with her mother; she is
equally practical, equally sober, equally energetic and equally
interested in money. They can have nothing in common because
they have grown up in different social circles. When Mrs.
Warren gave her daughter a good education she cut herself off
for ever. As it is impossible for Mrs. Warren to give up her
profession, so it is unthinkable that Vivie should accept the
money earned by the practice of it. In the final scene with her
mother Vivie says that in her place she might have done the same,
but she could never have lived one sort of life and believed in
another.

What spoils this powerful drama is above all its tone, which is
too light for the subject with which it is dealing. The basic idea,
the need for harmony between one's life and one's belief, is as
rigorously moral as any of Ibsen's.

At that time it was found too indecent for public performance,
and it was not until thirty years after it was written that it was
played in England. In New York it was performed in 1905; it
was attacked but survived the test, though Shaw declared it to be
a deliberately immoral play.

Shaw's first three plays met with no success when they were
first performed. Since this also meant that they were of no use

for propagating his ideas, Shaw chose new forms of drama for
his next dramatic ventures. In *Arms and the Man* (1894) he went
over to French vaudeville-farce. This is the mould in which
several of his best plays have been cast, and particularly his most
celebrated *Man and Superman*. This free farce form, sometimes
turning into opéra-comique, operetta and even revue, suited
Shaw remarkably well. As he threw himself into the wild
absurdities of farce with full deliberation his social purpose was
all the better served, because no serious opposition reply could be
possible. The purpose of *Arms and the Man* is serious, being
directed against the false romanticism of war. The form it takes
derives from Labiche. A musical libretto has been made of the
play, and it has been used as the basis of an operetta. Shaw knew
perfectly well that he had adopted the farcical plot traditional in
the Second Empire. In the preface to *Three Plays for Puritans*
he says that the plays certainly include the latest mechanical
improvements. The action is not advanced by impossible monologues and asides, and people go in and out of a room without the
need of four doors where there should only be one. "But my
stories are the old ones; my characters are the familiar Harlequin
and Columbine, clown and pantaloon; my stage-tricks and
suspenses and thrills and jests are the ones in vogue when I was a
boy, by which time my grandfather was tired of them."

Of course Shaw has here been exaggerating his debt to the
traditions of farce in the Second Empire in order to disarm his
critics. But his adherence was quite deliberate. It amuses him to
serve up his ultra-modern ideas in the old forms of comedy,
which he mocks even as he uses them, and to allow his characters
to play the traditional roles, while beneath the surface he is
completely altering their nature.

Arms and the Man shows up the traditional hero in his true
light, and this is a theme to be repeated in other plays. The
unheroic but practical Bluntschli regards war as his profession
and accepts the rank of an officer because it is better paid. His
ammunition pouches are full of chocolate—it is pointless to carry
bullets. After the conclusion of peace—the play is set in the
Serbian war against Bulgaria in 1885—he cheats his opponent
in the exchange of prisoners, and completely defeats that distinguished and gallant Bulgarian officer, Sergius, for the hand of

the fair Raina. Bluntschli is the son of a Swiss hotel-proprietor and is thoroughly at home in all practical matters, which according to Shaw are the most important. It is only Don Quixotes and fools who believe that they can win anything by heroic courage or pretty gestures. The real soldier is a sort of commercial traveller who can take things without sentimentality, practically and egoistically. Bluntschli disarms the audience by his calm business-like attitude, and it is impossible to get the better of him, because he never takes anything seriously. The grandiloquent idealist, Raina, feels herself unmasked: "Do you know," she says, "you are the first man I have met who hasn't taken me seriously!" Bluntschli answers quietly, "Don't you mean that I am the first to take you at all seriously?" This little exchange might well indicate the relation between Shaw and his audience. He mocks our ideals and romantic notions with such charming impudence that we are ready to agree with his arguments: not until then do we realize that what we thought was a joke the author meant in deadly earnest.

Shaw's favourite theme, however, is that of a man who, when confronted by some desperate situation, reveals his true nature, casting aside all the romantic illusions which he has been cherishing. This is particularly true of *The Devil's Disciple*, written three years after *Arms and the Man*. It is played during the American War of Independence and is in outward form a popular melodrama. Dick Dudgeon is the black sheep of his family, and indeed of the whole town, and is therefore called the Devil's Disciple. He happens to be in the Minister's house when an English patrol arrives to arrest the Minister as a rebel. As Dick is sitting in his shirt-sleeves while the Minister's wife is delivering a sermon to him it is assumed that he is the Minister. In a sudden onset of heroic self-sacrifice he puts on the Minister's jacket and goes with the soldiers. He is taken before a court-martial and condemned to be hanged. The Minister's wife, who is present, has suddenly fallen in love with him, and betrays his real name to the court, but this makes no difference. The final act is played near the gallows, and the dilemma is solved by the arrival of the Minister as an envoy of the victorious rebels only a few minutes before the execution is due to take place.

Shaw has himself told us how an actor once wanted to help by giving him a suggestion of a plot for a melodrama. Shaw was offended at the idea that he could not devise a popular melodrama on his own, and decided, as he says, to collect all the boring incidents and the trite situations that had served for the ordinary stupid plays of the previous ten years, and combine them into a new melodrama which would sound like a profound modern play. He stresses, however, in the preface to the play that it has something new in it: "But the novelty is not some new discovery of my own, merely the novelty of modern thought in my day."

It is really a modern psychological problem that confronts the audience at the moment when Dick allows himself to be arrested instead of the Minister. We have already begun to suspect that this scoundrel is a better character than his harsh Puritanical relations consider him to be. Although he has been brought up to serve God, he has from the very beginning felt the Devil to be his natural master. In his gloomy childhood home he has sworn an oath that he will stand by the Devil both in this world and the next. When the Minister's young wife, Judith, visits him in prison she asks if he took the Minister's place because he regarded him as a more valuable person. Dick denies this, saying, "I had no motive and no interest; all I can tell you is that when it came to the point whether I could take my neck out of the noose and put another man's into it, I could not do it. I don't know why not: I see myself as a fool for my pains; but I could not and I cannot. I have been brought up standing by the law of my own nature, and I may not go against it, gallows or no gallows."

Dick acts from instinctive and irresistible impulse, because he is the child of Puritans, and brought up in Puritan traditions, because the instinct to save his own life is weaker than the instinct to follow his own nature, the inner moral command. This Puritanism has been latent in him, but it breaks out with irresistible strength when he is unexpectedly faced with an opportunity for self-sacrifice. One wonders if Shaw, when he created Dick Dudgeon, had come to realize that he himself also had a Puritan heritage.

Shaw's treatment of the Minister is as original as his treatment of Dick. He is a worthy man, placable and generous, but fails when it is incumbent on him to give his life to save Dick. He becomes red in the face, and looks murderous when he hears that the soldiers have been hunting for him, and flatly refuses to surrender to the court martial. He collects his money, takes his pistols and flies to the rebels. He wants his wife to persuade Dick not to give him away until he is out of reach. She asks if it is not enough to pray to God. But the Minister replies "Pray! Can we pray the rope off Dick's neck . . . You're a fool, Judith; you don't know the man you are married to." The danger has aroused his sense of self-preservation, but also capacity for action. By his swift measures among the rebels he rescues Dick at the last moment, and feels that both he and Dick have missed their proper vocation: "It is in the hour of trial that a man finds his true profession. This foolish young man boasted himself the Devil's Disciple; but when the hour of trial came to him, he found that it was his destiny to suffer and be faithful to the death. I thought myself a decent minister of the gospel of peace; but when the hour of trial came to me I found that it was my destiny to be a man of action, and that my place was amid the thunder of the captains and the shouting. So I am starting life at fifty as Captain Anthony Anderson of the Springtown militia; and the Devil's Disciple here will start presently as the Reverend Richard Dudgeon. . . . You may keep my coat, and I'll keep yours." Dick replies rather bitterly that he ought to have behaved in the same way, and saved himself instead of making a vain sacrifice. But the Minister says, "Not vain, my boy—It takes all sorts to make a world—saints, as well as soldiers." This is a modification of the anti-heroic attitude of *Arms and the Man*.

With light and skilful use of a melodramatic plot, Shaw has created a play that is unusually firmly and carefully constructed, as well as having a genuineness of characterization, and a profound theme.

Another highly-regarded play which was written two years later is *Captain Brassbound's Conversion*. Here Shaw has used a pirate drama to expose the fallacy that a gangster's life is glamorous. The bandit Brassbound is diverted from his determination to avenge his wronged mother by a middle-aged English woman, Cecily Waynfleet, one of Shaw's best female characters.

Shaw also tried to adapt the light comedy form which he was

using at this time to suit a historical subject. In the year after *Arms and the Man* he wrote a one-act-play about Napoleon, called *The Man of Destiny*. The qualities which distinguish the great military leader and the world conqueror are not those romantic or heroic ones which people popularly suppose: "There is no such thing as a real hero. . . . There is only one universal passion, fear." He is strong because he believes in himself and because he is not afraid to appear mean and selfish.

If this little comedy has not generally received much attention, it is, on the other hand, widely held in England that Shaw's next historical work, *Caesar and Cleopatra* (1899), is one of his more significant plays.

Shaw does not try to give any historical colour to his description because he feels it fantastic to suppose that the twenty centuries which separate us from Caesar signify any sort of progress. He also regards it as artistically worthless to try to increase the effect by archaisms, quoting in his support Shakespeare's realism in *Julius Caesar*. Of course he criticizes this play sharply in his famous preface, *Better than Shakespeare*, but he retains the right to depict his own age unhindered, just as Shakespeare presented his own. The characters speak in the style of 1890, and we continually find modern jargon, modern opinions and modern prejudices. The climax of this sort of thing is reached in Caesar's secretary, one Britannus, a barbarian from the British Isles, who represents English stiffness, respectability and prudishness. When it was suggested to Shaw that the British Isles in Caesar's day were not even inhabited by the same race of people as present-day Englishmen, he replied with a long argument about the effects of climate on national character.

The original quality of *Caesar and Cleopatra* does not derive from these shocking or amusing anachronisms in themselves. They also fulfil a serious purpose. Britannus, for instance, gives scope for a biting satire on English self-complacency. It is said of him somewhere in the play, "He believes that the customs of his tribe are the laws of nature." In the same way, Shaw's figure of Caesar, though set in a travesty of classical antiquity, about as unhistorical as the Bulgaria of *Arms and the Man*, is something more than another Captain Bluntschli, dressed in a toga. It is an attempt to show by what means a man attains power over men.

Shaw's Caesar is boyishly uninhibited and devastatingly frank. He is a dreamer of great political dreams, but when it is time for action he is wholly a realist. Though humane and liberal, he is not afraid of blood-letting when it is necessary. He is too wise to allow himself to be hampered by false notions of honour, or to sacrifice real advantages for a gesture, but he knows that a gesture at the right time can bring more advantages than action. He deceives his opponents by always doing the opposite of what they expect, and finding ingenious reasons for everything that he does. His first task when he arrives in Egypt is to tax the inhabitants so that the country's debt to Rome may be paid, and his war chests refilled. Resentful and surprised, the King's guardian, Pothinus, bursts out: "Is it possible that Caesar, the conqueror of the world, has time to occupy himself with such a trifle as our taxes?" Caesar, friendly but unperturbed, replies, "My friend, taxes are the chief business of a conqueror of the world."

Shaw's Caesar is admirably alive, and during the half-century which has passed since the play was written several people like him seem to have passed across the world stage. Shaw came to show a certain amount of sympathy for dictators. Unfortunately he has given Caesar a little too much of his own glibness, and the slight cloudiness of the composition prevents us from seeing how he realizes his great intentions.

Shaw's idea of writing a play about future history, under the playful disguise of antiquity, was to be later adopted by many dramatists. The closest imitation was probably by Giraudoux, in *La Guerre de Troie n'aura pas Lieu* (*The War of Troy will not take place*. 1935), with its prophesies of a coming world war.

With all their diversity, Shaw's plays up to this point have shown a certain family resemblance. The same thesis is urged in various walks of life and various situations. They are attacks on what Shaw calls "the romance"—the romantic attitude to life which confuses reality and idealism—on conventionality, unconscious emotions and morality. They support the attitude which Shaw loves to call scientific, a sober and realistic outlook on life which need not exclude idealism, far less morality, but which requires that a person be adapted to just such a morality or such an idealism. The insistence of Björnson and Ibsen on 'being in truth' is repeated in Shaw, but he sees the truth differently. At the end of one of his earlier prefaces he says, "To me the tragedy and comedy of life lie in the consequences, sometimes terrible, sometimes ludicrous, of our persistent attempts to found our institutions on the ideas suggested to our imaginations by half-satisfied passions, instead of on a genuinely scientific knowledge of nature." A number of Shaw's early heroes are shown from the first with just this clear-sighted realism. Julius Caesar is an example of the matter-of-fact hero of real calibre, while Bluntschli is his modern, but slighter, counterpart. Among women, Lady Cicely comes closest to them. They could almost be described as ideal Shaw types, forerunners of the Superman whom he was later to proclaim when he became a disciple of Nietzsche.

But Shaw realizes that not all human beings have this high intelligence and this control over their emotions, and that many would be ridiculous if they tried to acquire them. What he demands is that people shall not load themselves down with romantic fancies and ideas which do not accord with their nature, and which do not correspond with anything real. A group of his plays, therefore, shows how people are converted, not by believing in some new attitude, but by discovering that they are living in the wrong setting.

It is of course difficult to use the full sharpness of Shaw's critical attitude in matters of love and marriage. What is love without romance? How can its problems be treated soberly and rationally? This is presumably the reason why Shaw called the first and greatest of his marriage plays, *Candida* (1894), a mystery.

Here, too, Shaw has chosen a very commonplace plot. Candida is torn, as in so many French plays, between her love for her husband, and her affection for a young man, and dramatic tension is concentrated on the big scene at the end of the play, where Candida is compelled to choose between the two men. Candida herself asks if she is to be put up for auction. This scene is fundamentally as improbable as any of the great *scènes à faire*. But in spite of this, and though the characters say things to each other that can only be said as frankly as this on the stage, the play has a vigour of characterization and a truth of situation that one rarely finds in Shaw. He has also escaped in this play from the excessive brilliance and wit which prevents so many people from taking the plays as seriously as they were written. One has also the comforting feeling that this time Shaw is not certain that he has solved his problem finally.

The two chief male characters, the parson and the poet, are opposites, as so often in Shaw. Each lives in his own sphere of false romanticism. In the final scenes it becomes Candida's duty to show them reality and their own true natures, in so far as they are capable by temperament of understanding them. But not even her comments provide the last word in the argument. Shaw leaves us for once with the unusual feeling that behind the revelations we have witnessed there is a whole world of unconscious feelings.

In the parson, James Morell, Shaw has to some extent given us a portrait of himself as an eager and vociferous social reformer. The modern reformer of the world has now taken over the functions of a priest, and even suffers from his occupational disease, the satisfaction of hearing himself speak, and the capacity to turn aside all attempts at self-analysis with pretty phrases. In this portrait of a clergyman Shaw has presented one of the most typical figures of our present-day civilization—the modern drawing-room parson with progressive social ideas, a member of every Christian-Socialist society, a zealous philanthropist and lecturer, but never out of the pulpit, even in casual conversation. His exact opposite is the eighteen-year-old Marchbanks, whom Morell once rescued after finding him asleep on the Embankment. He is ill at ease, shy, and gauche in his behaviour, but he has one advantage over Morell, that he can see through himself—and other people—better. Morell has been told by Marchbanks that he is in love with Candida, and even that he and Candida both despise his gift of preaching. His pride compels him to invite Candida to choose freely between them.

With proud humility Morell explains that he has nothing else to offer but his strength and his authority. Marchbanks offers the opposite, "My weakness, my desolation, my heart's need." "A good bid," says Candida, and promises to marry the weaker of the two. Morell, who believes that she has chosen Marchbanks, collapses, while Marchbanks' face whitens like steel in a furnace. "I feel I'm lost," he says, "he cannot bear the burden." Then

T

Candida explains that Marchbanks has been harassed ever since he was a child, and has learned to live without happiness. Morell on the other hand has been spoiled and admired ever since he was a child, and needs happiness and comfort if he is to live. Marchbanks disappears into the night with a friendly good-bye to Morell: "I love you because you have filled the heart of the woman I loved." Candida tries to comfort him by reminding him that she is fifteen years older than he is. But Marchbanks replies, "In a hundred years we shall be the same age. But I have a better secret than that in my heart. Let me go now. The night outside grows impatient." He goes, and husband and wife fall into each other's arms, "But," in Shaw's words, "they do not know the secret in the poet's heart."

This final playful comment has caused endless discussion about the meaning of *Candida*. Some critics felt that Candida was a healthy reaction against Ibsen's heroines and their rebellious tendencies. Others accused her of being middle-class and prosaic, and saw in her a tendency of Shaw to make the wife a motherly type, choosing Morell because he needs her.

One must not read any doctrine of marriage into this play. Warned by Morell's example Shaw has this time really refrained from proclaiming any truth applicable to everyone. Candida chooses Morell because he is the weaker, and this means that she needs him as the object of her motherly instincts. Marchbanks has already seen this long before Candida explains it. When Morell on one occasion embarks on some sympathetic speculations about what will happen to Candida if she deserts him, and who will provide for her and be a father to her children, Marchbanks answers, "She does not ask those silly questions. It is she who wants somebody to protect, to help and to work for." Her devotion to Marchbanks comes from his helplessness, not his poetic gifts, which she does not appreciate any more than Morell's sermons. The moment she realizes that Morell needs her help most, and that he would have most difficulty in recovering from the shock, her love returns undivided to him. She has always loved him, even if she knows that this love arises partly from his need of her to play the part of his mother. The poet disappears into the night with his secret, which consists, according to Shaw's explanation, of his contempt for the stale and insipid happiness

enjoyed by the other two. Life is nobler than that. For once Shaw
has taken up a neutral position in the argument.

In 1899 came a break of four years in Shaw's dramatic work,
and when he returned to the stage in 1903, with *Man and Superman*, something had changed. Hitherto Shaw had not pretended,
any more than Ibsen, to present a philosophy in dramatic form.
His ineradicable desire to explain himself caused him to write prefaces and notes for his plays, but the play is the important thing,
and the explanations are only there to enable them to be enjoyed.

With *Man and Superman* a change has been effected. The play
is preceded by an immense preface of no less than fifty pages, and
is followed by The Revolutionist's Handbook, a work by John
Tanner which we hear spoken of in the play. The third act,
which takes up about half the play and is only rarely performed,
is a loosely attached exposition of Shaw's philosophy in dialogue
form.

As Shaw says in the preface, it was the challenge of a critic to
write a play about Don Juan which caused him to write *Man and
Superman*. The real Don Juan was at least a hundred years out of
date. Mozart's Don Juan was the last genuine one; Byron's
vagabond is from the philosophical point of view no more
interesting than the sailor with a wife in every port. Man is no
longer, as Don Juan was, the victor in the struggle between the
two sexes. In Ibsen and Tolstoy Don Juan had already changed
his sex and become Donna Juana, breaking out from her doll's
house and winning her place as an individual. Man, the deposed
Don Juan, no longer thinks about winning the battle of the sexes:
he has turned to intellectual interests. It is thanks to women's
energy in getting married that the human race survives. They
say, of course, that a woman must wait until a man woos her;
yes, she often waits, motionless like a spider waiting for a fly.
But the spider spins her web, "and if the fly, like my hero, shows
a strength that promises to extricate him, how swiftly does she
abandon her pretence of passiveness, and openly fling coil after
coil about him until he is secured for ever!"

At last Shaw himself got caught in the spider's web. Earlier
he had had the same conceptions of love as the poet Marchbanks,
that life is nobler than the mawkish happiness which two lovers
can give each other. There was an Irish millionairess, interested

in socialism, who had tried to capture him for two years, but Shaw was very doubtful about taking this step. He wrote to all his friends asking them whether he ought to marry her. Meanwhile he suffered a period of tiresome illness during which she nursed him, and this settled the matter. At the age of forty-two he married.

Shaw calls *Man and Superman* a comedy and a philosophy. That part of the play which earns it the name of comedy is really revue, the lightest form of comedy. It has all the right ingredients: a completely haphazard and incoherent plot, and changes of setting from place to place without reason or method.

The psychological moderation and observation of the unities with which Shaw was concerned in *Candida* have now been deliberately abandoned. The two chief characters, Tanner and Ann, are not primarily intended to be individuals, but types of Man and Woman. The artistic effect of *Man and Superman* is like that of Voltaire's satirical novels, such as "Candide," where a fundamentally serious point of view is expressed in a playful and improbable tale. Exactly as in Voltaire, the characters, though treated by the author as puppets, are startlingly human.

Shaw has never before or since so ruthlessly created a puppet to his own purposes, as when he created John Tanner. It is not enough that he is made the author of Shaw's Revolutionist's Handbook, which, incidentally, appears on the stage before the author, and lands in the waste-paper-basket. When he falls asleep among the robbers in the Sierra Morena he dreams a hundred pages of Shavian philosophy. He is not intended to be a self-portrait, nor does he seem like one, but he is a concentrated expression of Shaw's philosophical and human ideals, both gently caricatured. From the literary point of view he has many predecessors. He is a mixture of the old raisonneur and the hero of the farce, always with a wisecrack or a piece of witty impertinence on his lips, always badly off but never dismayed, always equally cheerful and unconcerned in the way he meets misfortune.

He has also something in common with the clergyman Morell in *Candida*. Tanner is an extravert, a man entirely absorbed in his activities, which are ultimately less fruitful than those of Morell because they are less practical. Tanner is an intellectual to his finger-tips, and that is why in the end he becomes the helpless prey of Ann in her lust for marriage. Morell's weakness is that he does not know himself; Tanner's problem, like Shaw's, is that he knows himself far too well, and that, like Shaw, he cannot take himself seriously. With all his positiveness, there is something negative in the way he proclaims his ideals. He throws out bold truths, but with an undertone of scepticism. Despite his vitality, his brain has nothing to bite on. He is not naive, like Morell; indeed his weakness lies in his lack of naiveté. But to Shaw he is the true personification of modern man, man who has become pure intelligence, pure brain, and whose lot is therefore to be destroyed in the duel between the sexes.

This character is the most original conception in the play. Ann is to represent the sexual instinct; she is the female successor to Don Juan, the blind but certain Life Force that ensures the continuance of the human race. Occasionally this life instinct finds spontaneous expression, as when she replies to Tanner's question about whether she would really sell freedom and honour and self for happiness, with the moving words, "It will not be all happiness for me, perhaps death." But it is only exceptionally that she shows this side of her nature. Her trouble is that she knows her mind only too well. She is a masterpiece of feminine wiles and cunning, and when one sees how cleverly she has succeeded in trapping the highly intelligent Tanner in her net one gets the impression that she represents the blind sex-instinct that is working against him.

The problem is fundamentally the same as in Shaw's earlier plays, though on a rather different plane, wayward romance as against sturdy reality. Tanner, with his intelligence untouched by life, represents a sort of intellectual romanticism, while Ann represents another sort of reality in her determination to force him into at least one practical measure, getting married. This situation is made clear in the final scene. The engagement has been announced, and Tanner makes a long mocking speech in which he begins by stating that neither he nor Ann is happy, but that they have sold their freedom and happiness for a home and family. One of the ladies cries out in agitation that he is a brute, but Ann looks up at him with loving pride and strokes his hand, "Never mind her, dear, go on talking." This is an exposure of false sentiment as thorough as any in Shaw's dramas.

According to Shaw's own statement, the significance of *Man and Superman* lies in its philosophic content, and the third act is meant to be " a revelation of the modern religion of evolution."

It is suggested that Shaw developed the theories of Nietzsche and Darwin independently, and that he anticipated the pragmatism of James, as well as Bergson's doctrine of *l'élan vital*.

At first glance Shaw's philosophy appears to be a hotchpotch of all the ingredients of philosophical thought at the turn of the century. The most important result of this new approach to philosophy by Shaw is that it modified, if it did not entirely bring to an end, his terrifying rationalism. Both in his belief in the Life Force, and in his expectation of a Superman to come, he has developed a kind of mysticism which remains mystic even though it is based in scientific materialism. What matters in development is not the conscious will guided by reason; it is a blind force, the Life Force—Shaw even calls it stupid—which drives us on our way against our wills in order to create a Superman who will be as much an advance on man as we are above the apes. Everything which Shaw has hitherto condemned, romanticism, heroism, religious ecstasy and sexual passions—all these are now tools in the hand of the Life Force. Tanner would have left nothing more behind him than the Revolutionist's Handbook if the mystic Life Force had not lured him, against all the dictates of reason, to marry Ann in order to breed Superman. In the plays which followed this intellectual conversion there did not at first appear to be any perceptible change. Sober realism and romance are still opposed to each other, but even when realism wins the day, as in *Major Barbara,* we discover in Shaw something hitherto undiscernible, an undercurrent of sympathy for the irrational factors of existence.

Major Barbara (1905) is the first play to deal with a religious topic. Shaw told one of his biographers that he had long had in mind plans for a religious play, and that he had always seen it in terms of a conflict between the religious and the economic outlook on life. In the play the economic point of view is victorious. Shaw still regarded himself at this period as an atheistic mystic, so it came naturally to him to let religion be defeated. But what above all in the play catches the interest of the audience, and attracted the attention of critics, is Shaw's splendid, if somewhat mocking, presentation of primitive religious fervour. During his years as a public speaker he had rubbed shoulders at the street corners of the East End with the men of the Salvation Army. Their religion was something which the socialist atheist had to respect; a religion whose teaching and practice it was to seize people and force them to believe in the miracle of conversion. Shaw's eyes had been opened to the power of religion in life.

By making his heroine, Major Barbara, a daughter of the millionaire Undershaft, the armaments manufacturer, Shaw is enabled to discuss religious problems from an economic point of view. Undershaft and his daughter have not seen each other for a long time, and when they meet in the first act each tries to convert the other. They agree that on the following day Undershaft shall visit his daughter's Army headquarters. The day after she will go to his factory. The plot is somewhat improbable, and so, sometimes, are the characters, particularly Andrew Undershaft, a mild and agreeable man who preaches materialistic sermons about the power of money. His wife says of him that she could not live with him, because he gave the most immoral reasons for his highly moral behaviour. This must be quite contrary to the tactics of most millionaires. His social beliefs, which are set out in long and eloquent speeches in the last act, are mainly built round the surprising theme that poverty is a crime, yes, the worst of all crimes. Therefore it is quite pointless to try to convert a poor criminal by religious means: "It is cheap work converting starving men with a Bible in one hand and a slice of bread in the other. I will undertake to convert West Ham to Mahometanism on the same terms." The real way to put an end to crime and to convert the criminal is to give him a decent wage.

Undershaft is the spokesman for Shaw's social determinism, just as once Mrs. Warren was; indeed they are compared in the preface to the play. They have both been through the same mill. He tells his daughter that he has been an east ender himself, like her clients in the Army.

Beside this capitalist Superman, with his brutal ideas of power, Shaw has put his daughter. She has inherited her father's robust and energetic qualities, and that is why only in the Salvation Army has she found proper scope for her energy, and only here has she found the religious faith to suit her. The second act, at her headquarters, is undoubtedly the best in the play, and with its blending of pathos and humour it is one of the best that Shaw has written.

At a Salvation Army meeting a wild fellow called Bill Walker turns up. He is furious because the Army has converted his girl, and she has deserted him for a Salvation Army sergeant who used to be a heavy-weight boxer. He goes off to another Army centre to find his rival and deal faithfully with him, and comes back with a flea in his ear. He spat in his rival's face, to which the reply was, "Oh, that I should be found worthy to be spit upon for the Gospel's sake!" Whereupon the Sergeant finds no difficulty in knocking him down, kneeling on his chest and praying to God that he may break his stubborn spirit. This treatment proves effective against a tough fighter, and Bill Walker is now ripe for salvation. He makes a last attempt to buy his freedom for a pound, which he hopes will be reparation for having hit a woman soldier of the Army in the face. But Barbara refuses to accept the money; "No: the Army is not to be bought. We want your soul, and we'll take nothing else."

Now the chief Army Officer, Mrs. Baines, arrives, and says that Lord Saxmundham has promised to give the Salvation Army five thousand pounds, if they can collect as much again in other ways. Undershaft immediately offers to give this sum. Barbara is very distressed that the Army is prepared to accept this money. Her father's money was earned from armaments and Lord Saxmundham's from a whisky distillery. But Mrs. Baines has no doubts: after all, Lord Saxmundham is giving the money to the Army to fight drunkenness, money which may damage his own interests. Bill Walker, who has just seen his own offer rejected says, "What price Salvation now?"

The Army marches off, led by the band and Mrs. Baines, who carries her flag in one hand and Undershaft's cheque in the other. Barbara is left alone. In her agony she has torn off the Army's emblems from her collar. Bill says triumphantly to her, "You wanted my soul, didn't you? Well, you ain't got it," and Barbara replies, "I nearly got it, Bill. But we've sold it back to you for ten thousand pounds."

The purpose of the play is anti-religious. But the conflict of

souls between Bill Walker and Barbara is described with such
moving sincerity that even deeply religious people have been
carried away by this act, as also have admirers of the Salvation
Army. An untiring supporter of General Booth, W. T. Stead,
maintained that apart from the Passion Play at Oberammergau
he had never seen a play which presented so vividly the suffering
at Gethsemane, and the tragedy of the Crucifixion.

According to Shaw, the Salvation Army has preserved some of
the spirit of the early Church by its direct approach to the individual, and by talking the language of the people and entering into
their spiritual life. Its purpose is a practical one; it is anxious to
ease the suffering of the poor and to fight against their vices.
It has a gay, tuneful religion, which does not compel its adherents
to listen to soporific sermons, or scare them with threats of hell,
but invites them to coffee, singing and jollity.

There is a certain similarity between the methods of the
Salvation Army which Shaw praises in his amusing preface, and
his own. He also felt himself bound to proclaim a lofty, idealistic
and moral gospel, and, like the Army, he preferred to present it
in an easy, cheerful form. The public is given his lofty
Nietzschean ideas enlivened by the tones of merry marches and
popular songs.

In the rather less interesting final act it is Undershaft who wins
Barbara over to his economic gospel. She returns to the Army
determined to attack first the evils of poverty and to let religion
follow in the second place. It is all quite logical, but hardly
psychologically convincing.

We have the feeling that her surrender is only temporary. A
contemporary religious critic warned the public not to assume
that the faith preached by the wealthy armaments manufacturer
was Shaw's own; "Shaw is bound to acquire a better faith than
this. One day he will proclaim it to us, but not yet." His prophesy proved to be true, but it took twenty years.

Shaw's next play, *The Doctor's Dilemna* (1906), shows a retreat
from the intellectualism of *Major Barbara*, but the structure of
the play is similar. The amoral Bohemian artist, Dubedat, is
allowed to end his life as a saint. His counterpart, the intelligent
and scrupulous doctor, Sir Colenso Ridgeon, is at last brought
to realize that his jealousy has led him to commit what amounts

to a murder, although convinced at the time that he was acting
in full accord with social morality and justice.

Various people, including Oscar Wilde, have been suggested
as the original of Dubedat, but actually this wilful character,
who is fundamentally innocent and has the heart of a child, is
more reminiscent of certain figures from Russian literature,
notably in Tolstoy.

The short one-act play, *The Shewing-up of Blanco Posnet* (1909),
is Shaw's first attempt at a purely religious play, but although
Shaw declared that it was a tract in dramatic form the English
censor forbade its performance on the grounds that it was
blasphemous, and the première took place at Yeats's Dublin
theatre.

The play is set in America, and according to Shaw the title
is a piece of American slang. It means the revelation, the un-
masking, of Blanco Posnet, as a result of which most of the
remaining characters are revealed as hypocrites, while Blanco
Posnet himself remains as the criminal with the halo of a saint,
like a character in Tolstoy. When the play was reviewed in the
press, Tolstoy indeed expressed the desire to read it, because
for many people the power of human conscience is the only
proof of God's existence. Clearly Tolstoy felt as Shaw did, that
this power of conscience could best be shown if it was revealed
at work in an abandoned individual with criminal tendencies.
This opinion was passed on to Shaw, who sent Tolstoy a copy of
the play with a letter in which he acknowledged the use he had
made of the wealth of dramatic material which Tolstoy had
given later dramatists in *The Power of Darkness*.

Blanco Posnet spends the night with his brother in a small
community of settlers, but by morning he has disappeared, and
so has the Sheriff's horse which was in his brother's stable. He is
caught without the horse, but a witness swears that he saw him
ride away on it, and he is to be hanged without ceremony—for
in these parts horse-stealing is the worst of all crimes. Blanco
Posnet cannot be induced to say what has become of the horse.
In a conversation with his brother he lets fall some cryptic words
about God having sent him a woman and a child. He does not
believe that they were real; he saw them in the light of a rainbow.
They took his horse away. Preparations for the hanging have just

been completed when news comes that there is a woman outside
with a horse. Blanco Posnet is terrified: there was no real woman
—it was a rainbow-woman. She is admitted and tells how she
was given the horse by a man sent of God, when she was on the
way to a doctor with her child who was dying of croup. "The
man looked a bad man. He cursed me; and he cursed the child:
God forgive him! But something came over him. I was
desperate. I put the child in his arms; and it got its little fingers
down his neck and called him Daddy and tried to kiss him; for
it was not right in its head with the fever . . . . And then he gave
me the horse and went away crying and laughing and singing
dreadful dirty wicked words to hymn tunes like as if he had
seven devils in him."

The actual denouement, when Blanco Posnet is acquitted, is
somewhat of an anticlimax, but what is memorable is the way
Shaw has allowed natural incidents to catch a gleam of religious
miracle. It is in the same way that he shows the miracles in *Saint
Joan*.

In the preface to *Blanco Posnet* Shaw wrote that he had long
been meaning to write a play about the life of Mahomet, but
that he was afraid that the Turkish Ambassador would prevail
upon the Lord Chamberlain to ban it, as he had banned *Blanco
Posnet*. A few years later, in 1912, he happened to write a play
about a Christian martyr, *Androcles and the Lion*. It was intended
to be a play for children, to follow on Barrie's *Peter Pan*, but
Shaw knew little about children. The subject itself, the casting of
Christians to the lions in the Colosseum, is not suitable for
children, and in any case, the play was considered to be pagan.

This judgment is unjust because the play glorifies both faith
and readiness for sacrifice. According to the legend, Androcles,
who drew the thorn from the foot of a lion, and was in turn
spared by him in the arena, was an ordinary slave in Rome.
Shaw makes him not merely a Christian martyr but also a
Tolstoyan hero, something like Akim in *The Power of Darkness*.
Androcles is both ridiculous and sublime. He is a little Greek
tailor who endures patiently the nagging of his wife and loves all
animals.

The short two-act play is naive and half a parody, but it is also
moving. We see a gathering of the persecuted whose kingdom

is not of this world, together with Roman imperialism at its most
brutal Shaw was to some extent inspired by the medieval Miracle
plays, for the play ends in a similar manner. He has also found
expression for the faith which burned in the martyrs, and their
religious exaltation in the moment of death. Young Lavinia asks
herself why she has chosen the way of sacrifice. At first she
believes that it is because she refuses to burn incense to the
heathen gods, but in the moment of death she discovers that
everything in which she has hitherto believed pales before the
reality, as dreams do in daylight. She knows that she is to die
for something more than dreams and fables—for God.

In the epilogue of the play Shaw characterized Androcles as a
humanitarian nature-lover, and Lavinia as a fearless freethinker.
But the thought that there may be something higher than life
would not leave him, and the religious content of the play is
emphasized in the long preface which he wrote two years later.

Apart from these works Shaw produced a mixed bag of plays,
some of which were no more than small talk in dialogue form.
A few were witty but lacking in ideas, such as the successful and
very popular *Pygmalion*. The long dramatic satire, *Back to
Methuselah*, marked the nadir of his career. This play is a politico-
philosophical discussion. The first act deals with Adam and Eve
and the Serpent in Paradise. It continues to the present day, with
Asquith and Lloyd George in very transparent disguise, and then
jumps to A.D. 2,000 and 3,000, with a final act to be played "as
far ahead as mankind can see," that is to say, in the year 31,920.
The play was written in 1920, and the last act therefore was set
thirty thousand years ahead. The point of the title was to show
that if the human race is ever to achieve more sense, people must
grow as old as Methuselah. The play is a fantastic joke of no
great value.

Everyone was convinced that Shaw had written all that was in
him to write when in 1923 appeared his masterpiece, *Saint Joan*.
He had of course long been planning a play about a great religious
personality. Joan of Arc was canonized in 1920 and Shaw must
have read the various official reports on her case. He discovered
that the writers who had dealt with her previously had not done
her justice. In the preface Shaw declares that he is a mystic because
he believes in a superman power, a striving for development in

man: "The simplest French peasant who believes in apparitions of celestial personages to favoured mortals is nearer to the scientific truth about Joan than the Rationalist and Materialist historians and essayists who feel obliged to set her down as either crazy or mendacious."

How does Shaw conceive Joan of Arc? What he emphasizes above all are her strength of will and her self-confidence. This is already made clear in the admirable first act, in which the seventeen-year old peasant girl forces her way into the presence of a rough country knight in Champagne when he is completely absorbed in the irritating fact that his hens have ceased to lay. "You are to give me a horse and armour and some soldiers, and send me to the Dauphin. Those are your orders from my Lord." Saint Joan, with all her girlish gentleness, has some of the go-ahead quality of Major Barbara. "She is so positive, Sir," says the Steward, who has been unable to drive her from the door. At last she gets her way. When she has departed with the promise to save Orléans and to crown the Dauphin at Rheims, the Knight stands scratching his head and wondering at his folly in having given way to her demands. At that moment the Steward comes rushing in with an egg basket in his hand, crying, "The hens are laying like mad! Five dozen eggs!" The Knight grows pale and makes the sign of the Cross: "Christ in Heaven! She did come from God."

In the same way Joan succeeds in persuading the doubtful Dunois to cross the Loire and save Orléans. He obeys her advice, and the obstinate east wind which has been hindering them swings round to the west.

It is not the miracles which are convincing so much as Saint Joan's faith: "I believe the girl herself is a bit of a miracle," says her first protector, an old officer. "A miracle," declares the Archbishop of Orleans, "is an event which creates faith." It does not matter whether they are simple or remarkable events: "If they confirm or create faith, they are true miracles."

Saint Joan wins her victories through her purity, her firm faith, and her will-power, but her intelligence is by no means super-human. Shaw, who was generally so inclined to give his heroines his own intellectual powers, has allowed Saint Joan to retain her rural simplicity and her human weaknesses. She is afraid of the stake, and is for a time almost ready to sign a recantation. When she learns however that this will only substitute life imprisonment for the stake she tears up the document: "I could do without my war-horse; I could drag about in a skirt; I could let the banners and the trumpets and the knights and soldiers pass me and leave me behind as they leave the other women, if only I could still hear the wind in the trees, the larks in the sunshine, the young lambs crying through the healthy frost, and the blessed, blessed church bells that send my angel voices floating to me on the wind. But without these things I cannot live; and by your wanting to take them away from me or from any human creature, I know that your counsel is of the devil, and that mine is of God."

In the trial scene Shaw has been at pains to show that the judges were acting impartially and humanely. He has tried to show that even intelligent and tolerant people are incapable of understanding and following a great genius when one comes. This is still true to-day. In the Epilogue Saint Joan, who was acquitted after her death, is allowed to reappear. But no one can understand her message, and everyone tries to get rid of her. She brings the play to an end with the words: "My God that madest this beautiful earth, when will it be ready to receive Thy Saints? How long, O Lord, how long?"

Shaw once wrote that he wanted to depict Joan of Arc as the first Protestant, quite intolerable as all great original creators are. She is a Protestant in the same sense as Shaw is, because she fights freely for her ideas against every worldly or spiritual authority. She was created to arouse indignation.

In form the piece is a chronicle play. Shaw said that he wrote it as he believed Shakespeare would have done if he had lived in our day. He knows no more about the characters than Shakespeare knew about Falconbridge, Macbeth or Macduff. "In view of the things they did in history, and have to do again in the play, I can only invent appropriate characters for them in Shakespeare's manner." This is quite a different method of approach from that which Shaw used in *Caesar and Cleopatra,* where he was trying to shock historically-educated readers. He wrote to Sybil Thorndike, when she was about to play the title part, that for the trial scene he had used Saint Joan's exact words. Naturally Shaw also used modern dialogue, and his psychological approach was a modern one throughout, but the fact that despite his unruly imagination he followed historical sources so closely is proof of the seriousness with which he approached this task. Next to Björnson's *Beyond our Strength, Saint Joan* is the most moving presentation of a miracle that modern drama can show. It is strange that both these plays were written by professed atheists. It makes them more convincing than other plays written on similar subjects by believers such as the Catholic Claudel, or the Protestant Kaj Munk. Contemporary critics were astounded at this remarkable effort by the 67-year-old Shaw. The dramatic critic of *The Times* was a good friend of Shaw, who had dedicated *Man and Superman* to him. Yet he wrote, when it was announced that Shaw was busy with a play about Saint Joan, that this subject was too solemn and serious for an author of his calibre to attempt. He had to eat his words. The theatres were doubtful about a play which took four hours to perform. Shaw wished that no cuts should be made. But wherever it was performed it proved a rousing success.

After *Saint Joan* Shaw wrote a number of plays. The best of these is probably *The Apple Cart* (1929), in which a wise constitutional monarch shows his superiority to a capitalist democracy. Even his admirers agree that his later plays have been mere feeble repetitions and have had no significance for modern drama.

Shaw is the final point of a tradition of dramatic writing which largely dominated the drama of the 19th century, and is perhaps the most characteristic style of that century. This tradition was born with *Faust*, developed in the hands of Kleist, Hebbel and Schiller into the drama of historical principle, formed the modern problem play of the younger Dumas and Augier and reached its apex with Ibsen. It might be thought that *Saint Joan* was an exception, but only when the heroine is on the stage can it be called a chronicle play. The scenes in the English camp, both before the trial and during it, are those of a typical drama of principle, with spokesmen for the State, the Church, Nationalism and other interests opposing each other's arguments.

Shaw has more enthusiasm and fewer reservations about this type of drama than anyone else in our age. He has said himself that his plays are not written to induce pleasant dreams or romantic nonsense, but intellectual interest: "The pure drama of emotion is no longer the concern of the dramatist. It has been stolen by

the musician, after whose magic all tricks with words seem cold
and tame . . . Attempts to create a sort of opera without music
—and it is to this absurdity that our fashionable theatres have
been driven for some time without realizing it—are much less
hopeful than my own attempt to accept the problem as a normal
subject for drama." This comment of course takes no account
of symbolistic drama.

Shaw was entirely, as Ibsen partly, a preacher on the stage.
He reshaped drama to express his own opinions and views on the
world. At first he was content, like Ibsen, to have one character
representing his own views and another opposed to him, to speak
for the conventional attitude. Later, however, he went on to use
the stage as a platform for the discussion of ideas, neglecting to
this end all hitherto accepted rules of drama.

There was no form of dramatic art that he was not ready to
adopt, if it enabled him to convey his thoughts more effectively.
Hence comes the variegated assortment of dramatic forms, right
down to the revue, which we find in his earlier work, and hence
also the loose discussion form of his later plays.

He never succeeded in arousing popular controversy about the
problems he presented to the extent that he hoped. This was
partly because he presented them with so much bluster, and such
an air of superiority. In the preface to *Saint Joan* he says that
Socrates was brought to trial and condemned because his fellow-
citizens could not stand being revealed as idiots every time that he
opened his mouth.

Time passes quickly, and both the rationalism and mysticism
of Shaw are now out of date. What seemed shocking to Shaw's
own generation no longer has the power to move our spirits. It
may be, therefore, that Shaw's plays will not continue to hold
their place in the theatre. But his dramatic work will always be
read as the unique and artistic creation of a rich and original
personality. Along with his small talk and his paradoxes, his
bizarre and absurd notions, there is in Shaw a psychological
clarity, a capacity for capturing situations and moods, and a
pathos blended with the arts of the clown, all of which provide
the hall-mark of real genius.

JOHN GALSWORTHY

DESPITE his critical attitude to his fellow-countrymen Shaw remains an Irishman, both in his virtues and his faults. He has the glowing eloquence which characterizes the Irish, and their taste for exaggeration as well as their sparkling imagination, though he laughs at this last quality in *John Bull's Other Island*. His more symbolistically and romantically inclined contemporaries, Yeats and Synge—who together with Shaw are the greatest names in modern European drama—have, despite all differences, something in common with him.

Shaw's closest rival on the English stage, John Galsworthy, was, however, an Englisman to his finger-tips. He had none of Shaw's theories or rationalism, and even less of his vein of mysticism. He was an English gentleman, who took pains to make his work realistic, accurate, and above all, fair. He was so devoted to truth that he even refused to call himself a Naturalist.

Galsworthy's plays are often the exact opposite of Shaw's, and yet he had of course learned a lot from him, particularly from his early plays. In one preface he described the difference between Shaw and himself as follows: "About Shaw's plays one might say that they contain characters who express emotions which they do not possess. About mine one might say that they contain characters who possess emotions which they cannot express."

What gives Galsworthy's plays their distinction is precisely the English taciturnity of their characters. He places more reliance than any earlier playwright on gesture and facial expression. Often enough, an action has to serve as the reply, where Shaw would have expressed it in his own words or those of a character.

Galsworthy also lacks a trait which is irritating in Shaw, the desire to laugh at himself, his characters and his audience. He keeps his imagination under better control, but he has less of it. The characters in his plays are more like ordinary people than those of Shaw, but this is not because he is a better psychologist, but because he is often presenting the very type of a community, the average individual. The moral element in his plays is much less disturbing than that of Shaw, but is also more commonplace. The structure of his plays is never as ungoverned as in Shaw, but it is often cut to a standard pattern. He was a fine and gifted dramatist as well as an excellent novelist, but no genius—and indeed he did not pretend to be one.

Galsworthy was born in 1867, and published his first play, *The Silver Box,* in 1906, that is when he was nearly forty years old. He had then been writing novels and short stories for ten years, and had just achieved some distinction with the first part of *The Forsyte Saga.* He was therefore already a mature writer when he turned to drama, and his first dramatic work bears witness to this.

Galsworthy was the son of a successful barrister and he himself was trained for and had practised in the legal profession. Mention has already been made in this book of the predilection of 19th century playwrights for presenting their conflicts in the form of law cases, a tendency of which we find instances in Schiller and Kleist, the younger Dumas and Ibsen, to name only a few. No one, however, excelled Galsworthy in this type of playwriting. His whole dramatic production might well be defined as a series of court reports. In almost all his plays there are interviews with solicitors, details of legal procedure and court scenes, and even when these are lacking the drama almost invariably takes the form of a discussion of legal and moral issues. All Galsworthy's dramatic writing sets out to show the difference between moral and legal justice. His method is to investigate one case and then to try to cast further light on it by impartial inquiry in other directions.

His drama is not built on conflicts of character, or on problems, in Ibsen's sense of the word, but on concrete situations, on the sort of incident which we read about in the papers—a theft, a fraud, a dispute over property or some love-affair. This means that his plays often resemble detective stories. Both his first play, *The Silver Box,* and his most famous one, *Loyalties,* are concerned with criminal investigation, introduce detectives on to the stage and contain a tension which is partly that of a detective play. Galsworthy, however, is interested not in discovering the criminal, but in analysing the moral peculiarities inherent in man's attitude to crime. What he wants to show is how incapable ordinary everyday people are of rising to unusual occasions, how they fail to act in accord either with their own principles or with those of morality when they are suddenly exposed to the unexpected problem, different in kind from those which they usually have to decide. He points out particularly how class-conscious our conventional morality is. In one of his plays, *The Skin Game*, Galsworthy allows his point of view to be directly expressed by his hero, a sensitive and humane patrician. In a dispute about property he has been led to destroy the good name and happiness of a *nouveau-riche* family which lived near him: "What is it that gets loose when you begin to fight, and makes you what you think you're not? What a blinding evil . . . what's gentility worth, if it can't stand fire?" To some extent Galsworthy is dealing with Ibsen's fundamental problem. His heroes behave as unworthily as Helmer in *A Doll's House*, but in Galsworthy this conflict between absolute and conventional morality is not treated with the full vigour that Ibsen brought to it. He holds that people in exceptional situations always behave heartlessly.

Galsworthy's first play, *The Silver Box*, is already typical of him. It opens with a night scene in which we see young John Bartwick returning home completely drunk. He enters the room with a purse in his hand which he has stolen for a joke from the girl with whom he has been spending the evening. He is accompanied by a rather less drunk working-man, who met him outside the house and helped him to find the keyhole for his key. Bartwick falls asleep and Jones, the working-man, seizes the opportunity to steal the street girl's purse, and the silver cigarette-box from the table.

The play then goes on to show how different are the consequences for an upper-class and a lower-class criminal. Young Bartwick is visited by the girl, who demands her purse back but is satisfied when his father instead gives her a generous sum of money. Jones is sentenced to a month's hard labour, but no one thinks of connecting the purse, which the police have found, with young Bartwick. When the sentence is announced Jones mutters angrily, "Call this justice?... 'E was drunk, 'e took the purse ... 'E took the purse, but it's 'is money that got him off—Justice!"

Galsworthy has already worked out a technique of parallel scenes that contrast sharply. He has not yet achieved that impartial distribution of light and shade that he was later to be so concerned about. This point, however, he had achieved in the play that is commonly conceived to be his masterpiece, *Strife*. With methods that he was to use again, but never so successfully, he manages to make the individuals who represent the extremist point of view, old Anthony the employer and Roberts the Union leader, seem likeable and impressive, while those who are prepared to be reasonable and conciliatory seem merely to compromise and lack any idealism or real enthusiasm.

Strife treats of the settlement of a long-standing strike that has been going on at the Trenarth works. It has lasted all winter, the workers are almost at the end of their tether, and the company's resources have been sadly depleted. Galsworthy does not, like Hauptmann in *The Weavers*, show the strike from the point of view of the bitter need of the strikers, and their rebellious spirit. Apparently at this date he did not know of Hauptmann's play. With the exception of one single melodramatic episode, *Strife* deals with a strike from a modern point of view, presenting the negotiations between employers and workers' leaders. This method has enabled Galsworthy to observe the unity of time; the play begins at midday and the story is concluded at six o'clock in the afternoon.

The directors of the company are prepared to compromise, but are prevented from doing so by the authority of their chairman. Old Anthony, who is now nearly eighty, is the real founder of the works. He has been an employer now for fifty years, and refuses to depart from his principles. To give way now would mean a constant struggle, in which the employers would always have to give way.

With the same impressive adherence to principle as Anthony, Roberts fights for the cause of the workers. For him it is a question of justice, and therefore he refuses to listen to talk about the workers' strike being pointless, because no similar factory pays higher wages. There are also in the two camps, parallel characters in the trade union official, Harness, a calm and confident negotiator, who has advised against the strike from the first, and the company secretary, who even before the strike began had helped Harness to draw up a draft for an agreement—which was rejected by both sides.

Devotion to principle is winning the day, when Roberts' wife dies of hardship and starvation. This scares the workers, and is taken by the directors as a warning that public opinion may go against the company if it seems too ruthless. The agreement is accepted by both sides. Old Anthony resigns from the chairmanship, and Roberts is set aside also. He visits Anthony, in a state of great emotion: "They have done us both down, Mr. Anthony."

"One woman dead and the two best men both broken," says Harness mournfully to the company secretary. He replies "D'you know, Sir—these terms, they're the very same we drew up together, you and I, and put to both sides before the fight began. All this—and what for?" And the hardened Harness answers, with a wry grin, "That's where the fun comes in."

This is a picture of a strike as it works out in our day. But it is also, as someone has said, a picture of a general tendency in contemporary society. There is less and less room for men of conviction and strong ideas. It is moderate men who win the day with compromises and half measures. Our mass-produced culture breaks the wills and lays waste the lives of men, to win results that satisfy no one. By morning there will be peace at the Trenarth works, but how long will it last? Sooner or later the struggle between Roberts and Anthony will have to be fought to a finish.

In his earlier plays Galsworthy often described people from the upper classes who merely through their instinct for conventional justice set in motion the juggernaut which crushes all that comes beneath its wheels. In an agreeable little comedy, *The Pigeon*, he has done the exact opposite, showing very amusingly a gentleman who opens his door and his purse to every vagabond on the road. This play is almost the only one of its kind in Galsworthy's dramas. The chief character, Wellwyn, an old painter, has more flesh and blood than any other of

Galsworthy's stage characters, and the play's easy construction makes it less artificial than Galsworthy's other plays.

Wellwyn is, as his seventeen-year-old daughter declares, the despair of all social reformers. He cannot bear to inquire into the morals of those who seek help from him, to cross-examine them and see if they really deserve his sympathy. As long as he has a penny he is ready to give it away; he gives away his last garment, and lets the homeless spend a night in his studio as long as there is a spare corner. By the end of the play he has yielded to his daughter's persuasions and is moving to a quieter place. One can see, however, that it will not help much, for he has already given his clients visiting-cards with his new address. He excuses himself by saying that the welfare problem is so complicated that he has never really had time to study it.

We are also shown the grave representatives of various charitable organizations beginning to argue about each other's methods in Wellwyn's studio, and the play shows the deplorable effects of trying these methods out on three protégés of Wellwyn's, the armless cab-driver, Timson, a flower-girl Guinevere Megan, and a tramp of French extraction, by name Ferrand. Old Timson is taken to a home for alcoholics, given a diet of milk, and released. He then drinks steadily for a week and finally tries to commit suicide. The unhappy Ferrand has lain down in the cold by the side of the road to die, but is taken to an institution, and then transferred to two more. Each of them is a palace, in which nothing is lacking but understanding for the human heart: "There is in some human souls, Monsieur, something which cannot be tamed." This Ferrand feels is just what institutions, however benevolent, fail to recognize: "Leave us to live, or leave us to die where we like, in the free air."

A confirmation of this need comes at the end of the play, when an obliging police constable brings in Guinevere Megan, who has sunk to being a street girl, and has thrown herself into the Thames in her despair, but has been dragged out. After many efforts they succeed in reviving the poor creature, but in spite of his desperate entreaties she is not allowed to stay with the kindly Wellwyn. Attempted suicide is a serious crime. "Not a soul in the world wants her alive—and now she's to be prosecuted for trying to be where everyone wishes her," laments the good Wellwyn. Later the philosophical Ferrand says: "That makes the third of us, Monsieur. We are not in luck. To wish us dead, it seems, is easier than to let us die."

Galsworthy's desire to present the working-class in a more favourable light than the upper class becomes tedious in the long run. One of his English biographers said in 1916 that he could not resist the temptation to weep over every creature who came his way, and whose clothes were not quite so good as his own.

Perhaps Galsworthy realized the truth of this criticism, for in his later plays he avoided any direct contrast between rich and poor. Both *The Skin Game* (which was mentioned above) and *Loyalties* are set in a purely upper-class milieu. There are still class distinctions—and they determine the course of both plays—but they arise within one section of society.

The title refers to the false solidarity which exists in all social groups, and which sometimes threatens to grow into a caste morality. The play gradually shows that the ambitious young Jew, De Levis, is justified in his suspicions that he has been robbed by the man with whom he shares rooms, the aristocratic Captain Dancy. Dancy's friends consider that an attack on his honour is an attack on theirs, and when De Levis is heard to have voiced his suspicions at a London club, they compel Dancy to sue him. When the case looks like turning against Dancy, De Levis's lawyer throws in his hand, and De Levis himself does everything he can to hush the matter up. But the affair has already become too public, and Dancy shoots himself just as the police arrive to arrest him.

During the last fifteen years of his life—he died in 1933—Galsworthy had time to write several plays which were successful in England. But they do not indicate any growing powers. They really confirm the impression one receives from his novels, that the social revolution brought about by the first world war made him an even more bitter enemy of the "new rich," and an even more loyal advocate of the old English ideal of a gentleman.

Galsworthy's naturalism became more complete with the years. *The Roof* (1929) treats of a fire in a Paris hotel. There is no plot, but, like Chekhov, Galsworthy tried to substitute atmosphere. He had, however, too thin a vein of poetry to succeed with such experiments. The interesting aspect of his dramatic work is his concern with modern problems, and his sure characterization. Compared with the rather extravagant types produced by Wilde and Shaw, Galsworthy's characters are more ordinary, and they speak like the average man, not like a born orator. They are clear and distinct, drawn with the sure pen of a novelist, but there is not much to discover beneath the surface.

IRISH DRAMA

ALTHOUGH the English and the Anglo-Irish drama both saw light within the boundaries of the same kingdom, and use the same language, the difference between them is considerably greater than that between Austrian and German drama as regards style, choice of subject and general atmosphere. This remains true, even though two of the most famous English dramatists at the end of the 19th century, Shaw and Wilde, were both Irish by birth. The distinction can hardly be better illustrated than by two quotations, one from Shaw and one from Yeats. In *John Bull's Other Island* an Irishman is grumbling about his fellow-countrymen's dreamy nature: "An Irishman's imagination never leaves him in peace, never convinces him, never satisfies him. But it means that he can never look reality in the face, never shake hands with it or overcome it . . . If one wants to interest him in Ireland one must call that unhappy country Cathleen ni Houlihan, and say that she is a little old woman. It saves thinking, it saves work, it saves everything except imagination."

These words sound almost pagan when set beside Yeats's letter to Lady Gregory, in which he tells her how he found inspiration for his great play, *Cathleen ni Houlihan:* "One night I had a dream, almost as clear as a vision. I saw a cottage, with the comfort and warmth of a fire, and the people were talking about a marriage. Suddenly there came into the cottage an old woman in a long cloak. It was Ireland herself, Cathleen ni Houlihan, about whom so many songs have been sung, so many stories have been told, and for whose sake so many have gone to their deaths."

This new world of emotion of which Shaw was so scornful, and which Yeats glorified, was the creation of the Irish renaissance of the last quarter of the 19th century, and its finest expression was Anglo-Irish drama. The story of its development closely resembles that of Norwegian drama and its release from Danish bondage by Björnson and Ibsen, whose names are often quoted by the Irish.

The writers of the Irish renaissance, like the Norwegians, used the language of their old rulers, and like the great Norwegians they reshaped it into a more or less independent idiom. In Ireland, as in Norway, this was partly due to the good use made of the country's early legends and the living speech of the people. English as used by the Irish dramatists, like Norwegian in the early works of Björnson and Ibsen, included a sprinkling of archaisms. Moreover, in the construction of sentences and the choice of words philologists can detect traces of the old Gaelic forms. These have given Irish drama a strange flavour.

Ibsen and Björnson fought a war on two fronts; against the Danish influence and the stifling of everything truly Norwegian in character, but also against those who agitated for the wider use of the country dialect. In the same way Yeats and Synge and their friends have had to struggle both against those who did not wish Irish literature to differ in any way from English literature, and also against the tenets of the finally victorious Sinn Fein party. They wished to do away with English for writing in favour of Erse, and regarded every realistic representation of Irish peasant life with suspicion, as being profanation and treachery.

As in Norway, a few scholarly works opened the way to a national renaissance. During the years 1878-80 there appeared a history of Ireland by Standish O'Grady which gave a colourful account of ancient Irish legends, in the belief that they were a piece of real Irish history. Of almost equal importance was the history of Irish literature by Douglas Hyde, later to be President of Eire, as well as his collections of Irish folk-tales, folk-songs and folk-lore. Through these two scholars Ireland had acquired a treasure-house of its own historical and literary traditions to look back on, and to use as a store-house of inspiration for modern writers. The heroes of the Cuchulain and Ossian cycles had become the property of the whole people.

During the 19th century there had, of course, been writers in Ireland who wrote in English, in verse and prose, about their country's traditions, their legends, and their ballads. The new renaissance began at the end of the 19th century, when the temporary relaxation of political tension left people with leisure to develop their intellectual and poetic interests. Yeats wrote his first play, *The Countess Cathleen*, as early as 1892, and in the same year he founded the National Literary Society, to pave the way for Irish literature. In 1899 he at last succeeded in founding the Irish Literary Theatre in Dublin, which had to bring in English actors at first, but included Irish plays in its repertory. The inaugural play was *The Countess Cathleen*. To this theatre came many members of that young Irish generation which was later to become famous, and foremost among them Lady Gregory. At about this time, Gaelic plays were beginning to be performed by native Irish amateur actors. They showed themselves to be superior to the English company, even in the interpretation of the new Anglo-Irish drama, and in 1902 were acknowledged as the successors of the Literary Theatre company. Now there was a real Irish theatre in existence, which two years later acquired its own premises in Abbey Street in Dublin. In 1903, when Synge began his short but brilliant career, a new dramatic force appeared in Ireland. In a few years the reputation of the Abbey theatre, and the new and vital dramatic activity that was going on there, spread throughout the English-speaking world on both sides of the Atlantic, and later through all Europe. It is probably the most remarkable national contribution to the development of modern drama since the Norwegian revival.

Although both Yeats and Synge are dead, and the political conditions for the growth of this Anglo-Irish movement are much less favourable, people are still writing this sort of drama in Ireland. It has also exercised a great influence on modern peasant drama in other countries in our own time.

The real founder of the movement was William Butler Yeats. His talents were admittedly more lyrical than dramatic, and Synge's dramatic powers have caused even Irish judges to wonder whether Yeats's plays are not really meant for reading only. But they contain such a remarkably fine store of poetry that they deserve a place of their own in the category of symbolistic drama.

Yeats, who was born in 1865 and died in 1939, became the patriarch of the Irish renaissance. An admirably catholic taste enabled him to play a significant part in the encouragement of all aspects of this revival. To some extent he played the same role for Anglo-Irish literature as Mistral for Provençal literature, or Björnson for Norwegian. More than anyone else, he contributed to the support of promising ventures, and encouraged every enterprize which might further the cause of literary revival. Yeats however was in no way a typical literary impresario. On the contrary, he was a striking example of the dreamer, remote from the world, filled with the mystic's ecstasy. He claimed to have conceived many of his plays in moments of mystical revelation, and his finest works are set in a world that is half heaven, half earth, which for him, quite clearly, had objective validity. Their main theme is the longing of men to escape from the fetters of material existence to the land of the ideal, of eternal beauty and ineffable bliss.

In Paris Yeats had associated with the exponents of French symbolism, and had there made the acquaintance of Sar Peladan, Strindberg's master in the magic and occult arts. He continued for the rest of his life to believe in magic and the intervention of superhuman powers in the incidents of everyday life.

This was the reason why Yeats was able to enter so completely into the early Irish legends, about heroes who disappear to an unknown dream kingdom, and girls who are carried off to the land of heart's desire. The superstitious element in symbolism, which even in Maeterlinck, and still more in Hauptmann, seemed sometimes to be simply the fashion of the moment, was in him a natural expression of sincere conviction. In Strindberg, too, the world of spirits has the same quality of genuine experience, but in him it was contrasted—sometimes to an almost grotesque degree—with his naturalistic tendencies. Naturalism was entirely strange to Yeats, and therefore his supernatural world becomes more unified, more full of poetry, but also, in the long run, more monotonous and colourless. His rich and extremely delicate style made him one of the finest lyric poets of our age.

Yeats's first play, *The Countess Cathleen*, was written before Ireland came to possess a national theatre, and without any thought of performance. It was published in a collection of poems. Later, when Yeats was revising it for the stage, he complained of the restraint that this imposed on his poetic gifts: "We have made a prison of colour and texture, in which we have as little freedom as we have under our own roofs, for there is no freedom in a house made with hands. All art moves in the cave of a chimera, in the garden of the Hesperides, or in the quiet house of the Gods, and neither cave, garden nor house can reveal itself clearly except to the eye of the soul."

Yeats took the story from an Irish medieval legend, which he only knew from a French source. The still undiscovered original appears to have been a *conte dévot*, of the same kind as inspired Maeterlinck's *Sister Beatrice*. It was probably a familiar story in various parts of Europe in the Middle Ages. There was a famine in Ireland, and two demons appeared, dressed as merchants, who tried to make the starving people sell their souls to hell. The noble Countess Cathleen sells all that she has to save her people from starvation. At last, when all her money is gone, she sells her own pure and unspotted soul to the demons in order to save her people. She dies of grief at what she has done, but the agreement is annulled by God, and she is taken up to Heaven.

Yeats reproduced this charming legend in his magical verse, and transported the audience to a wonderland where the superhuman creatures of the legend move and have their being among simple Irish peasant men and women. The first and last acts are set in an Irish cottage, and give us at once that atmosphere which we shall find again and again in Irish peasant drama. The two middle acts are played in the castle of Countess Cathleen. This setting was inspired by Maeterlinck, and it is by his discreet methods that Yeats suggests the ghost-like atmosphere of the first act: we hear the dog bark, the owls hoot, a hen fluttering in terror, and the holy image fall from its niche, all with a sense of foreboding, before the merchants come in with their sacks of gold.

The Countess Cathleen differs from Yeats's later plays by its length and its carefully worked-out plot. This form did not suit him. He was more a creator of atmosphere than a delineator of character, and even such a straightforward figure as the Countess Cathleen lacks the qualities which would make her come really alive. We hear talk of her self-sacrificing idealism, but the play itself hardly gives us a convincing impression of this quality. We see her first in the company of her old foster-mother and her lover, the dreamy minstrel, Aleel. There is a trace of literary symbolism in this play, but it disappeared in his next works, which were mostly one-act plays, affording Yeats the opportunity to reduce his plots to the minimum, and allow his characters to appear as vague shadowy figures behind a veil of fantasy and dream. The verse is as melodious and movingly sincere as it always was to be in Yeats's drama.

His next play, written two years later, *The Land of Heart's Desire*, is his masterpiece. It was the first of his plays to be produced, and has remained one of his most popular works. He remains faithful to his Celtic peasant setting, which in this case is a little Irish village where the people are supposed to speak Gaelic, although the play is written in English with Gaelic phrases and turns of speech. The story is based on an old folk tradition that on Midsummer Eve, when the fires are lit, the fairies carry off human children. The play is also a poetic reflection of the way in which Yeats has been beguiled by the world of Irish legend.

In the kitchen of Maurteen Bruin's cottage the old peasant, his wife and the priest are sitting round the table. Shawn, the son, is laying the table for supper. His young wife, Mary, whom he has just brought home, is completely absorbed in the reading of an old yellow book, an heirloom from her grandfather. She is reading a fairy-tale about the princess Edain, a daughter of the king of Ireland, who one summer evening hears a voice singing, and follows it half asleep until she comes to the land of the fairies, where no one grows old or bitter. She is still there, deep in the heart of the forest, dancing in its dewy shade, while the stars wander above the mountain top. His old parents grumble because ever since she was married Mary has neglected all her household duties, and has buried herself in her dreams. The old priest warns her about the fairies and their temptations. She has brought misfortune to the house because she has given fire and food to two strange visitors, a little man dressed in green and an old woman. The peasants are convinced that they come from the fairy people. The only one to defend the girl is her husband, Shawn, who knows how sensitive and remote from the world she is.

At last Mary calls to the fairies to come and fetch her, and soon afterwards she hears a voice singing in the distance, and thinks she sees a pale child with golden-red hair. A moment later a voice is heard outside the door. The old peasant opens it, and in comes a young girl in a pale green dress, just like the child that Mary saw in her vision. She is given bread and honey, and as she is afraid of the crucifix on the wall, the kindly priest carries it into another room with the intention of teaching her the true Faith. Then the fairy girl begins to dance and talk about the country from which she comes, where the old are beautiful, and the wise are gay, where the fairies dance in a ring with their white feet, and raise their white hands in the air. She strews a ring of primroses round the young peasant bride, to the horror of the others, who feel helpless now that the crucifix has gone. Mary dies at last, falling into the arms of her husband, and the fairy girl dances out through the door, singing her magic song. Mary has been carried off to the kingdom of the fairies, to the Land of Heart's Desire.

Between the fairy girl and the dwellers in the cottage there is no gulf; they belong to the same world. The creature who reveals herself in their midst has sprung out of their own faith. Of the artificiality which so often seems inherent in symbolic drama there is no trace here: the verse is smoother and lighter than in almost any other play by Yeats.

With his next play, *The Shadowy Waters* (1900), Yeats is for the first time in country which was henceforth to be his own, He took the name and some of the incidents from that early Irish poetry which Mary Bruin was reading so eagerly in her old book. The plot, however, is his own invention.

We are on board Forgael's ship, bound for the world of dreams and fantasy. There has been a mutiny of the sailors, quelled by Forgael with his harp. Queen Dectora, whom he captured when his crew slew her husband, first tries to murder him, and then to persuade him to change his course. In the end she falls in love with him, and they are both smitten with the same irresistible longing for the land of eternal happiness. The play ends with them drifting together in his boat to the world of immortality. He is on his knees, playing his harp, and draped in her fair golden hair; "For we shall not look long upon this world."

Forgael's dream world is closely linked with Yeats's own

romantic and aesthetic notions, and also with his mystic ideals. He has rarely written work which so clearly reveals his inner-most self. He says himself that the play was woven out of his visionary experiences, and that he saw, as clearly as if he had been looking at them with his own earthly eyes, the counterpart of the young lovers in *The Shadowy Waters*.

An illustration of his belief that poetry had a higher value than any other form of existence was that Yeats, contrary to tradition, took the side of the poet when retelling the old legend of Seanchan in his beautiful verse play, *The King's Threshold*. Seanchan was an old bard who was denied access to the board and council of King Guaire, and therefore starved himself to death.

Some of Yeats's plays confine themselves entirely to the world of Irish legend, and the most remarkable of these is *Deirdre*, a tragedy after the style of *Romeo and Juliet*. Deirdre has been brought up to be his queen by old King Conchubar, but she escapes from his castle with young Naisi. Yeats is only concerned with the end of the story, in which, after spending seven years wandering in the forests, the young lovers are lured back to Conchubar's castle with false promises of mercy . They are taken prisoners, but Naisi can have his life on condition that Deirdre agrees to marry Conchubar. She is prepared to sacrifice herself, but Naisi refuses, and Conchubar has him executed. Deirdre then pretends that she loves the old king, and asks as a last favour to be allowed to see the body of her lover. The request is granted, and beside his body she stabs her breast with a dagger. It is a strong and passionate love drama, and its barbaric force contrasts strangely with Yeats's gentle and melodious verse.

Apart from these verse plays, which treat of legendary subjects and the heroes of Ireland, Yeats has also written a number of prose plays. For the most part they are slighter, for Yeats's creative and poetic gifts were closely connected, and his prose lacks dramatic power. One of these plays, however, is better than any of his other work, and, together with Synge's *Riders to the Sea*, marks the finest achievement of Irish drama; it is the little one-act play, *Cathleen ni Houlihan*. Yeats wrote it in co-operation with Lady Gregory, for he believed he was not sufficiently familiar with the country people's way of expressing themselves to do justice to the theme alone. However, it resembles Yeats's earlier dramatic work so closely that one is convinced that the poetic elements in the play are his own. The plays which Lady Gregory composed by herself do not achieve anything like the same heights.

The completed play follows the dream described above fairly closely. Yeats changes the date of the story to 1798, when a French expedition landed in Ireland and was joined by a number of Irishmen who were anxious to escape the English yoke. We find ourselves in the cottage of Peter Gillane on the eve of his son's wedding to a wealthy peasant girl, Delia Cahel. Michael is a happy young man; his wedding clothes are lying on the chest, all ready, and he has a bag which contains the dowry. Then an old woman, Cathleen, the daughter of Houlihan, comes in and begins to talk. She has come from afar, driven out of her home by strangers, and she has lost her four green fields. Now she hopes that her friends will help her to regain the lovely fields. She sings to herself a strange song of the people, about the golden-haired Donough who was hanged at Galway. Michael asks her why he was hanged, and she replies that he died for love of her: "Many a man has died for love of me." She speaks of O'Donnell and O'Sullivan, of all the champions of Irish freedom, of heroes who died for her hundreds of years ago, and those who will die for her to-morrow. They offer her money, but she says it is not silver she needs. Those who want to help her must give themselves. Suddenly Michael says that he will go with her, and she warns him of the fate that awaits him: "It is a hard service they take that help me. Many that are red-cheeked now will be pale-cheeked: many that have been free to walk the hills and the bogs and the rushes will be sent to walk hard streets in far countries. Many that have gathered money will not stay to spend it; many a child will be born, and there will be no father at its christening to give it a name." She leaves the cottage, but even through the door she can be heard singing how those who died for her will live on in memory and song.

Young Michael is deaf to all but her. They want to persuade him to try on his new suit for the wedding next day, but he has forgotten both the wedding and the new clothes. The bride comes in, bearing the news that the Frenchmen have landed in

x

the bay. She asks him why he looks at her as if she was a stranger, and he does not answer. She and his parents become anxious whether he will leave them to join the French. A few words of the old woman's song are heard through the door, and, as if drawn by a magnet, Michael leaves his kinsfolk without a word and rushes out. The play ends with the father asking the youngest son, a lad of twelve, "Did you see an old woman going down the path?" The answer comes, "I did not, but I saw a young girl, and she had the walk of a queen." Ireland herself grows younger as the young men join the fight for freedom.

The connexion with the theme of Yeats's earlier plays is easy to see. Mary Bruin in *The Land of Heart's Desire* is carried off to the land of the fairies; Forgael, in *The Shadowy Waters,* cuts the hawser and lets his boat drift to the land of eternal bliss, to a certain death; so the young bridegroom on the eve of his greatest happiness is taken away to a task which for him also will mean a death of sacrifice. But the mysterious powers, which in Yeats's earlier plays capture the hearts of his heroes, are replaced here by a more comprehensible ideal, that of fatherland and freedom.

Later, Yeats was to appear as an even more convinced Irish nationalist, as for instance in *The Dreaming of the Bones.* Here there appear to a young Irish revolutionary two spirits who can find no peace in the grave, King Dermot and his mistress, Devorguilla. Seven hundred years ago, Dermot was defeated in battle by Devorguilla's husband, and called in the Normans to help him. The young Irishman, who is himself waiting to be arrested and shot, refuses to forgive the penitent couple who were the cause of centuries of slavery for Ireland. *The Dreaming of the Bones* is a bold experiment in form, in the Japanese style, and despite its lack of action it has a strong dramatic rhythm. But *Cathleen ni Houlihan* seems a greater play because of its low tones and its simplicity. With this play Yeats opened the way for a new development in Irish drama which was to dominate it more completely than Irish legend had done, namely the peasant play, of which his pupil, Synge, was to be the foremost exponent.

Next to Yeats the name of John Millington Synge is the greatest in Irish drama. There have even been those who have claimed that he was the greatest writer for the stage in the English language since Shakespeare's day.

Synge's life was short and his output very small. Perhaps this has helped to increase his fame. He was born in Dublin in 1871, and when he left school he roamed about on the Continent with a small income, which he supplemented from time to time by writing travel articles for the press. It is believed that during his visit to Germany he was impressed by Hauptmann's peasant plays. In Paris, where he lived for two years, he revived his knowledge of Gaelic and moved among the Irish colony. In 1898 he was discovered by Yeats in an attic in the Latin Quarter. He showed Yeats some poems and essays in the decadent style, which Yeats declared to be completely worthless. Yeats advised Synge to leave Paris and to give up his studies of French literature and his plans for becoming a critic: "Go to the Aran Islands. Live there as if you were one of the people themselves, and then portray a way of life that has not yet found an artist to paint it." Synge went to the Aran Islands, wrote down the sayings of the peasants, learned their language and wrote a book of sketches which was not immediately published because no publisher would accept it. In 1903 he began to write plays and when he died he had six to his credit, of which two were one-act plays and only one could be considered a full-length drama.

It is on this quantitatively slight production that Synge's still-growing reputation rests. During his lifetime he was anything but popular in his native land. When his very first play, *The Shadow of the Glen,* was produced it roused a storm of indignation in the powerful Nationalist party. They were annoyed because the Irish peasant woman was depicted as frivolous; the agitators always represented her as a model compared with English and Scottish housewives. Four years later Synge wrote *The Playboy of The Western World,* his most far-reaching and finished play, in which a son boasts of having killed his father. Its production caused an absolute uproar in the theatre and in the press. The Sinn Fein party declared open war on this play which blackened the name of the Irish people, and at the second performance the opposition had arranged for such a din of shouting and trumpets that the actors could not be heard. The newspapers demanded that the play be taken off. The theatre directors, Yeats and Lady Gregory, refused to give in and continued to present the play, which was also performed in

London and America—to the accompaniment of demonstrations by the extreme Irish Nationalists. Far from being excluded from the theatre, Synge became a co-director with Yeats and Lady Gregory, and the sensation caused by *The Playboy of the Western World* helped to spread his fame through Europe.

If any literary works can arouse interest in Ireland, it is just these plays by Synge which were so hotly denounced by the Irish Nationalists. Yeats was primarily concerned with legendary settings, and Lady Gregory's plays, though often dealing with modern topics, had a plainly patriotic purpose and no great distinction, whereas in Synge's dramatic works we get a living picture of Irish peasant life. The Irish are among the most eloquent people on this earth and it would be completely absurd to make them talk laconically. Synge's dramas give an impression of the wordiness of the Irish peasantry, and though in various points he is the faithful pupil of Maeterlinck, there are no staccato lines in his plays. Synge has a capacity for not overloading the plot, for keeping it simple and alive, for avoiding all merely theatrical effect and talking for talking's sake. He throws himself straight into the story, and the dramatic tension never slackens. Critics with a naturalistic bias have reproached Synge for giving hair-raising and improbable descriptions of Irish peasant life. A comparison between the plays and their source, Synge's own sketches, shows that he has not invented a single one of his plots; he used stories which he had himself heard told by the peasants. But he has compressed them, given them an edge and an impetus. They do not pretend to be reasonable, but they treat of events which the peasants themselves consider to be real, not fairy-tales. In the preface to *The Playboy of the Western World*, Synge writes, "Anyone who has lived in real intimacy with the Irish peasantry will know that the wildest sayings and ideas in this play are tame indeed, compared with the fancies one may hear in any little hillside cabin in Geesala or Carraroe or Dingle Bay." Although the plot in at least two of his plays and their content of ideas are not unrelated to symbolism, Synge is a realist in the carrying out of his ideas. His character-drawing is confident and often meticulous, and he is above all careful to reproduce exactly the tone of peasant conversation. He explains in the same preface that he has only used one or two words in his plays which he has

not heard in use by the peasants, or used himself as a child before
he learned to read the newspapers. The words and the sequence
of words are those of peasant speech, but the melody of the
sentences is Synge's own. Although the plays are written in the
usual Anglo-Irish peasant dialect, the lines often sound as if they
were taken from some ancient epic. Yeats said that Synge's
plays reproduce the speech of a people who speak in English
but think in Gaelic.

Synge studied Elizabethan drama in his youth, and avails
himself of the Elizabethan technique of describing the setting of
a scene in the course of the dialogue. He does not need the endless descriptions of scenery to which contemporary dramatists
generally resort. In a single line he can often indicate the whole
poetic atmosphere of a play.

Another characteristic of Synge is his grotesque humour. Not
even the most serious of his plays, *Riders to the Sea*, is wholly
tragic. The plot is a confusing medley of comic and tragic
elements.

The Shadow of the Glen, Synge's first play, performed in 1903,
is quite typical of him. It is the story of an old peasant, taken
directly from his sketches in the Aran Islands. Synge has himself
pointed its relationship with the then popular *Matron from
Ephesus*, but also points out its independent origin.

The opening scene is romantic and weird almost to excess.
A young peasant wife is watching over her husband's corpse,
when a vagabond knocks at the door. The conversation then
shows us that the husband had died that very day, and that his
death is not untimely, for the wife has long been thinking about
marrying a young shepherd. She is now thinking with satisfaction of the money and the hundred sheep which her husband has
left. She goes out, leaving the vagabond to watch over the corpse,
but while he is muttering 'De Profundis' the supposedly dead
man rises from his bed. He has been pretending to be dead, in
order to learn the truth about his wife, but lies down again
when she returns with the shepherd. When the husband wants
to beat the shepherd and drive out his wife, the shepherd does
not try to protect her.

Now it is the vagabond's turn. In some speeches cast in clumsy
peasant dialect, but inspired by Synge's poetry of the wilds, he

describes the glories of a wandering life compared with the sad fate of growing old and ugly by the side of a whining old man; a night of frost and rain, the herons crying out over the black lakes, the cry of the grouse and the owl: "It's fine songs you'll be hearing when the sun goes up, and there'll be no old fellow wheezing, the like of an old sheep, close to your ear."

The wife makes her way out with the vagabond, but the shepherd is called back by the once-dead man who wants to drink a glass with him. In the original story the old man ended by giving his rival a bloody head with his stick.

Riders to the Sea was written at the same time as *The Shadow of the Glen*, and performed a year later. It is no exaggeration to compare this little one-act play to a Greek tragedy. There is probably no other instance in modern drama of a play which, without departing from the naturalistic convention, gives such a strong impression of Fate in the classical sense.

Very little happens in the play. There is a fisherman's widow, Maurya, and her youngest and last surviving son, Bartley. There were once six sons, but all the rest have gone down in the battle with the sea. Bartley rides off to a horse-fair, and as he passes along the rocky shore in the storm a great wave seizes him and hurls him down "where there is a great surf on the white rocks." We are reminded of the poems of Ossian, where the setting is similar, and sometimes the theme also; a man drowned out at sea, and those who are left to weep on the shore. Synge had of course been present at such scenes in real life when he visited the Aran Islands, and he describes them in his book with words that recur in the play. The play begins with two of the daughters in the kitchen, sorting out a bundle of clothes belonging to a drowned man. They fear that they may belong to Michael, who set out to sea nine days ago and has not returned. They are terrified lest their mother should come in while they are doing this, for she has already been so anxious about Michael, and now Bartley, the last surviving son, has this day gone off to Galway. By the end of the play they have decided that the clothes are Michael's and at the same time the body of Bartley, taken from the sea, is brought in.

As in Maeterlinck's *The Intruder* and *The Interior*, the story of the play consists of a death, foreshadowed from the beginning and confirmed by the end of the play. *The Interior* was performed at the Abbey Theatre in Synge's day, and he had also admired Maeterlinck during his stay in Paris. But here all the artificiality of Maeterlinck's atmosphere has gone and the dramatic tension is, if possible, even higher. As in Maeterlinck also, the chief character is really Death, the fate which crushes all it meets. But it has become more comprehensible because it is personified by the stormy sea, the sea which has devoured the whole family, generation by generation, brother after brother, and has now finally made an end of the family by taking Bartley before he has had time to leave any heirs. The play is a lament for a family, whose fate symbolizes that of a whole population.

All the time everybody's thoughts are directed towards Bartley's ride to the sea, which is regarded as the beginning of a journey to death, even though death actually comes earlier than is feared. But the play has none of the monotonous atmosphere which characterizes Maeterlinck's play in this style. Even in this mournful tragedy we find traces of Synge's grotesque humour. In this tale of a simple fishing family thoughts of past and present misfortune are mingled with all the trivialities of everyday life. From the first moment, when the characters are concerned with the clothes of the dead Michael, they discuss the family's great treasure, the black-footed pig, and how he has been eating the rope that Bartley needs for his journey. Whenever Maurya thinks of the dangers threatening the life of her son, she talks of the fine white boards that she has ready for a coffin. When finally his body is carried in, an old man is asked to nail together the coffin wood and it is discovered that she has forgotten to get hold of nails. A neighbour says reproachfully, "It's a great wonder she wouldn't think of the nails, and all the coffins she's seen made already." The daughter replies, excusing her mother, "Its getting old she is, and broken." Even pathos has a sober and prosaic quality. "If it was a hundred horses, or a thousand horses, you had itself," says Maurya to her youngest son, trying to dissuade him from the journey: "What is the price of a thousand horses against a son, where there is one son only?"

When Bartley goes, the women remember that he went off without a loaf of bread or his mother's blessing. She must catch him up at the turn of the road and give him the bread and the blessing. Maurya returns, a broken woman, having seen the most terrible sight in the world. Bartley was riding the red mare, with the grey pony behind, but on the pony his mother saw Michael sitting, in fine clothes and new shoes. The words stuck in her throat so that she could say nothing. Now she is convinced that Bartley is also doomed to die, and she begins to mourn all those whom the sea has taken from her, her husband and her father and her sons. Some were never found, others were brought home on a board. She remembers how she sat with Bartley, a babe on her lap, when four women came in, crossed themselves and said not a word. The men followed, bearing something in a red sail, and water dripped from it. It was Patch, who had been drowned. While the mother is recounting these memories, some old women come in silently, cross themselves and fall to their knees, pulling their skirts up over their heads. Maurya asks, as in a dream, "Is it Patch or is it Michael, or what is it?" The daughters then have to reveal the secret which they have hitherto concealed from her, that Michael has already been found and buried up in the North, and that his clothes have been recognized. The old women whisper that Bartley has been thrown from his horse, and in a moment he is borne in on a plank, covered in sail-cloth which leaves a trail of wet drops on the floor. But old Maurya raises her head and speaks as if she did not see the people round her: "They've all gone now, and there isn't anything more the sea can be doing to me . . . I'll have no call now to be up and crying and praying when the wind breaks from the South . . . I'll have no call now to be going down and getting Holy Water in the dark nights after Samhain (The Gaelic word for late autumn), and I won't care what way the sea is when the other women will be keening." She asks for the Holy Water, sprinkles some over Bartley's body, and over Michael's clothes also when she has spread them out. "It isn't that I haven't prayed for you, Bartley, to the Almighty God. It isn't that I haven't said prayers in the dark night, till you wouldn't know what I'ld be saying; but it's a great rest I'll be having now, and it's time surely. It's a great rest I'll have now, and great sleeping in the long nights after Samhain, if it's only a bit of wet flour we do have to eat, and maybe a fish that would be stinking." The daughters are surprised that she is so calm now, she who mourned for nine days in despair when Michael went. But the mother continues resignedly, "They're all together this time, and the end is come ... Michael has a clean burial in the far North, by the grace of Almighty God. Bartley will have a fine coffin out of the white boards, and a deep grave surely. What more can we want than that? No man at all can be living for ever, and we must be satisfied."

The fundamental idea, which is the calm unconcern of the old peasant woman when she has nothing more which the sea can take away from her, can also be found in a passage from Pierre Loti's "*Pêcheur d'Islande*," which Synge read just before he began to write *Riders to the Sea*. But in the novel we have the author's analysis of the inmost heart of the old woman; in the play the mother expresses this attitude in her own words, without giving the audience any impression of heartlessness.

Synge tended to be whimsical and unsymmetrical in his construction of plots. His characterization was shrewd but not subtle. He did not take sides or point morals. He was in consequence more effective in short than in long plays. The least significant of his plays is the short farce, *The Tinker's Wedding*, which was the first play he planned, but it was never performed during his lifetime. It does, however, reproduce admirably the way of life of the wandering craftsmen.

The Well of the Saints is set in an uncertain period of the past and for once a supernatural element plays a part. We see a beggar and his wife, both blind, sitting at a cross-road and receiving coins from passers-by. They are satisfied with their lives, and their only grief is that they cannot see each other. The old man believes that his ugly wife is a beauty—people with ordinary sight have called her in jest, "the great wonder of the West." A saint who is passing by with a can of holy water restores their sight to them, but they are so disgusted with each other that they nearly come to blows.

Fortunately they are soon blind again, and can once more enjoy their existence. When the saint returns and tells them that this time he proposes to restore their sight for good, the old man knocks the can out of his hand; "for if it's a right ... some of you have to be fasting and praying and talking holy talk the like of yourself, I'm thinking it's a good right ourselves have to be sitting blind, hearing a soft wind turning the little leaves of spring, and feeling the sun, and we not tormenting our souls with the sight of the gray days, and the holy men, and the dirty feet is trampling the world."

The saint declares them to be sinners, and the pious will no longer tolerate their presence. Satisfied with their lot, the beggars wander to the cities of the South, where they have not seen too much of the reality about them.

The play has a medieval flavour, and the theme has been found in one of Chaucer's Canterbury Tales. Synge says that he took the idea from a French farce, whose name he had forgotten. The play has been compared with Maeterlinck's *The Blind*, where the fine hearing of the blind, and their great awareness of nature are also described. But Maeterlinck conceived of the blind as profoundly unhappy, while Synge praises their happiness, and the advantages of illusion as against bitter reality.

Synge's most famous play is *The Playboy of the Western World*, (1907). It made his name known, thanks to the uproar with which it was received, and many people consider it his best play. Synge took the idea for the play from a story about a boy who, in a fit of temper, killed his father with a spade. The story is told in the Aran Islands. The remarkable part of the real story is that the islanders sympathized with the murderer, hid him from the police, and helped to get him over to America. Apart from this, the plot is an invention.

One evening there comes rushing into a country inn young Christy Mahon, a lean and pitiable figure. He tells the young daughter of the landlord that he happened to kill his father with a spade after a quarrel, and that the police are searching for him. The young girl looks after him with tender care, and her protective instinct soon turns to admiration and love. Christy notices that every time he tells how he killed his father he impresses the visitors more. At first he was terrified, but now he becomes bolder and more boastful, and his account of the murder ever more exaggerated. In the final version he claims to have split his father's body into two, right down to the waist. The young girl's feelings also grow warmer, all the more so because she has to fight for him against a widow, a comical character, who wants him for a husband, as well as against the

other girls of the village who swarm around him. She breaks
off her engagement to a wealthy young man, whom she nevertheless persuades to lend a decent suit to the stranger, and Christy
is soon spoiled with kindness and showered with presents. He
reproaches himself for not having put an end earlier to his
disagreeable and quarrelsome old father, since his action has
brought such delightful consequences. There are no obstacles
to the marriage as the girl's father, a persistent drunkard, has
given his consent.

At a most unsuitable moment Mahon, the father, whom everyone had thought to be dead, arrives with a dirty bandage tied
round his head. He rushes up to Christy, followed by the crowd,
knocks him down and begins to beat him. In a trice the aura of
heroism which has surrounded the boy vanishes, and people
realize that he was only a braggart after all. The girl turns
contemptuously away, and the crowd jeer at him. To regain his
lost prestige, he once again seizes a spade and rushes out through
the door in pursuit of his father, who has fled. When he returns
he discovers the gulf that lies between a wild story and a shabby
deed. The crowd, who have been so anxious to protect him,
now want to hang him, and he is only saved because his father
returns, quite uninjured this time, and drags him away, leaving
the poor girl to weep over her shattered illusions.

This play has generally been hailed as Synge's masterpiece,
one of the greatest creations of modern drama, and as a powerful
realistic play in the Elizabethan tradition, which indeed Synge
claims that it is in his preface. The hero has been called a caricature of a national type—a symbol of humanity. He has been
compared to Don Quixote, Tartarin, and—perhaps most suitably
—to Peer Gynt.

It is a burlesque of a popular joke, to which Synge has given a
realistic frame. The improbable plot is convincing because of
the remarkably skilful characterization. To the love-scene
between the landlord's daughter and the supposed parricide he
has imparted an atmosphere of peasant poetry. The young girl
in particular is an irresistible and magical creature.

During the controversy about the play, Synge wrote a short
note for a Dublin paper. He maintained that the play had no
purpose, in the modern sense of the word, and that it was only

partly intended to be extravagant comedy. "A good deal of what is to be found in it, and even more behind it, is perfectly serious, if one looks at it in a certain light. I believe this often to be the case with comedy, and that no one to-day is sure whether Shylock or Alcestis is meant to be played seriously or not." That this was indeed his attitude is confirmed by a contemporary letter to a friend, in which he stresses the serious element in his play.

It appears as if Synge was provoked by the opposition which the play aroused to exaggerate its gravity and its probability as a study of peasant life. In his letter he writes that the plot is in essence reasonable, if due regard is paid to the spiritual atmosphere of the setting.

To think of playing Christy Mahon tragically is impossible. But naturally *The Playboy of the Western World* is meant to do more than merely amuse for an hour or two. With all its farcical exaggeration, it provides a brilliant insight into the Irish temperament, the ease with which it flares up and as quickly dies down again, and its inability to distinguish between right and wrong, and between truth and falsehood. Without the suggestion ever being made in the play, one cannot help feeling that it is a satire on national character, created by a writer who has devoted his life to the study of the peasantry, whose faults he castigates precisely because he recognizes them in himself.

That the controversy about *The Playboy of the Western World* made a deep impression on Synge is apparent both from the article he wrote, and from the letter. It has also been said to have contributed to the illness from which he never recovered. He was occupied to the very end with a play which was not produced until after his death, and which to some extent reflects his own mood.

Even before the *première* of *The Playboy of the Western World* Synge had told Yeats that he was tired of the Irish peasant world, and he chose for a subject this time the most popular of early Irish legends, the tale of *Deirdre of the Sorrows,* which had already been dramatized by Yeats and others. He did not, however, entirely abandon his old peasant setting, nor did he, like Yeats, retain the old patina of the legend, for he largely modernized it

and treated the characters in an entirely original way. Yet his
Deirdre does not seem an anachronism. He has a natural sense of
style which saves him from many a fault, and with all its naiveté,
his dialect has an epic tone which is well suited to a legendary
period. His Irish peasants, too, with their powerful imagination
and their primitive wildness, do not need much disguising to
serve as the legendary heroes of a thousand years ago. Synge's
Deirdre is heavier, more compact and more gloomy than Yeats's,
which has more of the elegiac about it. The character of the
queen is also different. She is less charming and conforms less to
the spirit of the legend, but is a more original and forceful figure.
Synge's Deirdre is dominated by the fear of growing old, of
seeing her cheeks grow pale, her hair grey and her limbs stiff.
She is afraid of no longer being able to fill the heart of her
beloved Naisi. Listening to a conversation, she discovers that he
is already tired of the solitary life they have had to live, for fear
of the King's cunning plans, and she prefers her love-story to
come to an end before the glow fades. Fully realizing the danger,
she persuades Naisi to accept the King's treacherous invitation,
which she knows will cost him his life and compel her to commit
suicide.

This conception of the tragic moment in life, when the peak
has been reached and the path henceforth leads downwards,
this fear of withering, is always present in Synge. It is already
apparent in his first play, *The Shadow of the Glen,* where the young
wife leaves her home and husband for the same reason that moves
Deirdre to return to the King's country, in order to escape a
comfortless old age. The same motive causes the blind couple
in *The Well of the Saints* to long to be blind again. Perhaps the
theme fascinated Synge because he was himself doubtful how
long he would remain at the peak of his powers. His fears were
not realized. It is generally held that *Deirdre of the Sorrows* would
have been his masterpiece if death had not prevented him from
completing it.

From the short prefaces to his plays we learn that during the
last period of his life he was critical both of the Ibsen problem-
play and of symbolistic and naturalistic drama. He found
symbolism artificial and naturalism joyless, and believed that
intellectual drama—"look at Ibsen and the Germans,"—would

soon be as old-fashioned as Galen's pharmacopoeia. "But the best works of Ben Jonson and Molière can no more grow out-of-fashion than blackberries on a hedge." As a salvation from such schools of drama he pointed to peasant drama: "In Ireland, for a few years more, we have a popular imagination that is fiery, and magnificent, and tender; so that those of us who wish to write start with a chance that is not given to writers in places where the springtime of the local life has been forgotten, and the harvest is a memory only, and the straw has been turned into bricks."

Synge realized that only in certain places and for a short time could peasant drama have anything new to contribute, and he was indeed to grow tired himself of peasant themes before he died. Other dramatists of peasant stories have often set their plays many years back in time, as did O'Neill with *Desire under the Elms*, or described ancient and traditional customs, as Lorca did. But some of the fresh scent of blackberries is to be found in their works also. It was Synge's great contribution to awaken to life a dramatic tradition which many believed to be doomed in our industrial age, and to have created some of the most unforgettable masterpieces in this tradition.

EUGENE O'NEILL

AMERICA has known other significant playwrights before
O'Neill, but with him American drama makes its real entry
into the world theatre. He is played all over the world, and
translated into every language. There is a touch of American
boldness and creativeness in his dramatic work. It is also
noticeable that O'Neill experiments with various forms of
dramatic art, partly because he does not really feel at home with
any of them except the one-act play with the sea as its theme,
with which he first won his reputation. As a Naturalist he lacks
restraint; the content of his symbolistic plays is often confused,
while his attempts at expressionism often stop half-way. The
technical reforms which he thought so important, such as the use
of a thought-dialogue along with the ordinary one, the introduction of masks, and simultaneous scenes have not led to
subsequent imitations, and have been entirely abandoned in his
latest plays.

O'Neill's great dream appears to have been the creation within
drama of a counterpart to the modern novel. He has on several
occasions spoken of using his own life for a series of plays, on
the lines of "Jean Christophe" or "War and Peace," and during
recent years he has been engaged on the dramatic representation
of the history of an American family through various generations for a hundred and thirty years. This project was intended
to fill eleven plays, and reminds us of the long family chronicles
that we find both in English and French literature. O'Neill
seldom tries to achieve unity of time, and is quite ready to allow
long periods to elapse between acts. It would be perfectly natural
if his dramatic work was ultimately to swell out into something
resembling the modern cycle of novels.

O'Neill's production is uneven, and includes a number of

failures alongside his masterly works. Everything of his, however, has a certain dramatic intensity—action, characterization,
dialogue and even stage directions. From the very first, O'Neill
proclaimed himself a disciple of Strindberg, whom he read in
the year that he wrote his first play. "To me," he says," like
Nietzsche in his own sphere, he remains the master; still more
modern than any of us, even to-day; still our leader."

Though O'Neill has repeated this statement on several
occasions, Strindberg's influence is more difficult to detect in his
work than that of Nietzsche, which is plainly evident. It is not
correct to say that O'Neill's attitude to women and marriage
was determined by Strindberg's, except in one or two of the less
successful plays, such as *Welded*. It is even less possible to agree
with those critics in America, hostile to O'Neill, who claim that
plays such as *Desire under the Elms, Strange Interlude* and the
Electra trilogy are direct imitations of *Miss Julie*.

Up to a point, however, these comments show us something
of the truth, in so far as it is the naturalistic element in Strindberg,
both before and after Inferno, which has influenced O'Neill.
Even if there are some similarities between *Days without End*
and *To Damascus*, Part I, there is no trace of the dream atmosphere
of Strindberg in his American disciple. It is the art of writing a
dialogue that is both everyday and dramatically tense that
O'Neill has inherited from Strindberg. Indeed, the dialogue
is even more powerful in O'Neill, who has also achieved a
tighter construction than Strindberg.

This may well be connected with O'Neill's liking for stylized
drama. Once in the Thirties he insisted on the use of masks, even
for some earlier plays which hardly seemed suitable, such as *The
Emperor Jones,* and the *Electra* trilogy. With all his great talent,
O'Neill still lacks Strindberg's impulsiveness, his ebullient
imagination and his flights of poetry.

Eugene O'Neill was born in 1888, significantly enough in
Broadway, the theatre's own street in New York. His father,
James O'Neill, was born in Ireland, but had been brought over
to the United States at an early age, and had become a much
respected actor. His mother was born in America, but also of
Irish ancestors. Eugene O'Neill's early one-act plays, and his
peasant dramas show the influence of Synge. In *Anna Christie,*

which was first performed in Sweden, the sea plays the role of Fate as it does in Synge's *Riders to the Sea*. But he does not achieve Synge's poetry. Some claim to have noticed the influence of Shaw in O'Neill's work, and it is plainly apparent in such a play as *Lazarus Laughed,* in which O'Neill treats the biblical legend with the same wanton disregard of chronology as Shaw does in similar cases. But he was heavier by nature, and despite his taste for paradox he lacks Shaw's wit.

Eugene's father, James O'Neill, had a real talent for acting great roles, particularly the Shakespearian characters. Unfortunately, as early as 1883, he made a tremendous hit in a dramatised version of Dumas' *Monte-Christo*. Year after year he toured with this play all over America, often earning as much as 50,000 dollars in a season. "He considered that he simply could not afford to play in anything else," his son tells us. "But in later years he was full of bitter regret. He thought that *Monte-Christo* had ruined his dramatic career."

This experience of his father's obviously played a big part in O'Neill's life: "I decided that I would never sell myself," he is supposed to have said. Time and again we find in his dramatic work the picture of a man who has sold his soul and attained worldly success, without ever being really able to make full use of his wealth, and without even realizing the happiness to be found by other means. We meet this character in various disguises: the farmer's son in *Beyond the Horizon*, Marco Polo in *Marco Millions,* and the energetic and successful business man in *The Great God Brown*.

Opposed to him we often find a contrasting character, the confirmed romantic, who prefers to live in a world of dreams but never really sees his dreams fulfilled. This is clearly a picture of the author himself.

O'Neill had a very varied career before he threw himself into dramatic work. As a child he travelled round with his father on the Monte-Christo tours. Later he was sent to various Catholic schools—his parents were fervent Catholics—and in 1906 he went to Princeton, from which he was sent down for having broken a window-pane while making merry with his friends. Now began the years of adventure. After a few months in an office he went off to Honduras to look for gold. Then came a

number of sea voyages, on one of which he sailed as a cow-hand
in a cattle-boat from Buenos Aires to Africa and back again. On
his return, since he had not a penny, he was allowed to take a
small part in the evergreen *Monte-Christo,* and also spent some
time as a reporter, writing rhyming commentaries for a small
town newspaper. His parents regarded him as a hopeless wastrel,
and he was a regular customer at the seamen's tavern, which he
afterwards described in *Anna Christie.* During these stormy
years, however, his lungs had suffered, and towards the end of
1912 he entered a sanatorium.

   This period of enforced rest drove him to mental activity,
"particularly because by temperament I always was excitable
and nervous." His temperament was not to change. But when in
the spring of 1913 he was released with a clean bill of health, he
threw himself into dramatic work with the same zest that he had
previously shown for travel and changing jobs. He spent the
next twenty years in creative work, producing, apparently without any pause, some thirty plays, and suddenly stopped.

   Ever since his childhood he had been familiar with everything
that was performed on the American stage. As a convalescent
he read, he tells us, everything that he could lay hands on; "The
Greeks, the Elizabethans, practically all the classics, and of course
all the moderns, Ibsen and Strindberg, especially Strindberg."
In the autumn of 1914 he enrolled at Harvard as the pupil of
Professor G. P. Baker, who cherished the conviction that it was
as possible to train pupils to write plays as to paint pictures.
Under the Professor's guidance he wrote a couple of plays which
he later destroyed. Baker, a cultured man, and a well-meaning
scholar, had written a book about dramatic technique in which
he warned his pupils against the two extremes of one-act plays
and too long plays. O'Neill managed to ignore both these
pieces of advice. Teacher and pupil alike spoke kindly of each
other afterwards, but Baker's advice was wasted on the young
man, who even before he embarked on the course was a com-
petent writer.

   More important was the fact that O'Neill became acquainted
with one of the independent amateur theatres, that at Provincetown, which was founded in 1915 and 1916 on the European
model, and which was also intended to stage American plays. The

management of this theatre had heard that O'Neill had a caseful of plays, and asked him for one of them. He chose *Bound East for Cardiff*, which Baker had said was no play. After this several other plays of his were performed. O'Neill has expressed his gratitude to this company for encouraging him, and performing his plays: "But I cannot honestly say that I would not have gone on writing plays all the same. I had already gone too far to stop." Even before the première at Provincetown he had published a small collection of his one-act plays. But it was through this small private theatre that he first became known in the United States and then in Europe.

It was the memories of his life as a sailor that he reproduced in a series of one-act plays performed at Provincetown, the author himself sometimes taking a part. These sketches of life aboard ship are among O'Neill's finest works. Some of them, though in no way connected with each other, are set on the cargo-steamer *Glencairn*, and contain more or less the same characters. A good example of one of these is *Bound East for Cardiff*, and particularly, as O'Neill explained twenty years later, because it contains the seeds of that attitude to life which was to appear in all his later work.

The play has no real plot; perhaps this was why Baker did not consider it a proper play. It deals wholly with the death-struggle of a sailor called Yank. He has fallen down on to the deck from a ladder, and no one, least of all himself, doubts that he will die. But the play has a poetic atmosphere and dramatic rhythm. The ship is lying quietly in a fog out in the Atlantic, and poor Yank has very little hope of achieving the object of his desire, to be buried on land. To his best friend, another sailor called Driscoll, whom he has persuaded to stay with him to the end, he admits that a life at sea is only worth while when one is young.

Swiftly, events from his past life go through his mind. He is tormented by the memory of a knife-fight with another sailor at Capetown, and he also remembers Fanny, the barmaid at the Red Stork in Cardiff: "She was good to me, she tried to lend me half-a-crown when I was broke there, last trip. Buy her the biggest box of sugar-candy you can find in Cardiff." At the moment of death he believes he sees "a sweet lady dressed in black." When he has died the rest of the crew come into the

forecastle, where the play is set. The mist has gone and all is
once again life and movement.

This little play is usually included with O'Neill's early
naturalistic plays. But it might just as properly be called symbolistic. With all its brevity, it has more to say about life and
death than O'Neill was to proclaim when he later assumed the
mantle of a prophet. He has since declared that the one-act play
is an unsatisfactory form because it cannot reach far enough,
and added, "The one-act play is an excellent medium for a
poetic thought, a lofty conception which cannot be sustained
throughout a full-length play."

There is, of course, nothing to prevent a playwright from
sustaining the lyric atmosphere throughout a full-length play,
but O'Neill was too little of a poet to succeed at the first attempt,
and he is said to have burnt his first full-length play. Many of
his later plays tend to deal with a whole life-story, in which the
more interesting psychological changes are confined to the
middle acts.

This is true of his first full-length play to be performed, which
happens also to be a peasant play, *Beyond the Horizon* (1918).
It deals with a theme that recurs frequently in O'Neill's dramatic
work. There are two sons on a farm, one a romantic dreamer,
the other a vigorous man of action, and both have fallen in love
with the same girl, the daughter of a neighbour. Robert, the
dreamer, who has longed to go beyond the horizon, finds his
love answered and stays at home, and it is his brother Andrew
who goes off to sea. The marriage does not turn out well, and
the farm is neglected, but when the more practically-minded
brother Andrew returns it appears that he has not been able to
profit by his experiences either. He has become a restless pleasure-
seeker, and none of his speculations have been successful. For
the first time we see an instance of the Peer Gynt type who loses
his soul in the hurly-burly of the world, of whom O'Neill the
dramatist is so fond.

O'Neill has written that he got the idea from a Norwegian
shipmate, who was always grumbling because he had left his
father's cottage to come to sea: "I thought then, what would it
have been like if he, with all his wanderlust, had stayed on the
farm?" This comment shows that already in this play O'Neill

was concerned to express a fundamental problem, the difficulty experienced by every individual of finding a place in life where he belongs, where he can feel at home. The issue may not be quite so clear in *Beyond the Horizon,* because he has split his model into two characters.

Sentimentality and faulty psychology spoiled O'Neill's last real sea-play, *Anna Christie,* which was completed in 1920, and was particularly popular in Sweden because the chief characters are Swedish. With all his old virtuosity, O'Neill returns to depict again the setting of ships and ports with which he had been familiar. The title part is a reincarnation of the Lady of the Camellias, and repeats her predecessor's claim to have been purified by love. O'Neill seems to have realized the resemblance between this play and *The Lady of the Camellias,* for in a letter he makes the defence that simple people like Anna Christie can only express their emotions in terms taken from the films and novels with which they are familiar: "In moments of extreme tension life copies melodrama." This explanation is probably an afterthought. Apparently O'Neill himself no longer appreciates *Anna Christie.* In some of his other full-length plays it is noticeable that he is not yet able to make his primitive characters convincing throughout a play of several acts. He succumbs to the temptation to elaborate and refine until they become too sensitive.

O'Neill won a European reputation with *The Emperor Jones* in 1920 because he returned to the shorter form, and concentrated all his attention on one character with untamed and violent emotions. He also ignored some of the tenets of naturalism, merely retaining those which enabled him to give colour to the dialogue, and introduced visions and scenes which were only half-real. In this he may have learned something from Strindberg, but he also has to a certain extent been influenced by film technique.

O'Neill tells how he got the idea for *The Emperor Jones* from a story about President Sam of Haiti, who claimed that no one would ever kill him with an ordinary bullet; he would kill himself with a silver bullet. O'Neill had also read about the beating of the drums on the Congo, and how passions were aroused by them at religious feasts, and his gold-mining expedition in Honduras had shown him the effect of tropical jungles on the imagination. No doubt he was also affected by his childhood favourite, Kipling.

In any case, *The Emperor Jones* is one of the most original works of modern drama. In form it is monologue; only in the first and last scenes do other characters appear. The rest is all a series of monologues in which we see the Emperor Jones in the jungle, struggling with hallucinations which grow the more terrible as the sound of the pursuing drums grows louder.

The value of the play lies in the excellent characterization of the hero. Jones is an American negro who has been a Pullman-car attendant. After a murder he has escaped to an island in the West Indies, and become the sole ruler of it, because he has managed to convince the foolish jungle negroes that he cannot be injured by an ordinary bullet, and can only be killed by a silver bullet. When at last he is compelled to fly to the jungle he lacks the instinctive confidence with which others of his race can move in it. In so far as we come into touch with culture, by so much we lose contact with nature. Jones has not succeeded in acquiring more than the merest rudiments of civilization, but they have made him a stranger in the jungle where his forefathers lived. He is without a defence and a home in life.

This idea is worked out fully in *The Hairy Ape* (1922). As the original of the stoker, Yank, O'Neill mentions a man whom he knew in his sailing days. But it is really only in the first scene that Yank has a fully human appearance. Here we see him proud of his strength, jeering at an Irish shipmate who has been regretting the passing of the sailing ship: "Ugh, you make me sick. You don't belong here." But when a millionaire's daughter, whom he meets in the boiler-room, is appalled at the sight of him, and calls him a filthy beast, he throws up his job as a fireman. Thereafter it is the feeling of not belonging anywhere which forms Yank's tragedy. After signing off in New York he goes to Fifth Avenue and looses a punch at a passer-by for no particular reason. He is then thrown out of his Trade Union branch for his wild and revolutionary plans. Having been rejected by mankind he goes to the zoological gardens, in the hope that he will find the gorilla a better companion. But when he is about to shake hands with the gorilla he is killed. According to O'Neill the play symbolizes Man, who has lost his old harmony with nature, the harmony which he had as an animal, and has not yet acquired a corresponding harmony in matters of the spirit: "Yank can't go forward, and so he tries to go backward. That is the significance of his shaking hands with the gorilla. But not when he goes backward either can he find a place where he belongs. The gorilla kills him. The subject is the same as it has always been, and always will be for drama, man and his struggle against destiny. The fight used to be waged against the Gods, now it is against man's own self, his past, and his attempt to find where he belongs."

This is, as it were, a pessimistic version of Rousseau or Darwin, not untouched by Strindberg, whom O'Neill even then hailed as his master. But he expressed the same idea more effectively in *The Emperor Jones*.

With *The Emperor Jones* and *The Hairy Ape* began something which O'Neill himself described as super-naturalism. He was very anxious to stress that these plays were written before he knew anything positive about German Expressionism. In his next plays naturalism and symbolism wage an internal war against each other. He gradually introduces more and more of the technique of expressionism and draws closer to Nietzsche, whom he knew of old, and the psychoanalyists who were at that time fashionable in America.

After a number of uncompleted plays, O'Neill wrote in 1924 one of his finest works, the peasant play, *Desire under the Elms*. Like *Mourning becomes Electra*, it is set in New England.

The story reminds us of Tolstoy's *The Power of Darkness*, the greatest naturalistic play. In both works we have a picture of untamed passion and a primitive rural population. In *Desire under the Elms* also the murder of a child occurs, and, as in *The Power of Darkness*, the play ends with the guilty being seized by the hand of justice. The religious ecstasy of Tolstoy's play is, however, lacking. On the contrary, as in several of O'Neill's plays, the bias is against Puritanism, a Puritanism terrifyingly and impressively represented by old Cabot. At the age of seventy-five he has taken to himself a new wife, whose only motive for marrying him is to get at his land. To succeed in this she has to provide her husband with a child, and she therefore enters into a relationship with Eben, who is the son still living on the farm.

When Eben discovers her intention, she kills the child she has had by him, in order to convince him that it is him she really loves. Horrified at the murder of the child, he denounces her to the sheriff, but by the time this officer arrives he has decided to share her fate. Unmoved and without emotion, old Cabot hands them both over to the law. Neither Eben nor his step-mother feels any sense of guilt at their incest. It is for the crime of killing the child that she is ready to accept punishment, and when Eben says that it was "the child of our sin," she replies, "I do not repent that sin; I have not even prayed God to forgive it."

We see already in this play the influence of Greek tragedy. It is the farm that tempts the step-mother to seduce her step-son, but they soon find that an all-powerful fate has struck them. As symbols of this fate stand the great elms, one on each side of the house: "They bend their trailing branches down over the roof —they appear to protect and at the same time subdue; there is a sinister maternity in their aspect, a crushing, jealous absorption. ... They develop from their intimate contact with the life of man in the house an appalling humaneness. They brood oppressively over the house; they are like exhausted women resting their sagging breasts and hands and hair on its roof, and when it rains their tears trickle down monotonously and rot on the shingles."

This description of the setting foreshadows the fateful home of the Mannon family in *Mourning becomes Electra*. It sets the tone for the action which takes place on the stage. The ownership of the old farm, with all its memories of suffering and death, is the key to the heavy tragedy which hangs over the play.

In the two kindred plays, both completed in 1926, *The Great God Brown* and *Marco Millions*, O'Neill treats what he himself calls "The visionless demigod of our new materialistic myth —a success—building his life of exterior things, inwardly empty and resourceless." The point is clearest in the play about Marco Polo, which shows us a man so obsessed by the desire to amass wealth and success that he does not even notice love when it is offered to him.

The Great God Brown is the more significant play. Here we have a contrast between the successful, conceited and yet unsatisfied financier Brown, and his opposite and rival, Dion Anthony, who is a poet and a dreamer and wins the woman whom Brown has been vainly pursuing, but whom for lack of an inner harmony he has been unable to love or be happy with. The play is moving, but extremely complicated, both on the stage, because masks are used, and also in the actual content, because of the elaborate symbolism which O'Neill tries to introduce. It is interesting to note that O'Neill is already trying to tackle the Faust idea which is to dominate his later play, *Days without End.*

O'Neill first made his name with one-act plays, and for many years he did not dare to abandon the miniature form and the small theme, but his greatest fame was to be won with plays so excessively long that they could only be presented at a single performance by special arrangement. There are nine acts in *Strange Interlude,* and thirteen in *Mourning becomes Electra,* and O'Neill has now let it be known that he is engaged on a cycle of eleven plays.

A relevant point here is that although he has written practically nothing but plays, his gift is for narrative. The one-act plays of his youth are evocative short stories, and his mammoth dramas are half-novels. *Strange Interlude* gives us the history of the heroine, her circumstances and her development throughout her life, while *Mourning becomes Electra* gives us the downfall of a whole family. An illustration of this narrative tendency in O'Neill is his habit, in almost all his plays, of going into such detail with stage directions about scenery and the appearance and movements of the characters, that they go far beyond what might be justified by the needs of stage production. Even when O'Neill uses masks, they have to convey numerous emotions. Really to appreciate his plays, one must read them as well as see them. In this respect he goes further even than Shaw.

Strange Interlude is an extreme instance. Its remarkable length is not needed because of any wealth of action, but because the author makes the characters converse with each other, and also indulge in a second dialogue of thoughts. This is not merely a question of secret motives being expressed; they are often conveyed by tone and facial expression. The whole subconscious mind is laid bare in the 'thought-dialogue,' which takes more time, and is often more interesting, than the openly expressed dialogue. Any resemblance to the 'asides' of older drama is therefore purely superficial.

An objection that can be raised against this experiment is that the unexpressed thought is not always so clearly formulated as to enable it to be effectively presented in long speeches, and that, above all, the characters themselves cannot in this way be aware of their inner feelings; after all, this is clear from the very words, "unconscious," "subconscious." It has been said that O'Neill shows us his characters both as they are in ordinary life, and as revealed by X-rays. The absurdity lies in O'Neill's insistence that while they are talking they are looking at the X-ray photographs of themselves.

A performance of the play, therefore, leaves us with an impression of artificiality, but when read it is exciting. It is the novelist's trick of describing ordinary events, and interspersing the half-conscious reflections of the characters, that O'Neill is adopting.

We meet the heroine, Nina, at the beginning of the play as quite a young girl; by the end she is a white-haired old lady, the victim of emotional frustration. In her youth she had been engaged to Gordon Shaw, a war pilot who had crashed. Because her father prevented her from belonging to Gordon, she believes it her duty to pay the debt which she owes him by giving herself freely and without discrimination to the wounded soldiers in the hospital where she is serving as a nurse.

In the hope of giving the world a new Gordon she marries a good friend of his, whom she does not really love. But when she hears that her husband's family suffer from a hereditary mental disease, she arranges to have a son by the house-surgeon. Her son deserts her, her husband dies of a stroke, and at the last she is a lonely and disappointed woman. She then marries a family friend, one Marsden, in whom the well-known Oedipus complex is seen in caricatured form. He is deeply attached to his mother, whose loss he still continues to lament although he is a grown man. Nina's emotional life is ruined because she was never able to realize her youthful dream of belonging to Gordon. This is the point of the title; the present is a strange interlude between the past and the future.

The trilogy, *Mourning becomes Electra,* was published in 1931, though O'Neill had been working at it for several years. From the notes he published one can see that he was working on the same fundamental idea as Schiller. As early as the spring of 1926 he wrote, "Is it possible to create for drama a modern psychological counterpart of the Greek belief in Fate, such that an intelligent modern audience, which does not believe in Fate or supernatural vengeance, could believe and be moved by it?"

O'Neill constructed his plot to resemble closely the *Oresteia*, a connexion which he also indicated by his choice of title and the names which he gave his characters. He realized that his grim conception of fate might appear out of place in our present day, and therefore set his play in the final stages of the American Civil War. This enabled him to portray the adamant Puritanism which he had already dealt with in *Desire under the Elms*, also a Civil War play. He speaks in his first notes of the Puritan conviction that man is doomed to sin and punishment, and adds, "Orestes' Furies are within him, his conscience."

At the same time O'Neill was anxious to write a psychological play in which heredity should take the place of family guilt. There are other, but less important, ingredients of classical drama, the suggestion of a chorus of chattering women, and the attempt to keep to one scene as long as possible, namely the house of the Mannon family. The play corresponds at so many points to the *Oresteia* that it is hardly necessary to name them. General Ezra Mannon returns from the Civil War, just as Agamemnon returned from Troy. His wife, Christine, who has been carrying on an affair with a sea captain called Brant, conspires with him to poison her husband. Her act is discovered by her daughter, Lavinia, the Electra of the play, who hates her mother and is jealously in love with her father. She persuades her brother, Orin, to help her to murder Brant and scare her mother into committing suicide. After this, Lavinia, like Electra, has to comfort her brother when he is tormented by pangs of conscience, which correspond to the Erinyes. At the end of the play the dominating theme is the Oedipus complex, and the play develops rather differently from the *Oresteia*. Orin had regarded his mother with a sickly devotion and detested his father, and after his mother's death he becomes as unhealthily devoted to his sister, who grows more and more like her mother. He tries to prevent her from marrying, and in order to ensure that she will not marry he demands that she give herself to him. When she rejects his proposal with hard words he shoots himself, and Lavinia, the sole surviving member of the family, shuts herself away for ever in the gloomy family house.

It might be thought that *Mourning becomes Electra*, over-burdened as it is with a load of out-of-date psychology, would lose by re-reading, but, in spite of everything, the trilogy has a very powerful effect, and seems despite its period flavour to be timeless. Its similarity to classical tragedy has given it a stature not attained by any other works of O'Neill. The chief characters seem to have superhuman dimensions. Characters such as Ezra Mannon and Lavinia seem to be endowed with a legendary grandeur; their words fall like hammer-blows. Long before O'Neill wrote this trilogy, an American critic had pointed out his natural affinity with Aeschylus. It is this which has enabled him to create, after the model of the *Oresteia*, one of modern drama's most powerful and significant works.

The charming comedy, *Ah, Wilderness* (1933), shows that O'Neill was not as lacking in humour as might be supposed from his earlier dramas. It has usually been taken to be something of an autobiography, but O'Neill has categorically denied that it represents his family, or his youthful experiences. The portrait of the young schoolboy who has read so much modern literature, and is full of pathetic quotations from Ibsen and Shaw, must be something of a self-portrait, even though O'Neill himself did not make the acquaintance of these authors until he was older.

It is also uncertain how far *Days Without End* can be regarded as a personal confession. The play was published in 1934, but written earlier, and was intended to be the second play in a trilogy of which the first was published in 1929, the year after *Strange Interlude*, with the title *Dynamo*. *Dynamo*, which also contains a 'thought' dialogue as well as the ordinary one, is intended to show that fanatical atheism is as one-sided as the orthodox Puritanism which O'Neill so often attacked.

It is the story of an intolerant Calvinist minister, who adopts a materialistic faith in electricity, which he regards as the source of all life and God himself. He worships the dynamo, which

it is his duty to tend, as a savage worships his fetish, and at the
end of the play he throws himself into it.

O'Neill wrote later about this strange play that in it he was
trying to dig up by the roots the sickness of our age, "the death
of an old god, and the knowledge that materialism cannot provide
a new one which would allow our remaining religious instincts
to find a meaning in life, and a comfort against the fear of death."

He was already saying then that *Dynamo* was to be followed by
another play, called *Without Ending of Days,* and that the last one
in the trilogy would be *It cannot be Mad*.

Really, *Dynamo* shows us very little of the human struggle to
find a new god, as the young hero's development occurs entirely
off stage. But the fact that a confirmed hater of Christianity,
as O'Neill proved himself to be in his first plays, is here equally
opposed to the bigotry of Puritanism and the bigotry of atheism,
is a warning of what was to come, as are also his words about
the purpose of this rather unsuccessful play. His attitude was to
become even clearer in *Days without End,* where the hero is
finally converted to Catholicism, and thereby enabled to resolve
the mental conflict which has been tormenting him.

Days without End is both an autobiographical work and a
problem play. John Loving is an American business man, but the
social, philosophical, and religious attitudes which he has held
from time to time since his youth correspond more or less with
O'Neill's own development. This business man is engaged in
writing a novel, in which he describes in slightly disguised form
an occasion when he was unfaithful to his wife. He tells his wife,
who is recovering from a serious illness, about the novel which
he is planning, and she understands that it is of his own unfaithfulness that he is speaking. She hovers between life and death,
and accuses him of secretly wanting her to die. It is primarily
because he is afraid of losing her that he enters an old church,
and fervently prays for mercy before the altar.

O'Neill was never one for half-measures, and here what he
wanted was to create a new Faust. Two days before the publication of *Days without End* he said that Goethe's *Faust* is closer to
us than any other classical work: "When this play is produced,
I should like Mephistopheles to wear a mephistophelian mask of
Faust's face. For does not the whole of the truth of Goethe for

our day rest in the fact that Mephistopheles and Faust are one and the same—*are* Faust."

In his own play O'Neill has tried to introduce this Faust interpretation by splitting his chief character, John Loving, into two. One of these, John, represents the Faustian side of his being, while the other, Loving, wears a mask which is John's death mask, and represents that part of him which struggles longest against salvation and constantly gives a cynical and derisive twist to everything that happens.

The other characters cannot see Loving, but they take his words to be those of John. O'Neill has to some extent combined his old liking for masks with the double dialogue of *Strange Interlude*. Loving gives expression to John's unconscious thoughts and wishes. When John in the final scene makes his confession of faith, Loving at last falls at the foot of the Cross, and it is John Loving himself, now an integrated personality, who calls out, in a mystic ecstasy, the last words of the play: "Life smiles again with the Love of God, life smiles with love." It is the same Nietzschean faith, that life is a thing of joy, that was apparent in *Lazarus Laughed,* and was condemned earlier in the play.

That O'Neill could not rest content with this vague optimism is shown by his most recent play, which was produced in 1946, with the somewhat biblical title, *The Iceman Cometh*. It is a play about the agony of life, like *Days without End*. In one place it is suggested that the Iceman symbolizes Death. But it rejects all faith in life and all cheap salvation.

When the play was first performed, American critics hastened to point out its dependence on *The Wild Duck* and Gorki's *The Lower Depths*. O'Neill has not tried to refute these suggestions. With a repetitiveness that sometimes becomes tedious his play shows the inevitability of some 'life-lie' for the average human being, here represented by various clients in the tavern who have all gone off the rails, but who cannot abandon their dream of some time resuming their proper places in the community. At his first entry the commercial traveller, Hickman, who urges his friends to lead a new life and not put off everything until to-morrow, sounds rather like another Gregers Werle, and the surly tavern philosopher, Larry, might at a pinch be taken as a new Dr. Relling. The relationship with *The Lower Depths* is even clearer. The tavern becomes the centre of the drama, as does the lodging-house in Gorki, and we are introduced to the dregs of humanity, abandoned creatures who cannot raise themselves to a decent human level. In Gorki there is a counterpart to Hickman in the pilgrim Luka, whose attempt to persuade the lodgers to climb out of their degradation and begin an honest life is as ineffective as Hickman's.

These considerations, however, do not prevent the play from being a typical O'Neill work. The thought is less clear than in Ibsen, and the conclusion is somewhat different. Of the social purpose in *The Lower Depths* there is little trace in *The Iceman Cometh*. The clients of the tavern have brought their misfortunes on themselves, and to some extent they realize this. The play is more universal than Gorki's, while at the same time it also seems more of a personal confession. The slight knowledge one has of O'Neill's private life prevents categorical statements. We have to rest content with comparing it with other plays by him, where the personal elements are more obvious.

Days without End is the play nearest to it in time, and contemporary critics have insisted, despite O'Neill's denial, in regarding it as a Catholic credo. The inner conflict which was there presented in the persons of John Loving is here found in Hickman. Even the idea of his murdering his wife, because he found it so terrible that she should continually forgive his sinful life in bars and brothels, is fore-shadowed in *Days without End*. There the hero's lower self, Loving, urges him to finish off his ailing wife by allowing the deceived wife in the novel to die. There, as in *The Iceman Cometh*, one notices how the hero is both moved and infuriated by his wife's irrepressible hope that he will mend his ways.

Hickman on his visits to Harry Hope's bar has always suggested jokingly that when he is away on business the Iceman calls and makes love to his wife (hence the title). When he confesses that he shot her, he claims to have said afterwards, "Well, now you know what your dreams of the future are worth, you damned swine." The next moment he denies that he said this, but his words are to some extent confirmed by young Parritt, who betrayed his anarchist-communist mother to the police, thereby condemning her to a life sentence in prison. He claimed originally to have done this in order to get money for girls, but after Hickman's confession he bursts out, "I didn't care a scrap about the money. It was only because I hated her." Both men have felt themselves psychically "bound,"—in a Freudian sense—Hickman to his wife and Parritt to his mother. By killing his wife Hickman has at last rid himself of "all damned dreams and illusions," and himself rings for the detectives who will look after him on his way to the electric chair. Parritt, who considers that his crime is worse than murder, throws himself out of the window. Death is the only way of escape from the world of the "life-lie."

O'Neill goes beyond Ibsen in the blackness of his pessimism, because his conception of mankind is a purely determinist one. The gang at the bar are excellently, almost too carefully, drawn, a group of individuals who have at one time or another slipped out of the social machinery, but have never lost hope of resuming decent human standards of life. When Hickman urges them to pull themselves together, and try to realize their dreams, he fails miserably. They do not belong anywhere.

The individual's only way, according to Hickman, is to "accept himself as he is." But man is afraid of life, and even more of death. Is this the view of the half-crazy Hickman, or of O'Neill himself? One cannot forget that many of O'Neill's plays deal with the man who has lost his soul, and in a press interview at the première of *The Iceman Cometh* he described America as being in the same dilemma: "To America everything has been given, more than to any other nation in history, but we threw away our soul when we tried to possess something outside it, and in the end, as always happens with that sort of behaviour, we shall lose both our soul and our external possessions. But why go on—the Bible puts it much better; for what does it profit a man if he gains the whole world, but loses his soul?" It sounds as if this is the main theme of the great cycle of plays of a hundred and thirty years of American history, on which O'Neill has been engaged for over ten years. It is called *A Tale of Possessors Self-dispossessed*. This is probably true of other places as well as America. We recall O'Neill's words about *The Hairy Ape*, that man has lost his old harmony with nature, and has not yet acquired a new spiritual one.

In spite of all differences in subject, style and aesthetic value, O'Neill's plays have one thing in common. They attract and retain the interest of reader and audience alike with a grasp which is seldom relaxed. He struggles with the problems of life, and tries to find an answer for them. Sometimes he fails completely, for he is no clear thinker. But he is a great dramatist, together with Synge the greatest to make an entry in the 20th century. He digs deep, even when he runs the risk of losing sight of his objective. Once in the 1920's he said that a writer whose main purpose is not to find a meaning in life, and a comfort in death, is only "scratching the surface of things."

LUIGI PIRANDELLO

LUIGI PIRANDELLO was born in 1867, but he did not really begin to write plays until the first world war, when he was about fifty years old, and he is the last significant writer of the drama of ideas, the drama whose greatest exponents had been Ibsen and Shaw.

Italy was the country in which Ibsen was played more frequently than anywhere except Germany and Scandinavia, and research workers there have been most anxious to trace resemblances between the drama of Ibsen and Pirandello, but as far as one can see they are very slight. There are many more resemblances in the work of Pirandello's predecessors, Giuseppe Giacosa and Roberto Bracco, who sometimes followed Ibsen almost slavishly. He himself felt much closer to Strindberg, whom he admired greatly.

Pirandello started his dramatic life in the Naturalist school; he was a Sicilian and a good friend of Verga. Strange as it may seem, he remained a Naturalist in theory, and was much opposed to the symbolism in Maeterlinck's vein which D'Annunzio fancied. But he was not a Naturalist who described everyday things; for subjects he chose unusual and preferably eccentric cases.

That this naturalism could find expression in such a fantastic play as *Sei personaggi in cerca d'autore* (*Six Characters in Search of an Author*) was due to a belief which Pirandello frequently expresses, namely that we live two lives, one in reality and one in a world of illusion, and that in us there are two persons, the one we really are, and the one we think we are, or seem to be. Those who wish may of course try to trace this theory back to the doctrine of the 'life-lie.' But there can never be any real connexion, because Pirandello with the quick and subtle mind of

Southern Italy, and the light and airy imagination which is a national heritage, is made of quite different stuff from Ibsen.

Such information as we so far have about his life is mainly contained in a biography which he helped an Italian architect to write. It clears up a good many points in his dramatic work, which at first seemed he inventions of his brain. Some of his own experiences were indeed as fantastic as those of the heroes in his plays.

Pirandello's father was the owner of several sulphur-mines in Sicily, and when his son showed no aptitude for business he sent him to study in Rome and Bonn, where he took his degree. He had fought for Garibaldi in his youth, and was a powerful man but something of a tyrant, and unfaithful to his oppressed wife. He had at one time a very talented friend, Portulano, and in order to combine their business interests these two men agreed that Luigi should marry Portulano's daughter, Antonietta. The young couple had never seen each other before the engagement, and were never left alone in a room together before they were married. She was in a convent school and guarded very strictly by her father. This marriage, arranged by the parents for commercial reasons, made Pirandello's family relations even stranger. His father-in-law was a widower, whose wife had died of puerperal fever because she had refused to call in a doctor lest her husband's abnormal jealousy should be aroused.

Pirandello's marriage was tolerable as long as the family fortune survived. When floods ruined his father's sulphur mines, and his wife's dowry, which had been invested in them, was also lost, Antonietta received a shock from which she never recovered. Pirandello had to give lessons in Italian to foreigners at five lire an hour, to take a job as a teacher at a women's seminary in Rome and to write for a living. His wife's disturbed state of mind, which also evinced itself in the same jealousy that her father had shown, compelled him to cut himself off from his friends, and she watched his every step. At one time he had to hand over every *soldo* he earned, and she would allow him fifty *centesimi* a day for cigarettes and fares. It was during these unhappy years that Pirandello made his name as a novelist, and at the time of the first world war he won a European reputation as a dramatist. His plays sound like improvisations—and so they are. He has said himself that in one year he wrote nine plays, and two of the best of these only took him a few days to write.

This sounds like mass production, but it was not. A good many of Pirandello's dramas were based on his own short stories. It was to the flower of the literary work of a lifetime, that at the age of fifty he gave dramatic form. It was only then, in his old age, that he won the fame and wealth that would have served him so well in the difficult years at the beginning of the century, a fact which he regarded, as is plain from one or two autobiographical plays, as the irony of fate. In any case the wealth was to disappear as rapidly as it had come. Pirandello founded a national theatre in Rome in 1925, and with its company he went on tour in England and on the Continent. In this theatrical venture he lost 600,000 lire. The last years, during which he had no home or property, he spent travelling from country to country, arranging for the stage or film production of his works.

During his journeys around the world Pirandello was often told that his drama was too obscure and intellectual. In a discussion he defended himself on one occasion by saying that his contribution to modern drama was to turn reason into passion. But his logic is more devastating than Shaw's, and sometimes leads to conclusions which seem even more hair-raising to conventional morality.

A good example of this is the amusing and also moving comedy, *Pensaci, Giacomino!* (*Think it over, Giacomino!*). It contains an eccentric Sicilian schoolmaster, Toti by name, who at the age of seventy is looking for a young wife, so that the Finance Department will have to pay a widow's pension for many a long year. He learns that the school porter's daughter is expecting a child by one of his former pupils, Giacomino. The girl's parents refuse to let her marry the young man, so Toti marries her himself on condition that Giacomino remains her lover and promises to marry her after his own death. The resulting *ménage à trois* is a very happy one, and Toti is devoted to the child. The townsfolk, however, decide that the situation is scandalous, and at last Giacomino's sister summons a well-known priest, "almost a saint," to lead her brother back into the paths of righteousness. They engage him to another girl, and try to persuade Toti to say that Giacomino is not the father of the child.

But Toti refuses, seeks out Giacomino, leading his child by the hand, and threatens to tell the truth to his new fiancée. This threat carries weight, and with his child in his arms Giacomino returns to Toti's home. "It is a mortal sin," warns the Holy Father, "I believe . . . " But Toti interrupts him contemptuously, "Believe? You don't even believe in Christ." It is the old schoolmaster who acts in the spirit of Christ.

While this play and others like it only turn conventional morals upside down, there are yet others which seem to deny the existence of a truth which holds good for all. There is no absolute truth, explains Pirandello's mouthpiece in the witty comedy *Così è se vi pare* (*Right You Are—If You Think You Are*). People and circumstances are not something fixed by nature, which can only be understood in one way. This little play, which is called a parable, is more complicated than a short reference here might indicate.

The Prefect's new secretary, Ponza, makes his wife and mother-in-law, Signora Frola, live in different houses, and they are not allowed to visit each other. All over the small town where the action takes place, everybody is bursting with curiosity about the reason for this.

Ponza lets it be known that his first wife died in an earthquake four years ago. Two years ago he remarried, but his first wife's mother is mad, and believes that her daughter is still living. To preserve this illusion he must pretend to be madly jealous, and prevent her from meeting his new wife.

The mother-in-law's story is that Ponza has remarried his first wife. As a result of his violent jealousy she was conveyed, on doctor's advice, to a convalescent home, giving Ponza the impression that she was dead. When he met her again he did not recognise her, and a pretended new marriage had to be arranged for them. Now he is afraid that this wife too will be taken from him, and so he refuses to let her see anybody.

Nobody can quite understand where the truth lies in these stories, and all papers which might elucidate the mystery have vanished. At last the inquisitive folk of the little town contrive to secure a visit from the wife herself, Signora Ponza. She appears, heavily veiled, and explains that she is Signora Frola's daughter and Ponza's second wife. They try to force her to confirm one of the alternative versions. She replies, "No, for my own part, I am what people think I am." Then she says of her husband and Signora Frola, "Their misfortune is such that it should remain concealed from the world, for it would be too heavy to bear if it was not hidden by the merciful veil with which pity has covered it."

In several of Pirandello's plays the tragedy arises just because this veil has been torn away. This point is particularly clear in *Vestire gli ignudi* (*Naked*, or *Clothing the Naked*). The heroine is a nurse who has been found halfdead in a park in Rome; she has tried to poison herself. While she still believes that she is bound to die, she tells a journalist that she has taken poison because she was hounded from her post in a Consul's house in Smyrna by his jealous wife, and because her fiancé, a naval officer, deserted her to become engaged to someone else. Her life is saved, and when she emerges from hospital she discovers that she is the sensation of the moment in Rome. An elderly author of some distinction takes her to his home, with the intention of turning her story into a novel. Her former fiancé beseeches her to marry him; he has been summarily dismissed by his new fiancée as soon as she read the story in the newspaper. Meanwhile the Consul and his wife return from Smyrna; it transpires that the nurse was really the Consul's mistress, and that in the course of love-making they had allowed his little daughter to fall off the terrace. All those who were enchanted by her romantic story now turn away in indignation, and for a second time she takes poison. In the hour of death she confesses the reason for her action. She has never succeeded in becoming anything here in the world. We all try to look our best, and she hoped that at least she would go to the grave in a decent dress. Even this comfort was denied her. Unveiled, naked and degraded she is taken to the grave.

The same notion, that we all play a part which is different from our real self, lies behind Pirandello's famous *Enrico Quarto*. A young man once went to a masquerade to play the part of the Emperor Henry IV. He is thrown from his horse, and suffers an injury to the brain. After this he continually suffers from the delusion that he is the Emperor Henry. His wealthy sister keeps him in a villa where there is a throne-room like that at Goslar. There he resides with four secret advisers, that is to say, four nurses, and all visitors have to put on period costume and pretend to be people of the 11th century. When the play begins this strange carnival has been going on for twenty years. A group of visitors arrive, among them the girl he used to love and his former rival Belcredi, all dressed in medieval costume, in order to establish whether he is still insane. The self-styled "Henry IV" then admits that for the past eight years he has been quite sane. He has continued to play the part because his friends and the girl he loved have abandoned him, and because he knows that if he returns to life people will point the finger of scorn at him: "I realized that I was standing there like a man who arrives ravenously hungry at table, to discover that the guests have gone and the table has been cleared." The visitors are annoyed that he has deceived them so long, and Belcredi is particularly cutting in his comments. "Henry IV" replies complacently, "I am cured, gentlemen, because I know very well how to play the lunatic, and I do it calmly and quietly. What is sad is that your madness drives you to such lengths, and that you neither see nor acknowledge it." Gradually his anger with Belcredi grows; he now remembers that it was he who pricked the horse which threw him. When Belcredi insults him he draws a sword from the scabbard of the attendant standing near at hand, and with a lightning movement plunges it into him. Belcredi is carried out, and the visitors go too, leaving "Henry IV" in terror because he has played his part too well, and become a criminal: "Now there is no return, now I must continue." For a moment he has been tempted to take off his mask, but now he must keep it on until his death.

The play which made Pirandello world-famous was *Six Characters in Search of an Author,* which originated in one of his short stories. In it Pirandello describes how he used to be visited by the characters from future stories. One evening he was reading a long novel which had been sent to him, and later that night he was visited by its chief character, who had come to complain about the bad treatment he had received from his author. Here we already find the key phrase of the play, word for word, in which the Father explains that anyone who has been born as a living character can never die: "Man dies, an author dies, but the figure he has created by his imagination does not die." Sancho Panza will live for ever.

In a letter from Pirandello to his eldest son we learn that as early as 1915 he was thinking of writing a novel with the title 'Six Characters in Search of an Author.' It is therefore of himself as an author that he writes in the play seven years later, the author who brought six characters to life, and then either could not or would not complete the work for which they had been created.

In the play, as is wellknown, the six characters turn up at a rehearsal on the stage, and demand to be given parts. These characters have become detached from their creator, and have only an illusory existence, but their mouthpiece, the Father, considers that it is the actors who should question the reality of their own existence, "however living and real it may seem to you to-day, because, like yesterday, it is doomed to appear as an illusion to-morrow." A character created by an artist actually has an advantage over human beings in that it does not change from day to day, or die and disappear. Its existence is limited by immutable boundaries.

Pirandello's play is called a *commedia da fare* (cf. the French *Scène à faire*). The play presented by the characters to the actors is more akin to the improvised Sicilian plays which Giovanni Grasso—much admired by Pirandello—used to present with his company. The great scene is that where the Father, separated for some ten years from the Mother, who has had three children by his former secretary, pays a visit to Madama Pace's famous fashion shop. In a backroom he is introduced to his unknown step-daughter, who is just about to undress behind a screen when they are both interrupted by the Mother. This life story is a moving one when presented by the characters themselves, but when presented by the actors it is distorted into melodrama. The Father becomes a ridiculous old man, while the *prima donna* plays the step-daughter as such a commonplace Lady of the Caméllias that the original character bursts out laughing. After a somewhat melodramatic conclusion the producer curses both illusion and reality, which have made him lose a whole day's rehearsal.

The fundamental idea about the superiority of poetry over

reality is worked out in *Six Characters* with an irresistible logic, and the actual *mise-en-scène* is masterly. In contrast to the actors, who are merely doing their daily jobs, the characters seem like disembodied apparitions from another world. Without losing any of the dramatic tension of the play, Pirandello manages to introduce his personal philosophy into it. This play contains more ideas than any of his others, but it perhaps lacks some of their intensity.

Some of Pirandello's last plays are the only ones which seem autobiographical. He enjoyed towards the end of his life a short Indian summer of love, in which he became passionately attached to the leading lady of his company, Marta Abba. But his world reputation prevented him from enjoying the youth that he thought for a moment he had regained. This is the theme of his fine play, *Quando si è qualcuno* (*When You Are Somebody*, 1933). An author has already become so famous during his lifetime that a statue of him is erected, and he is not allowed to deviate from the stereotyped impression of him that people have formed. He has fallen in love with the sister-in-law of his nephew, Veroccia, and the poems which he has composed for her have been published by his nephew under the pseudonym Délago, and have created a sensation in the world of literature. He is then told that his own style is now old-fashioned, and that the younger generations have come to admire such poetry as that of Délago. Veroccia urges him to proclaim the truth, but he refuses: 'If I reveal that I am Délago, if I cry aloud that I am Délago . . . then Délago is done for; then he becomes my mask, you see, a youthful mask which I have put on for a joke."

Against his will his nephew publishes another book by him in the same style, and reveals that Délago is his pseudonym. Opinion changes when people learn that it is the old poet who has written these youthful love-poems. It is held to be undignified for a man of his years to write such things. The family takes a hand, and the poor author has to admit that he wrote the Délago books for a joke. Once again he is buried in the mausoleum of his fame. Veroccia is bitter because she thinks his love for her was only a mockery, and she breaks with him. He has to remain content with being celebrated and hailed as a genius.

When You Are Somebody is interesting, not only because it is

an autobiographical play written according to the same recipe as
Pirandello's earlier works. The elderly poet is as firmly bound
to his role as Henry IV was. With a bitter glance at his own
failings, Pirandello has also given expression in this play to his
grief that his stream of poetry is drying up.

In one of his earlier plays where the audience in the body of
the theatre are given their say, as in Tieck's neo-romantic plays,
there are some who grumble that in Pirandello it is always the
same old charade, that everything always pivots on the same
hinge. But others answer that one idea can be expressed in many
ways, to reflect fully the many-sidedness of life.

By the end of his life Pirandello was certainly tired of "the
same old charade," but he could not get away from it once the
critics had so extensively expounded the thought of his drama.

He himself knew that the notion that truth varies with the eye
of the beholder was as old as philosophy itself. It was his gift
that in an inimitable personal way he could give dramatic form
to this ancient thought. He had the light touch and the vivid
imagination of the Italian. Without being a great dramatist
he was graceful and witty, and his influence on modern drama is
greater than might be supposed. His own plays are showing a
tendency to disappear from the theatres, but from time to time
we find new dramatists who are working with his tools.

SPANISH PEASANT DRAMA

THE original feature of modern Spanish drama is the rise of a peasant drama, which reaches its highest point with Lorca. It has, however, its roots further back in Spanish literature. Its founder may be regarded as the Catalan dramatist, Angel Guimerá, who was born in 1847, and had already aroused much interest by 1890 with his plays depicting the life of the peasants in his own region. The best known of these is *Terra Baixa*, (*Lowlands*), which was used for the libretto of Eugen d'Albert's opera under the title of *Lowlands*. It contains in a modern peasant setting the familiar theme of a young girl whom the Lord of the Manor takes as his mistress, and then marries off to a simple shepherd from the mountains. He intends to get married himself, but hopes that in this way he can keep up his relations with the girl. But she tells her husband the whole story, and together they decide to fly from the corruption of the plain, and to lead a good life up in the mountains. When the Lord of the Manor seeks to prevent them he is strangled by the young shepherd. The heroine, Marta, is really the best-drawn character in the play. But the shepherd, Manelich, became such a great popular favourite that a statue of him was put up in one of Barcelona's parks, as the ideal type of Catalan.

There is a more convincing presentation of ordinary life in Guimerá's second peasant play, *Maria Rosa,* which deals with road-workers. There is, however, no particular social purpose behind the play. The beautiful Maria Rosa has lost her husband, a wine-trampler who was sent to prison on the suspicion of having murdered his foreman, and there died of typhus. After a year's mourning, she marries Ramon, who has been in love with her for a long time. At the wedding feast, which is a tremendous affair, Ramon becomes drunk and tells Maria Rosa that it was he who murdered the foreman, and let suspicion fall on her husband by slipping the bloody knife over the threshold into their bedroom. Thereupon Maria Rosa immediately seizes a knife and strikes the bridegroom dead. These two plays, which lack psychological depth but are 'good theatre,' have been translated from Catalan to Spanish by Echegaray.

His successor as a Nobel Prize winner, Benavente, has written two dialect plays which are held to have been inspired by Guimerá. The best known of them is *La Malquerida* (*The Passion Flower*), and the heroine is again a young woman, by name Acacia. Her step-father, Esteban, is secretly in love with her, and, by murder and other means, has prevented several men from marrying her. When in the final act he is about to leave the home, Acacia allows herself to be persuaded by her mother, and overcomes her loathing of her step-father sufficiently to embrace him. Once in his arms she realizes that hate is only the obverse of overpowering love, and she admits that she has never loved any other man. Esteban shoots his wife, and as she dies she comforts herself with the reflection that she has separated her husband and her daughter for ever.

Benavente has tried to make his heroine more convincing by the use of modern psychology, but this has spoiled the peasant atmosphere of the setting. The action takes place in a wealthy peasant home, but it might just as well have occurred in the aristocratic circles in which Benavente preferred to move as a dramatist.

Frederico Garcia Lorca was 37 years old when he was killed by the Fascists at the beginning of the Spanish Civil War, and superficially he may be regarded as a pupil of Guimerá and Benavente. The three plays which he wrote about peasant life had, like theirs, a woman as the chief character, and they have the same powerful conclusion. Lorca is closest to his predecessors in *Yerma*, where the heroine strangles her husband on the stage. The mockery of love is also the basic theme of all three plays. Family vengeance is an element in *Bodas de Sangre* (*A Fatal Wedding* or *Bitter Oleander*), as in *The Passion Flower*.

But, while Guimerá and Benavente can only stress the realistic element in their peasant plays, Lorca was principally a poet. Before he began to write plays he had already published

Romancero Gitano, which is said to be the most widely read book of Spanish poetry in this century. In simple folk-rhythms borrowed from romance, the Andalusian poet has written about the gipsies as he remembers them in his childhood. This collection was published in 1928, and the following year Lorca went to New York. There too he became interested in the simple and natural quality of negro life, which seemed to him a counterpart to that of his gipsies at home. His remarkable ode to the King of Harlem (*Oda al rey de Harlem*) is written in unrhymed modern verse, and contemplates, with a mixture of admiration and anxiety, the negro race which is to dominate the world. It is said that Lorca, in a conversation after his return to Madrid, described New York as a "Senegal with machinery," but this ironic comment does not fit in with the spirit of his New York poem.

An English literary historian, Edwin Honig, has written a study of Lorca, comparing him with Synge, though without venturing the statement that Lorca knew his great Irish predecessor. It is probable, however, that Lorca had either seen or read Synge's *Riders to the Sea*.

Lorca entirely lacks Synge's grotesque humour. This may partly be because he is more part of the world he describes. With Synge we feel that he is an observer, sometimes completely fascinated, at others ironically detached. He has buried himself in the world of Irish folk-lore with extraordinary intensity, but in himself he still remains to some extent the lyrical poet, the symbolist who has re-discovered the strange people and nature of his own country. Lorca had also learned much from the French symbolists, and while writing his peasant plays, and even before, he was also writing stylized and symbolistic drama. The finest play in this vein is *Rosita La Soltera,* which combines a rather static plot with some extraordinarily beautiful lyric writing. His peasant plays also contain elements of symbolism, but he never quite seems to escape from the magic circle which his native Andalusia made for him. That is why with their lyrical beauty and their strangeness they are so enchanting.

When the three plays, *A Fatal Wedding, Yerma* and *La Casa de Bernarda Alba* (*The House of Bernarda*) are grouped together as a trilogy, this is not merely because they all have a peasant setting. Though the characters and atmosphere in each are distinct, they treat the same fundamental theme; as Hjalmar Gullberg has said, they deal with the tragedy of motherhood. In *A Fatal Wedding* we find a mother watching her only son fall a victim to the common lot of the family, the knife. Yerma is completely obsessed by her longing for a child, and when she strangles her husband in her fury because he will not give her one, she thereby deprives herself once and for all, according to Spanish convention, of the chance of becoming a mother. Bernarda Alba watches over the chastity of her seven daughters with all the care of a dragon guarding treasure. By this very strictness she ruins their lives, and drives her youngest daughter to her death, but all she is concerned about is that no one shall discover that the daughter committed suicide because of an unhappy love-affair. Lorca seems to disapprove of Catholic bigotry, as O'Neill did of Puritanism, but to regard it as inseparable from the Spanish temperament.

A Fatal Wedding (1933) made Lorca world-famous. It was first played abroad in Spanish America, was then translated into French, English and Russian, and must now have been performed all over the world.

The plot is a simple one. On the very eve of the wedding the bride allows herself to be carried off by her former fiancé, Leonardo, who is now married to her cousin. They fly, but the bridegroom catches them up and the two men kill each other with knives. But round this story Lorca has spun some wonderful poetry. There are wedding songs, cradle songs and songs of mourning after the two men have died. In one passage of fantasy the moon, which has witnessed the grim struggle, also has a song to sing. In none of his other peasant plays has Lorca laid such a strong emphasis on folk-lore. The characters are taciturn and afraid of betraying their innermost feelings, and yet their profiles are clearly outlined against the dry Spanish summer landscape, particularly the sullen bride, and Leonardo, whose marriage has not been happy. Particularly tragic is the part of the bridegroom's mother, who is conceived as a Cassandra. She is anxious for her son, her only surviving son. His father and his elder brother have both been killed by members of Leonardo's family, and she fears that he will share their fate. She is always dreaming of knives, which have cut off her dearest possessions.

The basic theme is already indicated in the first scene, when the son asks his mother for a knife with which to cut the grapes. She mutters between clenched teeth, "The knife, the knife ... damnation to all knives, and to the wretch who first thought of them." By the end of the play her fears have been realized, and she is alone. The family light has been quenched, but now, for the first time after all her anxiety, she can breathe in peace: "Here, here I want to stay. And to be still. For now they are all dead. At midnight I shall be sleeping, sleeping, without knife or gun to frighten me any more. Other mothers can stand by the window when the rain is beating down and look for their sons. But not I. My sleep shall be a cold ivory dove, which will carry camellias of hoar-frost to the churchyard."

We are reminded here of the words of the fisherman's widow, Maurya, in *Riders to the Sea,* when she, who has grieved because the sea has taken her husband, her father and her sons, now feels easier when her last and youngest son is lost to the waves, and she has no one left for whom to be anxious: "They are all gone now, and there isn't anything more the sea can do to me ... and I won't care what way the sea is when the other women will be keening ... It's a great rest I'll be having now, and great sleeping in the long nights ... "

The similarity is undeniable, but where Synge keeps to what the people really do and say, Lorca becomes lyrical. This is seen at its most beautiful in the mother's famous last song:

> Women: with a knife,
> With a small, small knife,
> On a fixed day, between two and three,
> The two men killed
> Each other in love.
> Just with a knife,
> A small, small knife,
> Which a hand can almost cover,
> But which cuts sharply
> Into the dark flesh
> To stay where our cry
> Trembles at its hidden roots.

A Fatal Wedding is Lorca's finest play, and one of the greatest

peasant plays in world literature. It has an incomparable wealth
of colour and lyrical brilliance.   A premonition of what was
going to happen to the writer himself seems to creep in to the
constantly repeated strophes about Death reaping lives at their
fullest flowering:

> "He was a fine rider,
> And now a snowflake only."

Lorca's next play, *Yerma*, was produced in 1934. The construction resembles that of *A Fatal Wedding*, but there are fewer
lyrical passages. There is also a certain amount of symbolistic
mask play between the Male and the Female, who represent the
basic idea of the play. This is also indicated in the name of the
heroine, which she herself explains when she says that she is a
dry field. Her tragedy is that her husband does not desire any
children, and her sense of honour will not allow her to form a
connexion with anyone else, though she does feel attracted to a
childhood friend, Victor. At last, when her husband mocks her
scornfully, saying that he certainly does not want children and
will never give her any, she strangles him in a burst of rage, and
then falls into the depths of despair, because now she will never
be able to have a child: "I shall rest, and not wake up in terror
to see if my body warns me of another new body to be born.
Rest with my body dry for ever."

For the greater part of the play, Yerma has been an obedient
wife, fulfilling all the desires of her jealous husband, and allowing
herself to be guarded by his sisters, two silent old crones. She
had married Juan on her father's orders, and had faithfully
carried out her wifely duties, but only because she wanted a
child: "I gave myself to my husband that time for the sake of a
child, and I will continue to do so in hope of a child, but never
for my own pleasure."

For most of the play she is uneasy whether the lack of a child
is the result of her own infertility, and at last she visits a wise
woman who has a reputation for curing childlessness. In the
end, however, her suspicions are confirmed, that her childlessness
is due to the fact that her husband only seeks sensual satisfaction
with her, and does not wish for a child. A Spanish student of

literature, Barea, has made it quite clear that this is founded on a popular Spanish belief.

The idea that marriage was instituted for the procreation of children, and not for sexual satisfaction, is inherent in all Christian morality. But in *Yerma* it is given such a tense expression that a Scandinavian reader is immediately reminded of Ibsen's highly idealistic conception of the relations between the sexes. There is, however, no doubt that Lorca himself held the opposite view. In the symbolic scene between the Male and the Female especially, the subjects of married love and child-bearing are treated with fearless enthusiasm. The greatest heights of poetry reached in the play are found in the description of Yerma's disappointed mother-love, and her dreams of the child that she wanted. For her importunate husband her feelings are cool, while her love for Victor is suppressed by her Spanish notions of honour. We already notice here the same hostile attitude to conventional religion which is to be found in Lorca's last play.

The House of Bernarda was written shortly before Lorca was murdered. He only had time to read it to some friends, and biographies now available make only brief reference to the play which was published posthumously.

The House of Bernarda shows a more positive trend towards realism than *Yerma*. There are not merely no passages in verse—with the exception of a harvest song which drifts in through the window—but there are no symbolical scenes, such as were used in *A Fatal Wedding* and *Yerma*. Lorca may have wished to show those critics who attacked his earlier plays as the work of a poet who had wandered on to the stage that he could tie up the ends of a plot in perfect style, and could carry a plot to a tragic conclusion without making use of his lyric gifts. Slowly and imperceptibly detail is added to detail, and, as in an Ibsen play, the audience has to listen to every revealing line in order to understand the conflict.

The title character, Bernarda Alba, a widow who has just lost her second husband, has carefully prevented her five daughters from ever meeting a man. She treats them tyrannically, not merely because she is a domineering woman, and as her faithful servant Poncia says, "consumed with suppressed hunger for love." She is also dominated by Spanish conventions and notions of

AA

honour, and desires a 'clean facade' at any cost, as she says. She curses the village where she lives, which has no river, and where the wells are poisoned, and she is mortally afraid of its gossip.

The house has endured her harsh rule ever since her father died, and the daughters are spiritually stunted and at the same time the prey of suppressed desires. There is one excellent scene where a lively stallion in the stable can be heard kicking at his stall, while all the daughters, who are forbidden by their mother to look on a male creature, stand trembling and listening.

But the youngest daughter, Adela, has not yet had her joy of life quenched. The finest fellow in the village, Pepe Romano, has seen her, and begun an affair with her. After the father's death the eldest half-sister, the ugly Angustias, seems a better match, and Pepe is compelled by his parents to pay court to her. But after the customary serenades at Angustias' window, he continues his meetings with Adela in the stable. They are discovered by another sister, the hunchback Martirio, who is also hopelessly in love with Pepe.

Finally, a whistle is heard from the stable. Adela tries to get out, but is hindered by Martirio, who calls for her mother. In a rage Adela reveals the truth, and Bernarda rushes after Pepe with a gun and shoots at him. He vanishes, but Martirio has already had time to give Adela the false news that he is dead. Adela shuts herself in her room and hangs herself. "Happy, a thousand times happy, is she who could be his," cries Martirio, but Bernarda shows no grief. "Take her down," she orders. "My daughter has died a maiden . . . No one can say anything." The last words of the play are hers, telling everyone to be silent, in this home which is now more than ever a prison.

In the person of Bernarda, unconcerned about human life, but determined to preserve an appearance of decency in the grim house where she reigns, Lorca has created his most complete female character, a counterpart to old Cabot in O'Neill's *Desire under the Elms*. No more than O'Neill has Lorca succeeded in explaining the psychological reasons for the triumph of ruthlessness and bigotry over ordinary human instincts. Both Cabot and Bernarda are terrifying personifications of this bigoted attitude. O'Neill's play is bolder and more generous in conception, but in spite of all the attention to realism, *The House of Bernarda* has an inner lyrical quality which O'Neill lacks. Both these peasant plays show how Ibsen's basic problem, the conflict between individual and social morality, is expressed in the terms of peasant life. It is significant that O'Neill, in order to make his play convincing, had to move it back to the more primitive conditions of last century. Lorca has been able without undue difficulty to set his play in contemporary Spain, and gains thereby in genuineness, both of setting and plot. He was himself to fall a victim to the barbarous attitudes and customs which he depicted, when he was murdered by Franco's minions, although he had taken no part in the civil war. In him there died not merely Spain's, but modern drama's, youngest playwright of really great calibre.

INDEX OF PLAYS AND AUTHORS

Play titles printed in italics; Bold numbers indicate main reference to play or author